FODOR'S
SWITZERLAND
1986

(Including Liechtenstein)

Area Editor: Kay Gillioz-Pettigrew

Editorial Contributors: Robert Brown, Sean Conolly, Andrew Heritage, Frances Howell, Kenneth Loveland, Ira Mayer, David Tennant, Rosemarie Weber-Stocker

Editor: Richard Moore

Deputy Editor: Thomas Cussans

Maps: Brian Stimpson, Swanston Graphics

FODOR'S TRAVEL GUIDES

New York

Copyright © 1985 by FODOR'S TRAVEL GUIDES
ISBN 0-679-01279-6 (Traveltex edition)
ISBN 0-340-38367-4 (Hodder and Stoughton, London edition)

No part of this book may be reproduced in any form without permission in writing from the publisher.

The following Fodor's Guides are current; most are also available in a British edition published by Hodder & Stoughton.

Country and Area Guides

Australia, New Zealand & The South Pacific
Austria
Bahamas
Belgium & Luxembourg
Bermuda
Brazil
Canada
Canada's Maritime Provinces
Caribbean
Central America
Eastern Europe
Egypt
Europe
France
Germany
Great Britain
Greece
Holland
India, Nepal & Sri Lanka
Ireland
Israel
Italy
Japan
Jordan & The Holy Land
Kenya
Korea
Mexico
North Africa
People's Republic of China
Portugal
Scandanavia
Scotland
South America
Southeast Asia
Soviet Union
Spain
Switzerland
Turkey
Yugoslavia

City Guides

Amsterdam
Beijing, Guangzhou, Shanghai
Boston
Chicago
Dallas–Fort Worth
Greater Miami & The Gold Coast
Hong Kong
Houston
Lisbon
London
Los Angeles
Madrid
Mexico City & Acapulco
Munich
New Orleans
New York City
Paris
Philadelphia
Rome
San Diego
San Francisco
Stockholm, Copenhagen, Oslo, Helsinki & Reykjavik
Sydney
Tokyo
Toronto
Vienna
Washington, D.C.

U.S.A. Guides

Alaska
Arizona
California
Cape Cod
Colorado
Far West
Florida
Hawaii
New England
New Mexico
Pacific North Coast
South
Texas
U.S.A.

Budget Travel

American Cities (30)
Britain
Canada
Caribbean
Europe
France
Germany
Hawaii
Italy
Japan
London
Mexico
Spain

Fun Guides

Acapulco
Bahamas
London
Montreal
Puerto Rico
San Francisco
St. Martin/Sint Maarten
Waikiki

MANUFACTURED IN THE UNITED STATES OF AMERICA
10 9 8 7 6 5 4 3 2 1

CONTENTS

FOREWORD v

FACTS AT YOUR FINGERTIPS

Planning Your Trip; Getting to Switzerland; Arriving in Switzerland; Staying in Switzerland; Getting around Switzerland; Leaving Switzerland

THE SWISS SCENE

SWITZERLAND AND THE SWISS—Heritage and Achievement
Kenneth Loveland — 37

THE CONFEDERATION THAT WORKS—A Synopsis of Swiss History — 47

CREATIVE SWITZERLAND—A Collision of Cultures — 60

FOOD AND DRINK—Cuisine? . . . Kochkunst? . . . Cucina? — 75

PARADISE FOR SPORTSMEN—Always in Season — 80

THE FACE OF SWITZERLAND

BERNE AND THE BERNESE OBERLAND—Arcades, Bears and Fountains — 93
Map of Berne — 97

BASLE, BASEL-LAND AND THE NORTHWEST—Switzerland's Rhineland — 123

THE JURA, NEUCHÂTEL AND FRIBOURG—Where 'East *ist Ost*' and 'West *est Ouest*' — 135

LUCERNE AND CENTRAL SWITZERLAND—Historic Heart of a Nation — 150

ZURICH—Prosperous and Protestant — 173
Map of Zurich — 177

EASTERN SWITZERLAND—Charm and Creature Comforts — 188

LIECHTENSTEIN—Postage-Stamp Principality — 204

CONTENTS

THE GRISONS AND ENGADINE—Winter Playground of the World — 217

THE VALAIS AND THE ALPES VALAISANNES—A Journey up the Rhône — 242

THE LAKE GENEVA REGION—Lausanne, Vevey and Montreux — 260

GENEVA—Cosmopolitan Corner of the Lake — 276
  Map of Geneva — 280–1

THE TICINO—Canton of Contrasts — 289

SUPPLEMENTS

ENGLISH-FRENCH-GERMAN-ITALIAN VOCABULARY — 307

MAP OF SWITZERLAND — 315

INDEX — 319

FOREWORD

Switzerland is the heart of the matter of Europe. Not only is it geographically right in the center, but its network of roads-with-tunnels, plus telephone, telegraph and postal services and the Swiss Federal Railways, are firm spokes to all of the continent. And its scenery is unmatched—with alpine peaks, rolling fields, vast lakes with comfortable lakeboats, and a southern canton (the Ticino) where palm trees line the lakefront and Italian traditions give a new look to the Switzerland you have been led to expect.

Switzerland has for long been regarded as one of the most expensive holiday destinations in Europe, but this is no longer the case. Over the last few years the Swiss have kept a tight rein on their prices, especially where hotels and restaurants are concerned, and, although it is certainly not a budget country, it no longer ranks among the most expensive for the visitor. It is a tribute to the way the Swiss manage their affairs that they have had an incredibly low rate of inflation compared to most other countries, and this happy state of things makes life much easier for anyone wishing to visit the country.

Modern tourism started in Switzerland and the country is still right at the top when it comes to the art of looking after people on holiday. You would be amazed how many hoteliers around the world have been trained in the demanding school of Swiss catering. But the Swiss approach to tourism has not rested on its considerable laurels. The National Tourist Office is always coming up with attractive new schemes to draw the people of the world to its clean and efficient country. Setting a precedent now followed by several of its neighbors, Switzerland was the first to offer a Holiday Card for its extensive and admirable rail and postal coach network, a move copied subsequently by many European countries. Since the national network of trains, postal coaches, trams and lakeboats ties the entire mountainous mass together, you can go anywhere at whatever time you wish, at a fee you have already paid.

The goal of the effective and informative Swiss National Tourist Office is to open its country to travelers and show them the best ways to tour on their own—whether their interests run to mountain climbing, learning to yodel, bicycling, studying languages, or just plain wandering around at will. The Swiss make it easy.

The principality of Liechtenstein, a special fragment of Europe, is covered in a separate chapter, with background, hotels, restaurants and touring suggestions.

In a country that has four national languages, most travel routes are clearly identified by symbol. You'll have no problem getting around, and we urge you to do so with a minimum of baggage—mental and actual. The democratic Swiss have never made a fuss over finery. The less you carry with you in the way of luggage, the happier your travels will be.

We would like to thank our many friends in Switzerland, New York and

FOREWORD

London for their assistance in creating this 1986 edition. Above all, we would like to thank Kay Gillioz-Pettigrew for her efforts on our behalf. Our thanks go also to Mr. Franz Blum, Press Officer at the London office of the Swiss National Tourist Office. We have also received considerable assistance from the regional tourist offices in Switzerland itself.

*

We would like to emphasize that our hotel and restaurant listings represent only a selection of the wealth of establishments available. Wherever you travel in Switzerland you will find well-run, comfortable places to stay and eat.

All prices quoted in this guide are those available to us at the time of writing, mid-1985. Given the volatility of European costs, it is inevitable that changes will have taken place by the time this book becomes available. We trust, therefore, that you will take prices quoted as indicators only and will double check to be sure of the latest figures.

*

Acts of God and governments, sudden changes in the standard of hotel or restaurants service, the unexpected closing of a museum, avalanches and floods, can all affect the reiiability of a guidebook. We make every effort to ensure that our information is up-to-date and accurate. To help us in this task we welcome letters from our readers, telling us of their experiences and making suggestions. Our addresses are—

in the US: 2 Park Avenue, New York, NY 10016;
in the UK: 9/10 Market Place, London W1.

SuperEurope:
Sail QE2 One Way, Fly Concorde The Other—Only $549 Extra.

Together, the supersonic Concorde and the superliner Queen Elizabeth 2 represent the ultimate transatlantic travel experience.

Choose from specially reserved British Airways' Concorde flights between London and New York, Miami, Washington, D.C. and several other U.S. cities. (Or enjoy free British Airways economy-class airfare between London and 57 North American cities; you can upgrade to Club Class or First Class by paying the difference.)

On QE2, recipient of the two highest ratings in <u>Fielding's Worldwide Cruises</u>, you dine splendidly at an unhurried single sitting. Enjoy casino gaming, dancing, disco and the Magrodome Indoor/Outdoor Center, with international entertainment day and night. And experience the famed "Golden Door Spa at Sea,"® with yoga and aerobics, a gym and jogging deck, saunas, swimming pools and Jacuzzi® Whirlpool Baths.

Consult your travel agent about choice European tours that include a five-day QE2 crossing; European hotel discounts available to QE2 passengers; and European cruises on QE2 and Vistafjord, which may be combined with a crossing.

Or for all the facts, including any requirements or restrictions, write Cunard, Dept. F85, Box 999, Farmingdale, NY 11737.

Certain restrictions apply to free airfare and Concorde offers. All programs subject to change; see your travel agent. QE2 is registered in Great Britain.

© 1985 CUNARD

QUEEN ELIZABETH 2 · SAGAFJORD · VISTAFJORD

Experience Europe at its best, and have fun on a Maupintour escorted tour!

You want to see and do and have fun, and be with people who are enjoyable companions. And, you want someone to take care of the details, give advice and take the bother out of travel. That is what Maupintour is all about. Come join one of over 150 quality escorted tours within the USA and all over the world.

Discover the Maupintour difference: ☐ uncommonly good quality ☐ well-planned itineraries ☐ accompanying tour manager ☐ limited size group ☐ interesting companions ☐ pleasant balance of activities and free time ☐ for one price, everything is included ☐ voted America's #1 tours abroad in *TRAVEL/HOLIDAY* poll.

Maupintour escorted tour programs include:

- ☐ Africa
- ☐ Alaska/Yukon
- ☐ Alps
- ☐ Arizona
- ☐ Art/Culture
- ☐ Asia
- ☐ Australia
- ☐ Austria/Bavaria
- ☐ Belgium
- ☐ British Isles
- ☐ California
- ☐ Canada
- ☐ China
- ☐ Christmas Tours
- ☐ Colorado
- ☐ Cruise Tours
- ☐ Death Valley
- ☐ Ecuador
- ☐ Egypt/The Nile
- ☐ Europe
- ☐ Fall Foliage
- ☐ France
- ☐ Galapagos
- ☐ Germany
- ☐ Greece/Aegean
- ☐ Hawaii
- ☐ Historic East
- ☐ Holland
- ☐ Hungary
- ☐ Iceland
- ☐ India/Nepal Kashmir
- ☐ Ireland
- ☐ Israel
- ☐ Italy
- ☐ Japan
- ☐ Mexico
- ☐ Middle East
- ☐ Morocco
- ☐ National Parks
- ☐ New Year's Tours
- ☐ New Zealand
- ☐ Nile Cruise
- ☐ Opera Tours
- ☐ Orient
- ☐ Pacific N.W.
- ☐ Peru
- ☐ Poland
- ☐ Portugal
- ☐ Scandinavia
- ☐ South Pacific
- ☐ Soviet Union
- ☐ Spain/Portugal
- ☐ Switzerland
- ☐ Turkey
- ☐ USA East
- ☐ USA South
- ☐ USA West
- ☐ Winter Tours
- ☐ Yugoslavia

Free tour brochures! Ask your travel agent, call or write Maupintour, 1515 St. Andrews Dr., Lawrence, KS 66046. Telephone toll-free 800-255-4266.

quality escorted tours since 1951

FACTS AT YOUR FINGERTIPS

Take a travel expert along on your next trip...

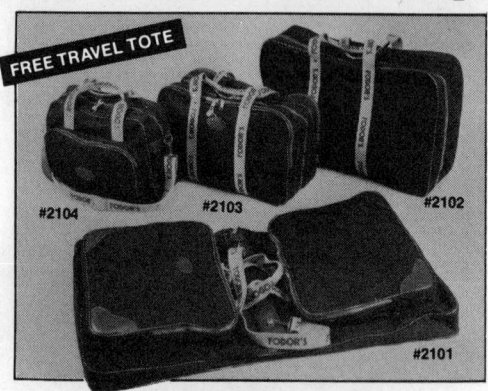

FODOR'S®
the travel experts.

When you spend fifty years in the travel business you're bound to learn a few things about quality luggage.

Basically you want it to be ruggedly made so it withstands the inevitable stresses of not-too-careful handling, and you want it to keep its good looks after many miles of hard use. Sounds simple. The problem is, luggage like that often costs a lot more than your whole vacation. **Not any more.**

Fodor's has found a line of luggage produced in the U.S.A. that meets our highest standards yet sells for a surprisingly reasonable price. We like it so much, in fact, that we've put our own name on it. We're sure you'll agree, this is truly a travel bargain.

100% cotton canvas treated for storm and water repelency, genuine saddle hide leather trim. Hand crafted made in U.S.A., durable extra strength cotton webbing, YKK nylon zippers.

Buy the complete set and save $50.00 plus you will receive a matching 18" travel tote free. Retail value $20.

Special Introductory Offer: **$280** *Complete Set*

Also available as separate pieces:

Item 2101 — 46" Garment Bag with adjustable should strap, holds 4 suits or 6 dresses with many large compartments for all your accessories. Specially designed zipper closing creates an extra large storage compartment **$145**

Item 2102 — 26" Pullman Bag easily handles all your travel items **$65**

Item 2103 — 21" Triple zipper multipurpose carry on with convenient adjustable shoulder strap and special hanger fixture for one suit **$70**

Item 2104 — 16" Multi compartment tote with shoulder strap and multipurpose back pocket which will accommodate a tennis racket **$50**

All styles available in either brown or navy canvas with genuine saddle hide leather trim.
1 year guarantee against all damages with normal wear.

Order Now. Call 1-800-228-2028 Ext. 204

Charge it to your VISA or MASTER CARD
If lost or stolen you can reorder at a 10% discount.
We will gold stamp up to three initials free of charge.
Add $7.50 for shipping and handling. New Jersey residents add 6% sales tax.
Identification tags free with purchase. Allow 2-3 weeks for delivery.

FACTS AT YOUR FINGERTIPS

Planning Your Trip

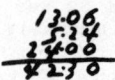

WHAT WILL IT COST. Switzerland has an air of expensive plush and ingrained affluence that tends to discourage many potential vacationers. But the fact of the matter is that, while the country does have an admirably high standard of living, it is not expensive to visit. The reason for this apparently paradoxical state of affairs lies largely in the positively legendary efficiency of the Swiss. While much of the world has been grappling with the many-headed monsters of inflation, unemployment and recession, and for the most part none too successfully, Switzerland has continued largely undisturbed on her quiet course of economic expansion and prosperity.

But while prices have remained so stable in comparison to those in the bulk of other western countries, services, what you actually get for your money that is, have emphatically not declined. The hotels are still as comfortable and as clean, the restaurants as excellent and welcoming, the trains as punctual and fast and, perhaps most important of all, the people as hospitable and courteous.

Of course you can still go to Switzerland and live as luxuriously and expensively as anywhere in the world—and where better to do so than in Switzerland—but you can also have a splendid and delightful holiday, in either the summer or the winter, without sending your bank manager into paroxysms of rage or committing yourself to the poorhouse for the rest of your natural span.

Nonetheless, there are still some points to bear in mind if you want to keep costs down. Stay away from the really smart winter sports resorts such as St. Moritz, Davos, Arosa or Zermatt during the height of the winter season. These places are still genuinely expensive and prices, particularly for hotels and restaurants, can be very high. Similarly, the major cities, especially Zurich and Geneva, are significantly more expensive than most other areas of the country. So investigate some of the quieter and less well-known areas such as St. Gallen in the northeast or the Jura in the northwest where, incidentally, the skiing can be pretty good. Make a point of avoiding the more obviously expensive luxuries; whiskey and other imported spirits are expensive, as are taxis and the more fashionable restaurants. And try to take advantage of the many excellent special deals offered by the Swiss National Tourist Office, not least the now-famed Swiss Holiday Rail Card which, for an extremely modest outlay, offers unlimited travel by rail and postal coach as well as reductions on many lake steamers and cable cars. You really don't need to do a lot of traveling to make significant savings.

Traveler's checks are still the standard and best way to safeguard your travel funds; and you will usually get a better exchange rate in Europe for traveler's checks than for cash. In the US, Bank of America, First National City Bank and Republic Bank of Dallas issue checks only in US dollars; Thomas Cook issues checks in US, British and Australian currencies; Barclays Bank in dollars and pounds; and American Express in US, Canadian, French, German, British, Swiss and Japanese currencies. Your choice of branch will depend on several factors. American Express checks are widely known, Bank of America has some 28,000 correspondents throughout the world, Thomas Cook about 20,000. The best-known British checks are Cook's and those of Barclays, Lloyds, Midland and National Westminster banks.

Major credit cards are accepted in most large hotels, restaurants and shops.

The Swiss monetary unit is the franc, which is divided into 100 centimes (or Rappen). There are nickel-silver coins of 5, 10, 20 and 50 centimes (or ½ franc), 1 franc, 2 francs and 5 francs. There are notes of 10, 20, 50, 100, 500, and 1,000 francs.

The rate of exchange at time of writing was Fr. 2.80 to the US dollar, Fr. 3.00 to the pound sterling.

A typical day's basic costs for two people

	francs
Hotel (Moderate) double room with bath and breakfast	120
Lunch, no wine, day's special	55
Dinner, including wine	36
Transportation (2 buses, 1 taxi)	10
	215

Sample Costs. Cinema (moderate seat) Fr. 8 to 10; theater (this can vary greatly) Fr. 10 to 30; museums are normally free; coffee Fr. 2; carafe of wine (3 dl.) Fr. 3.50. (Swiss wine is very much more expensive).

Hairdressers are very expensive in Switzerland, so have your hair done before you come!

SWISS NATIONAL TOURIST OFFICES. The major source of all information for anyone planning a vacation in Switzerland is the Swiss National Tourist Office, an organization of extraordinary efficiency. They will be able to help you with information on every type of vacation from painting holidays to trips on steam trains, and can supply details of car hire, hotel and restaurant prices, documents, insurance, camping and just about any other

FACTS AT YOUR FINGERTIPS

vacation information you might need. They can also advise on the multitude of tour operators offering trips of every kind to Switzerland.

Within the country there are local tourist offices in all main cities and tourist regions. You will always find someone who speaks English. Remember that tourist offices are called *Verkehrsbüro, Office du Tourisme* or *Ente Turistico* in the German-speaking, French-speaking and Italian-speaking areas of the country respectively. We list addresses of all these local tourist offices in the Practical Information sections at the end of each chapter.

The addresses of the main Swiss National Tourist Offices overseas are:

In the US: Swiss Center, 608 Fifth Ave., NY, NY 10020 (tel. 212–757 5944). 250 Stockton St., San Francisco, Ca 94108 (tel. 415–362 2260).

In Canada: Commerce Court West, PO Box 215, Toronto, Ontario M5L 1E8 (tel. 416–868 0584).

In the UK: Swiss Center, 1 New Coventry St., London W1 (tel. 01–734 1921).

CLIMATE. Switzerland is almost unique among European countries in having two quite separate tourist seasons; the winter sports season, which runs from around Christmas to the middle of April, and the summer season, which runs from around the beginning of May to the end of September.

Summer in Switzerland can be delightful. The weather is generally warm and very sunny, though of course the higher you go the colder it gets, especially at night. In many of the alpine valleys, however, it is frequently very hot. Spring and fall can also both be charming, the former especially for the profusion of wild flowers in the Alps. But both can also be rather dull and wet. The Swiss winter is cold everywhere. In the low-lying areas the weather is frequently damp and overcast, while in the Alps, though there are often brilliantly clear days, it is guaranteed to be very cold and very snowy.

The only exception to the general weather patterns of Switzerland is the Ticino, the Italian-speaking canton in the south of the country. Here, protected by the Alps, the weather is positively Mediterranean and even in the winter is normally significantly warmer than in the rest of the country.

Average afternoon temperatures in degrees Fahrenheit and Centigrade:

Geneva	Jan.	Feb.	Mar.	Apr.	May	June	July	Aug.	Sept.	Oct.	Nov.	Dec.
F°	39	43	51	58	66	73	77	76	69	58	47	40
C°	4	6	11	14	19	23	25	24	21	18	8	4

OFF-SEASON TRAVEL. This has become increasingly popular in recent years as tourists have come to appreciate the advantages of avoiding the crowded periods. Transatlantic fares are slightly cheaper and so are hotel rates. Even where prices remain the same, available accommodations are better, the choicest rooms in the hotels, the best tables in the restaurants have not been pre-empted, nor are you harried by fellow tourists at every turn. Moreover, if you really want to get under the skin of a country, the time to do it is when its inhabitants are going about their regular daily routines, not when they're all away on vacation, too.

However, if you are planning to visit Switzerland in the off season, particularly in the winter, do bear in mind that the weather can be rather bad. This is especially true of the cities, all of which are in low-lying areas. For winter sports, on the other hand, there are many positive advantages to be had from coming in the off season (basically from just after the New Year to around the beginning of March, and from after Easter to the end of April). The snow is just as good as during the peak periods, but everything is both less expensive and less crowded, except at weekends when the Swiss take to the slopes *en masse*.

SPECIAL EVENTS. Twice a year the Swiss National Tourist Office publishes a free booklet— *Events in Switzerland*. Here are some you may not want to miss:

January. Notable for two sets of celebrations—the *Schlittedas* of the Engadine and the *Vogel Gryff* festival in Basle. The first is an informal excursion on fine Sundays when unmarried boys and girls in traditional costume go on delightfully decorated sleighs from one Engadine village to another. The Basle celebration, which in English would be the Feast of the Griffin, occurs in the middle of Jan. (not always on the same date, so inquire when it is to take place) and begins with the arrival by boat of the Wild Man of the Woods, who is greeted by the Lion and the Griffin; afterwards a mummers' parade keeps the streets lively for the entire day. Wengen stages the International Lauberhorn ski races.

February. Also marked by a folk fête, the burning of Old Man Winter (the Homstrom) at Scuol, in the Lower Engadine, usually on the first Sunday of the month. Carnival is wildest at Basle, where it begins with another mummers' parade on the Monday after Ash Wednesday. Lucerne celebrates the Thursday before Ash Wednesday with its parade of the Fritschi family through the streets, when oranges are distributed to children, the carnival continuing into the following week. At the same time, Schwyz has a mummers' procession of harlequins, called *Blatzli*. In Ticino, at Mardi Gras, is the *Festa del Risotto*, when risotto and sausages are served in the squares. International speed skating championships at Davos; horse racing on the frozen lake at St. Moritz.

March. The month for Geneva's auto show and the Engadine Skiing Marathon, Maloja-Zuoz. Davos stages the Parsenn Derby international downhill ski race. Easter is celebrated in a number of Catholic communities by the footwashing ceremony on Maundy Thursday, and in Fribourg the bishop, in token of humility, kisses the feet of the faithful in the cathedral. Religious processions occur on Good Friday in many southern towns. Mendrisio's is a survival of a medieval Passion Play, and occurs on both Maundy Thursday and Good Friday. Annual Locarno Concerts (through June).

April. The Landsgemeinde meetings, where you can see Swiss democracy at work in its oldest and most direct form, take place in Appenzell, Hundwil or

FACTS AT YOUR FINGERTIPS

Trogen, Sarnen, Stans and elsewhere. Other events in April are the *Festa delle Camelie* at Locarno, and the Sechseläuten festival of Zurich, when centuries-old guilds parade, and the Böögg, a straw scarecrow representing winter, is burned at the side of the lake; the blessing of horses, donkeys and mules at Tourtemagne (Valais) on April 23; and the pilgrimage from the Centovalli across the Italian frontier to the shrine of the Madonna di Rè on the 30th. There is also the Swiss Industries Fair at Basle and the Golden Rose Television Festival at Montreux.

May. May Day is celebrated with particularly colorful ceremonies at Bad Ragaz (St. Gallen), Romainmôtier (Vaud) and Juriens (Vaud). At Cartigny (Geneva) the first Sunday in May is dedicated to the festival of the Feuillu, when the children who have been crowned King and Queen of the May lead a procession from house to house, and on the same day the Landsgemeinde is held at Glarus. Ascension is celebrated elaborately at Beromünster (Lucerne), when priests carrying the sacrament ride on horseback around the district blessing the crops, a ceremony dating from 1509. Corpus Christi is observed at Appenzell by strewing carpets of flowers underfoot; at Kippel (Valais) by a procession headed by the Grenadiers of God, in 19th-century uniforms; and at Bulle, Romont, Fribourg, Châtel St. Denis, Einsiedeln, and Lucerne by colorful rites and pageants. Around mid-May, Neuchâtel has its Musical Spring festival, and Lausanne starts its festival of music and ballet.

June. Geneva makes a considerable to-do about the rose, exhibiting some 100,000 of them, and accompanying Rose Week with concerts, shows, and other amusements. If you want to see cows fight, this is the month when they are pitted against each other in the lower Valais. It's a month full of music. Lausanne has its International Festival Weeks of music and ballet; Zurich, its International June Festival (music, opera, drama, etc.); Berne holds an Art Festival. If you want to look down at it all, go to Mürren for the International High Alpine Ballooning Weeks.

July. Weggis (near Lucerne) has its Rose Festival, and this is the month to see crossbow shooting in the Emmental, and the famous William Tell play which starts at Interlaken and goes on through August. For those who can't get enough skiing in the winter there's the giant slalom on the Diablerets glacier and the summer ski race on Jungfraujoch. Montreux holds its International Jazz Festival.

August. The Geneva festival with a battle of flowers and much jollification takes place now. As does Lucerne's music festival and the film festival at Locarno. Folklore is in full swing. Swiss wrestling in the Emmental and elsewhere, folkfests at Interlaken, the National Horse Fair with costumed riders on the strong Jura horses at Saignelégier, and the Menuhin festival at Gstaad. August 1 is the Swiss national day, with celebrations and lots of fireworks all over the country, but shops and offices mostly remain open.

September. Lausanne stages its big industrial and agricultural fair, the Comptoir Suisse, and the *Knabenschiessen,* or boys' shooting contest, is held at Zurich. Einsiedeln has the *Engelweihe,* a religious festival marked by spectacular torchlight processions. Montreux and Ascona both have important music festivals.

FACTS AT YOUR FINGERTIPS

October, there are vintage festivals everywhere, especially Lugano, Neuchâtel, and Morges. This month there are also Geneva's garden show and the picturesque fair of La Chaux-de-Fonds, the Braderie, a tremendous flea market without fleas, and the great Olma agricultural and dairy fair at St. Gallen. At Lausanne there's the Italian Opera Festival.

November. A month of open-air markets, dancing and kermesses, the most quaint being the *Zibelemärit* (Onion Market) of Berne.

December. The Spengler ice hockey tournament at Davos is one of the year's most notable sports events. Christmas merriment begins on St. Nicholas' Day, Dec. 6., with particularly colorful practices in the Goms Valley (Valais), Kaltbrunn (St. Gallen), Küssnacht and Arth, goes on through the riotous Escalade festival at Geneva on the 11th and 12th; and ends, after Christmas itself, with the noisy masquerades of St. Sylvester (New Year's Eve).

WINTER SPORTS. Though Switzerland is of course a wholly delightful country to visit at practically any time of year, it is perhaps most popular as a winter sports destination. Indeed, even today, Switzerland remains the number one winter sports destination in Europe. The main reason for this is of course the incomparable skiing offered by the Swiss Alps, but almost as important is the characteristic efficiency with which the Swiss operate their winter sports resorts and the consequent range of accommodations, ski schools, hire shops, package deals (of all types), plus the variety and excellence of runs and, last but not least, après ski available. Though we give more details in our chapter *Paradise for Sportsmen* (see page 80), it would be helpful to give a few brief pointers here.

There are, first, many hundreds of package deals available for the winter sports enthusiast, many of them offering all-inclusive and extremely reasonably-priced trips to resorts the length and breadth of the country. Those for groups, particularly staying in chalets, are especially numerous and competitive. But at the other end of the scale, there is certainly no lack of possibilities for those wanting to make their own arrangements, either expensively or inexpensively.

Your best bet, therefore, is to talk to your travel agent or contact the Swiss National Tourist Office and find out from them which resort and/or package is best for you. They will also provide details on ski schools, reduced-price cable car or lift tickets and hire (or purchase) of equipment. Inquire too about off-season benefits, as these can be considerable. And don't forget bobsleighing, tobogganing, skating, curling and langlaufing (cross-country skiing), all of which feature prominently in the winter sports curriculum.

But whatever type of deal you opt for, it is essential that you are adequately insured. Broken bones, though expertly cared for in Switzerland, are *very* expensive. For details of accident insurance, see Health and Insurance (page 10).

FACTS AT YOUR FINGERTIPS

WHAT TO TAKE. Travel light. Airline baggage allowances are based on size rather than weight. Outside first class, you may take free two pieces of baggage, provided that the sum of their dimensions—height plus length plus width—is not over 106 inches, and neither one by itself is over 62 inches. For first class the allowance is two pieces up to 62 inches each, total 124 inches. The penalties for oversize are severe. In any case, traveling light simplifies going through customs, makes registering and checking baggage unnecessary, lets you take narrow-gauge mountain trains with room for hand baggage only, and is a lifesaver if you go to small places where there are no porters. The principle is not to take more than you can carry easily yourself (unless you travel by car.)

Clothes. Except at the most chic of international resorts you won't need formal evening dress. Nonetheless, women visitors staying at first-class and better medium-grade hotels will be glad to have something smart, but lightweight, for the evening and men, a lounge suit. That said, elsewhere and on other occasions Switzerland is a country where you can get along most of the year on sports clothes, shifting with the seasons from the summer to the winter variety (and of the latter, in particular, you'll find a tempting selection in Swiss shops, though they are not cheap). In the summer, don't forget a sweater or two; high up in the mountains it grows chilly even on August evenings. Also something to drape over your bathing suit to protect yourself from the sun is advisable if you burn easily; there are a couple of thousand feet less of atmosphere than at sea level to screen you from the sun's rays.

PASSPORTS. American citizens. Major post offices and many county courthouses process passport applications, as do US Passport Agency offices in various cities. Addresses and phone numbers are available under governmental directories. Renewals can be handled by mail (form DSP-82) provided that your previous passport is not more than eight years old. You will need proof of citizenship, such as a birth certificate; two identical photographs on non-glossy paper and taken within the last six months; $35 for the passport itself, plus a $7 processing fee if you are applying in person (no processing fee when applying by mail) for those 18 years and older, or, if you are under 18, $20 for the passport plus $7 processing fee if you are applying in person (again, no extra fee when applying by mail). Adult passports are valid for 10 years, others for five years. You will also need proof of identity. When you receive the passport, write down its number, date and place of issue: if it is lost or stolen, notify either the nearest American Consul or the Passport Office, Department of State, Washington DC 20524, as well as the local police.

Canadian citizens. Application forms for passports may be obtained at any Post Office. Send your completed form to the Canadian Passport Office, 200 DuPortage, Place du Center, Hull, Quebec, K1A 0G3, together with a remittance of $20.

British citizens. Apply on the form obtainable from travel agents or main Post Offices. Send your completed form to the Passport Office for your area at least four weeks before the passport is required. There is a fee of £15. Validity is 10 years.

British Visitors' Passports are also valid for Switzerland. These cost £7.50 and are valid for one year. They can be obtained from any main Post Office.

Visas. American, Canadian, British, EEC and most Commonwealth citizens do not require a visa to enter Switzerland. You must of course have a valid passport though.

HEALTH AND INSURANCE. There is no free medical treatment in either Switzerland or Liechtenstein, and charges are high. For a clinic consultation expect to pay around Fr. 50, for a doctor's visit at least twice as much. And if you wind up in hospital, you can conservatively expect to pay approximately the same as at the most expensive deluxe hotel in the country. Medical expenses insurance is therefore largely essential for anyone planning a trip to Switzerland. If you are going on a winter sports holiday, it is vital.

Basic Blue Cross/Blue Shield policies cover health costs incurred whilst traveling. They will not, however, cover the cost of emergency transportation, which can often add up to several thousand dollars. Emergency transportation is covered, in part at least, by many major medical policies such as those underwritten by Prudential, Metropolitan and New York Life. It is essential to check any policy carefully before buying to make sure you are getting the cover you need. It is also important to note that most insurance issued specifically for travel does not cover pre-existing conditions, such as heart disease.

Two other organizations Americans and Canadians might contact are *IAMAT* (International Association for Medical Assistance to Travelers Inc.) and *Intermedic*. IAMAT, 736 Center St., Lewiston, NY 14092 (tel. 716–754 4883), or 188 Nicklin Road, Guelph, Ontario, NIH 7L5, furnishes, free of charge, a directory of English-speaking doctors who have trained in the U.S., Canada or Britain. In Switzerland, IAMAT has an office at 17 Gotthardstrasse, 6300 Zug, and correspondents in 12 cities. Uniform fees are: office call, $20; house or hotel call, $30; night, Sunday or holiday call, $35. A similar service is furnished by Intermedic, 777 Third Avenue, New York, N.Y. 10017 (tel. 212–486 8900). There is an initial membership charge, of $6 for an individual, $10 for a family; thereafter the fees are somewhat higher than those of IAMAT.

Other varieties of travel insurance cover everything from lost baggage to trip cancellation. Sometimes one blanket policy covers everything: alternatively, certain aspects may be covered by existing policies you have for health and/or home. Before purchasing separate travel insurance, be sure to check your regular policies carefully, or consult your insurance agent.

Flight insurance, which is often included in the price of the ticket when the fare is paid via American Express, Visa, or certain other major credit cards, is often included in package policies, providing accident cover as well. These policies are available from most tour operators and insurance companies.

FACTS AT YOUR FINGERTIPS

Should you become ill abroad, or for some other reason be unable to continue a trip (particularly non-refundable charters), you may have to buy a new one-way ticket home. Trip cancellation insurance is usually available from travel agents.

Travel Assistance International, the American arm of Europ Assistance, offers a comprehensive program providing medical and personal emergency services and offering immediate, on-the-spot medical, personal and financial help. Annual membership is $5 per person and trip protection ranges from $30 for an individual for up to eight days to $220 for an entire family for a year. Full details from travel agents or insurance brokers, or from Europ Assistance Worldwide Services, Inc., 1333 F St., N.W., Washington, D.C. 20004 (800–821–2828). In the U.K., contact *Europ Assistance Ltd.,* 252 High St., Croydon, Surrey (01–680 1234).

TRAVEL FOR THE HANDICAPPED. Major sources of information are: the book *Access to the World: A Travel Guide for the Handicapped,* by Louise Weiss, available from *Access,* Facts on File, 460 Park Ave. S., New York, N.Y. 10016 ($14.95); the book *Travelability,* by Lois Reamy, published by Macmillan; the *International Directory of Access Guides,* a listing of publications describing access facilities in specific countries and cities, including Switzerland, published by *Rehabilitation International,* 1123 Broadway, New York, N.Y. 10010 (tel. 212–620 4040); the lists of commercial tour operators who arrange travel for the disabled published by the *Society for the Advancement of Travel for the Handicapped,* 26 Court St., Brooklyn, New York 11242 (tel. 212–858 5483); and the *Travel Information Center,* Moss Rehabilitation Hospital, 12th St. and Tabor Rd., Philadelphia, Penn. 19141 (tel. 215–329 5715). *International Air Transport Association,* of 2000 Teel St., Montreal, Quebec, H3A 2R4, publishes a booklet, *Incapacitated Passengers' Air Travel Guide.*

Information on Europe is also available from *Mobility International,* 62 Union St., London SE1; the *National Society for Mentally Handicapped Children,* 123 Golden Lane, London EC1; the *Across Trust,* Crown House, Morden, Surrey, England (they have an amazing series of 'Jumbulances,' huge articulated ambulances that can whisk even the most seriously handicapped across Europe in comfort and safety and staffed by volunteer doctors and nurses). But the main source in Britain for all advice on handicapped travel is *The Royal Association for Disability and Rehabilitation (Radar),* 25 Mortimer St., London W1 (tel. 01–637 5400).

LANGUAGE. Language in Switzerland is a complicated matter. Yet as ever the Swiss contrive to make it easy for the tourist. There are four official languages; German (or more properly Schwyzerdütsch, the Swiss variant of German, though high German is also spoken), French, Italian and Romansch. This last is spoken only in the Grisons and Engadine in the southeastern corner, and though a number of groups are active in promoting its use it is not likely to be encountered by many visitors. It is, in truth, a dying language artificially preserved. Italian is spoken only in the Ticino, the canton to the south of the Alps, while French is spoken only in the more westerly parts of the country, in those areas around Lake Geneva (or Lac Léman as the Swiss call it) and in the cantons of Fribourg, Jura, Neuchâtel and Vaud. But the large majority of the population (73%) speak Schwyzerdütsch. Notices in all public places appear in French, German and Italian.

But if anyone feels alarmed at the prospect of having to cope with not one but three foreign tongues simultaneously they need not worry. First, German is very much the predominant language (only 20% of the population speak French and only 5% speak Italian). Secondly, the divisions between the various language areas are distinct and it is most unusual to encounter more than one language simultaneously. But, and more to the point, English, the lingua franca of the modern world, is spoken widely. All tourist offices will have at least one person who speaks English (probably more), and the same goes for hotels, restaurants, airlines and rail road personnel. But if you can master a few phrases your efforts will be warmly appreciated by the Swiss.

CUSTOMS. Residents of non-European countries, over 17 years old, may import duty free into Switzerland 200 cigarettes or 100 cigars or 50 grs. of tobacco, plus two liters of wine and one liter of spirits. Residents of European countries, over 17 years old, may import duty free into Switzerland 200 cigarettes or 50 cigars or 250 grs. of tobacco, plus two liters of wine and one liter of spirits. There are no restrictions on the import or export of currency.

Getting to Switzerland

From North America

BY PLANE. Swissair, the national carrier of Switzerland and without question one of the finest airlines in the world, is the main operator between North America and Switzerland. Direct flights leave from several major cities in the U.S.A. and Canada, and through-flights with one stop-over can be arranged from most other points.

Fares. Air fares across the Atlantic are in a constant state of flux and it is generally best to consult a travel agent for the latest information. But a brief run down on the available fares is nonetheless useful. In descending order of cost, you have the choice of First Class, Business Class, Apex and Budget tickets. The first two are the most flexible and easiest to book, but they are also the most expensive by a long way. Apex generally represent the best value for money, but they must be booked and paid for about 21 days in advance and you must stay in Switzerland for at least six days and no more than six months. Budget tickets are even less expensive but you can only choose the week you want to fly. A

FACTS AT YOUR FINGERTIPS

few charters are also available to Switzerland; again an agent will be able to recommend the best.

From Britain and Ireland

BY PLANE. Switzerland is easily accessible by air from all parts of Britain, and services are operated by several airlines. From London (Heathrow) to Zurich there are a minimum of seven non-stop flights daily, with a journey time of around two hours 35 minutes. They are by Swissair and British Airways. From London (Gatwick) Dan Air has a service to Zurich. Zurich is also served by a direct flight daily by Swissair from Manchester. Geneva is well served from London (Heathrow) by Swissair and British Airways with a minimum of five flights daily. The journey time is around two hours 30 minutes. The airport at Basle (Mulhouse) is served by a minimum of two non-stop flights on week days from London (Heathrow) by Swissair and British Airways with a journey time of two and a half hours. The Federal Capital Berne has flights on several days a week run by Dan Air from Aberdeen and Newcastle, both of which call and can be boarded at London (Gatwick) en route.

Fares. These vary widely and there is, as usual, a bewildering range. They will be dealt with in descending order of price. Euro-budget tickets are valid for one year, no break of journey is allowed and they must be paid for at the time of reservation and cannot subsequently be altered. Slightly cheaper are Excursion return tickets, valid for up to one month. A Saturday night must be included in the stay and again no break of journey is allowed. Slightly cheaper still is the PEX fare—for which the number of seats available is restricted. It has the same general conditions as the Excursion ticket except that it is valid for three months. The cheapest fare is the APEX return; this is also valid for three months and has the same conditions as the others but must be booked one month before departure. It is also possible to obtain discounted tickets for scheduled flights from many travel agents or tour operators; savings can be considerable and it pays to shop around. Also, especially in winter, tour operators offering skiing package holidays often have spare seats on their charter flights which can be obtained very cheaply. For these scan the Classified Ads in newspapers like *The Times, The Sunday Times, The Standard* and *The Mail on Sunday.* But be sure to check all the costs quoted and ask about extras. Not all are as cheap as they seem at first sight!

BY TRAIN. Access to Switzerland by rail is excellent, and with recent improvements in the European rail system journey times have been much reduced. From Britain, you have a choice of several routes depending on which part of Switzerland you are visiting, what you want to see and do on the way and, of course, on your budget.

FACTS AT YOUR FINGERTIPS

The classic route to northern Switzerland is from London (Liverpool Street) to Basle, sailing from Harwich to the Hook of Holland and then by Trans Europ Express to Switzerland. This is the stylish way to make the journey, especially as the Trans Europ Expresses may not survive much longer. You take the evening Boat Train from Liverpool Street to Harwich, then sail overnight to the Hook of Holland, reached in the early morning. The journey from the Hook of Holland is in two stages; first on the Rhein Express to Utrecht, and secondly on the famous Rheingold (TEE) for the remainder of the run to Basle. TEE trains are first-class only and require a supplement. Advance reservation is obligatory. The Rheingold has multilingual hostesses, *and* you can sample food and wines from the regions through which the train passes.

The same scenic route along the banks of the Rhine can be covered by modern Inter City trains which are airconditioned and very comfortable, especially in first-class. In this case first take the Rhein Express as far as Cologne and then change onto a through InterCity train for Switzerland. Both combinations will get you to Basle by late afternoon and Zurich by early evening. The main drawback—if it can be considered one—is that neither route is for the traveler in a hurry.

An alternative route to the above is from London to Basle via Ostend, Brussels, Luxembourg and Strasbourg. The channel crossing from Dover to Ostend is on the speedy Jetfoil which allows you to complete the entire journey in one day, leaving London (Victoria) at 8.15 in the morning and arriving in Basle just after 10 in the evening. The journey from Ostend is in two stages, first to Brussels (Midi Station), then change to the Edelweiss for the remainder of the journey through to Basle and Zurich. There is a supplement for travel on the Jetfoil and it is advisable to reserve seats for the whole trip in advance. The route can also be covered by using the conventional ferry service from Dover to Ostend, but the extra time taken for the Channel crossing means that the journey cannot be completed in one day.

The most rapid route from London to Switzerland is via Paris. The journey to Geneva, Lausanne and Berne can be completed comfortably in one day. Services are now so fast that it is possible to leave London (Charing Cross) at 10 in the morning and be in Geneva the same evening. The route is best considered in two sections: from London to Paris; and from Paris to Switzerland.

1. From London to Paris. There is a choice of several routes and combinations of transport. The quickest is by the Citylink rail–hovercraft–rail service operated by Hoverspeed from London (Charing Cross) to the Gare du Nord in Paris. The first stage of the journey is by train to Dover Priory Station where you transfer to the Hoverport for the cross-Channel "flight" to Boulogne. The hovercraft terminal there has its own railway station and it is a simple matter to change to the French Turbotrain for the fast run to Paris. By this route and combination of transport the journey to Paris takes under five and a half hours.

There are several other options open for the run to Paris, although most do not arrive there in time to catch trains which will get you to Switzerland the same evening. For example, Hoverspeed operate a coach and hovercraft service

FACTS AT YOUR FINGERTIPS

from London to Paris, the City Sprint service. Alternatively, you can go by train from London (Victoria) to Dover Western Docks, then by Sealink ferry to Calais (Gare Maritime) and thence by train to Paris (Gare du Nord). For travelers with heavy luggage this is the best all year round route. During the summer only there is a service from Calais to Venice; accordingly, there is no need to change trains and stations in Paris. On its way through Switzerland this useful train stops at Vallorbe, Lausanne, Montreux and Brig. However, during the winter the train runs in two halves, first from Calais to Paris (Gare du Nord) and then from the Gare de Lyon, making it necessary to transfer between stations at Paris. Another London to Paris possibility is from London (Victoria) to Folkestone Harbor, then by Sealink ferry to Boulogne (Gare Maritime) and on to the Gare du Nord. This is a useful summer-only route and takes around eight and a half hours to Paris.

Finally, for the traveler looking for something different. Travel in ritzy style by taking the recently resurrected and very luxurious Venice–Simplon–Orient Express from London, either to Paris or right through to Zurich. The train operates three days a week during the Summer and gets you to Zurich in the early morning the day after leaving London. For this you must book well in advance. Details from: *Orient Express,* Suite 2841, One World Trade Center, New York, NY 10048 (tel. 800–223 1588), or *Sea Containers House,* 20 Upper Ground, London SE1.

2. From Paris to Switzerland. The journey from Paris to the Swiss cities of Geneva, Lausanne and Berne has been revolutionized by the introduction of the magnificent *Train à Grande Vitesse* (TGV) and the construction of a new line exclusively for its use. As a result, journey times have been dramatically reduced. From Paris (Gare de Lyon) there are four TGVs a day to Geneva and four to Lausanne; traveling time in both cases is now a mere 3½ hours. Connections to all major Swiss cities are excellent and frequent. For details of these services contact either the Swiss National Tourist Office or French Railways. Note that it is necessary to book in advance for all TGVs and that a supplement is payable on most services. Further details are available in the useful *Traveler's Guide to TGV* produced by French Railways.

Fares. These vary widely depending on your route, the length of the channel crossing and type of accommodations, on ship or train, if traveling overnight. Fares for 1985 were not available at the time of writing, but every year the Swiss National Tourist Office publishes a full list—Fares list A—available free. They will also give a quotation for the complete through fare to any destination. If you have a Swiss Holiday Card (details of which are given in *Getting Around Switzerland,* page 24) you need only buy a ticket to the Swiss Frontier. Return tickets are valid for two months. Young people (under 26) should investigate the reduced rail fares offered by *Transalpino Travel.* They are able to offer a choice of routings—even with their discount fares breaks of journey are allowed. *Transalpino Travel,* 71 Buckingham Palace Rd, SW1 (tel. 01-834 9056/6283).

FACTS AT YOUR FINGERTIPS

HOVERCRAFT. The only hovercraft services across the Channel are operated by *Hoverspeed*. The "flights" are from Dover to Calais or Boulogne and journey time is 30–35 minutes. The Boulogne route is especially suitable for rail travelers but the service offered to car borne travelers is also excellent, road conditions on both sides of the Channel are good. The basic fare is calculated from the length of the vehicle and there is a standard charge for each occupant.

BY CAR FERRY. There are many drive-on, drive-off car ferry services across the Channel, but only a few are suitable as a means of getting to Switzerland. The situation is complicated by the different pricing systems operated by ferry companies and the many off-peak fares, and by the fact that the French charge tolls on some of their motorways; these add up, particularly if you drive long distances. To avoid the tolls, many people take a northerly route through Belgium or Holland and Germany where motorways are free. The crossings for this route are: Felixstowe, Dover or Ramsgate to Zeebrugge; Sheerness to Vlissingen; Dover to Ostend; and Dover or Ramsgate to Dunkirk. All these Continental ports have good road connections and Switzerland can be reached in one day's driving.

The short crossings from Dover and Folkestone to Calais and Boulogne do not give an ideal landfall in France for a fast journey to Switzerland. The first kilometers towards Paris are slow, then the *Periphérique* (ring road) around the capital has to be negotiated—not for the faint hearted! On the motorway from Paris to Switzerland and the south of France, the *Autoroute du Soleil*, tolls have to be paid. Travelers going the French route should consider using the sailings from Southampton/Portsmouth to Le Havre as road connections on both sides of the Channel are excellent. To use the Swiss motorways an extra tax is payable—either in advance or at the border. 1985 price $30/8Fr. Contact the S.N.T.O. for details for 1986.

Fares. These vary considerably according to season, journey time and length of vehicle. However, the approximate cost of crossing the Channel by one of the short sea routes in high summer, with an average vehicle of 14 ft. and two adult passengers, works out at around £85 one way. But traveling off peak, i.e. early morning or late evening, or in June and September, costs can be reduced.

BY BUS. International bus services to Europe are poor and do not offer a real alternative to the trains. *Wallace Arnold/Euroways* is the only operator with services from London to Switzerland. Their bus runs from London to Geneva via Paris. The service runs daily throughout the summer leaving London in mid-afternoon and arriving in Geneva late the following morning. Return fare to Geneva works out at around £70 return. But in addition there are several companies which offer organized coach tours. Details may be obtained from the Swiss National Tourist Office.

FACTS AT YOUR FINGERTIPS

From the Continent

BY PLANE. Switzerland has air connections with almost every European capital as well as with many other European cities. The bulk of these flights are to or from Zurich, the country's principal airport, but there are also many services to Geneva. The third main Swiss airport, Basle, is very much less used, but does have a number of flights from various cities in France, Germany, the Benelux countries and Italy. With the opening of the Geneva airport rail station, both main airports—Zurich and Geneva—will be plugged into the Inter City rail system. Coupled with this is the 'Fly Luggage' facility by which you can send your bags direct to your destination station—no lifting heavy luggage —ask for the 'Fly Luggage' leaflet.

BY TRAIN. Switzerland might well be called the international railway junction of western and central Europe as so many main line international expresses link it with all its neighbors—Germany, France, Italy and Austria —as well as more distant countries. For example, you can reach the land of William Tell by train without changing from places as far away as Hamburg, Amsterdam, Ostend, Calais, Paris, Rome, Venice, Nice, Brussels and even Barcelona. A number of TEE trains serve the country. All the international trains are electrically hauled and many, including the TEE services, are airconditioned. And they offer both daytime and overnight services.

It is well worth while buying the *Thomas Cook Continental Timetable,* if you want to be really knowledgeable about European trains. It is published monthly, but be sure to get the timetable applicable to the period of your visit. There are marked differences between the summer and winter schedules of Europe's national railway operators.

In the US, it is available from Travel Library, PO Box 2975, Shawnee Mission, Kansas 66201. In the UK, from Thomas Cook Ltd., Timetable Publishing Office, PO Box 36, Peterborough, or over the counter at any Thomas Cook branch.

BY BUS. In addition to the local and intermediate services from neighboring countries, Europabus operate routes from Munich to St. Moritz and from Besançon to Lausanne, neither of which are very useful. Even during the summer they are infrequent, with the first mentioned running only on Saturdays and the second only on Sundays. For details, contact Europabus, 747 Third Ave., New York, NY 10017 (tel. 212-308 3103).

BY BOAT. This is not quite the joke it may appear. There are regular sailings up the Rhine from April to October from the Netherlands (Rotterdam, Amsterdam and Nijmegan) to Basle. The trip takes four and a half days if you are going to Switzerland. From Switzerland (that is, going downstream) it is a little faster. The vessels are operated by several companies and are really miniature liners. Fares depend on the cabin and class you choose and also on whether you are going up or downstream. The single fares start at about $350 and go up to over $500; and if you travel deluxe then the cost is higher still. You can join all the boats at Cologne in Germany, whence fares are some 25% less.

You can also cross into Switzerland from France over Lake Geneva by lake steamer, and from Germany and Austria over Lake Constance (Bodensee in German). There are also lake crossings from Italy across Lakes Lugano and Maggiore.

Full details of all the Rhine services are available from all good travel agents in both the US and UK. Details of lake services can be had from the Swiss National Tourist Office.

Staying in Switzerland

HOTELS. Swiss hotels are the envy of hoteliers the world over, and for excellent reasons. At all price levels, they are spotlessly clean, impeccably run and excellent value for money. At the top end of the scale you will find luxury and superb service unequalled almost anywhere. And at the lower end of the scale, though frills and extras are obviously fewer, you are guaranteed shelter at the very least, but are more likely to encounter both extremely friendly service and comfort. There are not many bad hotels in Switzerland.

Our price gradings are divided into four categories, Deluxe (L), Fr. 220 and up (top prices can run as high as Fr. 500), Expensive (E) Fr. 150 to 220, Moderate (M) Fr. 120 to 150 and Inexpensive (I) Fr. 70 to 120. These prices are all for two people in a double room. They are all also averages only. Shower and half-board (one full meal a day) are frequently included in the prices quoted above. In the lists that follow, we have indicated where this is the case by the term "all inclusive." (This does not, of course, refer to *garni* hotels, which serve breakfast only.) Though Swiss hotel prices are not for the most part expensive, contrary to popular belief, in major resorts and cities they can be higher than those quoted here. Similarly, in the smaller towns and resorts, or in the off season and in more rural areas, they can be significantly lower.

For any one planning to do much traveling around within Switzerland, it is well worth while getting the official Swiss Hotels Association guide, available free from all Swiss National Tourist Offices and most regional tourist offices. It includes only those hotels that are members of the Swiss Hotel Association, but

FACTS AT YOUR FINGERTIPS

on the other hand these do account for approximately 80% of all Swiss hotels. The guide lists phone numbers, prices, number of beds and all facilities as well as providing a list of resorts, sports facilities and other information.

All major towns and many rail stations have accommodations offices. We list addresses of these in the Practical Information sections of each relevant chapter. Most charge a small fee, but it is extremely unlikely that they will not be able to find you a room for the night, even if it is only in a private house.

Among the excellent hotel chains operating in Switzerland is *Romantik Hotels*. If you wish to book with them before leaving the States, their address is 12334 Northrup Way, Suite C, Bellevue, WA 98005 (tel. 206–885 5805 or 800–826 0015).

Chalets. There are thousands of furnished chalets or apartments of all sizes and price levels throughout Switzerland. Off season, a simple but comfortable chalet-apartment sleeping four people could be rented for about Fr. 45 per person per week. But during the high season, a deluxe one sleeping five or six costs nearly ten times as much. Many travel agents can make rental arrangements for you, often incorporating reduced-rate travel. You can get an illustrated brochure describing many hundreds of chalets and apartments from *Swiss Touring Club*, Wasserwerkgasse 39, 3000 Berne 13, Switzerland, *UTO-Ring AG*, Beethovenstrasse 24, 8022 Zurich, Switzerland or *Inter Home*, Buckhauserstrasse 26, 8048 Zurich, Switzerland; or 383 Richmond Rd., Twickenham TW1 2EF, England.

In the US, contact *Villas International*, 71 West 23 Street, New York, NY 10010. (tel. 212–929 7585); or the Swiss National Tourist Office at 608 Fifth Avenue, New York, NY 10020, (tel. 212–685 4340); 250 Stockton St., San Francisco, Ca. 94108 (tel. 415–362 2260); Commerce Court W., PO Box 215, Commerce Court Postal Station, Toronto, Ontario, M5L 1E8 (tel. 416–868 0584). All can suggest firms.

Youth Hostels. Youth hostel organizations offer many benefits to tourists under 25, among which are reduced transportation fares. There are youth hostels all over Switzerland for cyclists and hikers, rates ranging from about Fr. 3 to occasionally Fr. 9 a night, the latter in big cities. Linen sleeping bags are compulsory. Youth hostels are called *Jugendherbergen* or *Auberges de la Jeunesse*. Information can be obtained by writing to the *Schweizerischer Bund für Jugendherbergen*, Hochhaus 9, Postfach 132, 8958 Spreitenbach.

Additional information about this type of travel can be obtained from: *The American Youth Hostels, Inc.*, 1332 I St. NW, Washington DC 20005 (tel. 202–783 6161).

In Canada: *Canadian Hostelling Association*, Place Vanier, Tower A, 333 River Road, Ottawa, Ontario K1L 8H9 (tel. 613–746 0060).

In Britain the addresses are: *Camping Club of Great Britain and Ireland*, 11 Lower Grosvenor Place, London SW1W OEY; *Youth Hostels Association*, 14 Southampton St., London WC2 7HY, (callers only), or Trevelyan House, St. Albans, Herts.

CAMPING. Switzerland is an ideal country for covering a good deal of your route on foot, carrying your luggage on your back, for sleeping under canvas or in youth hostels. It is a paradise for campers, or for trailer camping or taking the gear in your own car. There are hundreds of camping sites set aside expressly for that purpose. Rates vary widely; but for a family group of two adults, one child and car or camper the range is roughly Fr. 6 to 30 per night, with the average around Fr. 10-15. Organized camp sites are maintained, among others, by the *Swiss Touring Club* and the Federation of Swiss Camping Clubs. Both publish lists of their camps, which can be obtained from official Swiss Tourist offices, or by writing to the *Swiss Touring Club,* 9 Rue Pierre-Fatio, 1200 Geneva, or *Federation of Swiss Camping Clubs,* Habsburgerstrasse 35, 6000 Lucerne. The Swiss National Tourist Office also publishes a free folder, with map, listing over 200 camp sites.

To stay in a European camp you will have to produce the International Camping Carnet, which is also your third party (public liability) insurance. If you wish to obtain your carnet before leaving home, write to the *National Campers and Hikers Association,* 7172 Transit Road, Buffalo, NY 14221 (tel. 716–634 5433); or to the *Camping Club of Great Britain and Ireland Ltd.,* 11 Lower Grosvenor Place, London, SW1. In Europe, apply to the *Fédération Internationale de Camping et de Caravanning,* 78 rue de Rivoli, Paris. If you intend to camp with your family, apply for a family carnet as it costs less (rates vary from country to country). You can also obtain the carnet through a local branch of any of the European national camping clubs when you arrive there. Apply in person. Photographs will be required.

RESTAURANTS. As with hotels, so with restaurants; they are of a uniformly high standard in Switzerland, and though you can eat as expensively here as anywhere in Europe, the country also has a wealth of extremely reasonably priced and small eating houses all serving delicious food. As a general rule, restaurants in the French-speaking areas are rather more expensive than their counterparts in the German and Italian areas. Similarly, in the larger towns and resorts you will find prices higher, sometimes significantly, than in smaller towns and resorts. Chains, such as the excellent *Mövenpick*, normally have more than one price range and the same restaurant is often both inexpensive and expensive simultaneously. Be sure you go to the right part of the restaurant. All restaurants have menus and prices displayed in the window.

As one might expect, in the German-speaking areas German food predominates, while in the French and Italian areas French and Italian food respectively is the norm. But for a fuller picture of Swiss cuisine, see our chapter on Food and Drink in Switzerland (page 75).

Our price gradings for restaurants are divided into three categories—Expensive (E) Fr. 45 and up (there is no upper figure really, but Fr. 45 is not uncommon for a table d'hôte menu, while Fr. 25 is the minimum for an à la

FACTS AT YOUR FINGERTIPS

carte dish); Moderate (M) Fr. 18 to 25; and Inexpensive (I) up to Fr. 15. These prices are for one person only and include wine.

Note: all Swiss restaurants close one day a week.

TIPPING. By law, an automatic service charge of 15% is included in all hotel, restaurant, café, bar and hairdressing bills. This covers everything except that some people give the hotel baggage porter Fr. 1, Fr. 3 for much baggage. However, if anyone is especially helpful (e.g. the hotel desk porter in saving you money, or giving you advice on tours or nightlife) an appropriate reward would be appreciated. Station and airport porters get Fr. 1.50 for each article plus 10%. In a cloakroom where no fixed charge is made give about 50 centimes per person to the attendant. Give 12-15% to cabbies wherever service is not included, the larger percentage for shorter rides. Ushers and washroom attendants may expect Fr. 1; and if you feel that you have had special service from your hotel maid you can leave her about Fr. 2 extra. Theater ushers get Fr. 2 if they give you a program.

CLOSING TIMES. Usual shop hours are from 8 to 12:15 and from 1:30 to 6:30. Banks: hours vary from place to place, but usually 8 to 4:30 or 5. Closed for lunch and on Sat. and Sun. Foreign currency exchange windows at airports and larger railway stations are open daily from 10.

PUBLIC HOLIDAYS. January 1; March 28 (Good Friday); March 31 (Easter Monday); May 8 (Ascension); December 25-26.

August 1, Swiss National Day, is not a public holiday.

TIME. Switzerland is six hours ahead of Eastern Standard Time, and one hour ahead of Greenwich Mean Time.

MAIL. Current rates for letters (all mail goes airmail): to the US, Fr. 1.20 less than 10 grams, Fr. 1.50 less than 20; to the UK, 80 centimes up to 20 grams. These rates may well change during 1986.

TELEPHONES. The Swiss telephone system is excellent and extremely reliable. You can direct dial most places in the world, and of course everywhere within the country itself. There are booths with operators in attendance in all post offices and railway stations in larger towns and cities, but there are also other public telephones, some with instructions in English.

Every town and village has its own telephone code, all of which are listed in the front (pink pages) of telephone books. For information and inquiries, dial 111. If you have difficulty getting through or want to make a complaint, dial 112. For police dial 117, for fire 118.

Whenever possible, do not make international telephone calls from your hotel room. Most hotels will add as much as 400% on to the price of the call.

PUBLIC TOILETS. Lavatories in Switzerland, even in the simplest spots, are usually modern, and invariably clean. Look for a WC sign, or (in French, German and Italian speaking areas respectively) *Toilettes, Toiletten* or *Gabinetti.* Ladies: *Dames* or *Femmes; Damen* or *Frauen; Signore* or *Donne.* Gentlemen: *Hommes* or *Messieurs; Herren* or *Männer; Signori* or *Uomini.* Public lavatories are at stations, cable car termini and the like, and near major tourist attractions and features. Otherwise they are not very common. Use those in cafés, gas stations, department stores, etc. Normally free but might need a 20c. coin.

CASINOS. Some Swiss resorts have a casino but they are a far cry from Las Vegas or Monte Carlo. Boule, a modest version of roulette, is the favored form of gambling. The minimum bet is usually Fr. 1 and the maximum only Fr. 5. While this modest 4-to-1 ratio of lowest to highest wagers frustrates most systems, it also makes losing a fortune a major undertaking. The Swiss are opposed to big-scale gambling on moral grounds. But if you must try your luck, go to Lugano in southern Switzerland, cross the lake to the Italian enclave of Campione, and you'll find an eminently respectable high-stakes casino—or you might try Konstanz (Germany) just over the northern border. The popular French casinos at Divonne, only a few miles from Geneva, and at Evian, a pleasant boat trip across the lake from Lausanne, attract a cosmopolitan crowd.

STUDYING IN SWITZERLAND. If you are looking for a school at the preparatory or finishing school level, write to *Fédération Suisse des Ecoles Privées,* 40 rue des Vollandes, 1211 Geneva, giving all pertinent details—age of the prospective student, whether you prefer a one-sex or mixed school, type of course desired, whether to complete the pupil's education or prepare him or her for the university, and so forth. They will save you the trouble of plowing through catalogs by sending you the names of four or five schools which meet your requirements, thus narrowing the field. At the same time, however, ask them to send you the booklet *Federation of Swiss Private Schools,* which not only lists but describes and illustrates the more important ones. The Swiss National Tourist Office publishes a useful booklet, *Private Schools in Switzerland.*

At the university level, plenty of opportunities exist for study. For information, apply to any Swiss tourist office for the publications *University Studies in Switzerland—Information for American Students;* and *Lodging for Students at University Cities in Switzerland.* Semester and academic year programs are offered particularly at Fribourg and Neuchâtel.

There are special summer schools from early July to late August for 10- to 18-year-old youngsters. Details in booklet *Holiday Language Courses and Centers,* free from Swiss National Tourist Office. Languages (chiefly French), sports, excursions and hiking are part of the course. American parents can take advantage of special rates which include flights by *Swissair* and also cover living accommodations, 3 meals daily, any necessary medical services, and the tuition for the 8-week course. Brochures from travel agents and Swissair offices. The *American Field Services,* 313 East 43 St., New York, NY 10017 (tel. 212–949 4242), organizes home-stay-with-study exchanges for young people of high school age.

Student tours are organized by a number of tour operators in the United States, incorporating short courses at European universities that include Switzerland. Write to: *Students Abroad,* 179 N. Fulton Ave., Mount Vernon, NY 10550 (tel. 914–699 8335) or 2378 N.E. 28th St., Lighthouse Point, Florida 33064 (tel. 305–941 3889).

For information on work camps and opportunities for volunteer services, write to *Aktion 7,* Postfach, 8022 Zurich. Stays are usually 2–4 weeks, participants receive room and board, and some knowledge of either French or German is advisable.

SPAS. Switzerland is a country rich in natural mineral springs, of which there are nearly 300. Around the health-giving waters of many of these springs, medicinal spas have grown up. Some, like Bad Ragaz-Pfäfers, for example, have been known for centuries, are world-famous, and offer all of the expected trappings of an international watering place. Others are small, unsophisticated, and known to few.

Often the spas are fine, modern establishments; sometimes they are a little dated in their appearance. But all are spotlessly clean, and whether you are there for a thorough-going cure, for rest and relaxation, or for something in between, you will find they offer skilled and sympathetic attention at surprisingly reasonable prices.

The hotels at most of the spas have special all-in rates which include room, all meals, tips, and resort and other taxes. These special terms (called *prix forfait* or *Pauschalpreis*) operate, however, only when you stay at least three days.

A booklet describing many of the Swiss spas, and another listing hotels with their all-inclusive terms, can be obtained from the *Swiss National Tourist Offices,* as well as from most local tourist offices in Switzerland.

Getting around Switzerland

BY TRAIN. The Swiss public transport system is probably the best in the world. Despite its complex web of private and public transport companies and the extensive and equally complex links between train, bus, boat and mountain transport, the system functions as one smooth and immensely well-oiled body. The proverbial notion that you can set your watch by Swiss trains is not so far off the mark. And certainly Switzerland is perhaps the only

FACTS AT YOUR FINGERTIPS

country in Europe where it really isn't necessary to have a car to get the best out of the country. However, most Swiss trains are not especially fast, largely because of the mountainous terrain over which they often have to travel. But the steep gradients, sharp curves, long tunnels (much of the Swiss rail system represents a triumph of engineering) also mean superb views. And what the trains may lack in speed, they make up for in reliability and cleanliness.

Anyone contemplating a vacation in Switzerland using public transport should avail themselves of a number of essential purchases. One is a copy of the official timetable (*Offizielles Kursbuch* or *Indicateur Officiel*), price Fr. 8.50. Don't be put off by the appearance of this volume. It may be the size of a thick paperback but, despite being written in four languages (English, French, German and Italian), it is beautifully clear and easy to understand. The timetable gives schedules of the state network, the private railways, lake steamers, postal coaches, main cable cars and also details of the bus and tram routes in main towns and cities.

Also very useful is the Kummerly and Frey Rail Map of Switzerland, which includes postal coach routes, lake steamers and town plans. Both the map and the timetable can be purchased from any Swiss National Tourist Office. However, the most useful purchase you can make, especially if you plan to do quite a bit of traveling, is the Swiss Holiday Rail Card. Of course, if you also intend to travel elsewhere in Europe by train, you will probably find that the Eurail Pass (see below for details), perhaps with the addition of a Postal Coach Holiday Season Ticket, is your best bet. But for travel in Switzerland only, the Holiday Card is unbeatable value.

The card gives unlimited travel for periods of 4, 8 or 15 days or one month on all trains of the Swiss Federal Railways, and on nearly all private railways, lake steamers and postal coaches. In addition it gives reduced fares on many mountain railways and cable cars. (But if you are in any doubt as to precisely on which routes you qualify for reductions, the map on the reverse of the card marks them all clearly.) The first class card costs Fr. 215, Fr. 250, Fr. 300 and Fr. 420 for 4 days, 8 days, 15 days and one month respectively. The second class card costs Fr. 145, Fr. 170, Fr. 205, Fr. 285, respectively, for the same periods.

The card is only available to non-Swiss residents and must be purchased outside Switzerland, either through leading travel agencies or from any office of the Swiss National Tourist Office or Swissair.

There are also a series of Regional Holiday Tickets. These are good for train, postal coach and steamer travel and are valid for 15 days. They also permit unlimited travel, but only in the area for which they are good. But unlike the main Rail Card, you are allowed to travel free for only 5 out of the 15 days of the card's validity. On the remaining 10 days, you must pay half-fare. These regional cards are, with some exceptions, for second class travel only, and are available from April 1st to October 31st for the following areas: Montreux/Vevey (Fr. 64), Alps Vaudoises (Fr. 56), Bernese Mittelland (Fr. 66), Bernese Oberland (Fr. 102 in 2nd, Fr. 134 in 1st), Lake Lucerne (Fr. 112), Sargans/Walensee (Fr. 38), Grisons (Fr. 86 in 2nd, Fr. 134 in 1st), Locarno/Ascona (Fr. 46 in 1st), and Lugano (Fr. 50 in 1st).

FACTS AT YOUR FINGERTIPS

There is also a family rail ticket that enables a group of adults and children to travel at reduced rates. This is particularly useful for short stays: enquire at any rail station. All these cards conspire to make rail travel in Switzerland an extremely viable proposition, especially as the trains are otherwise very expensive; the railways charge by the kilometer and there are very few reductions. However, children under 6 travel free and those under 16 travel at half-fare.

The Eurailpass. A Eurailpass is a convenient, all-inclusive ticket that can save you money on over 100,000 miles of railroads, and railroad-operated buses, ferries, river and lake steamers, hydrofoils, and some Mediterranean crossings in 16 countries of Western Europe. It provides the holder with unlimited travel at rates of: 15 days for $260, 21 days for $330, 1 month for $410, 2 months for $560, 3 months $680; a 2nd class Youthpass (anyone up to the age 26) is available for $290 for 1 month and $370 for 2 months. Children under 12 go for half-fare, under 4 go free. These prices cover first-class passage, reservation fees, and surcharges for the Trans-Europ Express services. Available to US, Canadian and South American residents only, the pass must be bought from an authorized agent in the Western Hemisphere or Japan *before* you leave for Europe. Apply through your travel agent or the Swiss National Tourist Office, 608 Fifth Ave., New York, NY 10020 (tel. 212–757 5944); 250 Stockton St., San Francisco, Ca. 94108 (tel. 415–362 2260); 104 S. Michigan Ave., Chicago, Ill. 60603 (tel. 312–641 0050); Commerce Court W., PO Box 215, Commerce Court Postal Station, Toronto, Ontario M5L 1E8 (tel. 416–868 0584).

Excellent value as the Eurailpass is, remember that it is essentially for those who plan to do a lot of traveling, over considerable distances and in several countries. If you plan to stay mostly inside Switzerland you'll do better with one of the special plans offered by the Swiss railways for that country only.

Lake Steamers. Swiss Federal Railways provide regular year-round services on a number of lakes, among them: Geneva, Constance, Zurich, Neuchâtel, Bienne, Morat, Thun, Brienz, Lugano and Maggiore. Sailings are reduced out of season—see the official rail timetable for details or ask at the Tourist Office.

POSTAL COACHES. The postal coach network is excellent, and connects central towns with places off the rail network. The coaches are a bright buttercup yellow and still have the traditional and delightful 3-tone coach horn of days of yore as a warning to other drivers as they approach hairpin bends. If you have not got one of the holidays cards giving unlimited travel on both the railways and postal coaches it may be worth buying the Postal Coach Holiday Season Ticket. This is valid for one month and gives free travel on three days, which you can choose as you go along, and half price travel for the rest of the month. Also look out for the Postal Coach Weekly Cards which give unlimited travel over a section of the network. They are available for the following districts: Sion, Sierre, Oberwallis, Ilanz, Thusis, Appenzell, Toggenburg, and the principality of Liechtenstein. You buy the tickets at the local Post Office on arrival. And watch out for the booklets which give details of easy (and not so easy) walks which can be made using one of the postal coaches to return you to your base. Finally keep an eye open for special day or half-day tours; these are invariably good value.

PRESERVED STEAM TRAINS. The Swiss are addicted to the romanticism of steam train travel, especially when it is combined with excellent food and wine aboard a vintage rail car. This is a delightful enough prospect at the best of times, but when you also add beautiful and often dramatic scenery viewed at a sedate pace, you have the makings of a perfect day out. As ever, the Swiss have it organized to a fine art.

Every spring the Swiss National Tourist Office produces a booklet listing those lines that operate steam trains. These fall into three groups. First, those which operate steam trains to a regular timetable for public travel on certain Sundays of the month, usually from June to the end of September. Second, those which run steam locomotive-hauled trains once or twice a year (for which it is best to book in advance). Third, there are those which have operational steam engines, but only run them for groups hiring a complete train. The railways below are those which are of scenic interest, are easily accessible and on which you could see steam operation during even a short stay in Switzerland.

Chemin de Fer Touristique Blonay-Chamby. A museum line, run by enthusiasts, is situated on the hillside above Vevey and Montreux. The 3 km. (2 miles) route is operated using steam and electric traction. It can be reached by taking the Montreux Oberland Bahn from Montreux to Chamby or the line from Vevey to Blonay. For details of operating dates, see 120 (blue pages) in the Swiss Federal Railway timetable.

Brienzer-Rothorn-Bahn. Climbs the Rothorn from Brienz. This is the last mountain railway in Switzerland using steam locomotives in normal service. Operates from May to October.

Vitznau-Rigi-Bahn. Rack-and-pinion railway that runs from Vitznau on the shores of Lake Lucerne almost to the summit of Mt. Rigi. The views from the summit itself are spectacular. Steam services operate on the first and third Sundays of every month from June to September. But if you want a really special day out, make use of the 'Full Steam Ahead' excursion. You travel by historic paddle steamer to Vitznau from Lucerne and then go by steam train up the Rigi. After lunch, you return to Weggis and continue by paddle steamer to the Swiss Transport Museum on the lakeside at Lucerne.

Regionalverkehr Berne Solothurn operate a very efficient network of narrow-gauge suburban railways serving the Berne area. During the summer a steam special is run on the second Sunday of each month. Start your journey on the RVB platforms in the Berne main station and travel the short distance to Worblaufen, a modern suburb where the steam trips begin. The first, in the morning, is on the line to Worb; in the afternoon go to Solothurn. Both are attractive routes running through a mixture of garden suburbs and fields.

FACTS AT YOUR FINGERTIPS 27

Rhaetische Bahn. This is part of one of the largest meter gauge railway systems in Europe (the other principal parts being the Furka Oberalp and the Brig-Visp-Zermatt railways). The railway had in fact largely dispensed with steam engines as long ago as 1922, but two 2-8-0 locomotives (Nos. 107 and 108) have been maintained in working order for special trains. Public excursions are run on several Sundays from May to August and make a circular trip that takes in Landquart, Klosters, Davos, Filisur, Thusis, Chur and back to Landquart. It is an unforgettable day out; the views are magnificent.

It is also occasionally possible to travel on main lines behind steam locomotives. Swiss Federal Railways maintain some five engines for operation at festivals and displays, but they are usually only advertised locally.

The Mikado 1244 preservation society have restored a Liberation 2-8-0 built by the Montreal Locomotive Works in Canada in 1947 for French Railways (SNCF). This magnificent machine is based at Rapperswil and hauls several trains a year; they often include opulent former Orient Express coaches. Book well in advance, and have dinner on the train! Details from *Verein Mikado 1244*, Beethoven-Str. 11, CH-8002, Zurich, Switzerland.

Finally, the Swiss Transport Museum in Lucerne is well worth a visit. The museum covers the complete spectrum of transport in Switzerland from aircraft, through lake steamers, railways and postal coaches and includes exhibits on telecommunications. A large section of the museum is devoted to the development of the railway network including a superb automated model railway of the famous Gotthard route.

MOTORING. Switzerland has two associations which can be of service to the visiting motorist—the *Automobile Club de Suisse (ACS)*, Wasserwerkgasse 39, Berne, and *The Touring Club (TCS)*, Rue Pierre Fatio 9, Geneva 3, both of which have branch offices throughout the country. The TCS operates a 24-hour breakdown and patrol service. Your own automobile club can make contact with either of these two, but ask the Swiss National Tourist Office, before you leave, to give you their tourist map, a marvel of condensation, which on a single sheet gives you a route map for the entire country.

Swiss roads are usually well-surfaced but are mostly winding and hilly, not to say mountainous. It is not really possible to achieve high average speeds, and when estimating likely travel times it is sensible to take a close look at a map. There may be only 20 miles between one point and another, but there could also be a mountain pass among them. There is a well-developed motorway network, but it still has some noteworthy gaps, as for instance in the south along the east-west line roughly between Lugano and Lausanne. When the snows are down this makes motoring in the south a time- and petrol-consuming business, and the snows may well be down until the end of May. However, brilliantly engineered roads and tunnels make north-south travel a delight at any time.

Some mountain passes have railway tunnels beneath them through which cars can be transported by train, the passengers remaining in the cars—a rather curious experience, and often very cold. The latest pride and joy of the Swiss is the St. Gotthard road tunnel, opened in September 1980. At just over 9 miles, it is the longest of its kind in Europe and represents a magnificent feat of engineering. The safety features include SOS telephones every few meters with screens that flash 'We are coming' as soon as the receiver is lifted. The other long Swiss tunnel, the Great St. Bernard, levies a toll of Fr. 15 to 34 according to wheelbase. Useful information on the mountain passes, tunnels, use of chains and many other things is available in the leaflet *Switzerland by Car* obtainable from Swiss National Tourist Offices. As from Jan. '85 motorists are required to display a special tax disc costing Fr. 30 if they wish to drive on the motorways. A second disc will be needed for towed caravans or trailers. Discs will be good for one year of unlimited use.

Information of use to tourists is also broadcast daily, in English, at around 7 P.M. on Channel 1 Swiss Radio, and a daily tourist information bulletin is available on the Swiss telephone system by dialing 120; or 140 for round-the-clock motoring advice and emergency assistance; a road condition bulletin is issued from 8 A.M. onwards on 163.

If you take your own car to Switzerland the only documents you need are the car's registration papers and a valid driving license (minimum age 18), but it is wise to have an insurance Green Card. Caravans require the usual Customs documents (obtainable through your motoring organization). You drive on the right. In built-up areas the speed limit is 50 kph (30 mph). On motorways it is 120 kph (75 mph) and on all other roads, except where clearly marked to the contrary (eg, motorways), there is a strictly enforced speed limit of 80 kph (50 mph). It is compulsory to wear seat belts and children under 12 years old must not be carried on the front seats.

In Switzerland, as in most European countries, vehicles coming from the right normally have priority, and will expect it. The exceptions are on main roads marked by a yellow diamond sign, or by a blue road sign. In such cases *you* have priority over traffic coming from the right—but do *not* take it for granted.

Driving on sidelights only is no longer permitted in any circumstances. Vehicle lights—main, dipped or fog—must be on when traveling in heavy rain or poor visibility, while in road tunnels dipped headlights are obligatory at all times. Police are authorized to collect fines on the spot, *and they do.*

On mountain roads, which are marked with a road sign showing a yellow posthorn on a blue background, the yellow postal coaches have priority over all other vehicles. Such coaches have a distinctive 3-note horn that is used liberally to announce their approach around blind corners and narrow turns: when you hear it, allow as much passing room as the size of your car permits. If the road is too narrow for you and the coach to pass, you must follow the instructions of the driver as to backing up, pulling to one side, etc.

Traffic going *up* a mountain road has priority over all traffic, except postal coaches, going *down*. A useful booklet, *Handbook of Swiss Traffic Regulations*, is obtainable at customs offices, price Fr. 5.

Along mountain roads, where snow chains are frequently needed (and sometimes compulsory) in the winter, there is an established service to equip cars

FACTS AT YOUR FINGERTIPS

with them. Snow chain service posts are identified by signs bearing the words *Service de Chaînes à Neige.* Chains can be hired throughout Switzerland.

If your automobile breaks down, assistance can be hired through the local telephone exchange (ask operator for *Autohilfe*). Roadside repairs or towage are free to motorists with international touring documents.

Car Hire. Several airlines have plans whereby you may arrange when purchasing your plane ticket to have a self-drive or chauffeur-driven car awaiting you at the airport or your hotel. Swiss Federal Railways have a similar arrangement, available at most big stations.

There are dozens of car rental firms in the country; some of the larger ones are: *Avis,* main offices Gartenhofstrasse 17, Zurich and 42 rue de Lausanne, Geneva; *Hertz,* Lagerstrasse 33, Zurich and 60 rue de Berne, Geneva; *Europcar,* Badenerstrasse 812, Zurich and 63–65 rue de Lausanne, Geneva; *Inter Rent,* Lindenstrasse 33, Zurich and 37 rue de Lausanne, Geneva.

Most important car-rental companies have offices at Basle, Geneva and Zurich airports.

Minimum age required for hirer is 21 years. The hirer must have held a valid license for at least a year.

MAJOR ALPINE PASSES. Except in midsummer, it is advisable to check road and weather conditions before starting across any of the major passes. The sun may be shining down where you are, but that's no guarantee that snow and ice aren't turning the pass itself into a nightmare of poor visibility and slick surfaces, or that highway repairs necessitate one-way traffic along certain stretches that will delay you for hours. Both of the Swiss automobile clubs issue daily bulletins, otherwise dial 163 for constant road reports. With most of the important passes, somewhere on the approach road there is a prominent notice stating whether the pass is open or closed.

Swiss Touring Club mechanics in black-and-yellow cars patrol the most frequented mountain passes: St. Gotthard, Susten, Furka, Grimsel, Julier, Simplon, Flüela, Mosses, Pillon, etc.

Bernina. This pass, connecting St. Moritz with Tirano, across the Italian border, is among the most scenic in Switzerland, and is traversed by rail as well as highway. The principal attraction is the exquisite Piz Palü, with its sensational glacier, which is seen just beyond the 2,345 meter (7,700 ft.) summit of the pass. From Poschiavo onward, the atmosphere is distinctly Italian.

The pass is open most of the winter. Maximum gradient 10%. The narrow-gauge Bernina Railway takes three hours for the trip.

Great St. Bernard. The granddaddy of all Swiss passes. Although best known for the legendary lifesaving dogs kept by the monks from the famous hospice, the Great St. Bernard connecting Martigny with Aosta (Italy) is historically one of the most important passes in Europe. It was known and used by the Celts, and later, but long before the birth of Christ, by the Romans. The old pass road, which reaches a height of 2,470 meters (8,100 ft.), is relatively easy driving for

Swiss Touring Club mechanics in black-and-yellow cars patrol the most frequented mountain passes: St. Gotthard, Susten, Furka, Grimsel, Julier, Simplon, Flüela, Mosses, Pillon, etc.

Bernina. This pass, connecting St. Moritz with Tirano, across the Italian border, is among the most scenic in Switzerland, and is traversed by rail as well as highway. The principal attraction is the exquisite Piz Palü, with its sensational glacier, which is seen just beyond the 2,345 meter (7,700 ft.) summit of the pass. From Poschiavo onward, the atmosphere is distinctly Italian.

The pass is open most of the winter. Maximum gradient 10%. The narrow-gauge Bernina Railway takes three hours for the trip.

Great St. Bernard. The granddaddy of all Swiss passes. Although best known for the legendary lifesaving dogs kept by the monks from the famous hospice, the Great St. Bernard connecting Martigny with Aosta (Italy) is historically one of the most important passes in Europe. It was known and used by the Celts, and later, but long before the birth of Christ, by the Romans. The old pass road, which reaches a height of 2,470 meters (8,100 ft.), is relatively easy driving for an Alpine pass, having a maximum gradient of about 10%, but is narrow in parts. The summit section is usually closed about mid-Oct. to mid-June, but a fine 6 km.-long (3¾ miles) tunnel, which burrows some 680 meters (2,000 ft.) under the summit, now enables the crossing to be made throughout the year although chains may be necessary in winter.

There is a Swiss postal coach service from Martigny to the hospice, June-September, two and a half hours; an Italian one from the hospice to Aosta, two hours.

Julier, Maloja. The approach roads for both of these passes connect at Silvaplana, near St. Moritz. Open the year round, they provide an excellent connection between the Grisons and Italy, starting at Chur and passing through Lenzerheide and Silvaplana. On both, the highway is excellent and kept relatively free of snow in winter, although in January and February chains are recommended. The scenery is less rugged than along the western passes but no less pleasing. The countryside is heavily wooded even though the summits of both passes rise above 1,900 meters (6,000 ft.).

Julier: modern, well engineered; maximum gradient 12%. *Maloja:* modern road; gentle, easy ascent from Silvaplana; much steeper—9%—with hairpins coming from Italy.

Postal coaches run from St. Moritz to Lugano, an all-day excursion and one of the most rewarding trips you can make in Switzerland.

Oberalp, Furka, Grimsel. These three connecting passes constitute the primary east-west Alpine traverse, crossing the northern approach to the St. Gotthard at Andermatt. The Oberalp 2,040 meters (6,700 ft.) begins at Disentis near the source of the Rhine and is the boundary between the cantons of Grisons and Uri. The Furka, 2,440 meters (8,000 ft.), between Andermatt and Gletsch, affords a sensational view of the 13 km.-long (8 miles) Rhône Glacier, and at the western end connects with the Grimsel Pass road leading to the Bernese Oberland. The Grimsel, 2,163 meters (7,100 ft.), was known to be in use as early as the 13th century. The principal attraction now is the 304 meter-long, 115

FACTS AT YOUR FINGERTIPS 31

to. Also as a result of this new tunnel, the car rail service has been stopped. The tunnel is toll free. Pass usually open mid-May to mid-Oct. Max. gradient 10%.

San Bernardino. This new tunnel, almost four miles long under the old San Bernardino pass, has given this route added importance. The old road, although fairly easy, maximum gradient 10%, was usually closed mid-Oct. to June over its 1,071 meter (6,800 ft.) summit. With the new tunnel, this route connecting the central Grisons with Bellinzona and Lakes Lugano and Maggiore is now open throughout the year.

Simplon. This major route between Switzerland and Italy was completed at the beginning of the 19th century at the order of Napoleon Bonaparte. When the railway tunnel—the longest in the world—was opened in 1905 Napoleon's road over the pass lost much of its importance. Recently, the road—which reaches 2,080 meters (6,500 ft.)—has been much improved. As a result of new tunnels and snow galleries it is now open throughout the year and, as Alpine passes go, is a relatively easy drive. Cars can also be carried on trains through the rail tunnel between Brig and Iselle.

Swiss postal coaches join Brig and Domodossala in Italy, a 3-hour trip.

Susten. An alternative to the Furka/Grimsel pass route is the Susten, which connects Wassen, north of the St. Gotthard, and Andermatt with Meiringen. This is a first-class highway, the pride of all the Swiss Alpine passes. The Susten region is a favorite of mountain climbers. A quarter-mile tunnel underpasses the summit of the Susten.

Open mid-June to late Oct.; magnificently engineered; easy to drive; heavy weekend traffic; maximum gradient 9%.

There are several coaches a day from Meiringen to Susten, a 3½-hour trip.

Other Alpine Passes. Brünig. 1,005 meters (3,300 ft.). Usually open all year. Good surface, not too many hairpins. Maximum gradient 8%. Chains.

Flüela. 2,375 meters (7,800 ft.). Usually open during the winter, with a toll. Not too difficult. Maximum gradient 10%.

Forclaz. 1,525 meters (5,000 ft.). Usually open throughout the year. Good surface most of way. Maximum gradient 8%. Chains required in winter.

Jaun. 1,493 meters (4,900 ft.). Usually open most of the year, with chains. Good surface, but narrow. Maximum gradient 10%.

Klausen. 1,950 meters (6,400 ft.). Open from mid-June to mid-Oct. Some sharp turns, gravel over summit. Maximum gradient 9%.

Lukmanier. 1,920 meters (6,300 ft.). Open May to end Oct. Good surface. Maximum gradient 9%.

Mosses. 1,432 meters (4,700 ft.). Usually open all year. Relatively easy, modern road. Maximum gradient 8%.

Nufenen. 2,468 meters (8,100 ft.). Fairly narrow approach roads lead to new construction over summit. Maximum gradient 10%. Open June to end Sept.

Ofen (or **Fuorn**).2,163 meters (7,100 ft.). Usually open throughout year. Good surface, relatively easy. Maximum gradient 10%. Chains.

Pillon. 1,525 meters (5,000 ft.). Usually open throughout year. Fairly easy. Maximum gradient 9%. Chains.

Splügen. 2,102 meters (6,900 ft.). Open June to mid-Oct. Good surface but many hairpins and tunnels. Maximum gradient 9%.

Umbrail. 2,498 meters (8,200 ft.). Open late June to mid-Oct. Switzerland's highest pass, narrow and well-supplied with hairpin turns. Gravel surface otherwise not overly challenging. Maximum gradient 9%.

ALPINE TUNNELS. Alpine rail tunnels, through which cars and their occupants are carried by train, make possible year-round transit of the Simplon, Furka, Lötschberg and Albula passes; detailed information on timetables, charges and fares obtainable from the Swiss National Tourist Office or regional tourist offices. In addition, there are four splendid road tunnels—the Great St. Bernard, Mont-Blanc, San Bernardino and the St. Gotthard.

Albula. Rail tunnel Tiefencastel to Samedan. Automobiles about Fr. 82 one way, including driver. Up to 8-seaters; passengers Fr. 17 in 2nd class, Fr. 27 in 1st. Trains run about six times a day the year round.

Furka. Rail tunnel opened in 1982. From Oberwald to Realp. The newest Swiss rail tunnel provides all-year access for both motorists and rail travelers between the Valais and Central Switzerland/the Grisons. The car-carrying shuttle runs hourly and costs Fr. 33 for car and driver.

Great St. Bernard. Road tunnel. Martigny (Switzerland) to Aosta (Italy). Almost four miles long. The first Alpine road tunnel to be built. Tolls levied according to wheelbase; from 15 to 22.50 for car. Drivers are requested to carry either Swiss or Italian money for the payment of tolls.

Lötschberg. Rail tunnel. Automobiles Fr. 40 irrespective of length. Charges are for the journey Kandersteg to Brig, and include vehicle and up to eight passengers remaining in it during journey. (See below for the Brig-Iselle section through Simplon.)

Mont Blanc. Road tunnel opened in 1965. Connects France (Chamonix, near Geneva) with Italy (Courmayeur). For cars, tolls are based on wheelbase, and range from 50 to 270 French francs. Payment must be made in French, Swiss or Italian currency.

San Bernardino. From Hinterrhein to San Bernardino. A 6 km. (4 miles) long road tunnel beneath the old pass. Connects the Grisons with Ticino, Lakes Lugano and Maggiore. No toll charges.

Simplon. Rail tunnel. Brig to Iselle (Italy). Automobiles Fr. 37 irrespective of length; include vehicle and up to 8 passengers remaining in it during journey.

Kilometers into Miles. This simple chart will help you to convert to both miles and kilometers. If you want to convert from miles into kilometers read from the center column to the right, if from kilometers into miles, from the center column to the left.

Miles		Kilometers	Miles		Kilometers
0.6	1	1.6	2.5	4	6.3
1.2	2	3.2	3.1	5	8.0
1.9	3	4.8	3.7	6	9.6

4.3	7	11.3	55.9	90	144.8
5.0	8	12.9	62.1	100	160.9
5.6	9	14.5	124.3	200	321.9
6.2	10	16.1	186.4	300	482.8
12.4	20	32.2	248.5	400	643.7
18.6	30	48.3	310.7	500	804.7
24.8	40	64.4	372.8	600	965.6
31.0	50	80.5	434.9	700	1,126.5
37.3	60	96.6	497.1	800	1,287.5
43.5	70	112.3	559.2	900	1,448.4
49.7	80	128.7	621.4	1,000	1,609.3

CUSTOMS ON RETURNING HOME. Americans. US residents may bring in $400 worth of foreign merchandise as gifts or for personal use without having to pay duty, provided they have been out of the country more than 48 hours and provided they have not claimed a similar exemption within the previous 30 days. Every member of a family is entitled to the same exemption, regardless of age, and the exemption can be pooled. For the next $1,000 worth of goods, inspectors will assess a flat 10% duty based on the price actually paid, so it is a good idea to keep your receipts.

Included in the $400 allowance for travelers over the age of 21 are one liter of alcohol, 100 cigars (non-Cuban) and 200 cigarettes. Any amount in excess of those limits will be taxed at the port of entry, and may additionally be taxed in the traveler's home state. Only one bottle of perfume trademarked in the US may be brought in. However, there is no duty on antiques or art over 100 years old—though you may be called upon to provide verification of the item's age. Write to *US Customs Service,* Washington, D.C. 20229 for information regarding importation of automobiles and/or motorcycles. You may not bring home meats, fruits, plants, soil or other agricultural items.

Gifts valued at under $50 may be mailed to friends or relatives at home, but not more than one per day (of receipt) to any one addressee. These gifts must not include perfumes costing over $5, tobacco or liquor.

If you are traveling with such foreign made articles as cameras, watches or binoculars that were purchased at home, it is best either to carry the receipt for them with you or to register them with U.S. Customs prior to departing. This will save much time (and potential aggravation) upon your return.

Canadians. In addition to personal effects, the following articles may be brought into Canada duty-free: a maximum of 50 cigars, 200 cigarettes, or 2 pounds of tobacco and 40 ounces of liquor, provided these are declared to customs on arrival. The exemption is $300, and gifts mailed to friends should be marked 'Unsolicited Gift—value under $40'.

Britons. There are two levels of duty free allowance for people entering the U.K.; one, for goods bought outside the EEC or for goods bought in a duty free ing importation of automobiles and/or motorcycles. You may not bring home meats, fruits, plants, soil or other agricultural items.

Gifts valued at under $50 may be mailed to friends or relatives at home, but not more than one per day (of receipt) to any one addressee. These gifts must not include perfumes costing more than $5, tobacco or liquor.

If you are traveling with such foreign made articles as cameras, watches or binoculars that were purchased at home, it is best either to carry the receipt for them with you or to register them with U.S. Customs prior to departing. This will save much time (and potential aggravation) upon your return.

Canadians. In addition to personal effects, the following articles may be brought into Canada duty-free: a maximum of 50 cigars, 200 cigarettes, or 2 pounds of tobacco and 40 ounces of liquor, provided these are declared to customs on arrival. The exemption is $300, and gifts mailed to friends should be marked 'Unsolicited Gift—value under $40'.

Britons. There are two levels of duty free allowance for people entering the U.K.; one, for goods bought outside the EEC or for goods bought in a duty free shop within the EEC; two, for goods bought in an EEC country but not in a duty free shop.

In the first category you may import duty free: 200 cigarettes or 100 cigarillos or 50 cigars or 250 grammes of tobacco (*Note* if you live outside Europe, these allowances are doubled); plus one liter of alcoholic drinks over 22% vol. (38.8° proof) or two liters of alcoholic drinks not over 22% vol. or fortified or sparkling wine; plus two liters of still table wine; plus 50 grammes of perfume; plus nine fluid ounces of toilet water; plus other goods to the value of £28.

In the second category you may import duty free: 300 cigarettes or 150 cigarillos or 75 cigars or 400 grammes of tobacco; plus 1½ liters of alcoholic drinks over 22% vol. (38.8° proof) or three liters of alcoholic drinks not over 22% vol. or fortified or sparkling wine; plus four liters of still table wine; plus 75 grammes of perfume; plus 13 fluid ounces of toilet water; plus other goods to the value of £120 (*Note* though it is not classified as an alcoholic drink by EEC countries for Customs' purposes and is thus considered part of the "other goods" allowance, you may not import more than 50 liters of beer).

In addition, no animals or pets of any kind may be brought into the U.K. The penalties for doing so are severe and are strictly enforced; there are *no* exceptions. Similarly, fresh meats, plants and vegetables, controlled drugs and firearms and ammunition may not be brought into the U.K. There are no restrictions on the import or export of British and foreign currencies.

THE SWISS SCENE

SWITZERLAND AND THE SWISS

Heritage and Achievement

by
KENNETH LOVELAND

The biggest challenge Switzerland has to face is its own reputation. Every visitor arriving for the first time does so with a picture ready formed in the mind, either from carefully selected postcards sent by friends on holiday, or from films, from classic tales of travel or from legends.

The Swiss have always been able to rely on other people to do their advertising for them. Poets, painters, musicians, Mark Twain, Queen

Victoria, they all did their bit before the tourist explosion happened. Switzerland is the one country about which we can all claim authority before we have ever been there. The image having been established, Switzerland has to live up to it.

Mostly it does. Here is one of the remaining places on earth where arriving really does justify traveling hopefully. Yet here we encounter the Swiss paradox. It is fatally easy to be wrong about Switzerland. Delight at discovering the Swiss idyll can cause us to stop right there, to be happy with the half of the truth that is about places, and neglect the other half, which is about people. When we spare time for that other half, we uncover contradictions, and some of the ideas we have brought along in our luggage have to be thrown away. Tidily, of course, for Switzerland is a tidy place.

Memory may be allowed the luxury of recalling some of the goods Switzerland puts in its shop window. I remember a day when I sat on a rocky ledge high above Lake Lucerne. Below, steamers chugged their way from Vitznau across to Beckenried, from Brunnen down to Weggis, slashing the turquoise of the lake with minute wakes of white. Snow-clad peaks reached defiantly into an azure sky, green meadows were dotted with wild flowers, cowbells tinkled in happy indiscipline in the valley below. I ate my sandwiches enthralled, ravenous after a walk round the plateau of Klewenalp. Surely this was the Switzerland of the imagination?

There was a day when the sun was hot on the waterside terraces of Montreux, all flowers and sophistication, with the splendor of primitive nature watching from the distant mountains, the vineyards rising in orderly rows, an overlay of French style and elegance subtly suggested all around, and into a lazy mind ghosts intruded. Could this be Stravinsky and Diaghilev arguing out some new idea for the Russian ballet? Was that Tchaikovsky, out on an afternoon walk from Clarens, whence he fled after his disastrous marriage? By Lake Geneva—the visitor soon learns to call it Lac Léman—so much inspiration was born. How could it be otherwise?

Another day, clearly etched in the mind, happened in the Ticino. It was early October in Locarno. The roses had not yet retired, the summer flowers were still in profusion. Yet the trees were changing color, the streets were thick with the russet and gold of fallen leaves and, beyond, the snows were glistening white. There had been minestrone and pasta for lunch in a genial, noisy restaurant in a lakeside village. The chestnut festival awaited us. Three seasons were exchanging greetings amid a riot of color, and Italian brio was tempered with Swiss efficiency.

Days like these are dangerous. They can drug curiosity. And when the drug has worn off, and logic intrudes into the hour of recovery, *the*

SWITZERLAND AND THE SWISS

question starts to nag. In such a land, where three old European cultures of such marked contrast all form part, each with its inherited language, can there possibly be a national character? There is, and it expresses itself in ways that are positive but quiet. We should go in search of it.

Dispelling Illusions

Switzerland is a land which disproves the theory, cherished by propagandists, that you cannot have a national identity without a national language. If there was a national language here, it would be Romansch. According to the sympathies of the person you ask, Romansch is either dead, dying or recovering. But even those who claim that it is gathering strength would be hard put to claim for it much commercial viability. It is kept alive by sincere enthusiasts, which is the way of such things, but when I last sought definite statistics, I was told that it is the first language of no more than one percent of the population. For 74 percent, the first language is German, for 20 percent French and for 4 percent Italian. Romansch is still spoken by one percent. Mathematicians will point to a missing one percent, proof that Switzerland still attracts immigrant minorities.

This is the point at which to dispel, or at least modify, a longstanding legend that the Swiss all speak English. Not all of them do, and I have waited more than once in an attractive backwater village while an obliging landlady fetched a daughter who had progressed to high-school English. But mostly, they do speak English, and this is one of the features that makes Switzerland an ideal place for English-speaking visitors dipping a cautious first toe into the waters of European travel. So is the general desire to get things right.

It is, incidentally, an English with occasional American overtones. Americans will be reassured, British slightly surprised, to learn, at Zurich's fine airport station giving quick access to all the principal cities, that the next train arrives, not at platform four, but track four.

Two more illusions to be dispelled. After days spent walking through pine forests, following mountain tracks, hiking through meadows with only photogenic cows for company, it is easy to support the impression that Switzerland is under-populated and that most of its people must be farmers. Untrue. The average distribution of population works out at more than six times as many people per square kilometer as in the United States, and only seven percent of them are engaged in agriculture or forestry. Machinery tops the employment figures, chemical industries are next, and third place is taken by tourism—which must be another reason for approaching a Swiss holiday with confidence.

Peace, Perfect Peace

Harry Lime made one of the biggest mistakes about Switzerland when he delivered his cynical defense of violence while going round the great wheel of Vienna's Prater. Look at the cruel history of Italy, he argued, and the glories of art it produced. Look at Switzerland. Hundreds of years of peace, and what did it produce? The cuckoo clock!

Now, though Switzerland has produced no Shakespeare, no Mozart, no Michelangelo, the Swiss record in the creative arts is not insignificant, and in appreciation of them it is higher than most. The nations which produce the artists are not necessarily those with the widest taste. I have sat appalled in the countries which produced Beethoven and Haydn while audiences have mustered only grudging applause for masterpieces which happened not to be German or Austrian. I have been dismayed many times by the apathy of Italian audiences towards works which were part of the mainstream of world music but not part of their national tradition. But, on the other hand, I have often felt the audience at the Lucerne Festival to be the most receptive and broadminded in Europe, witness to an informed cosmopolitanism which is a healthy thread running through Swiss artistic life.

Where Harry Lime really got it wrong was in that crack about peace. True, the last time the Swiss were involved in a war with a foreign power was during the Napoleonic campaigns, though there have been conflicts at home, including the armed dispute between Catholics and Protestants in 1847. But Swiss nationhood had first to be bought with blood and fire.

Back home, the holiday over, it is easy to nod approval at the text books which claim that the William Tell legend is only partly true. But it is another thing to deny it when you are standing in front of Richard Kissling's defiant statue, in the square at Altdorf, where they will tell you he shot the apple from his son's head and braved Gessler. It is a cold-blooded disbeliever who does not feel the pulse quicken in the valley where the men of the cantons gathered to destroy Gessler's troops. If it was good enough for Schiller and Rossini, it is good enough for me. Only an unromantic cynic can walk the lush green plateau of the Rütli, and not warm to the thought of the representatives of the founder cantons taking their oath.

A long time ago? So it was. But it was on this same ground, they say, that the Swiss commanders gathered in 1940 when, surrounded by Axis powers, they decided on a plan of defense. Switzerland was not involved in the actual fighting of the two major wars in Europe during the 20th century—but she was not untouched by them. There were the hardships caused by the blockades of the first, there was the proximity

SWITZERLAND AND THE SWISS

of the second. The help given to Allied airmen and escaped prisoners of war during that time is a matter of history.

Peace and absence of war are not quite the same thing, as the world is beginning to learn. Realists ever, the Swiss determination to protect a hard-won independence is one of the strongest indications of a national character. It comes as a shock to the uninformed to learn that this nation with a reputation for peace has compulsory military service.

It was brought home to me when I was waiting for a train in Berne one Saturday morning. Surely I knew that uniformed figure, pack on back, rifle slung, boots polished? I did. It was a prominent businessman off to do his national service. Did he have to, I asked. Yes, he replied gloomily, and you could see that Sunday lunch was on his mind. Then, as the train came in, he brightened. "I am, in fact, a very good shot with a rifle," he proclaimed defensively.

In Switzerland, only disability or residence abroad qualify for exemption from military service, which must be bought with a personal tax. Every young Swiss man has an initial course of 17 weeks at the age of 20, and is allocated after basic training to the unit with which he will work in future. There will be recurring refresher courses of three weeks until he is 36, of two weeks each after that. The military obligation lasts until 55 for officers, until 50 for other ranks.

Even in years when he is not called for national service, he is not allowed to forget it. His equipment is always somewhere around the house, for the Swiss soldier is the only one in the world who keeps his rifle, ammunition, gas mask and other gear at home—he has to produce it for regular inspection and attend marksmanship courses.

Hardly what you would expect in a peace-loving nation. So as the train pulled out I asked the question. "Why, if you never have a war, do you need such a large trained army?"

He lowered the window. "That," he shouted, "is why we never have a war."

Tolerance and Enlightenment

So the Swiss are prepared to defend their own rights. They have, of course, always been generous in their championship of the rights of others. I was walking past the Place Molard in Geneva one morning when a plaque above an ancient gateway caught my eye. *Geneve, cité de refuge,* it read. So it has been, a city of refuge down the centuries.

What an assorted company they make, those refugees who came to Geneva. Here came Calvin, Knox and other fugitives from persecution at the time of the Reformation, and one of Geneva's finest statues catches them in a mood of collective disapproval, a stern "Thou Shalt Not" about to be delivered. De Beze, though, looks as though his mind is on other things. After all, he did marry his mistress before joining the Presbyterians.

What would the Calvinists have thought of some of those who came after them? Byron, in disgrace with London society and accused of incest with his half-sister Mrs. Leigh; Shelley, his marriage with Harriet Westbrook disintegrated; Liszt with his mistress the Countess d'Agoult; Wagner, on the run from husbands, creditors and politicians. Defenders of the word and freedom of thought, Voltaire, Victor Hugo, Balzac and others passed through the town where Rousseau himself was born. And in our own century, Geneva's role as the home of the League of Nations, then the United Nations, and as the birthplace of the Red Cross have won for it and the nation of which it is part a name as the protector of humanities. Tolerance is one word which comes to mind. Enlightenment is another.

All of which makes it rather odd that women in Switzerland should have had to wait so long for the vote. It did not come their way until 1971.

One day, while shopping in the vegetable market for a picnic, I took my courage in both hands and asked a woman if she felt deprived at not having the vote. "And what would I do with it?" she demanded. Waving a hand at a stall of mushrooms and tomatoes, "Would it buy me any more of these?"

The awful truth is that I cannot recall a Swiss woman ever telling me that she felt deprived at not participating in elections. No doubt some did. Neither have I spoken to any who feel that their lives have changed dramatically since women's suffrage was introduced. No doubt some do. I shrink before the impending assault of women's rights campaigners, but can only report. Switzerland seems to be the same happy, well-run country that it was before. Yet a little voice persists. Was it not odd that the land of humanities kept its women waiting so long?

In fact, there are still corners where they are not yet allowed to take part in cantonal elections, particularly where such elections are conducted in the open air by a show of hands (*Landsgemeinde*).

Transports of Delight

One senses a reluctance to change which contrasts oddly with the Swiss reputation for grasping the nettle of progress in other things. But one detects also a readiness to compromise. This is demonstrated practically in the partnership of state and private enterprise in the transport system, a genius for making the best of both worlds.

At a time when we hear of state-owned airlines plunging into deficit, it comes as a surprise to know that Swissair, the national carrier and

SWITZERLAND AND THE SWISS

a superb advertistment for Swiss standards everywhere it flies, is not, in fact, state-owned and actually makes a profit. Roughly two-thirds of its share capital is in private hands, and only about 30 percent in the hands of government institutions and local authorities. There is no direct government subsidy.

When we turn to the railways, the private sector is even more prominent. Spend a holiday in Switzerland, and you are almost certain to travel at some time or another on a private railway. They may have pulled up a few lines and put down one or two others since writing, but in round figures, something like three-fifths of the network is state-owned, and the rest is operated by 97 private railways.

Over the state lines run the crack expresses and an intricate design of local services. To this the private lines are an indispensable complement, reaching into delectable backwaters and adding to the personality of the areas they serve. I have had some wonderful experiences on the private lines of Switzerland, and if I remember the Montreux-Bernese-Oberland railway especially, it's just that this is the one that comes to mind at the moment.

I was commuting between the Festivals of Lucerne and Montreux. It was a glorious September day, golden and mellow, and I changed to the Montreux-Bernese-Oberland line at Zweisimmen. The line curved its way in and out of the mountains, taking steep gradients in its stride, giving unforgettable views of proud mountain peaks and sylvan valleys. Then, suddenly, we passed through clouds, and there was the blue spread of Geneva's lake below—there was Montreux, there was the Château de Chillon, immortalized by Byron, its gaunt walls washed by the waters of the lake, there were the sun-kissed vineyards, there were fields ablaze with wild narcissi. It was as though a master magician had suddenly drawn back the curtain on the unexpected and the exotic.

The triumphs of engineering and organization that have gone into the making of the Swiss railway design can be measured in statistics. We can be astonished to know that there are more than 5,000 kilometers of railway in such a small country, that Mount Pilatus (which Queen Victoria ascended on a mule the first time she went there) has the steepest rack and pinion railway in the world with a maximum gradient of one in two. We are impressed to learn that the Jungfrau railway's Jungfraujoch terminus stands at 11,333 feet, and is the highest anywhere in the world. We can thrill to the thought of the adventurous pioneering and engineering that gave Switzerland some of the longest tunnels, the 12 miles of the Simplon, the nine miles each of the Gotthard and the Lötschberg. The figures are a permanent record of the determination of a small nation to conquer a difficult terrain.

But what cannot be measured in statistics in the joy that Swiss railways, and particularly those mountain ascents, have given to millions of passengers. When Queen Victoria was helped from her mule at the top of Pilatus, she would have been rewarded by a panorama of the green Swiss lowlands, Lake Lucerne looking like a star-shaped mirror, and the ice-capped peaks of the Bernese Oberland—the Eiger, the Mönch, the Jungfrau—brilliant in the sunshine. You will find similar experiences at the top of most mountain railways in Switzerland. Statistics retreat at the memory.

I have often climbed into one of the red cars of the Rigi railway and watched Vitznau shrink into a dot as we rose ever higher. Not so long ago, I saw in a museum a notice announcing that for Fr. 16, you could hire a horse to take you to the top. That was in the 18th century. You could also be carried there in a sedan chair. But in 1871, they built the rack and pinion railway, and it's now the oldest of its kind in Europe.

It has long been electrified, but when the centenary was celebrated in 1971, they fetched out of retirement one of the splendid old steam engines that had been specially designed for the gradients in the early days of the line, and we savored the nostalgic smell of hot oil and felt ourselves to be a little corner of history re-lived as the old engine with the upright boiler puffed her way to the top.

No matter how much more efficient the railways are now that the steam engines have been put out to grass, a slice of romance has gone with them. The Swiss have a sentimental regard for them, and you will find some among other relics of their transport system preserved in the fine Lucerne Transport Museum, worth a day's browsing. During the summer, steam returns on several of the lines. When last I went up Rigi, I was delighted on leaving the steamer at Vitznau to see an engine belching smoke at the head of a line of carriages. It was like coming home. The Swiss know that, given the chance, we can be just as sentimental as they are, and steam can add a dimension of romance.

They call Rigi the singing mountain. Mark Twain might have had another name for it. The story is that, pursued by ardent Alpine horn blowers, he paid them off generously only to find their numbers doubled at the next village. The news had spread.

Rigi I love, Pilatus too. Wagner would have had a magnificent view of both. He took the villa at Tribschen, just outside Lucerne (it is a well-kept museum today) and there wrote parts of *The Mastersingers, Siegfried,* and *Twilight of the Gods,* as well as the *Siegfried Idyll,* a combined Christmas and birthday present for Cosima. I like to think that some of the most turbulent passages in the *Ring* might have been written with memories of days when storms swept the lake, and lightning flickered around the tops of Pilatus and Rigi.

Today, when one watches the *Cisalpin* rush out of the Simplon tunnel on its way from Paris to Milan, or stands on Basle station marvelling at the way they break up and re-form through expresses

SWITZERLAND AND THE SWISS

from all parts of Europe, it's amusing to recall that one of the practical reasons for the start of Swiss railways in 1847 was the liking of the Zurich aristocracy for hot buns with their breakfast. The buns were made at Baden, and an important assignment for Switzerland's first railway, 23 kilometers from Zurich to Baden, was to ensure that the buns arrived in time for breakfast. Out of such priorities grew one of the finest railway systems in the world.

The Varied Fabric

The Swiss are proud of their railways. They are, in fact, proud of anything to do with transport, and have a quite touching affection for it. It's an affection that's easy to share, whether it is lavished on the railways, the yellow postal coaches or those lovely old paddle steamers with the beautifully engraved prows and majestic lines, sailing down the lakes with all the elegance of swans. For me, drifting from one lakeside settlement to another on an old-fashioned steamer with a tall funnel is an ideal form of escape. The Switzerland of statistics and business acumen slips out of sight, and the romance is enhanced when a village band comes on board, or perhaps a choir in national costume, on the way to a folk festival.

Switzerland is rich in these folk festivals, and you can be quickly caught up in them. There are the grape harvest festivals of Valais; the beribboned cows on their way to their winter quarters in a score of villages; Alpine traditions jealously preserved—Lucerne's Martinmas Goose; the cheese distribution in the Justis valley; the risotto meals of the Ticino; religious festivals. Colorful costumes, masks, processions, dancing, quaint old customs are all part of celebrations which can be riotous, sometimes devout.

In the remote regions of Appenzell, I have been awakened by the drum heralding the dawn of carnival day; in Schaffhausen, I've been hauled on to the platform to become part of carnival itself. You need to know a little about local politics to get the best out of carnival. Much of it is involved in the lampooning of local figures, the burlesquing of recent events. The cartoon of a year's affairs passes before your eyes. And suddenly, another myth is exploded. Who said the Swiss have no sense of humor? They have, and what is more, they can stand being on the receiving end of the joke. At carnival time, the most unlikely people have to.

I was once told you can judge a nation by its capital. Experience makes me doubtful. But the Swiss, as a nation, are happily represented by Berne. On the one side, a city of fine shops and a transport center that is a model of 20th-century planning; on the other, the old town: graceful arcades that remind one of Italy, eleven decorated fountains in the old streets that lead from the Kramgasse to the Marktgasse, the onion market, the signs of the guilds, the medieval facades, geraniums tumbling from the window boxes, the 16th-century astronomical clock and, at the end of it all, the bears, Berne's very special pets, part of the town's history and celebrated on its coat of arms, regularly going through their performances in the pit watched by admiring children of all ages—Swiss sentiment beginning to show again.

You can step backwards in time so easily in Berne. So you can in Basle, by old Father Rhine, and in Zurich, where the quiet of medieval squares contrasts so strangely with the city's fame as a business center.

In Engelberg too, though in a different way; here it is not fanciful at all to imagine the shades of ecclesiastics dead for centuries, nor whimsical for the ear to catch the chants of forgotten monks in the grounds of the Benedictine monastery beneath the mountains. Here is peace of a kind that transcends time, and atmosphere is all. So it is at Einsiedeln, when I once sat hushed while a procession of pilgrims, their long journey over, filed slowly into the monastery and fell to prayer. It had been happening there for a thousand years.

But we started by looking, in a practical and reasoned way, for the Swiss national character, and we have been seduced from the path by the beauty of the country, by its diversity—just as we predicted would happen.

Yet in letting the fancy wander, in deserting hard facts for romance and color remembered, perhaps we have discovered something.

Perhaps a picture has emerged of a national character which is welcoming and is no less sincere because it is experienced: a peaceable demeanor with a strong streak of realism, and a firm willingness to stand up for itself. A personality wary of change for its own sake but open to persuasion and prepared to compromise, proud of achievement and jealous of heritage, be it from God or man. There is a surprising vein of sentimentality and a touch of poetry which can be aroused by such matters as the snows of the Jungfrau turning from white to pink in the sunset. There's quite a sense of fun, too, and a feeling for the fine things of life.

On the whole, just the kind of person to be found living in a land where distinctive cultures overlap—a place of dramatic mountains, time-soaked cities, busy industry, placid lakes, noisy carnivals and massive forest silences. He is the product of a small state with an amazingly varied fabric. May he never have to bring the equipment out of the cupboard to defend it. For Switzerland is contentment—a vanishing commodity in an angry world.

THE CONFEDERATION THAT WORKS

A Synopsis of Swiss History

Situated as it is at the crossroads of Europe's natural trans-Alpine routes, Switzerland was the scene of much coming and going—tribal migrations, armies and, later, merchant caravans—even before the curtain went up on the European stage.

Prehistoric man of the Iron Age has left traces of his passage at La Tène, the northeastern point of Lake Neuchâtel, where archeologists have found one of Europe's most important settlements of that period. At the dawn of recorded history Celtic tribes and especially the Helvetii migrated into the plateau lands, bounded on the west by the Jura mountains and on the east by the Alps, and wandered down into the Lake Geneva region. The Swiss of today, in poetry and in song and on solemn occasions, call their country Helvetia, symbolized by a lady of generous proportions. And, indeed, all official Federal documents bear the seal of the *Confoederatio Helvetica,* or Swiss Confederation.

The Romans, under Julius Caesar, interested in the conquest of Gaul, put an end to the migrations of the Helvetii in 58 BC and, via the Great St. Bernard Pass, brought in the wake of their armies the culture and prosperity of their civilizations to territories of the conquered tribes and also to Rhaetia (now known as the Grisons). But the Romanization of Switzerland was at best patchy, and the Alemani, of German origin, infiltrated and settled in the northeastern part of what is present-day Switzerland, and in the central plateau. Meanwhile, the Burgundians established themselves west of the Sarine, the river which flows through Fribourg. A relatively peaceful people already converted to Christianity, the Burgundians in course of time were assimilated by the native population. Latin was the language at first spoken in the region but over the centuries various French dialects came to the fore, to be replaced in comparatively recent times by the French that is spoken there today. The ancient boundary between the Germanic Alemani and the French-speaking Burgundians varies little, in fact, from the language frontier which exists today.

In Rhaetia, where the Romans had gained a strong footing, the native population, firmly ensconced in their mountains, were able to resist assimilation by the invaders. Latin remained the language spoken there and so in the Grisons today many thousands speak Romansch, Switzerland's fourth national language and one which sprang from an old Rhaetian dialect. South of the Alps, the Italian-speaking territory now know as the Ticino, and geographically part of Italy, remained untouched by these racial upheavals and for several centuries followed the destinies of Lombardy.

Aftermath of Empire

After the split-up of Charlemagne's colossal empire in the 9th century, the power of an insecure central government was broken: all over Europe, bailiffs, barons, lords, and overlords strove one against the other, eager to grasp power and wealth. West of the Jura, the house of Burgundy arose, to rule vast territories extending across the plateau to the shores of Lake Geneva. The Burgundian kings reigned wisely and well, introducing the cultivation of flax and the vine and many domestic crafts. Rudolf III of Burgundy made a gift of his lands to the Emperor of Germany and, at his death, in 1032, Conrad II formally took possession of his new territories and was crowned King of Burgundy at Payerne. Thus all the Alpine lands were incorporated in the German Empire.

THE CONFEDERATION THAT WORKS

Nevertheless, throughout this territory, far too vast for the wielding of a careful, centralized government, ducal families greedily continued to snatch what they could. During the 12th century, the Dukes of Zähringen owned most extensive estates reaching in a wide span from Lake Geneva to Lake Constance, and the populations under their sway strove in vain for freedom. However, modern Switzerland owes seven cities to the House of Zähringen: Fribourg, which was founded in 1178 by Duke Berthold IV, and Berne, founded in 1191, by Berthold V, who died childless in 1218, to mention but two.

A great opportunity was now to be had for the taking and one can imagine the eagerness with which the innumerable petty lords temporal of the dukedom—counts, barons, bailiffs—to say nothing of the lords spiritual—bishops and abbots—seized this great chance of dividing up the Zähringen estates.

The House of Savoy promptly invaded the north shore of Lake Geneva. Duke Peter extended his territories as far north as Gruyères and the Oberland. In the course of this victorious swoop, he built many castles and fortresses, among them Chillon, with the aid of English military architects from the Plantagenet court of Henry III. Peter of Savoy died in 1268. He remains a brilliant and heroic figure and his intelligent policies firmly established his family on the road that was to lead to the throne of Italy in the 19th century.

One mighty opponent stood barring Savoy's way to a more complete victory: Rudolph IV of Habsburg, whose family had risen slowly to riches and power amid the disruption of medieval empires. History says that Rudolph was a generous, godly man. He was certainly astute and ambitious. From his family seat at Habsburg, in Aargau, he cleverly made his bid until, in 1273, he achieved the supreme success of being elected Emperor of Germany. It was then purely an honorary title, for the imperial authority had been undermined by warring nobles. Rudolph had no intention of remaining a mere figurehead, however. He set the imperial house in order, brought his lords and princes to heel and, by creating at least the illusion of peace, encouraged the commoners to work. Nor did he neglect his own interests, not the least of his acquisitions being the Duchy of Austria. At his death, in 1291, the House of Habsburg reigned supreme in Central Europe and the Alps.

Economic and human conditions were not so good, however, under the Habsburg domination and, in the central Alps, men were beginning to dream of freedom. The three clans of Uri, Schwyz, and Unterwald sent their magistrates to hold a secret conclave, according to legend at the famous field of Rütli, a meadow overlooking Lake Lucerne opposite Brunnen. The outcome of this meeting was a pact of mutual allegiance and assistance among the people of Uri, Schwyz, and Unterwald. A document was drawn up in Latin to which the three seals were set on the first of August, 1291. It is still reverently preserved in the archives of the canton of Schwyz, for it is the foundation stone of the Swiss confederation.

From that time on, the House of Habsburg played a losing game in the Alps. Its bailiffs and soldiers were harassed by guerrilla warfare and were the butt of such tricks as those attributed to the legendary William Tell. In 1315, Duke Leopold of Habsburg decided to put an end to all this, but, unfortunately for him, his fine army was defeated by the confederate army at Morgarten. After this victory, the three allies made their intentions public in the Pact of Brunnen.

The wave of revolt spread. Other territories and cities, subject to the Empire and the Habsburgs, unhesitatingly stepped out on the road of freedom. Lucerne joined the confederates in 1332, Zurich in 1351, Glarus and Zug in 1352, and, finally Berne in 1353.

Understandably enough, the House of Habsburg was not prepared to lose such vast territories without a fight. Leopold II organized a strong expeditionary force against the confederates, but was defeated at Sempach in 1386 and again, two years later, at Näfels. The Habsburgs had had their lesson and, in 1394, were ready to sign a 20-year peace pact with their former vassals.

The Martial 15th Century

Meanwhile, the rest of the alpine territories were split up into countless small vassal states. The House of Savoy still possessed the greater part of the Lake Geneva region, except for the city of Geneva, which was held in the benefice of a powerful bishopric.

The eight confederate states had tasted victory and liked it. In 1415, they set out to wrest from the Habsburgs the old imperial city of Aarau. A few years later, Thurgau also passed into their hands. The newly won lands were divided up among the victors and became vassal territories.

Neighboring populations continued to wrest their freedom from spiritual and temporal overlords. Schaffhausen asserted its rights as a free imperial city. Appenzell revoked the suzerainty of the Abbey of St. Gallen and the Grisons revolted against the feudal domination of the Bishopric of Chur.

The activities of the confederates had not escaped the notice of the wily old fox, the French king, Louis XI, whose great rival was Charles the Bold of Burgundy. To further his own ends, Louis negotiated a perpetual peace pact between the Swiss and their old enemies the Habsburgs. That took place in 1474 and the confederates were free thereafter to expend their warlike energy in another direction. The Habsburgs were in conflict with Burgundy in regard to the territories of Alsace and Breisgau and it took little to persuade the confederates

THE CONFEDERATION THAT WORKS

that they should go to war on behalf of their new friend, Austria. So began the Burgundian wars.

The first round went to the Swiss, who won the battle of Héricourt in 1474 and followed up this victory with the invasion of Franche-Comté. Two years later, Charles the Bold succeeded in mobilizing a great army and marched against the Swiss. He was defeated, however, at Grandson and at Morat.

In the flush of victory, the confederates invaded the territory of Vaud (a fief of Savoy on the north of Lake Geneva) and then called an international conference in Fribourg. Delegates from France, Austria, Savoy, the Alsatian cities, and the confederate states decided that Vaud should be returned to Savoy, that Berne should hold certain communities in the Rhône Valley. Fribourg's status as a free and independent city was recognized.

The Burgundian wars flickered out with the death of Charles the Bold at the battle of Nancy in 1477. Thus France got rid of an annoying rival and the Swiss won great military prestige.

Having tasted power, the confederates continued to pursue their policy of territorial expansion. When, for example, Swiss merchants complained that their cattle had been seized by agents of the Duke of Milan, it was an excellent excuse for the occupation of Domodossola and the Valle Leventina, south of the St. Gotthard. Uri and Obwald retained a foothold in that region, despite peace treaties with Milan. Thus other vassal states were added to the steadily increasing territories of the eight Swiss cantons.

The allotment of war spoils is never conducive to harmony. Nor did the confederates find it so. Strife arose between the three prosperous cities of Berne, Zurich, and Lucerne and their poor relations, the rural cantons of Uri, Schwyz, Unterwald, Zug, and Glarus. Dissension was aggravated by the request of Fribourg and Solothurn to be admitted also into the confederation.

By one of those rare strokes of good fortune that sometimes befall a nation, the Swiss had in their midst a one-time farmer and political leader who had become a venerable hermit and mystic, by the name of Nicholas of Flüe. So in 1481 an emissary was dispatched posthaste to the great man by the Council of Stans, where the cantons teetered on the brink of civil war. His advice was earnestly sought, freely given and wisely followed, the member states reinforcing their pact by a convention breathing brotherly love and promising mutual assistance against aggression or the revolt of minority populations. Fribourg and Solothurn were allowed to join the confederation.

The member states now numbered ten. Later, they were joined by Basle, Schaffhausen, and, in 1513, by Appenzell.

In 1500, the lingering dispute with Milan was aggravated when Uri, Schwyz, and Unterwald seized and held the fief of Bellinzona, south of the Alps. Nevertheless, to prove their goodwill, the confederates broke their alliance with France (whose King Louis XII had occupied the Duchy of Milan in 1499) and took up arms in favor of Milan. In 1512, the confederate army swept across the Alps into the plain of Lombardy and won victory after victory over the French armies. They graciously re-established Maximilian Sforza in his dukedom. For three years the Swiss remained invincible and the taste of power was sweet.

But the throne of France changed hands. The proud Francis I succeeded sickly Louis XII and set about regaining the lost kingdom of Italy. At Marignano, in 1515, 20,000 Swiss, with only a small force of artillery, came face to face with 60,000 French and Venetian troops armed with the most modern weapons. The defeat of the confederates was final and the following year they accepted and signed a pact of perpetual peace with France. Truth to say, the Swiss were treated rather well by a magnanimous victor: they were allowed to retain the territories they had won in battle, except the Valley of Ossola, and furthermore received a generous financial indemnity.

Renunciation of Empire; the Reformation

It is now, after the defeat of Marignano, that occurs one of the most astounding—and wisest—changes of policy in the history of any nation. The thirteen confederate states, realizing that the methods of warfare had been changed by the introduction of modern artillery and that, with the limited means at their disposal, they could not hope to vie in the field with the great powers, renounced all thought of territorial expansion in Europe. Both the cities and the rural cantons settled down to achieve prosperity by commercial development and the arts of peace. True, this did not mean that all citizens within the confederation were free men: the sovereign cantons still held in fief many vassal communities and territories.

At this period, too, we find that the basic social structure of Switzerland began to grow and develop. Switzerland has no nobility, no aristocracy as understood elsewhere in Europe. The upper crust of Swiss society consists of old, and formerly rich and landed, patrician families, having their roots in both town and country. In the early days of the confederation such families provided military leaders and magistrates who actively pursued the federal interests and their own. In the 16th century, their descendants were sufficiently alive to the potentialities of trade and commerce to seek power and enrichment in this field.

THE CONFEDERATION THAT WORKS

For this reason, too, the 13 cantons of the confederation, having but little to export and an energetic population to sustain, found a way of killing two birds with one stone by 'exporting' their mercenary troops. For centuries to come, France, the German kings, and other European powers, great and small, were glad to avail themselves of the help of Swiss mercenaries in the fighting of their wars. These troops were commanded by their own officers and flew their own standards and were never assimilated into the armies amongst which they fought. The Swiss Guard of the Vatican is the last relic of this custom.

At home, also, for a certain period, men of the 16th century found ample opportunity to expend their energies in religious strife. The wave of reforms set going by Martin Luther and Ulrich Zwingli in the early years of the century led to the abolition of Catholic rites in Zurich in 1523. Berne listened to the inspired teaching of Berthold Haller; Basle to John Hausschein, known as Oecolampade. Geneva became the refuge and the fortress of the French Huguenots and their leader, William Farel, and his fanatical successor, John Calvin. By 1535, the power of the Bishop of Geneva had been entirely broken and the city became a sovereign republic.

These religious conflicts provided a glorious opportunity for the still territorially ambitious canton of Berne. Duke Charles VIII of Savoy, alarmed by the progress made by the Reformed Faith, commenced hostilities against Geneva. Berne came to the rescue and, at the same time, 'peacefully' occupied, 'liberated and annexed' Vaud, a fief of Savoy. The chief town of the district, Lausanne, remained the seat of the Bernese bailiff for two centuries.

Thus, gradually, the Swiss confederation was assuming the form and structure that we know today. Two religious faiths—the Catholic and the Protestant—were accepted by the 13 member states, seven of whom remained faithful to the Church of Rome: Uri, Schwyz, Unterwald, Lucerne, Zug, Fribourg, and Solothurn.

Until the French Revolution, in 1789, Switzerland's story remained more or less uneventful, at least so far as the outside world was concerned. The confederation ably succeeded in remaining clear of the Thirty Years' War (1618–1648) and obtained official recognition by the great powers of its status as a sovereign, neutral state by the treaty of Westphalia.

Nevertheless, at home, the course of Swiss life did not run quite so smoothly. The ascendancy of the urban cantons—Berne, Zurich, Lucerne, and Basle—over the rural communities gained rapidly. Vassal states were treated with anything but brotherly leniency: heavy taxation, tolls and statute labor filled the coffers of the all-powerful cantons whose administrations and government had passed into the hands of a few patrician families. Revolts of the peasant populations against this

THE SWISS SCENE

oligarchy were sternly suppressed, as in the Peasant War of 1653. Almost a century later, in 1728, the heroic patriot of Vaud, Major Davel, was put to death by the Bernese for championing his country's liberties. Throughout the 18th century, Switzerland smoldered with sedition and revolt.

Despite this, Switzerland appeared to contemporary Europe as an idyllic state. The fashion for travel among the romantic Alps and along the no less romantic shores of Lake Geneva had been set by Jean-Jacques Rousseau, the Geneva-born literary giant of the pre-Revolution period. His novel *La Nouvelle Héloise,* with its setting in Montreux and Chillon, had taken Europe by storm. Replete with cosy though dilapidated farmsteads, rugged mountains, and glittering lakes, Swiss rural communities still gave a reflection of peace in a Europe already tossed on the surge of revolutionary ideas.

The French Revolution

Close neighbor to France, Switzerland could scarcely escape the influence of the French Revolution. In Basle, Geneva, Zurich, and elsewhere, subject communities rose against their masters. In January 1798, the people of Vaud stormed against their Bernese bailiffs and proclaimed their independence, christening their new state the Lemanic Republic. The cry of 'liberty and equality' sounded throughout the confederation like a trumpet call.

This sudden dispersal of authority also served as an incentive for revolutionary France, whose armies invaded Switzerland in March 1798. First Vaud, then Berne, passed into their hands. The confederation of the 13 cantons was doomed and in its place the French government established a tottering satellite state, the Helvetic Republic. The Republic of Geneva was annexed by France in the same year.

The artificial structure of the new republic was foredoomed to failure. It became the butt of conflicting interests and political factions. Finally, in 1803, Napoleon Bonaparte intervened and imposed his mediation, obtaining the restoration of a federal regime. Six states joined the new confederation: St. Gallen, Grisons, Aargau, Thurgau, Ticino, and Vaud. Legislative powers were vested in a federal diet presided over by a chief Landammann, who remained in office one year. Under his regime, Switzerland enjoyed ten years of peace.

Unfortunately, as Napoleon's power began to fade in 1812–1813, and despite the diet's declaration of neutrality, the Austrian army—160,000 strong—marched into Switzerland at Basle and Schaffhausen. In December 1813, the diet annulled Napoleon's act of mediation and freed the confederation from the tutelage of France.

THE CONFEDERATION THAT WORKS

Attempts were then made by Berne and Zurich to restore the old oligarchy, but the new sovereign cantons, such as Vaud and Aargau, found an unexpected champion in the person of Emperor Alexander I of Russia. Under his sternly liberal eye, the diet was forced to elaborate a new federal pact that was presented to and accepted by the powers, gathered together in godlike assembly, at Vienna, in 1815, their purpose being to reorganize Europe. Switzerland's 1815 constitution included three more member states: Valais, Neuchâtel, and Geneva.

However, the political structure of Switzerland remained insecure, and the country did not escape the general political convulsions and turmoil that engulfed much of Europe in 1848. After a series of revolutionary movements and the religious Sonderbund war (effectively a Civil War) had swept the country, a new constitution was drawn up and accepted by the 22 cantons. This gave rise to a bicameral legislative body, the Federal Assembly, composed of a National Council and a States Council. Executive powers were vested in the Federal Council and the Federal Tribunal served as the Supreme Court of Appeal. The cantons all conserved their own governments and undertook not to form alliances amongst themselves and to leave to the federal government the care of conducting negotiations with the outside world. Berne was selected as the federal capital.

The new regime proved acceptable to all the cantons; it had been elaborated with the cooperation of them all and was not submitted to the approval of the great powers. The Swiss confederation thus took its place among the nations as a wholly independent, sovereign state.

Nevertheless, as time went on, it was found that the 1848 constitution was in many respects insufficient; it was revised and augmented in 1874. The powers vested in the federal government were increased, especially as regarded the army. Compulsory, free schooling was to be introduced throughout the confederation, although the application of the law remained a cantonal matter. Two liberties were introduced: the rights of initiative and referendum. By the former, any male citizen, provided he can obtain the signature of 100,000 of his fellows, may propose the introduction of a new law to the federal assembly. Referendum means that 50,000 signatures suffice to force the federal government to submit any enactment to popular approval.

On the 1st January, 1979, Jura became a new canton. This brought the number of full cantons up from 22 to 23. Jura, whose capital is Delémont, was the French-speaking part of the Berne canton. The various half-cantons are also lobbying for full cantonal status, which would entitle them to send two representatives, instead of one, to the States Council.

Switzerland Today

The structure of the Swiss federal constitution can be summarized as follows: a bicameral legislative body, the Federal Assembly, is composed of two houses: the National Council (corresponding to the US House of Representatives), to which one deputy per 22,000 people is elected, and the States Council (equivalent to the US Senate), in which sit two representatives of each canton. The executive body is the Federal Council, composed of seven members (elected for four years, but almost always re-elected), who rotate each year in the office of President of the Council and also of the Confederation.

Each canton is a republic, a sovereign state having its own government composed of an executive (State Council, Government Council, etc.) and a legislative (Cantonal Council, Great Council, etc.) branch. They have almost full control of cantonal affairs: education, public health, police, cantonal taxes, etc.

Federal and most cantonal elections are held every four years. But the civic-minded Swiss voter has quite a busy time. He is called to the polls frequently to voice his opinion (by ballot) on federal, cantonal, and municipal laws, policies and enactments. Voting days are always set for weekends, to ensure that as many voters as possible will go to the polls. Nevertheless, in recent years, there has been a marked falling off in number of votes recorded, indicating a certain apathy among the population.

Outdoor Parliaments

Three cantons and two 'half' cantons hold a popular open-air parliament once a year in spring. Every last Sunday in April and the first in May, voters of Glarus, Appenzell (Inner and Outer Rhodes) and Unterwald (Obwald and Nidwald) are convened to the Landsgemeinde, held in the main squares of the small capital towns of Stans, Sarnen, Trogen or Hundwil (alternatively) and Glarus. Voters elect their magistrates for the coming year and vote 'yes' or 'no' by show of hands for any new cantonal legislation that may be put before them.

Appenzell A. Rh. can boast of having the largest Landsgemeinde—10,000 to 12,000. They gather in the public square at Trogen or Hundwil, and the ceremony is opened by the arrival of the magistrates in office, headed by their chief, called the Landammann. They are preceded by a band of fifes and drums and take their stand on a central platform, from where they address the crowd. When the elections have been held and discussion on legislation is completed, the ceremony ends with a mutual exchange of vows. The Landammann takes an oath that

THE CONFEDERATION THAT WORKS

he will be faithful to the people who have elected him and he is answered by an oath of allegiance from the electors: 'And having understood fully all that has been read to me this day, I shall hold to its truth, faithfully and without swerving. So do I desire, and may God help me'.

A quaint ritual it is, in which religion and politics are closely intermingled: prayers, psalm-singing, and patriotic songs lend a solemn air to the ceremony. The men who are going to vote all carry a sword tucked into their Sunday suit, as a symbol of their rights and freedoms. Most remarkable to the onlooker is this crowd of black-clad men—Sunday suits are usually black, made of coarse serge and ill-fitting—with their clodhopper boots. Many of these rugged, weather-beaten faces are bearded, all are intense with concentration on the matter in hand.

The Landsgemeinde are ancient institutions, once common to all Swiss cantons, and date back to the 13th century. In the old days, they were convened whenever a nation-shaking decision had to be taken: in 1765, for example, the people of Schwyz were called 24 times to vote on one subject or another.

One important element in Swiss civic life is the commune. It is the town or village—in other words, the community—to which each family is bound by the accident of birth. Every Swiss, wherever he may live, remains legally attached to the commune of origin of his family, and his commune must help him in case of destitution. In the old times, burghership implied both obligations and advantages; today, there are few communes that still make gifts in kind to their burghers resident in their territory, gifts such as wood for the winter from the communal forests, cheese, butter, and so on.

By birth, the members of each family remain burgesses of the father's commune of origin. After marriage, a woman assumes the citizenship of her husband's commune. Citizenship of a commune can be obtained for the price of a donation to a designated charity, and this kind of 'naturalization' is necessary often for men of other cantons or communes who wish to hold administrative posts in their town of residence.

Switzerland was late in giving to its women the vote and full civil rights. The women's suffrage movement started about 1898 but made slow progress, partly because of apathy and lack of interest in politics and civil affairs by the women themselves. There was even a modestly active 'Women's League Against the Vote'. But in 1971 Swiss women were given the federal vote and representation in the National and States Councils, Cantonal Parliaments and Courts. In 1984 a woman was elected to the Federal Council for the first time.

The Swiss Army

The militia army of Switzerland is one of the most characteristic institutions in the country and unique of its kind.

Every able-bodied male citizen is a soldier. At the age of 19 he is called for medical examination to be passed or refused for military service, which begins the following year. The initial period of training, the recruit school, is of 120 days, and a strenuous one. When the young soldier returns home, he takes his uniform and full kit with him, so as to be prepared in case of emergency and also for the subsequent three-week periods of refresher courses he will have to serve ten times until he is thirty-six. Men up to that age belong to the Elite; those of thirty-seven to forty-eight to the Landwehr. An NCO's duty ceases at 50, an officer's at 55. Recruits aiming for rank have to serve an extra 148 days for non-commissioned officer and a further like period for second lieutenant. Men exempted from military service can serve in auxiliary forces (air raid wardens, etc.), or have to pay an annual military tax. Fireman's service is also compulsory, including foreign male residents up to the age of forty-five, but you can get around it by paying the municipal fire tax.

In peacetime, when there is no General Headquarters, the highest authority of the militia army is an officer selected by the Federal Assembly. In times of emergency, that is to say, on the first day of general mobilization, the Federal Assembly appoints a supreme army chief. The Commander-in-Chief holds office until all danger of war or invasion is past.

This organization, which is purely a defense weapon, is highly efficient and speedy in its working. For example, the Swiss frontiers were entirely manned, every officer and soldier at his post, before the British House of Commons had heard the announcement of the official declaration that World War II had begun.

And speaking of the Swiss army brings us to the question of Swiss neutrality, for the protection of which the military system has been devised. Neutrality is for Switzerland far more than a political line of conduct adopted to meet the contingencies of a decade or period: it is a fundamental necessity and a basic element of her national structure.

From early times, Switzerland has constituted herself the guardian of strategically important international routes, and the significance of this geographically imposed task was recognized by the Treaty of Westphalia in 1648, confirmed in 1815, when the Congress of Vienna explicitly announced its 'formal and unconditional recognition of Switzerland's neutrality', in 1919 by the Treaty of Versailles and again in 1920, when the Council of the League of Nations admitted the

THE CONFEDERATION THAT WORKS

'unique position' of Switzerland, 'conditioned by a centuries-old tradition explicitly incorporated in international law'. In 1939, also, the nations at war individually confirmed their recognition of this status.

The only nationalized utilities in Switzerland are the post office, telegraph and telephone and the main network of railroads (the Swiss Federal Railroads). Other utilities are private or municipal enterprises —gas works, streetcars, branch line railroads, and so on—but in some cases are subsidized by cantonal governments. Hydroelectric power plants are also owned by private companies under federal or cantonal grant. Freedom of trade and industry is one of the fundamental clauses of the federal constitution, and everything possible is done to encourage private enterprise.

Le Corbusier   Arthur Honegger   Carl Jung

CREATIVE SWITZERLAND

A Collision of Cultures

Switzerland, in many ways, is the most European of all European countries, rich in history and tradition, prosperous, elegant, civilized. One has only to walk through the lively and affluent streets of Geneva, an international city *par excellence,* or around the chic streets of Zurich or Berne, to be aware of the many-centuried layers which have combined to make Switzerland one of the most intriguing, sophisticated and culturally varied countries in the West.

All of Europe, it seems, is here.

As befits a prosperous and stable country, cultural activities are everywhere in evidence. L'Orchestre de la Suisse Romande in Geneva ranks high among the leading European orchestras; the Schauspielhaus in Zurich boasts one of the finest classical theater companies in Europe; Berne, the federal capital, is home to a whole host of museums, ranging

CREATIVE SWITZERLAND

from the Kunsthaus, which houses the Klee collection (the largest and most important of its kind in the world) to, at the opposite end of the scale, the Swiss Alpine Museum. The medieval cities of Basle—home to one of the oldest and most respected Universities in Europe—Lucerne, St. Gallen, Berne itself, Fribourg and Neuchâtel all contain a multitude of marvelous buildings from practically every period of the country's history. And throughout the last 500 years Switzerland has been home to some of the most advanced and influential of philosophers, teachers, artists and writers of Europe.

But, extraordinarily, this cultural crossroads has failed to produce any extended body of work that one can confidently call a Swiss school of painting or music, literature or architecture. How can one explain this strange cultural vacuum?

The unique geographical and political nature of Switzerland goes a long way toward providing the answer. Switzerland lies at the meeting point of three great European countries and thus at the meeting point of three powerful European cultures—France to the west, Germany to the north and Italy to the south, each with a long and rich heritage of national creativity. As might be expected of a small country surrounded by such very powerful neighbors, Switzerland has long been susceptible to their influence, all the more so in that it is only in relatively recent years that Switzerland has enjoyed real internal political unity, without which a national identity is hard to attain.

As a consequence of this three-way pull, there has been a natural tendency, still very much in evidence today, for Swiss artists to gravitate toward, and become a part of, the very well-established cultures of these countries.

The Cultural Exodus

The most extreme example of this cultural dominance occurs in literature. A francophone Swiss writer, for example, writing in French, automatically becomes part of the French literary tradition. Similarly, a German-Swiss writer, because he writes in German, becomes part of the German literary tradition. Hermann Hesse, winner of the Nobel Prize for literature in 1946 for his novel *The Glass-Bead Game,* though a naturalized Swiss, is always considered a German writer. This is not simply because he was born in Germany but because, writing in German, he could hardly be considered anything else. Similarly, Friedrich Dürrenmatt, perhaps the most important Swiss playwright of this century, is generally considered a German author first and a Swiss second. Without a unifying Swiss language, the possibility of a body of native Swiss literature is something of a contradiction in terms.

There is, however, one fairly important exception. Though the Swiss-Germans mostly speak pure German, their everyday spoken language is a dialect known as Schwyzerdütsch (literally Swiss-German). This is not spoken outside Switzerland. Consequently, any Swiss-German writer who elects to write in Swiss-German, and proclaim his Swissness, necessarily confines himself to a limited readership and can seem rather parochial.

The exigencies of language have created a more extreme situation for Swiss literature than the circumstances affecting the other arts, but much the same sort of dilemma faces the painter, architect or sculptor as faces the writer. Even in the 20th century—when, following the establishment of a very much more obvious national identity, one might expect to find native schools of Swiss art growing up and establishing themselves positively—nearly every single Swiss artist of international stature has been drawn to the established cultural milieu of his or her parent culture and has subsequently become firmly identified with it.

Le Corbusier (1887–1966) and Alberto Giacometti (1901-1966)—probably the two most important and influential Swiss artists of the 20th century—both spent the majority of their adult lives in France and are, to all intents and purposes, French artists. Le Corbusier, apart from belonging to an avowedly international school of architecture, claimed that he owed his cultural allegiance exclusively to France. Switzerland, for the most part, is noticeably lacking buildings by him.

Among slightly less well-known Swiss artists of the 20th century one finds a similar natural inclination to leave Switzerland in favor of the more stimulating and varied cultural climate abroad. The sculptor Jean Tinguely (b. 1925), whose exploding and disintegrating 'animated' sculptures have raised more than their fair share of artistic eyebrows the world over, followed Giacometti's example and settled in France, where he still works.

The composer Arthur Honegger (1892–1955), the leading Swiss composer of the 20th century, despite training at Zurich Conservatory, nonetheless spent most of his life in Paris where, with Francis Poulenc and others, he founded the avant garde musical group Les Six in 1917. Another important Swiss composer, Frank Martin (1890–1974), a leading figure of the post-war musical world, lived in Holland for long periods.

To trace these trends further back, to the 19th century, the painter Arnold Böcklin (1827–1901), though born in Switzerland, was trained in Germany, Flanders and Paris and subsequently spent many years in Munich and Rome. It is difficult not to see him as a German painter first and foremost.

The Baroque and Beyond

Before the 19th century, with Switzerland unified not even in name, this pattern is more pronounced and, from time to time, more confused. The painter Henry Fuseli (1741-1825), whom the Swiss have long claimed as one of their most important artists, spent his entire working life outside Switzerland. In fact it is difficult to see how any convincing case for considering him a 'Swiss' artist can be made, except by virtue of his birth. He trained in Berlin and London before journeying to Rome where he remained for eight years before returning to London. It was in London that he enjoyed his greatest success, which included full membership of the Royal Academy in 1790. He was highly thought of among artistic circles and his powerful, nightmare visions, poised somewhat incongruously between neo-Classicism and the fully-blown Romantic proved highly influential. His pupils included Constable and Landseer and he was highly admired by Blake.

Francesco Borromini (1599-1667), the most idiosyncratic and original architect of Roman High Baroque, presents a remarkably similar case. Like Fuseli he was born in the Ticino, the Italian-Swiss part of the country. But having traveled to Rome in his early twenties, he remained there for the rest of his life and is completely identified with the Italian Baroque.

The painters Conrad Witz (1400/10-1444/6) and Hans Holbein the Younger (1497/8-1543), both extremely influential, have stronger claims to be considered Swiss, but they are by no means convincing. Witz lived and worked in Basle and subsequently Geneva—at that time not a member of the Helvetic Confederation, though in other respects very closely allied to it—and it was there he painted his one extant masterpiece, *The Miraculous Draught of Fishes,* the background of which contains the first specifically recognizable landscape in Western painting. The greater part of his working life was spent in Switzerland, and the Swiss landscape was crucially important to his development of landscape painting, but Witz was born in Germany, where he received his early training, and the dominant influences on him were the Van Eyck brothers, who were Flemish. So the degree to which Witz can be considered a specifically Swiss painter is certainly debatable.

Holbein, too, was born not in Switzerland but in Germany. His father was an accomplished portrait painter and, as a young man, Holbein worked in his studio. He left Germany and settled in Basle, becoming a citizen in 1520, though in 1517 he left briefly to visit Italy. It was in Basle that he met the Dutchman, Erasmus, in 1523, the greatest of all the Humanist philosophers. Despite the fact that Holbein enjoyed great success as a portraitist and painter of religious pictures in Basle and that his style was consolidated there, much of his most successful and characteristic work was done in London for Henry VIII during two trips to England, the first from 1526 to 1528, the second from 1532 to 1536. Similarly, the dominant influences on him were Flemish and Dutch. And it is also interesting that his strikingly penetrating and psychologically charged portraits attracted only the lamest of imitators and disciples in Switzerland itself whereas his influence in Germany was very much more pronounced.

The Land As Influence

Ironic though it may perhaps seem, Switzerland's most distinctive and famous geographical feature, the Alps, Europe's largest mountain range, has also played its part in preventing the development of Swiss culture. Over 50 percent of the total land area of Switzerland is alpine, and about half of those alpine areas are entirely non-productive. Until the coming of the railways in the latter part of the 19th century, many alpine communities were entirely isolated even from their immediate neighbors for long periods during the winter months. For much of the country's past the Alps were the province of the peasant farmer and shepherd. Consequently, much of Switzerland's heritage centers around folk art and peasant culture.

A great deal of this is extremely attractive and ingenious: the delightfully painted and carved wooden houses of the Engadine, for example, the weird but wonderful Alphorn, today very much a national symbol, even the much-maligned cuckoo clock. Similarly, there are a number of festivals which owe their origins to peasant celebrations—the world-famous Fête des Vignerons held every 25 years at Vevey, or the Unspunnen Festival of Alpine Herdsmen, which draws vast crowds.

Folk music is still very popular in Switzerland and the visitor is likely to come closest to uncovering a genuinely Swiss atmosphere at one of the many festivals held in the summer. Folk music, of a sort, is also evident in one of the most instantly recognizable Swiss traditions, yodelling. But though this thriving heritage of popular culture may be both enduring and characteristic of Switzerland, it cannot really be considered a positive contribution to European cultural traditions. Folk art, however enjoyable it may be, is by definition derivative and decorative. It lacks the spiritual and intellectual content that the creation of great art must inevitably generate.

A Comfortable Culture

But the prevalance of a peasant culture and the dominance of Switzerland's neighbors cannot completely account for the strange lack of

CREATIVE SWITZERLAND

home-grown cultural achievement. There is another crucially important factor: the character of the Swiss themselves. Though it is always dangerous to generalize about a people, there is nevertheless no doubt that at heart the Swiss are an extremely sober and bourgeois people, fond of their creature comforts and dedicated to prosperity, banking and railway timetables. In the German-speaking areas in particular, the conspicuously conservative and careful attitudes one encounters do seem to be at odds with the probing imagination necessary for artistic endeavor.

In many ways this is rather paradoxical. The stability, peace and prosperity that the bourgeois attitudes of the Swiss have created might well be expected to have encouraged rather than to have stifled artistic life. The predominantly comfortable culture of Flanders and Holland in the 17th century, for example, produced Rubens, Rembrandt, Vermeer, Hals, Cuyp, the Ruisdaels, Van Dyck, the Brueghels and a score of other extraordinary painters. The arts always prosper during times of plenty—indeed this is an essential ingredient—and it is a Romantic myth to believe that there is something fundamentally incompatible between art and material wealth or that the reckless spirit of the artist must have turmoil and unrest to drive him on. Nearly all the most productive periods in the history of art have coincided with periods of peace and prosperity. But not apparently in Switzerland. Why this should be so to quite the extent it is remains a mystery. It is undeniable that there is in Switzerland's distinctive brand of bourgeois thinking something fundamentally inimical to the creation of art—although it provides rich soil for the growth of cultural awareness and the enjoyment of art in all its forms.

Craftsmanship in Print

But if the sobriety of the Swiss has inhibited the creative arts, it has paid dividends where craftsmanship is concerned. Since the Reformation the excellence of Swiss craftsmanship has been an acknowledged fact both in Europe and, latterly, through the world at large. In more recent times this expertise has reached its highest peak in sophisticated feats of engineering and technology. Watches are perhaps the best-known example. But from the standpoint of the arts, the finest flowerings of Swiss craftsmanship are found in printing in all its forms.

The first great period—it has been described as Switzerland's golden age—came in the 16th century when Holbein, Niklaus Manuel (1484–1530), Tobias Stimmer (1539–1584) and the extraordinary Urs Graf (1485–1527), poet, draughtsman, engraver, painter and mercenary, began a rich and longlasting tradition of skillful and sophisticated drawing and print making. The 17th and 18th centuries saw a number of competent draughtsmen and printers continue this tradition, though none of outstanding merit emerged. But in the 19th century Switzerland enjoyed something of a renaissance in printmaking, the principal and most influential figure being Rudolphe Toepffer (1799–1846), an engaging character who, among his other achievements, is credited with the development of the strip cartoon. His humorous and satirical lithographs, fluid and delicate, are today enjoying a well-deserved revival.

In the 20th century there are only a few figures to compare with the distinguished graphic artists of the past—and among those few Hans Erni must rank high—but the country is nonetheless a world leader in color printing in general and the printing of fine art posters in particular. There are a number of celebrated and sophisticated printing plants and many of Europe's leading artists of the 20th century have taken advantage of these facilities. They include Arp, Chagall, Henry Moore, Kokoschka and many others.

Patronage Par Excellence

Switzerland's bourgeois affluence has led to the establishment of a large number of cultural institutions. Being wealthy, Switzerland is consequently also rich in art. It is a curious fact that there is more art per capita in private hands in Switzerland than in any other country in the world. Among the outstanding private collections are three of particular excellence: that of Baron Heinrich Thyssen in Lugano (Villa Favorita), which ranks among the finest anywhere in the world; the Oskar Reinhart collection in Winterthur which includes Goya's last, unfinished, work as well as a very large number of French, Flemish and Dutch masterpieces; and the Hahnloser collection, now divided between Winterthur and Berne and which features 19th- and 20th-century works, many by artists who were close personal friends of Dr. Hahnloser. Three private collections of this sustained excellence in a country the size of Switzerland are eloquent testimony to the commitment—and spending power—of the country's private collectors. All three collections, however, were formed before the war, and it is doubtful if even the most assiduous and affluent collector could amass anything comparable today.

The federal and cantonal museums, despite their scale and numbers, do not for the most part rank among the leading European galleries, though there are exceptions. The Kunstmuseum in Basle, for example, contains important works by Holbein and Witz as well as a large collection of 19th- and 20-century French paintings, including a fine collection of pictures by Ferdinand Leger. The Berne Kunstmuseum is home to the Klee collection, certainly the most representative in

CREATIVE SWITZERLAND

existence, as well as to a number of very beautiful Kandinskys. The rest of the collection is, however, undistinguished. Zurich is the site of the third most important gallery in Switzerland. It organizes consistently stimulating and imaginative exhibitions of modern work, as well as possessing a large and important permanent collection that includes a number of Monet's enormous *Water Lilies* panels.

The Intellectual Heritage

Switzerland also has a thriving and varied intellectual heritage. In fact this fecund intellectual tradition may well constitute Switzerland's most persuasive claim to cultural importance. Basle, home to Erasmus and Holbein at the beginning of the 16th century, was the first city in Switzerland to rise to intellectual prominence, though during the same period the fiery presence of the Frenchman Jean Calvin in Geneva and Ulrich Zwingli in Zurich, both preaching the new doctrine of the Reformed church, ensured that Switzerland remained in the forefront of new ideas in Europe, as well as playing a leading role in the Reformation.

In the 18th century two other Frenchmen, the philosophers Jean Jacques Rousseau and Voltaire, continued this tradition of intellectual excellence. Both were forced to flee France as a result of their championing of enlightened thought and liberal ideas and both settled in French-Switzerland. (Rousseau was to proclaim himself proudly a "citizen of Geneva".) At the end of the 18th century Switzerland enjoyed a brilliant period intellectually. Zurich was the "little Athens of the north"; Geneva a cauldron of new political liberalism, "the political laboratory of Europe". The Académie of the Vaud, a Protestant college founded during the Reformation, held courses on diplomacy and civil administration—unknown elsewhere—and supplied diplomats, administrators and tutors to many European courts, most especially in Germany.

This period also saw the emergence of one of the handful of truly original and influential thinkers Switzerland has produced—the pedagogue, visionary and humanist, Heinrich Pestalozzi (1746–1827). His revolutionary approach to education, based on methods one can only call psychological, though he predated the discovery of psychology as a science by almost 75 years, and his precocious social conscience, allied to his insistence on the importance of love as the mainspring of all successful human relations, single out Pestalozzi as a man genuinely before his time.

Of the legion of botanists, chemists, philosophers, educators and men of letters that distinguish Switzerland's story in the latter part of the 19th century and into the 20th century, two men deserve special mention. Jacob Burckhardt (1818–1897), the historian whose work on the Italian Renaissance dramatically altered perceptions of that period as well as initiating a new approach to art history, and the psychologist Carl Jung (1875–1961), now considered the founder of a legitimate alternative to Freud's system of psychoanalysis, since he placed more emphasis on what he felt to be the naturally religious character of the human soul, and displayed a creative flexibility in his thought that outreached the rigid doctrinaire legacy of the Viennese master.

The Brain Drain in Reverse

Switzerland has attracted a large number of foreign exiles, especially since the end of the 18th century. A fair percentage of them have been artists and intellectuals of the highest caliber. This trend can be traced originally to the early 16th century, with the presence of Witz, Holbein and Erasmus in Basle. But it is not until the arrival of Rousseau and Voltaire in Geneva around 1760, both of them coming to Switzerland as exiles from the Ancien Régime in France, that the notion of Switzerland as a place of exile for the dispossessed of Europe began to take firm shape. With the subsequent confirmation in the Constitution of 1848 of neutrality and tolerance as the bedrock of Swiss foreign policy, the number of exiles in Switzerland swelled dramatically, though for much of the remainder of the 19th century these were principally political rather than artistic refugees.

However, the innumerable European artists that poured into Switzerland in the early 19th century were basically tourists, inspired largely by Rousseau's powerful polemics on the glories of the dramatic Alpine landscape. Hardly a single major figure from this period did not at some time or another visit Switzerland, many staying for lengthy periods, among them the English historian Gibbon, author of *The Decline and Fall of the Roman Empire,* who settled in Geneva, and the Frenchwoman Madame de Staël. Her château at Coppet on the shores of Lake Geneva became a focal point of liberal thought in Europe. It was she who first propounded the notion of a Europe without frontiers where the free exchange of ideas would not only be possible but actively encouraged; prophetic indeed.

Other giants of the Romantic age who came to Switzerland were— Goethe; his fellow German Schiller, who gave fictional flesh to the greatest of all Swiss folk heroes, William Tell, in his play of the same name; Byron, still looked upon in Switzerland as the very embodiment of the Romantic ideal, largely as a result of his poem, *The Prisoner of Chillon,* which celebrated the six-year incarceration of Bonivard in the Château de Chillon during the Reformation; and Keats and Shelley (whose wife Mary wrote *Frankenstein* in Switzerland in 1816).

CREATIVE SWITZERLAND

Among the many painters who drew inspiration from the towering misty peaks and gushing waterfalls of the Swiss landscape, perhaps the most famous was Turner who, during a number of visits, sketched, drew and painted the Alps in every weather and all lights, seeking to extract the maximum of mystery and majesty from their mighty masses. The many albums of prints he produced proved essential visual complements to the literary outpourings inspired by the Alps for the People of Quality throughout Europe.

Two later 19th-century visitors to Switzerland were the German composer Richard Wagner and the philosopher Friedrich Nietzsche, both having made life more than a little hot for themselves in their native lands. Wagner began his massive operatic epic, *The Ring of the Nibelung,* in Zurich and, during a later stay in Lucerne, completed *The Mastersingers of Nuremburg.* Nietzsche taught at Basle University and conceived the idea for his Zarathustra and Superman during a holiday in the Engadine.

In the 20th century—largely as a result of the vast upheavals caused by World War I, the Russian Revolution, the rise to power of the Nazis and World War II—a large number of exiles, principally, but not exclusively, German, settled in the safe bourgeois bosom of Switzerland. Among the most distinguished were Einstein, who did much of the groundwork for his Theory of Relativity in Berne; the novelist Herman Hesse; the playwright Bertolt Brecht; Thomas Maria Rilke, perhaps the leading German 20th-century poet; the innovatory Russian composer Stravinsky; and the Russian painter Kandinsky who lived for a time in Berne, when Paul Klee was there.

Klee, in fact, of all these artists, has the best claim to be considered Swiss. Not only was he born in Berne, though of German parents, he long nurtured a fervent hope of obtaining Swiss citizenship, though this was never to be. However, at the same time it has to be said that his most productive periods were all spent in Germany where he was a member of the Blau Reiter group, "founders", as it were, of abstract painting. He also enjoyed a long and fruitful association with the Bauhaus in Weimar (Prussia), until its dissolution by the Nazis the leading avant garde art school in Europe.

This influx of refugees, both political and artistic, led to one extraordinary simultaneous gathering of unlikely figures in Zurich in 1916. These were Hans Arp and Tristan Tzara—co-founders of Dada, the anti-art, anti-bourgeois movement—Lenin and Trotsky—fathers and prime movers of the Russian Revolution—and James Joyce, *enfant terrible* of English literature. Tom Stoppard's successful play, *Travesties,* is based on this strange concatenation of characters.

Today, foreigners have continued to make Switzerland their home, but their motives have been influenced more by favorable tax concessions than persecution at home.

Switzerland Performs

Music is a universal language, transcending the limitations of tongue. Appropriately, the multilingual Swiss are great listeners. That is not to imply that they do not produce great performers, but that their programs are designed without the narrow prejudices which sometimes invade nations with greater creative classical traditions, and without the inborn reservations of some of their audiences.

A winter tour of their opera houses can be a stimulating experience, and since the country is so concentrated and well-connected, it can be undertaken in a few days. It is something for the visitor who has out-grown mere worship of stars—there will not be many of these—but who has come to understand opera as a team integration of singing with imaginative production and design, meaningful orchestral playing and intelligent acting.

Geneva's Grand Théâtre, rebuilt after a disaster in which a fire scene rehearsal became too realistic, is a handsome theater casting its net wide for its repertory and staging mostly new productions of established works. Zurich's Opernhaus has an enterprising policy judiciously mixing in tradition and, like Geneva, combining it with a school where maturing young singers can get practical experience, producing many famous names. Berne's Stadttheater achieved international recognition when in 1981 it staged a modern dress *Rigoletto* which exemplified the Swiss spirit of innovation, and the Stadttheaters of Basle and St. Gallen are others where exciting things can happen. The Swiss opera seasons run from early autumn to summer.

Orchestral music abounds. Every city has its permanent symphony orchestra and if we single out one for special mention, it does not mean that the others, such as the Zurich Tonhalle formed in 1867, are unimportant. But L'Orchestre de la Suisse Romande in Geneva, through their numerous recordings, have carried the flag of Swiss excellence to the four corners of the world. Formed in 1918, they were conducted for almost half a century by the great Ernest Ansermet, famed for the lucidity of his Stravinsky performances. The orchestra retains its high international esteem.

A remarkable ensemble is the Basle Chamber Orchestra, formed in 1926 by the enthusiastic Paul Sacher when he was only 20. He still conducts it—his youthful vigor was astonishing at the golden jubilee concerts—and the orchestra still specializes in contemporary music. Among the composers who have written specially for it have been

CREATIVE SWITZERLAND

Britten, Bartok, Stravinsky, Prokofiev, Honegger, Martinu, Martin, Tippett, Hindemith and more recently, Henze and Berio. Some list.

Swiss festivals abound for the summer visitor, and the most important is Lucerne, begun by Toscanini and Walter in 1938, and still playing host to the world's top orchestras and conductors every August in the concert hall by the lake. It is a favorite summer date for music lovers.

Montreux in September follows a similar design. It includes the Clara Haskil piano competition, and stages some of its events in such picturesque settings as the Château de Chillon. Other festivals of note are Zurich (June), where the accent is on opera, and Gstaad (August), high in the mountains above Lake Geneva and enjoying an illustrious association with Yehudi Menuhin. But the visitor should also keep an eye open for the less publicized festivals in small towns which often yield unexpected delights and unfamiliar music in lovely old baroque churches.

If we have concentrated on operas and concerts, it is because they present few problems of communication. But it should be added that most Swiss communities have healthy drama companies, and though a limited command of the local language may blunt the message it need not obscure it. You could, for example, enjoy a play of Dürenmatt with only minimal German, follow his de-bunking of inbred conservatism and out-dated pomposity, and emerge feeling you have enjoyed a Swiss Ibsen.

In the summer there are numerous special festival productions. One of the most famous, which takes place every five years, is Einsiedeln's *Welttheater,* with its theme of the life and death of man, played out in the great arena that forms a natural openair theater in front of the Benedictine monastery. Altdorf ensures that the motto on the William Tell statue ('The story of William Tell will be told as long as the mountains stand') becomes an annual reality by staging Schiller's drama in the town from which the Swiss patriot fought.

Ballet is performed regularly throughout the year and there are workshops and experimental theater wherever you find the conventional stage. Plenty of specialist theaters, too, such as the puppets of St. Gallen, Fribourg and Geneva.

A Cultural Calendar

Here are the most important cultural events in the Swiss calendar, taking place every year at about the same time—

| March/June | Locarno | The Locarno Concerts |
| April/June | Lugano | The Lugano Concerts |

THE SWISS SCENE

April	Montreux	International Choral Festival
April/beg. May	Montreux	*Golden Rose of Montreux* International TV Festival
April/beg.May	Berne	International Jazz Festival
May/June	Lausanne	Lausanne International Festival
June	Zurich	International June Festival Weeks
Mid-June	Berne	Berne Art Weeks
July	Montreux	International Jazz Festival
Mid-July	Braunwald	Braunwald Music Week
July/August Mid-July	Interlaken	William Tell Festival Plays
Mid-August	Engadine	Engadine Concert Weeks
July/September	Sion	Tibor Varga Music Festival
Mid-August/ beg. September	Lucerne	International Festival of Music
Mid-August	Geneva	*Fête de Genève* (Geneva Festival)
August	Locarno	Locarno International Film Festival
August	Gstaad	Yehudi Menuhin Festival
September	Montreux-Vevey	Montreux-Vevey International Music Festival
September/October	Ascona	Ascona Music Festival Weeks
2nd half September	Geneva	International Competition for Musical Performers
end September	Diablerets	International Alpine Film Festival
October	Zurich	International Jazz Festival
Mid-October	Lausanne	Italian Opera Festival

The Cinema

Switzerland's contribution to the cinema has been limited, but nonetheless telling. Two leading actors of the early screen gained their initial experience on the stage in Zurich. Emil Jannings (1884–1950) was to move to Max Reinhardt's theater in Berlin in 1914 and from there set out on a substantial career as a serious male lead for the UFA studios. His best work includes *The Last Laugh* (1924), *Tartuffe* (1925) and *Faust* (1926), all directed by F.W. Murnau. His role in von Sternberg's *The Last Command* (1928) gained him the Best Foreign Actor Oscar. In Hollywood from 1927–29, he returned to Germany to play the obsessed professor in von Sternberg's *The Blue Angel* (1930). In

1940 he was made director of the UFA studios and oversaw the production of numerous films approved by the Nazis, which led, after the war, to his retirement.

Michel Simon (1895–1975) crossed Switzerland's western borders to become one of France's best loved stars, most memorable in *L'Atlante* (1932, Vigo) and *Boudu Saved from Drowning* (1934, Renoir). His remarkable talent for improvisation, an almost chameleon-like ability to defy type-casting, and immense energy led to a long and fruitful career, crowned by his performance in *Blanche* (1971, Borowcyk).

By contrast Ursula Andress (b 1936) cannot be said to have made many films, and few of distinction. But her statuesque features remain an essential icon of the 1960s, and her first international appearance, striding from the waves in *Dr. No* (1962, Young), remains a cornerstone in the development of the modern popular cinema, a Botticellian Venus of our times.

Swiss directors mirror, in reverse, these actors. Marcel Allegret (1900–73) made a long and distinguished series of films over a span of 50 years. In his youth he was private secretary to André Gide, who wrote *Les Faux-Monnayeurs* for him. His films remain potboilers of little thematic consistency, although he may be remembered as Roger Vadim's mentor.

Two young Swiss directors of distinction appeared in the 1950s, on the fringe of the European Free Cinema. Claude Goretta and Alain Tanner collaborated on a short film *Nice Time* (1956). Both their careers have been checkered but influential. Tanner has, for the most part, developed directly from the dogmatic social concerns of the Free Cinema, itself prefiguring the New German Cinema of the 1960s and 1970s. *The Salamander* (1969) was his first international success, and revealed an enquiring concern with the middle-European bourgeois consciousness. His work since has mixed moody doubt with an assertion of cautious human optimism in *Le Milieu du Monde, Jonah who will be 75 in the year 2,000* (1976, co-written with John Berger), *Messidor* (1979), a strictly Swiss and beautiful film, and the misguided *Light Years Away* (1980). A naturalistic counterpart to Jean-Luc Godard, his career seems now equally fragmented and confused.

Goretta, on the other hand, moved rapidly in the opposite thematic direction, consciously avoiding discourse in favor of asserting individual human values as the subject of film. *Le Jour de Nous* (1971) was a tribute to his mentor Jean Renoir, whose paternal influence is also felt in *L'Invitation* (1973). From 1977–78 Goretta was heavily involved in a French/Swiss/British co-production examining the later years of the 18th-century philosopher Jean-Jacques Rousseau, in *The Roads of Exile*. Shown unfinished at the London Film Festival in 1978, this film most accurately revealed Goretta's concern with the thinking individual and his relation to the society about him, and showed the influence of the Italian director Roberto Rossellini.

Goretta's greatest success came with *The Lacemaker* (1977), a delicate and fatalist love story which gained its young star Isabelle Huppert international renown and an Oscar nomination. The unfortunate Francophilia which permeates Goretta's career (in contrast to that of Tanner) seems to have reached a climax in the angst-ridden *Girl from Lorraine* (1981).

FOOD AND DRINK

Cuisine? . . . Kochkunst? . . . Cucina?

Swiss cooking, like the patchwork that is Switzerland, is a medley drawn from several countries. It has borrowed from the French *cuisine,* the German *Kochkunst,* and the Italian *cucina.* Gastronomic pleasures are appreciated by the Swiss, and their home cooking has been brought to a fine art without the aid of tinned or packaged foods.

However, the traveler in Switzerland is more concerned with the art of the professional chef, and in many reputed restaurants and hotels he will catch glimpses of highhatted *maîtres queux,* master cooks commanding a bevy of skilled helpers. Innumerable inns and small restaurants all over the country do a thriving trade with Swiss and local patrons, who know that here—or there—one can enjoy a specialty dish. Many popular regional dishes relished for centuries in farmstead kitchens now appear on the best menus.

Originally devised in Vaud, Valais, or Geneva—no one quite knows which, for all three of these cantons claim priority—*fondue* is the dish that set the fashion for dunking when it was introduced to the United States at the Swiss Pavilion at the 1939–40 New York World Fair. It is a concoction of cheese, mainly Emmentaler and Gruyère, melted and skilfully mixed with a soupçon of garlic, a teaspoonful of flour, white wine, and a little Kirsch (*eau de vie* made from cherries). The richly aromatic whole is brought to the table in the pipkin and placed on a flame in the center of the table. Guests armed with long-handled forks spear small squares of bread which are thrust in turn into the steaming dish.

The eating of fondue is a fine art. Each guest who fails to withdraw his morsel of bread from the pipkin is called upon to offer a bottle of wine to the company.

Guests are warned never, *never,* to drink water or beer with or after fondue. White wine, Kirsch or tea are suitable beverages. The season for fondue begins in early September and continues merrily until late spring.

Where Cheese is an Art Form

It is understandable that, in a country famed for its dairy produce, cheese is an important food item. A great variety of cheeses are made in Switzerland, ranging from the widely exported Gruyère and Emmentaler to the less known Jura delicacy Tête de Moine, which must be scraped from its sugarcone-shaped cake. Vacherin is a fine cream cheese, made in Jura and Alpine pastures during the summer and stored by the cowherds in round boxes made of tree bark; it is ripe in late November and adorns the Christmas and New Year table. The Valais produces the slightly insipid, rather hard and very delicate Bagnes and Conches, also made in Alpine pastures and used for *raclette*. The Ticino favors the locally made Piora and Muggio or, for grating, Sbrinz (rather like Parmesan). Schabzieger, made with herbs, is a Glarus specialty.

Among the cheese dishes popular in Switzerland, the Valais raclette runs a good second to fondue. It is not served at just any restaurant, for its making requires an open fire to which a half cake of Conches or Bagnes is exposed; as it softens, it is scraped directly onto your plate, to be eaten with potatoes boiled in their skins, pickled spring onions, and gherkins.

Salées au fromage, or cheese quiches, are eaten all the year round and can be bought in most bakers' shops. Nevertheless, their yearly climax of popularity is at the Lausanne Swiss Comptoir, the national autumn trade and agricultural fair. Big brother to the Salée is the

FOOD AND DRINK

Gâteau au fromage. Then, too, there is the *Croûte au fromage,* the Swiss version of the Welsh rarebit.

Meat and Fish Specialties

Kässuppe, or cheese soup, is a specialty of central Switzerland, served in Lucerne, Zug, and neighboring cantons.

In the western lake district of Switzerland (Lakes Geneva, Neuchâtel, Bienne, Morat) delicious fish specialties are served in summer, when fresh-water fishermen can ply their trade to their heart's content. *Friture de perchettes* (fried fillets of small lake perch) are served piping hot in butter. With a glass of local white wine and a romantic view at hand, what better end to a warm summer's day can a gourmet wish? Pike (*brochet*), grayling (*ombre*), char (*ombre chevalier*), and trout also appear on western Swiss menus. Blue Lake trout (from the hatcheries at Blausee on the Spiez-Kandersteg route) are a great delicacy.

Croûtes aux morilles (delicious little mushrooms served on toast) are much prized when in season as a lunch or supper dish. And Fribourg cooks are specialists in the making of mushroom sauces.

Country-cured pork meats abound in this region and weekly markets are replete with sausages of all kinds: *saucisse au chou* and *au foie, saucisson, boutefas,* neighboring with smoked hams and pork chops. Served with creamed leeks or French beans, they make a most appetizing dish. Genevans are partial to *pieds de porc au madère* (pig's trotters with Madeira sauce). *Choucroute garnie* (sauerkraut with boiled ham and Vienna sausages) also agreeably replenishes the inner man.

A Valais and Grisons specialty in great demand is *viande séchée* or *Bündnerfleisch* (dried beef or pork). The meat is not cured, but dried in airy barns where the air is crisp and dry. Cut wafer-thin, with some pickled spring onions and gherkins it makes a delectable, if somewhat expensive, hors d'oeuvre.

In Berne you will find *Bernerplatte* listed on the menu; it is a Rabelaisian dish of sauerkraut or French beans 'garnished', that is to say piled high, with broiled ham, pork chops, Vienna sausage, smoked sausages, and other delicacies. *Röschti* is the German Swiss form of fried potatoes, excellent when served with small squares of fried bacon; it often accompanies *Geschnetzeltes* (chopped veal in cream sauce). *Mistkratzerli* is a dish much favored in the Rhine cantons—young roast cock fresh from the farmyard served with baked potatoes.

St. Gallen has *Schüblig,* a special type of veal sausage; Zurich its *Zürchertopf* (macaroni, minced meat, tomato sauce, oven-baked *en casserole*), *Geschnetzeltes* (chopped veal with thick cream sauce) and *Leberspiessli* (liver skewered and fried). Basle is partial to *Klöpfer,* a particularly succulent cervelat sausage.

In the Ticino, much has been borrowed from Italian cooking. Here menus list *ravioli al pomodoro* (ravioli with tomato sauce), *risotto con funghi* (which means 'with mushrooms'), *fritto misto alla ticinese* (mixed grill), and *polenta*. *Coppa* and *zampone* are Ticino sausages and *busecca* is a soup made from tripe, while *zuppa del paese* is a thick, vegetable broth. Snails—*lumachi*—are served with a walnut paste and *panettone* is a plain fruit cake, shaped rather like the northern *Gugelhopf*, an importation from Lombardy.

In these regions, too, you will find delicious lake and river fish: trout, pike, red mullet, ferra (a type of Central European salmon).

Lucerne has a specialty called *Kugelipastete*, a *vol-au-vent* served with *Luzerner Allerlei*, a vegetable and mushroom salad.

Pork meat in sausage form has a variety of names, each locality having a special recipe for its making: *Knäckerli* and *Pantli* (Appenzell), *Mostmöckli*, and *Kalberwurst* (the latter being made of calf's liver). The Grisons boasts of its *Salsiz* (small salami), *Bierwurst, Engadiner Wurst*, and *Leberwurst*, as well as the previously mentioned *Bündnerfleisch*.

Calories Unlimited

Pâtisserie—all those temptingly displayed little cakes seen in tearooms and bakeries throughout Switzerland—is not a western Swiss specialty. But in the region under review, you will find *petits pains de Rolle* (sugar buns); the *cuchéole* of Fribourg (large sweetened bread loaves made with eggs); *merveilles*, crisp, sweet wafers, fried in oil and served on high days and holidays; *gâteau au nillon*, a rather stodgy salted cake made from *greubons*, the dialect word for the residue of melted lard; *bricelets*, a square, wafflelike, sweet wafer; *tresse*, fine white bread in plaited form.

Cakes and sweetmeats are equally varied in this part of the world. *Leckerli* are Basle specialties that have found favor all over Switzerland; they are a sort of spiced honey cake, flat and oblong in shape, with a thin coating of sugar icing on top. In Berne, they are sold with a white sugar bear for decoration. *Fastnachtküchli* are a sort of *merveille* eaten in Zurich at Mardi Gras festivities. *Gugelhopf* are large, high bunlike cakes with a hollowed center, useful for stuffing with whipped cream. *Schaffhauserzungen*, which as the name implies are made in Schaffhausen, are cream filled cakes; *Fladen* and *Krapfen* are rich fruit pastries made with pears, nuts, and almond paste. *Birnbrot* is a less interesting teabread made chiefly of dried pears.

The Land of the Friendly *Deci*

The Swiss, especially the populations of the west and south, are great drinkers of wine, which is for them what beer is to an Englishman or an *espresso* to an Italian. That is to say, when two Swiss buddies get together for a friendly drink, they order three *decis* (deciliters) of open wine. White wine is appreciated as an appetizer in preference to a cocktail or vermouth. Travelers in Switzerland soon learn to value the advantage of being able to drink, at any café or wayside inn, at any hour of the day, a glass of these excellent vintages.

Much of the vine stock cultivated in Switzerland is the Chasselas, imported from Burgundy. In Canton Valais, Rhineland stock, especially the green Sylvaner, has been imported, together with the famous Black Pinot from Burgundy. Ticino wines are produced mostly from Nostrano, Americano or Isabelle and a little Bordeaux stock. It is said that the Romans first introduced the vine into Switzerland. At all events, in the 10th century, Good Queen Bertha of Burgundy encouraged her vassals in the Lake Geneva region to carry on this husbandry.

Vaud wines are divided into two major groups: Lavaux (Dézaley, Epesses, Rivaz, St. Saphorin, etc.), and La Côte (Féchy, Luins, Bégnins, etc.). A third, smaller group is the Vaud Chablis wines, produced in the Alpine foothills from Montreux to Aigle. A fourth wine-producing region in the Canton is at the southern end of Lake Neuchâtel (Bonvillars, Vully, Concise).

Valais has a dry climate and long, hot summers, ideal for the cultivation of vines. Fendant is a popular white wine and Dôle the most popular red. Specialty wines of delicious bouquet are also produced: Johannisberg (similar to Rhine wine), Riesling, Hermitage, Malvoisie (a sweet dessert wine).

Neuchâtel produces light, sparkling vintages, usually sold under the name of their canton of origin. A Neuchâtel wine is said to be 'excellent' when a star forms in the glass after it has been poured.

Ticino is a great producer of wine, but until recent years the vintages here have been of inferior quality. Modern methods of viniculture and the introduction of new stock have brought forth smooth, fruity white wines (Nebbiolo, Bonarda, Freisa, Merlot) and the rich red Nostrano. Genuine pure Nostrano is, unfortunately, available only in small quantities. It is hard to find anywhere, unless you know some Swiss gourmets.

Central Switzerland has Herrliberg, Meilen, Erlenbach, and Limmat. Schaffhausen boasts of its Blaurock, Hallauer and Käferstein; the Grisons of the light red Maienfelder, Fläscher and Zizerser.

PARADISE FOR SPORTSMEN

Always in Season

Switzerland is a land of sports. You can watch or take part in almost any sport that strikes your fancy; that is, unless you are a surfboard enthusiast. The country of the Alps and lakes has its peculiar national sports such as Swiss-style wrestling (Schwingen), the regular Sunday morning shooting, gymnastics, and Hornussen, a game American visitors have baptized 'Alpine baseball'.

If you like to sit back and watch international sporting events, Switzerland has more than its share to offer. Automobile Grand Prix racing has been forbidden, but there are still some thrilling uphill events and rallies. The grueling Tour de Suisse cycle race will make you wonder what happened to the leg muscles you once had. In addition, there are the usual sporting events such as international tennis, golf and ice hockey tournaments as well as soccer, sailing, swimming, and skating

PARADISE FOR SPORTSMEN

championships. If you want a thrill, you can watch or participate in skijoring (with horse, jeep, or airplane), mountain automobile races, Alpine fishing, horse-races on frozen lakes, curling, bob-sleighing and tobogganing. But above all: Switzerland is the land of skiing and mountaineering.

Skiing Regions

The three best-known regions of Switzerland for Alpine skiing are the Valais, the Grisons, and the Bernese Oberland. The last area is bounded on the north by the lakes of Thun and Brienz and to the south by the Bietschhorn, Finsteraarhorn, Oberaarhorn, and Breithorn mountains, the southern slopes of which descend into the Rhône Valley. As soon as new snow has settled and danger of avalanches has gone, peaks such as the Eiger, Mönch, Jungfrau, Schreckhorn, and Wetterhorn can be reached by experienced skiers. The inner part of this mountainous region, with peaks averaging between 2,370 meters and 3,200 meters (7,800 and 10,500 feet), offers countless opportunities to the skiing enthusiast. The Swiss Alpine Club has established dozens of huts, one of which has over sixty berths, and access to the area is made easy by the Interlaken—Lauterbrunnen—Kleine Scheidegg—Jungfraujoch mountain railway. If you are an experienced skier, you can combine skiing with a visit to some of the most beautiful mountain country in the world.

The second main region for all-year high Alpine skiing is the southern Valais, limited to the north by the Rhône and to the south by the Italian border, and such peaks as the Grand Combin, Mont Collon, the Matterhorn, and Monte Rosa. Recently La Haute Route (The High Route) between Martigny, on the Rhône River, and Zermatt, has become famous as one of the most beautiful skiing-climbing itineraries in the entire chain of Alps. One can race over the middle part of La Haute Route in twenty-four hours, as do Swiss army patrols, or one can take it easy and spend days or even weeks climbing peaks and skiing through the valleys. There, too, huts such as the Val-des-Dix, the Britannia, Cabane Bertol, and Hörnli offer the possibility of establishing mountain headquarters or spending a night or two between two legs of a trip through this strange region where three entirely different languages are spoken—the old German dialect, French, with the rolling accent of the Valais, and Italian, which, although only spoken along the border region, influences the pronunciation and syntax of the entire area.

The third region where the ski enthusiast can enjoy his sport, whether it be January or August, is in the Grisons. In the area around the Albula Pass, flanked by the Piz d'Err and the Piz Kesch, skiers can establish their headquarters in any one of a number of huts, and they will find the scenery magnificent.

Ski Schools and Equipment

Skiing in Switzerland accounts for more than 40% of total returns from tourism, and, as a result, the Swiss have spent much time and effort over the last ten years improving their already excellent skiing facilities. Large sums of money have been spent on improving transport facilities to and from ski resorts; on roads and hotels; on the construction of aerial cableways and ski lifts; and on the preparation and improvement of ski runs, winter footpaths and cross-country trails. Another important development in the expanding winter sports industry offered by the Swiss is the linking up of adjacent resorts by the construction of new lift systems, so that skiers can take advantage of more than one resort at a time.

There are so many ski resorts in Switzerland that it is not surprising that the winter sports industry accounts for such a high tourism return. Most resorts have their own ski school (SSS) and every winter 4,000 ski instructors give a total of approximately 2.9 million half-day lessons throughout the season.

If you are a beginner, lessons are vital as it is almost impossible to teach yourself. Language should not be a problem—most Swiss instructors speak English. When you first sign on in a ski school, an instructor will test you to see how proficient you are. He will then put you in a suitable class. All ski schools have five or six classes, and your instructor will move you from class to class depending on how quickly you master the sport. It is important to bear in mind that the smaller the class, the faster you learn, so try never to be in a class with more than eight other people.

Until a few years ago, people learned to ski on long skis, but many resorts now teach beginners on short skis as they are generally considered to be easier to learn on. The best length ski for beginners should be about shoulder or head height. However, many people find that as they improve they prefer longer skis.

Having the right equipment is very important for all classes of skier. All resorts have their own ski hire shops, and the beginner is well advised to hire all his or her equipment in the resort rather than buying it before going out there. Ski boots which don't fit can be agony, and once you've bought them and taken them to the resort, you won't be able to change them. If you hire a pair of boots in the resort and find that they are not right after a few days, the shop will change them for you. Hiring equipment is not expensive, although costs will obviously vary between resorts.

PARADISE FOR SPORTSMEN

There are many different types of ski boot available. It is best to have a pair that is too big, rather than too small, or they will pinch your toes and your feet will get cold. And if they are too big, you can always put on another pair of socks. It is also important to have a boot that gives sufficient support and which doesn't rub your legs when skiing. Most ski boots today are made of plastic and have adjustable hinged clip fasteners and flo-fit inner boots which are removable. When putting your boots on, make sure your socks are pulled up tight and that they don't have wrinkles in them. If they do they will rub against your feet and legs and will be very uncomfortable.

What skis you use will depend on how well you ski. Hire shops will always advise on what types there are, but there is no point in having a racing ski if you are a beginner! Skis are usually made of either metal or plastic, or a combination. They have metal edges and if you have your own skis, it is important to keep these edges sharp, and the bottoms waxed. But if you are hiring them, the shop should ensure that the skis are in good condition. If you find your skis sticking to the snow on the slopes, it usually means that they need waxing; if you don't feel like doing this yourself, the local shop will do it for you.

Safety bindings are as important as comfortable ski boots and they can, more importantly, prevent broken legs. Bindings come in two varieties—step-in and plate. Both kinds should have heel and toe release and should be correctly adjusted and checked regularly. When you fall, the bindings should automatically release the boots from the skis, with the safety strap stopping you from losing the ski.

For the beginner, proper clothing is a necessity, especially as you will probably spend a lot of time in the snow rather than on it. It doesn't matter how your clothes look providing they are warm and waterproof. Salopettes or dungarees are recommended for warmth, together with a jacket. Equally important are all the small accessories, such as gloves, socks and hats, particularly in December and January. Gloves should be waterproof. The best gloves are made of leather rather than plastic, because they are warmer. If you get cold hands, silk liners worn inside your gloves will help keep your hands warm. As the weather gets milder, many skiers wear ordinary trousers and sweaters.

Other necessary accessories are sun glasses or goggles. In bright sunlight, glasses are better because they keep the glare out of your eyes. But if the weather is overcast, goggles are preferable, because they are made of special glass or plastic which cuts down snow glare, making it easier to see the bumps. If you wear neither when the sky is overcast you will discover that you are skiing in 'white out' conditions, when none of the bumps is visible.

Don't forget your sun tan lotion. The thin air and the combination of sunlight and reflection off the snow can cause bad sunburn. It is also advisable to keep some lip salve with you to protect your lips against the sun and wind.

Choice of Resorts and Best Ski Runs

With so many Swiss resorts to choose from, it is up to the individual to decide which is their own favorite resort. Everyone will require different facilities at a resort. Good skiers will tend to choose resorts where there is a wide range of runs. Some people like the scenery and ambience of a particular resort, while others will consider the night life to be the deciding factor between resorts. Your final decision may also depend on how much you want to spend, since a top resort will obviously be more expensive than a lesser known one. It is difficult to find any two people who have the same opinion as to the best ski run in Switzerland. A pool, however, was recently held among the experts, and these dozen or so runs were selected as the best and fastest.

Resort (Altitude in meters and feet)	*Starting Point of Run*
Davos, 1,555 m. (5,100 ft.)	Weissfluhjoc, 2,835 m. (9,300 ft.)
Zermatt, 1,615 m. (5,300 ft.)	Furrggjoch, 3,350 m. (11,000 ft.)
Wengen, 1,280 m. (4,200 ft.)	Lauberhorn, 2,470 m. (8,100 ft.)
Grindelwald, 1,035 m. (3,400 ft.)	Männlichen, 2,225 m. (7,300 ft.)
Mürren, 1,655 m. (5,400 ft.)	Schilthorn, 2,970 m. (9,750 ft.)
St. Moritz, 1,828 m. (6,000 ft.)	Corvatsch, 3,350 m. (11,000 ft.)
Arosa, 1,828 m. (6,000 ft.)	Weisshorn, 2,650 m. (8,700 ft.)
Klosters, 1,219 m. (4,000 ft.)	Weissfluhjoch, 2,835 m. (9,300 ft.)
Gstaad, 1,035 m. (3,400 ft.)	Wasserngrat, 2,133 m. (7,000 ft.)
Engelberg, 1,005 m. (3,300 ft.)	Kleintitlis, 3,020 m. (9,900 ft.)
Flims, 1,155 m. (3,800 ft.)	Cassonsgrat, 2,680 m. (8,800 ft.)
Verbier, 1,490 m. (4,900 ft.)	Mont Gelé, 3,020 m. (9,900 ft.)
Meiringen, 590 m. (1,950 ft.)	Plan Platten, 1,800 m. (5,900 ft.)

The longest of the popular ski runs in Switzerland is the one from the Weissfluhjoch, near Davos, to Küblis, ten miles away and 1,655 meters (5,400 feet) lower than the starting point. While participants in the Parsenn Derby cover this stretch in less than a quarter of an hour, the average skier may expect to spend an hour or more making the descent. But if you are seeking speed, the fastest of the standard Swiss runs is the Windspillen stretch, near Gstaad, where the experts average over fifty miles per hour. Another extraordinary run is the one from Gornergrat to Zermatt, where contestants in the races cover slightly over five and a half miles in about eight minutes.

For the Non-Skier

Not everybody wants to spend their winter holidays skiing, and most resorts offer alternative sports for non-skiers. There are also many people who like to ski in the morning and then try a different sport in the afternoon. For skiers and non-skiers alike, Switzerland has a wide range of sporting activities.

Tobogganning has always been a popular sport for the non-skier and Switzerland has one of the best tobogganing runs in the world. Called the St. Moritz Cresta Run, it is a steep ice channel through which you flash on a four-inch-high, 35–50-inch-long, and 20-inch-wide steel sled called a skeleton. You lie on your stomach, head to the front, and steer with steel hooks attached to your shoes. It looks easy—try it! The record time from the top is a mere fifty-five seconds. Speeds of over 80 miles per hour cause little astonishment, but if I were in your toboggan, I would hold the speed to a mere 50 miles per hour. That's fast enough to keep you from becoming bored. The eight hairpin turns, which have been given the promising names of Stable Junction, Church Leap, Battle Dore, Shuttle Cock, Stream Corner, Bullpetts Corner, Scylla, and Charybdis, are guaranteed to keep you from worrying about your income tax, but the thought of inheritance taxes may flit through your mind from time to time.

Today, the high class St. Moritz Tobogganing Club counts several hundred members. Its books have carried such famous names as those of Charlie Chaplin, Douglas Fairbanks and Jan Kiepura, and even now the payment of a modest membership fee will put your name on the club rolls along with such well-known persons as Lord Brabazon of Tara, Henri Martineau, Jr., Ralph Harbour, Carl Nater-Cartier, and Count Theo Rossi di Montelera. It does not cost much to risk your neck in such expensive surroundings. Non-members may rent their skeletons for only a few francs a day.

For those who do not care to slide around corners at 50 miles per hour, it is also a spectator sport. There are various contests during the winter season, the best known being the Curzon Cup, and the Grand National. There are also bobsleigh runs at St. Moritz, Davos, Mürren, Gstaad, Klosters, Engelberg, Crans, and several other resorts.

Ski-joring (a kind of water-skiing on dry land) and ski bobbing (tricycling on skis) are two different snow sports often seen in Switzerland, but neither one is as exciting as skiing, and both are only variations on a theme.

Summer Skiing

Summer skiing is becoming more popular all the time in Switzerland although it would be more accurately called glacier skiing since it takes place on glaciers, which retain their snow all year. But it is only possible until lunchtime, as the snow gets very slushy towards the end of the morning. Most summer skiing resorts keep their slopes open until September, and feature a wide range of après-ski activities. The best resort is Zermatt, but others are: Pontresina, St. Mortiz/Silvaplana, Andermatt (only until July), Engelberg, Gstaad, Jungfraujoch, Mürren, Les Diablerets, Crans/Montana and Saas Fee.

Cross-Country Skiing or *Langlaufing*

Langlaufing, unlike ordinary skiing, is a sport which has no age limits, and which is increasingly popular throughout Switzerland. Cross-country skiing equipment can be hired at most resorts and most ski schools offer langlaufing courses. Unlike downhill skiing, langlaufing needs no great skill and it is cheap because there are no charges for using the cross-country trails.

Each year at the beginning of March, about 11,000 langlaufing enthusiasts gather in the Engadine area of Switzerland to compete in the Ski Marathon, the country's biggest cross-country skiing event. The 26 mile course stretches from Maloja past the Upper Engadine lakes to Zuoz, and the competitors must complete the course in under six hours. This race is as popular with spectators as it is with competitors, and each year, thousands of people line the track to watch.

There are also excellent and interesting routes in the Neuchâtel-Jura area. One center for the sport is the Tête-de-Ran and La Vue-des-Alpes region (where there are also ten ski lifts for those who want to ski downhill). A circular tour runs from La Vue-des-Alpes via Pertuis; another is a 50 kilometer (33-mile) 'Trans Jura' route that connects with the Jura trails. You can go from Les Bugnenets via Pertuis, La Vue-des-Alpes, Tête-de-Ran, La Tourne, Les Ponts-de-Martel and La Brévine to Les Carnets near the French border.

The Valais also has many cross-country trails, one of the most fascinating being the Upper Goms Valley, where the sides of the valley have been rubbed smooth by the Rhône glacier's passage. A 19-kilometer (12 miles) trail is cleared each morning in season between Oberwald, where the train stops, and Blitzingen, and both Oberwald and Münster have cross-country instruction.

For details on the main areas offering facilities for cross-country ask the Swiss National Tourist Office for the booklet on *All-inclusive arrangements for cross-country skiers and ski-roamers.*

For those who don't want to go cross-country skiing, there is always ordinary walking, and all Swiss resorts have footpaths. If you are going to walk around a resort, remember to wear shoes or boots with non-slip soles, because you're as likely to slip over on ice and break a leg as you are to fall on the ski slopes and hurt yourself.

Curling and Skating

One sport which has recently experienced an astonishing boom is curling. To the uninitiated, a curling party from afar looks like a group of elderly ladies and gentlemen pushing metal hot water bottles over the ice. As a matter of fact, you do not have to be elderly to enjoy the game, but the rest of the description is not unjust. As the rules of curling are long and involved, we will not go into them at this time. Suffice it to say that curling is a team game. Each team has four players, each of whom has two hot water bottles, or, to use the parlance of the game, 'stones'. The players push their stones, which are 40-pound granite blocks with metal handles, toward the center of the target area (the 'tea' or the 'dolly'). Stones barring the direct line to the tea can be avoided by in-handling or out-handling one's own stone, but once the stone has been tipped, it glides over the ice in a curved rather than a straight line. The team whose stones are nearest the tea at the end of 9, 11, or 13 'heads' is the winner.

Incidentally, curling is highly recommended for married couples. A rule prohibits players from talking to each other. They may only address their words of endearment, or whatever other sentiments they may have, to the stone. Some of the most popular curling centers in Switzerland include Davos, Grindelwald, Gstaad, Lenzerheide, Villars and Zermatt.

Next to skiing, ice skating is probably the most popular winter sport in Switzerland and many ski resorts have natural ice rinks. There are about 140 natural and 80 artificial ice rinks throughout the country. Davos has one of the best speed-skating rinks in the world. It is a center for speed and figure-skating as well as ice hockey. There are also good rinks in most of the cities, and you seldom have to go far to reach a lake.

Each season there is a large number of international hockey matches, and tourists with a minimum of experience will be welcomed by the local hockey clubs at the various resorts. Skates can be hired in all of the resorts for a small daily rate, and skating lessons cost between Frs. five and ten an hour.

Other Winter Sports

Besides the various winter sports mentioned above, there are other sports available and these include tennis, swimming, riding, hot-dogging and, for the brave, hang-gliding.

Many resorts now have indoor tennis courts for tennis enthusiasts, and at Flims, Grindelwald, Leysin, Saas-Fee and Zweisimmen, you can take a combined course in tennis and ski lessons. Indoor swimming pools are also becoming increasingly popular and more and more hotels are providing them to give their guests the opportunity of swimming all the year round. Frequently there are also saunas close to the pools.

Riding is available in some resorts and Arosa and St. Moritz are both well-known winter horse racing centers. Racing on snow is a specialty sport, but Gstaad offers a winter horse-jumping show in its programme of events, and Davos has an annual show-jumping competition which is open to international entries.

Hot-dogging is also catered for in Switzerland, and special courses are held in Grächen, Lenzerheide and Riederalp for those who want to learn the art of ski-ballet or ski-acrobatics.

Hang-gliding is a relatively new sport in Switzerland, and whatever the season, it is exhilarating. The view is perhaps more spectacular when the snow is on the ground, but whatever the weather, hang-gliding is not a sport for the fainthearted!

If you do go hang-gliding, proper instruction is absolutely essential, even if it is expensive. You learn to hang-glide on a two-seater, the instructor going up with you. Once he considers you to be proficient, he may let you fly solo. It is much easier to hang-glide with skis than without them, because taking off and landing are simpler. It looks like an easy sport, but it isn't, so if you do try it, be careful.

Summer Sports—Golf, Tennis, Riding, Cycling

Switzerland has a reputation for being the home of winter sports, but for those persons visiting the Helvetic Confederation during the summer months there are innumerable forms of recreation. During the May to November golf season there are numerous tournaments on the magnificent courses situated in alpine surroundings. In the better clubs there are hefty greens fees but you can watch the International Open Championship of Switzerland at Crans-Montana for little or nothing.

Like golf, tennis is a popular sport in Switzerland, and the visitor will find suitable courts in all of the major tourist areas. If he is the guest

PARADISE FOR SPORTSMEN

of one of the hotels that have their own courts, and a great many do, his problems will be solved, but other tourists may play at a local club for a small fee.

If you like watching tennis best, over 30 open tournaments are held in Switzerland each year. The most important is the International Championship of Switzerland, which holds the stage annually in June or July. Star players from all parts of the globe take part, and many of them stay to compete in the matches at Villars, St. Moritz, and Gstaad.

Other events attracting participants from abroad are the International Horse Shows at St. Gallen, Lucerne and Geneva (all held every other year). There is horse racing in spring and autumn in a dozen towns, while Davos and Arosa have horse shows or races on snow in the late winter.

Tourists who are willing to content themselves with a dip in one of the lakes will be able to relax in the bright summer sun for the price of a bus or tram ticket. Of course, there are artificially heated pools in many of the resorts as well as some of the big cities, but if you insist on the lake, the swimming season, even in the low country, is limited to the period between June and September. Water skiing is popular on most larger lakes and fees are quite reasonable.

For the cost of a few francs you can combine swimming with sailing. Sailboats can usually be hired on all the big lakes, and a sailing school exists on the Lake of Thun. Here you can learn all the best techniques while living in picturesque alpine surroundings. Licenses can be obtained in some cantons easily, not so easily in others, and you must have one to take a boat out (or else hire a sailor to accompany you).

Cycling is a sport that attracts many of the younger tourists. It provides plenty of exercise, and at the same time it is an economical way of touring the country. In rural Switzerland half of the population seems to move on two wheels. If you do your traveling on a bicycle, you are certain to get a better view of the country and to get closer to the people than you would whizzing along in an automobile or a train. And you can hire a bicycle at any Swiss rail station, dropping it off at any other station. Rates for cycle hire are extremely reasonable. But, if you feel a bit short of wind and leg muscle, cycling is also a spectator sport. Among the Swiss people the annual Tour de Suisse is the most popular single sporting event of the year. In eight days, professional bicycle racers from all parts of Europe cover about a thousand miles of grueling mountain and valley roads, and at every stage of the race the route is lined with rows of eager spectators waiting for a chance to cheer their favorite as he pedals past. There are several other road races as well as the track seasons at the Zurich and Basle Velodromes and occasional track events at Lausanne.

Automobile uphill racing has become very popular since Grand Prix racing on the road circuits was forbidden for safety reasons. The Geneva Automobile Rally in spring and heats for the motorcycle cross-country World and European Championships are other annual motoring events. The uphill races draw big crowds. The drivers, starting at regular intervals, cover anywhere from one to 15 miles, climbing sharp gradients. A fine driving technique rather than horsepower usually decides these contests on the narrow, winding roads.

Fishing

You need a license to fish in Switzerland, but these are easily obtained from local authorities. License in hand, you can then try your luck at casting, trolling or pulling them in with a net. Some of the lake trout are said to weigh as much as 20 pounds, but if you prefer casting in a river or stream the many icy torrents that rush down should provide you with a wide choice of locations.

THE FACE OF SWITZERLAND

BERNE AND THE BERNESE OBERLAND

Arcades, Bears and Fountains

Berne, the seat of government of the Swiss Confederation, ascribes an exact date to its foundation—1191. It also possesses a legend of how it came about, and how the city got its name. According to one version, Berthold V, Duke of Zähringen, had decided to build a city on the bend of the River Aare where Berne stands today. He was hunting in the forest, which at that time stretched on both sides of the river, and told his followers that the new city would be named after the first animal he killed. It happened to be a bear. Coincidence it may be, but the name of Berne differs only slightly from the German word for bear, and to this day a bear is the principal feature on the city's coat of arms.

It does not matter much whether or not the legend is true, but the rise of Berne can definitely be ascribed to the Zähringen family (although in 1191 there was already a fortified position here—the fortress of Nydegg). As for the name, modern philologists smile at the bear story, and some attribute it to a local deformation of the name of an Italian city from which some early settlers in this region are supposed to have come—Verona. Since 'B' and 'V' are interchangeable in some languages, Berne, it is argued, is simply Verona with a Swiss accent. But, be that as it may, on Sundays the children of Berne, uninterested in these semantic disputes, still carry carrots to the famous occupants of the Bear Pit by the Nydegg Bridge.

In 1353 Berne became the eighth 'state' to join the Confederacy, started by the three cantons of Uri, Schwyz, and Unterwalden in 1291. Almost immediately the city's hard-headed merchants and patricians began to establish a supremacy over their colleagues that was to result in Berne becoming the nation's center of government.

In 1405 a major fire swept through the city destroying most of the houses, then made mainly of wood. It was rebuilt in sandstone, and as a result has a pleasantly unified architectural appearance. Later additions barely disturb this impression (for example the baroque and rococo refacings of the 17th and 18th-centuries which most of the buildings received); and if you find yourself in the city's 'diplomatic quarter' (Elfenaustrasse, Thunstrasse, Marienstrasse, and the other streets around the Helvetiaplatz), you will see just how well these stately 19th-century mansions blend in with their older surroundings.

Berne also has many modern buildings, some, such as the city's enormous glass railway station, fantastically so. But these, although certainly not eyesores, are restricted to a few clearly defined areas. Elsewhere there are strict laws which say, in effect, that anything can be done to the inside of a building as long as the facade remains unchanged.

Lively in Its Fashion

Some visitors complain that Berne is lacking in highlights, liveliness, and fun; that it is dull and drab. But to pass this judgment is to have misunderstood the city's personality. One of its greatest charms is that the places of interest and entertainment are provided for the citizens, rather than for the tourist. The animated local markets are a good example of this, in particular the centuries-old festival known as the Zibelemärit (Onion Market), which is held on the fourth Monday of November. This, like the fountains which are Berne's trademark, has a spirit which is lively without being raucous. The people of the city

BERNE AND THE BERNESE OBERLAND

know how to have a good time, but without making an exhibition of themselves.

Berne is primarily a patrician city, the product of long-established families and a conservative tradition, conscious of its responsibilities. The emphasis is on the serious pursuit of government, rather than politics. Perhaps more than any other nation the Swiss have come nearest to eliminating politics, in the unsavory sense of the word, from their corridors of power. Berne, being staunchly Swiss, has also avoided most of the cosmopolitan influences which come from the international element in any capital city. Its traditions tend towards a more sober, unmistakably bourgeois, style of life. Business and diplomacy are conducted around the conference table, rather than in restaurants and at cocktail parties.

Exploring Berne

It is not difficult to cover the principal attractions of Berne in a comparatively short time, since the geography of the city has compressed its sights into a restricted area, albeit a hilly one. The old town is perched on a high rock that juts into a loop of the River Aare. Most of what the visitor wants is contained within this loop, and the few places outside it lie just on the far side of the bridges.

As you stroll through the streets of the capital, three architectural features will almost certainly impress you—arcades, fountains and towers. The arcades, which roof the sidewalks of so many of Berne's streets, are one of the city's chief characteristics. These *Lauben,* as they are called, are a welcome asset in the main shopping streets. With their low, vaulted roofs, they extend to the edge of the pavement, where they are supported on sturdy 15th-century pillars. Under their protection, comfortable window shopping is possible even in the worst weather. Most of the arcades (and there are over eight kilometers, or five miles, of them) are in the old town; the most famous being on the Spitalgasse, Marktgasse, Kramgasse and Gerechtigkeitsgasse.

The brilliantly colored and skilfully carved fountains, their bases surrounded by flowers, are for the most part the work of Hans Gieng, and were set up between 1539 and 1546. They provide light relief from the often severe structure of the medieval houses that form their background. The Fountain of Justice might seem less than original with its figure of the blindfolded goddess with her sword and scales, perched on a high column, until you glance at the severed heads that lie at the base—not only those of the emperor, the sultan and the Pope, but even, striking nearer home, of the mayor of Berne! The Ogre Fountain shows a giant enjoying a meal of small children. Then there are the Bagpiper, the Messenger, Moses, the Zähringer Fountain (with its harnessed bear and its cubs feasting on a bunch of grapes), Samson (overcoming a lion), and many others, some of them sculptured references to historical events. All the fountains have lately been restored and treated with a protective plastic paint.

A Berne Walk

Start on busy Bahnhofplatz in front of the Schweizerhof Hotel, facing the mirror-like glass walls of Berne's futuristic railway station. To your left, and at the top of Spitalgasse, is the Church of the Holy Ghost, finished in 1729 and now plainly uncomfortable amid the modernity and bustle of the eighties. If you now walk down Spitalgasse you will quickly come to samples of Berne's fountains and towers. The Bagpiper Fountain stands in the middle of the street with the Prison Tower (Käfigturm), a city gate in the 13th and 14th centuries, beyond it. Straight down Marktgasse and past the Anna Seiler and Marksman Fountains, you'll come to Kornhausplatz on the left and its Ogre Fountain. To your right is Theaterplatz and in front of you Berne's colorful showpiece and trademark: the Clock Tower (Zeitglocken Turm).

The 'Zytgloggeturm' (as it is called in the local dialect), was originally built as a city gate in 1191, but since then has been extensively restored, while the interior has been converted into a small museum. In 1530 an astronomical clock and a series of mechanically operated puppets were installed on the eastern side; and every hour, when the clock strikes, they put on a delightful, and justly famous, performance.

To see the show it is best to take up position at the corner of Kramgasse and Hotelgasse at least five minutes before the hour. You won't be the only one there. For photographers, the best time in summer is 10 or 11 A.M. At two or three minutes to the hour, heralded by a jester nodding his head and ringing two small bells, the puppet show begins. From a small arch on the left a couple of musically inclined bears—a drummer and a piper—appear, leading a procession of a horseman with a sword, a proud bear wearing a crown, and lesser bears, each carrying a gun, sword or spear. When the procession comes to an end a metal cockerel on the left crows and flaps his wings in delight, after which a knight in golden armor at the top of the tower hammers out the hour, while Father Time on a throne in the middle beats time with a scepter in one hand and an hour glass in the other.

From the Clock Tower our route continues down Kramgasse. It's a lovely old street with many guildhouses, the inevitable arcades and needless to say, a couple more fountains—the Zähringer and the Samson. At the next intersection it is best to make a brief diversion and turn

BERNE AND THE BERNESE OBERLAND 97

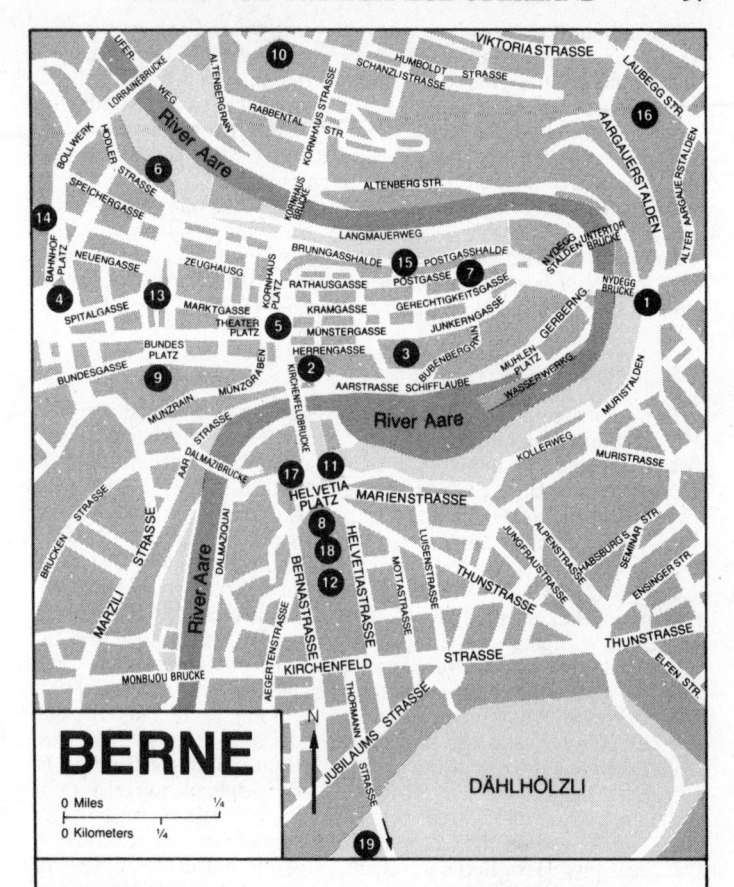

BERNE

0 Miles ¼
0 Kilometers ¼

Points of Interest

1. Bear Pits
2. Casino
3. Cathedral
4. Church of the Holy Ghost
5. Clock Tower (Zeitglocken Turm)
6. Fine Arts Museum (Kunstmuseum)
7. Fountain of Justice
8. History Museum
9. Houses of Parliament
10. Kursaal
11. Modern Art Gallery (Kunsthalle)
12. Natural History Museum
13. Prison Tower (Käfigturm)
14. Railway Station
15. Rathaus
16. Rose Gardens
17. Swiss Alpine Museum; PTT Museum
18. Swiss Rifle Museum
19. Zoo

left down a short, narrow lane. This will bring you to Rathausplatz and the Rathaus (Town Hall) itself, seat of the Cantonal Government.

Originally built in the 15th century after the great fire which destroyed most of Berne, the Rathaus is a pleasingly simple building in the late Gothic style. The markets once occupied the ground floor, and city business was conducted above. But today, after several restorations, it has become the center of both city and cantonal government, the council chamber being a really charming old room. In the courtyard is a lovely fountain which, although modern, shows a distinct affinity with the medieval ones outside. The Rathausplatz in front of the Town Hall is a beautiful little medieval square with delightful dimensions and lines. It contains the Venner (Ensign) Fountain.

Berne's Bears

If you now leave the Rathausplatz, return down the lane and turn left at the intersection, you will walk down Gerechtigkeitsgasse and past the Justice Fountain. A left turn at the bottom will take you steeply down Nydegg Stalden through one of the oldest parts of the city, past the fountain depicting a 16th-century messenger with his bear companion, and on to the 15th-century Untertor Bridge over the River Aare. From here it is a short, steep climb to the far end of the high Nydegg Bridge which will later take us back over the river. However, if you are feeling energetic it's well worth while crossing the road and then either climbing up the little path to the left, turning right at the top, or walking up Alter Aargauerstalden, and then turning left. Both will bring you to the entrance (free) of the splendidly arranged and kept Rose Gardens. Allow a little time here, to enjoy not only the 200 varieties of roses, and the fine plants and shrubs, but also the best panoramic view there is of the city tightly squeezed in the bend of the river. On a hot summer day, too, you'll find it difficult to resist a rest in the cool shade of the trees before returning to the Nydegg Bridge where, at the end on the left, you'll find the famous, but surprisingly drab, bear pits. Here Berne's mascots, alive and not made of metal or stone as on the Clock Tower or fountains, will put up a fine bit of clowning if you dangle a carrot above their heads.

Leaving the bears we now cross the Nydegg Bridge and at the far end turn left up Junkerngasse, a street notable for its fine old houses. At the top you come to the pride of the city—the magnificent Gothic cathedral. Started in 1421 by master mason Matthias Ensinger on a site formerly occupied by an older church, it was planned on lines so spacious that half the population could worship in it at one time. Its construction went on for centuries. Even the Reformation, which converted it from a Catholic to a Protestant church, did not prevent work

BERNE AND THE BERNESE OBERLAND

being continued. Daniel Heinz directed this for 25 years (from 1573 to 1598), completing the nave and the tower. The finishing touch, the tip of the 300-foot-high steeple, was not added until 1893.

The cathedral has two outstandingly fine features, one on the outside and one inside. Outside is the main portal, with a magnificent sculptured representation of the Last Judgment (1490) whose 234 carved figures may distract attention from the admirable statues of the Wise and Foolish Virgins. This work was completed immediately before the Reformation, but fortunately escaped destruction by the iconoclasts who emptied the niches of the side portals.

Inside the church, while the elaborately carved pews and choir stalls are worth attention, the real attraction is the stained glass. Possibly the best are the 15th-century windows of the choir, but Berne has not been content to rest with the heritage of the past. Many fine windows have been added in recent years, like that of the Dance of Death which, though modern in execution, is old in design, for it was made from a sketch by Niklaus Manuel Deutsch, Berne's artist-statesman-warrior of the 16th century. Before leaving the cathedral, walk across to the terrace at the back where, from the walls, there is a splendid view down on to the river.

If you walk from the cathedral up Herrengasse or Münstergasse, you will quickly reach the Casinoplatz and the Casino, which stands at the northern end of the Kirchenfeldbrücke. This contains a concert hall (frequent concerts), restaurants and banqueting rooms. Unlike most Swiss cities, Berne also has a Kursaal (usually they have one or the other), which lies on the northern side of the river and is devoted to rather lighter entertainment than the Casino. One of its attractions is a gaming room where boule is played to a five-franc limit. Further south on the same side of the river—opposite the Casino—is Helvetiaplatz, reached from the other bank by the Kirchenfeldbrücke. This historic square is surrounded by a cluster of Berne's most fascinating museums; including the History Museum, the Natural History Museum, the Swiss Rifle Museum, the Swiss Alpine Museum and the Modern Art Gallery (Kunsthalle). Beyond Helvetiaplatz is the fine residential quarter of Kirchenfeld, and, a little further on still, the zoo.

Returning to the Casinoplatz, turn left down Münzgraben and then right along the terrace behind the Houses of Parliament. Here there's another fine view across the river and, in good weather, to the distant Alps. At the bridge end of the parapet there is a diagram which will help you to pick out the principal peaks. You can walk round the end of the Parliament building into Bundesplatz, and then into the traffic free Bärenplatz. On Tuesday and Saturday mornings and Thursday afternoon and early evening, there is a colorful and lively market here and in some of the surrounding streets. It is at its best during the summer and fall.

This walk should give you an idea of what is most notable in Berne. But there are other areas to explore if time permits. To the south of the city you can go by funicular up the Gurten Kulm and enjoy not only a fine view of the city but also a famous one of the Alps to the south with Jungfrau in the middle. The return fare from anywhere in Berne to Gurtem Kulm is about Fr. 4.50. There is another excellent view of the city from the fine park behind the railway station.

Beyond the park is the university with its famous law and medical schools. The students sometimes add a touch of color to the city's streets but as a rule they find their fun in the Stämme, the fraternity meeting places. The north side of the river offers not only the Kursaal, already mentioned, but also the nearby botanical gardens.

Finally, if you exhaust the attractions of the city itself, you will find it an excellent headquarters from which to make excursions to other parts of Switzerland. It is an important rail and road junction, and round-trips to many of the country's tourist centers can be made from it within one day. Zermatt or Jungfraujoch, to mention only two places, can be comfortably visited on day excursions.

Aristocrat of Alpine Scenery

The Bernese Oberland covers an area of around 4,600 square kilometers, (1,800 square miles), and comprises nine valleys, and the lovely lakes of Thun and Brienz. There are also a number of 'lakelets' in the heart of the mountains. Notable among these are Bachalp-See, which lies at a height of 2,254 meters (7,400 feet), just below the summit of Faulhorn; and Oeschinen Lake—one of the most beautiful—above Kandersteg. The mountains are there as well, lots of them, with a beauty and grandeur which have to be seen to be believed.

The Bernese Oberland was discovered as soon as traveling as an independent pastime began. Jean-Jacques Rousseau was one of the first who praised the beauties of these wild mountains, and in the early 19th century fashionable Paris society started to visit the Interlaken district. Madame de Staël, Necker, and La Rochefoucauld were among those who came. During the 19th century, the district was frequently visited by English royalty, and by a number of poets and writers. Byron stayed on the Wengernalp in 1816, and others who stayed and worked here include Goethe, Shelley, Thackeray, Ruskin, Matthew Arnold, Longfellow and Mark Twain. Other famous visitors include Brahms, Mendelssohn, and Weber; and some respected painters—Lory, Koenig, and Wocher—have completed well-known canvases in the area.

BERNE AND THE BERNESE OBERLAND

The inhabitants of the Bernese Oberland are mainly German, or rather Schwyzerdütsch-speaking Swiss. Decent, hardworking, modest and friendly, they are mostly farmers, craftsmen, or hoteliers. But although foreign visitors are extremely important to them they do not exploit their tourists. They prefer to please their guests so that they will want to return.

The wide variety in altitude creates a great diversity of scenery. Around the Lake of Thun you will see fig trees, vineyards and even southern vegetation; in two hours' time you will reach the region of Alpine plants, and after another hour and a half you are in the land of eternal snow and ice. On an early July morning you may bathe comfortably in Lake Thun, and in the afternoon ski on the slopes of the Jungfrau.

Even the two neighboring lakes, Thun and Brienz, vary greatly in character. The former has a mild climate and a relatively open situation, although the hills rise steeply along the northern shore. It is surrounded by fertile land, flowers, orchards, vineyards and fig trees, the whole sprinkled with ancient villages, castles, and manors. But the Lake of Brienz on the other hand is encircled by wild mountain ranges, rocky cliffs, and dark forests. While traveling around it you will constantly hear the thunder of waterfalls. Lake Thun is much the larger, 20 kilometers (13 miles) long, and about three kilometers (two miles) wide. The lake of Brienz is just over 13 kilometers (over 8 miles) long, and two and a half kilometers (one and a half miles) wide.

However fascinated you are by the natural beauty of the district, do keep an eye on the little towns and villages you pass, for in architectural charm the Bernese Oberland is almost unsurpassed. Whether you travel by bus, car, or train, you will see enchanting houses with terraces and graceful little towers, their gardens bursting with color in summer.

Costume and Craftsmanship

On Sundays you might see women and children dressed in local costume; but the thick, boned bodices are not very comfortable and are infrequently worn these days. However, the Swiss Society for the Preservation of Historic Sites is increasingly concerning itself with the conservation of the national dress, and its branches organize festivals and pageants to encourage its use.

The men's traditional dress has almost entirely disappeared—except in a few almost unapproachable villages and on special occasions—but the women's is much better preserved. Many girls still possess a Hasli, a chemise with starched sleeves, worn in white on Sundays and blue for the rest of the week. With it goes a heavy woollen ankle length skirt, fastening at the front, and blue or purple stockings. A small black cap, known as a Zitterli, completes the outfit. But the costume varies a great deal throughout the Bernese Oberland. Ribbons may be added or taken away, and in Emmental, for example, the girls wear black knitted mittens in summer and long gloves in winter, usually with a bracelet over one glove.

The world famous Swiss woodcarving industry originated at Brienz in the last century. A man named Fischer started carving pipes of horn and later of maple. Soon he applied his knowledge to carving napkin-rings, boxes, egg-cups and cigarette holders and eventually experimented with figures—first trying William Tell, of course. Gradually his neat, artistic work gained a following, and Fischer's whim became a vast industry. Some 20 years ago they started doing cabinetwork, and although these large and impressive pieces of furniture may not be particularly comfortable or easy to clean, they are nicely designed. Another form of woodworking takes place at Frutigen, where matches and matchboxes are made.

Lacemaking is one of the oldest industries of the Oberland, and handweaving is still practiced on a small scale. The handmade torchon lace of the Lauterbrunnen Valley is well known and justly admired. First-rate fancy leather articles are manufactured by a firm in Spiez, and the artistic and lovely pottery made at Steffisburg is gaining popularity.

Apart from the craftsmen and the hotel-keepers, the inhabitants of the Bernese Oberland, as mentioned earlier, are mostly farmers. If you are traveling by car, you have to stop every now and then to let the cows pass, and wherever you go you hear the tinkle of the bells hung around their necks. Even in the elegant streets of Interlaken—a world famous, sophisticated resort—you will meet the herd coming home every evening.

Exploring the Bernese Oberland

At the point where the River Aare leaves Lake Thun lies the town of Thun, a picturesque place which has managed to retain much of its medieval character and charm. It is dominated by the four-turreted Zähringen Castle, which with the church and the town hall forms a coherent photogenic group approached by steep streets and flights of stairs. Down on the lakeside is another castle, called Schadau, built in the English style.

The town is an excellent center for a number of fascinating walks. Within pleasant walking distance are the heights of Goldiwil, Heiligenschwendi and the Grusisberg. A morning's gentle walk will take you to several small resorts around the end of the lake, or to the bird sanctuary at Einigen. If you are a glutton for exercise (although you don't need to be a mountaineer), you can make the pleasantly tiring climb up Stockhorn (2,163 meters, 7,100 feet). Alternatively, if walking doesn't appeal, there are good boat services from Thun, bus services around the lake, and trains along the southern shore.

On the northern shore of Lake Thun, between Thun and Interlaken, are a string of interesting villages, all of them fairly well known resorts. During the season these places are filled to capacity, but being smaller and less worldly than either Interlaken or Thun, they are quieter and, of course, less expensive. Hilterfingen, the nearest resort to Thun, has a yachting school and, like adjacent Oberhofen, is notable for its gardens and lush vegetation. Oberhofen, on a lovely bay, has a picturesque 12th-century castle on the waterside. Next comes Gunten, a water-skiing center, which is also well known for its rich southern vegetation and very mild climate. From here, one can take a bus to the hillside resort of Sigriswil. A little bit farther on is Merligen, a lakeside resort at the entrance to the Justis Valley where every September cheese produced during the summer is gathered together for solemn division between the dairymen and cattle-owners of the district at the ceremony known as the Kästeilet. Just beyond, at the shore terminal of Beatenbucht, you can take the funicular up to Beatenberg (1,157 meters, 3,800 feet) and then a chairlift on to Niederhorn (1,919 meters, 6,300 feet), both of which are winter sports and summer resorts with remarkable views. Farther on still is the entrance to the illuminated Beatus caves.

Spiez

If, from Thun, we travel along the southern shore of the lake in the direction of Interlaken, the first locality of note that we touch is the small town and popular holiday resort of Spiez. Here you can still breathe the air of ancient poetry and hear the songs of troubadours. It was Rudolph II, King of Burgundy, who built the present castle of Spiez, then called 'The Golden Hall of Wendelsee'. Afterwards it belonged to the Strättliger family one of whom, Heinrich, was a great troubadour. But the poets and troubadours of the 13th century frequently fell upon hard times, and Heinrich von Strättliger was forced to sell his castle. It was bought by a nobleman called Bubenberg and later acquired by the von Erlach family, to whom it belonged from 1516 to 1875. Now it is the property of a public foundation. Appropriately, concerts and open-air theatrical performances are periodically held there.

Leaving Spiez, we pass through some villages that are less well known and less popular with visitors than the resorts on the opposite shore. They include Leissigen, Darligen, the small sailing resort of Faulensee, and behind it (at 850 meters, 2,800 feet), Aeschi, which caters for both winter and summer visitors.

Interlaken

Gateway to the Bernese Oberland, for generations Interlaken had one purpose only, to attract summer tourists. Out of season most of its great hotels, tearooms and bars closed down. But nowadays more and more are open year round as winter sports enthusiasts begin to realize the wealth of superb facilities so readily accessible.

Interlaken, as its name implies, is situated 'between two lakes'—Thun and Brienz. On a strip of flat, grassy land bisected by the River Aare, it is surrounded by a superb mountain panorama. The west and east sections of the town are connected by the Höheweg, the central esplanade lined with trees, formal gardens, hotels and souvenir shops. A quaint touch is given by the fiacres as they clip-clop alongside modern motor coaches, but it's a nostalgic touch, too, for they are among the few remaining relics of 19th-century and Edwardian Interlaken. The older hotels have been pulled down or modernized and new ones have arisen, such as the skyscraper Metropole with its breathtaking views from the upper floors.

Halfway along Höheweg, on the north side and almost hidden behind shops, is Interlaken's Casino, standing in beautiful gardens with a gigantic flowerbed clock. In the Casino, a building of curiously mixed styles both inside and out, you can try your luck at the gaming tables (maximum stake five francs), or listen to a constantly changing program of symphony concerts, dance bands, and even yodeling.

During the summer Interlaken has a tradition of open-air performances (but the audience sits in a splendid covered grandstand) of Schiller's *Wilhelm Tell,* a drama with a large cast which perpetuates the memory of the legendary hero and the historic overthrow of the house of Habsburg. The resort also has an outstandingly fine eighteen-hole golf course at Unterseen, close to Lake Thun, but golfers claim that they are put off by the magnificent scenery.

Obviously Interlaken has many restaurants, cafés, bars, dance halls, cinemas and all the trappings that go to make a successful resort but, first and foremost, it is a center for excursions, and as such has few rivals throughout Europe.

Interlaken as an Excursion Center

The Swiss are justly famous for their remarkable engineering ability and throughout the Bernese Oberland they have fully developed this

BERNE AND THE BERNESE OBERLAND

special skill in providing mountain transport. It seems, in fact, as if every peak and crag has been tunneled for trains or elevators, or bound with cables of aerial cabins and chairlifts. Cogwheel trains scurry up and down mountains; motor coaches add a touch of contrasting color to winding roads; cable cars and chairlifts soar silently aloft. Thus sightseers can alight at heights varying from around 500 meters (about 2,000 feet) to the Jungfraujoch's 3,453 meters (11,333 feet). The latter is possibly the finest excursion in Switzerland—some say in Europe—and maybe the most expensive one, too. But first let's take a look at something more modest.

Only five minutes' walk from Interlaken's West station is the lower terminal of the funicular railway up to Heimwehfluh (669 meters, 2,200 feet), where there are magnificent views of towering Jungfrau, Eiger and Mönch. At the top, there's an elaborate scale-model railway. On the other side of the town, not much farther away, is the funicular which will take you on the fifteen-minute ride up to Harder Kulm (1,310 meters, 4,300 feet), and so to an even finer mountain and lake panorama. There are splendid walks along prepared paths, and you may even see a wild ibex, for they wander freely hereabouts. Just a short distance from the top station is an attractive restaurant with a terrace where you can drink in both the view and something stronger.

Now let's venture farther afield and a trifle higher. From Interlaken East station the Bernese Oberland Railway will take you in six minutes to Wilderswil, a charming little spot with a view of the Jungfrau that, according to Ruskin, is one of the three great sights of Europe. At Wilderswil we change to a cogwheel train for the steep, fifty-minute climb to Schynige Platte (1,965 meters, 6,450 feet). Even by Bernese Oberland standards the view from here is remarkably beautiful and fully justifies its fame. Almost as famous is the Alpine Botanical Garden near the summit station, where hundreds of different Alpine plants have been laid out in natural surroundings. If you are looking for a really memorable evening there are moonlight walks organized along the ridge from Schynige Platte. All you need is to be reasonably fit, well shod, and suitably clothed. Check with the Interlaken tourist office for details.

Note: Mountain sickness affects few people, but it is at best an unpleasant experience and it can be dangerous. It is important that anyone suffering from heart trouble, weak lungs, or high blood pressure consults a doctor before embarking on either of our next two expeditions—to Schilthorn and Jungfraujoch.

The Schilthorn and Mürren

It takes about one and a half hours to get from Interlaken to the top of Schilthorn; starting with a train journey to Lauterbrunnen and then a ten-minute coach ride to Stechelberg, where you'll see the Mürrenbach, said to be Europe's highest waterfall, tumbling over the cliff. Incidentally, even more impressive and famous are the Staubbach Falls near Lauterbrunnen, and the Trümmelbach Falls some three kilometers away. At Stechelberg the real trip begins—a four-stage cable-car journey lifting you silently in little more than a half-hour to the summit of Schilthorn, some 2,970 meters (9,750 feet) above sea level. It was here that scenes were shot for the James Bond film *On Her Majesty's Secret Service*. And if you go into the circular Piz Gloria restaurant above the cable-car terminal, you can sit and watch an Alpine panorama—so grand that it seems faintly unreal—slowly roll past your window, for the whole restaurant revolves continuously. Sit there fifty minutes, and you'll have gone the full circle.

On the way up one of the cable-car stations is Mürren (1,663 meters, 5,400 feet), the highest village in the Bernese Oberland. Impressively perched among clifftop pastures almost 800 meters (2,600 feet) above the Lauterbrunnen Valley, Mürren enjoys an incomparable view of Jungfrau and its snow-capped colleagues. It's a first-rate resort, tailor made for those yearning to escape from the noise and hurly-burly of city life since it is inaccessible by road, leaving the streets blessedly traffic-free. For winter sports, Mürren is world-famous. Especially notable is the funicular to Allmendhubel (1,910 meters, 6,270 feet), where a bobsleigh run begins, and descends through hairpin bends to the finish over 300 meters (1,000 feet) below.

Instead of going by cable car, a slightly quicker and more interesting way to reach Mürren is by train from Interlaken to Lauterbrunnen, then by funicular up the steep cliff to Grütschalp, and finally by mountain railway along the cliff edge to the resort itself.

The Jungfraujoch

From Interlaken the journey to the Jungfraujoch is in two parts, the first via Lauterbrunnen or Grindelwald to Kleine Scheidegg, and the second from there to the summit station. The usual outward route is from Interlaken East station (578 meters, 1,900 feet), past Wilderswil and Zweilütschinen to Lauterbrunnen (791 meters, 2,600 feet), noted for its mountain torrents, beautiful waterfalls and lace. You may not see the latter but you will certainly notice plenty of rushing and falling water. Just before Zweilütschinen, if you look to the right of the train,

BERNE AND THE BERNESE OBERLAND

you'll get a glimpse of the confluence of the rivers Schwarze (Black) Lutschine and Weisse (White) Lutschine, and where the waters join you'll clearly see the difference in color. The 'white' is glacier water and the 'black' comes from rocks.

At Lauterbrunnen we join the green cogwheel trains of the Wengernalp Railway, popularly known as WAB, and the steep climb to the top really begins. The train twists and turns through tunnels and over viaducts, giving a succession of camera-clicking views of yet more mountain torrents and waterfalls, of the Lauterbrunnen valley down below with the funicular to Mürren up the other side, and of an unending, constantly changing vista of peaks. In early summer the track is lined with a superb display of wild flowers.

The first main stop is at Wengen (1,297 meters, 4,200 feet), a famous, long established, and well equipped all-year resort which is still no more than a mountainside plateau village at the foot of the Jungfrau. Nor is its peaceful atmosphere disturbed by cars, since it cannot be reached by road. The sunset is one of Wengen's claims to fame. You may have admired many sunsets, but here the glow which bathes surrounding peaks and slopes and casts a pink and flame-red light over the entire scene is unique.

Rocks, Snow and Ice

The train which takes you onwards from Wengen must be classified as one of the miracles of Swiss engineering. It seems incredible that the steeply climbing train can find a route through the rocks, snow, and ice.

At 1,873 meters (6,150 feet) you pass through Wengernalp, where Byron stayed in 1816 and is reputed to have conceived the idea for *Manfred*. Soon afterwards, at a height of 2,059 meters (6,760 feet), you will reach Kleine Scheidegg, a quiet little winter and summer resort. It doesn't quite belong to the land of eternal snow but it is high enough for skiing right into late spring.

At Kleine Scheidegg we change over to the smart little brown-and-cream train of the Jungfrau Railway which climbs more than 1,370 meters (4,500 feet) over the next 9.5 kilometers (6 miles), which leads to the summit station. Over 7 kilometers of this distance (4.5 miles) is in a tunnel which runs through the Eiger and Mönch mountains. The line took 16 years to build and was opened in 1912. Even today it is still one of the marvels of the world's railway systems.

Leaving Kleine Scheidegg, where there is a good moderately priced station restaurant, the train passes through pastures with views of Mönch and Grindelwald, as well as the treacherous Eiger North Wall, which we'll see better on the way down. Just before the next station,

Eigergletscher (2,318 meters, 7,610 feet) which has a small hotel and restaurant, you'll see on the right-hand side of the track the kennels of the husky dogs which pull the sleighs at the summit, and next to them a pen containing a colony of the small, furry marmots which inhabit the high Alps.

Now the train plunges into the long tunnel which leads steeply up to Jungfraujoch—a forty-minute journey. The next station is Eigerwand (2,864 meters, 9,400 feet), which lies only a few meters inside the precipitous North Wall. From the station platform short tunnels lead to enormous windows cut into the North Wall, and all trains stop long enough for passengers to walk across to take in the view. Given fine weather, you'll see a magnificent panorama of Grindelwald far below, Lake Thun in the distance, and a multitude of mountains, valleys, fields and forests. At the next station—Eismeer (3,154 meters, 10,350 feet)—windows are also cut into the mountain face a few yards from the platform, but here the view is very different and even more impressive. Here for the first time you realize you are in a white world of ice, glaciers and snow.

On Top of the Jungfraujoch

From Eismeer it is only about eleven minutes to the Jungfraujoch terminus at 3,453 meters (11,333 feet). Remember that from Interlaken you have risen a total of 2,887 meters (11,333 feet), and that the air, however pure, is also rarefied. Those who move around too quickly before they are adjusted to the altitude may feel giddy, or even become ill. So take it easy; move slowly. Or, as the Swiss guide said, 'For the first fifteen minutes, please forget that you are young'.

From the trainside of the Jungfraujoch station—the highest in Europe—a rocky corridor used to lead to the Berghaus, Europe's highest hotel and restaurant. Alas, this was all burned down in 1972, but it has been replaced by the fine Inn-above-the-Clouds restaurant and cafeteria, seating 290.

If, when you leave the train, you take the free elevator behind the post office and souvenir shop, it will take you to the corridor leading to the Ice Palace. It's quite a long one, much of it cut through a glacier, its walls, ceiling and floor being of solid ice. On the way you'll pass a full size car sculptured out of ice, and a replica of a bar complete with tables, chairs, counter and a whiskey barrel. Down a few steps at the end is the great hall, also cut out of ice.

Back at the station, another corridor—the Sphinx Tunnel—leads from the lower end of the platform to yet another free elevator, this one whisking you up 111 meters (367 feet) in ninety seconds to the famous Sphinx Terrace. Here there's not only a research institute and as-

BERNE AND THE BERNESE OBERLAND

tronomical observatory but, from the observation terrace, an incomparable panorama of rock, snow, ice and clouds that is one of the wonders of Europe. Facing south you'll see the primeval Aletsch Glacier, a 16 kilometer (10 mile) ribbon of shattered ice, divided into strips by thin traces of black. To the southwest, apparently little more than arm's length away, is the 4,157 meter (13,640 foot) peak of Jungfrau, and behind you, to the northeast, the peaks of Mönch and Eiger. On a fine day you may see the Jura and Vosges, the Black Forest, and the lakes of central Switzerland.

If you have never been on skis before, but want to try just for fun, you can do so on top of Jungfraujoch at the summer ski school. The school is reached along a path from the Sphinx Tunnel exit. The services of an instructor and rental of skis and boots will set you back about ten francs an hour. But although there's a skilift, it's a simple slope and of little interest to serious skiers. Should you want something a little less strenuous, near the ski school for one franc you can have a five-minute sleigh ride, weather permitting, pulled by the husky dogs we saw down at Eigergletscher.

To vary the homeward journey, at Kleine Scheidegg you can get a train which goes via Grindelwald (your ticket is valid both ways), giving you, as it descends steeply around the Eiger, superb views of the North Wall towering above. The North Wall was first climbed in summer in 1938, but it was not until 1961 that the first group of climbers successfully conquered in winter the almost vertical rock face, braving subzero temperatures, and falls of rock, ice and snow. It took them six days to reach the top. As you look up from the comfort of the Jungfrau Railway train, the surprise is not that about 40 people should have lost their lives on the North Wall, but that anyone, even in summer, should have succeeded. If your eyes are good, from near Alpiglen station you can just see, almost in the center of the North Wall and about halfway up, the windows of Eigerwand station through which we looked on our upward trip.

Grindelwald (1,035 meters, 3,400 feet) is a fairly large, year-round resort noted for its glaciers and views. From it Wetterhorn (3,702 meters, 12,150 feet), Eiger (3,962 meters, 13,000 feet), Finsteraarhorn (4,267 meters, 14,000 feet), and countless other peaks can be seen, as can the Lutschine valley. Perhaps the greatest attraction is the Firstbahn, Europe's longest lift, which in half an hour carries you from Grindelwald to an altitude of 2,163 meters (7,100 feet) at First. In summer it's the views which are spectacular; in winter, the skiing, although Grindelwald also has skating, curling and ice hockey.

From Grindelwald it is only about forty minutes back to Interlaken. On our Jungfrau trip we've taken part in many records. We've been on the highest railway in Europe to the world's highest underground station; stood on Europe's highest mountain observation terrace; looked down on the Aletsch glacier, the greatest in the Alps; been on what is almost certainly Europe's finest and most spectacular excursion; and traveled on the world's most expensive railway! But, like some 400,000 people every year, it's a fair bet you'll think it was worth every franc.

Lake Brienz

Returning to our starting point, Interlaken, let us now take a tour around the Lake of Brienz, bordered by steeply rising mountains. Along the wild southern shore, the winding narrow road only goes about halfway. At the end, among green hilly meadows between steeply wooded mountainside and the lake, is Iseltwald. A charming, unsophisticated village resort, it lies partly on a picturesque peninsula jutting out into the quiet waters of the lake, and partly around a small bay formed by the peninsula itself. From Iseltwald, a beautiful forest walk of about an hour and a half brings you to the Giessbach Falls, where 14 cascades rush down through the rocky cliffs to the lake. Along the northern shore, the road passes through several small resorts before reaching Brienz at the northeastern end.

Although only a small town this is the largest place on the lake, and as well as being a popular resort it is also the home of the Swiss woodcarving industry, as you will gather from the shop windows. Switzerland's last steam-driven cogwheel train also runs from here, up to the summit of Brienzer-Rothorn—346 meters (7,700 feet) above the town. Many artists have settled here, and the town's school of woodcarving is subsidized by the government.

Brienz again represents the milder beauties of the Oberland. Its climate—though not quite so mild and southern as Lake Thun's Guntenen—is much warmer than that of neighboring regions.

The Swiss Open Air Museum of Rural Building and Home Life at Ballenberg, near Brienz, is open again to the public. (April to October, 9-5). At certain times old crafts such as linen weaving, baking, basket making, are demonstrated.

About 12 kilometers (8 miles) beyond Brienz, we reach Meiringen, the main town in the Hasli Valley, and the center of the valley's homeweaving industry. It is popular with mountaineers and particularly with tourists, for roads lead north to the Brünig Pass and Lucerne, east over the Susten Pass to Andermatt, and south along the Hasli Valley to the Grimsel, Furka and St. Gotthard passes.

The rocky Hasli Valley is renowned for its dramatic scenery, for the 1.5 kilometers (a mile) of the Aarschlucht (an eerie 180 meters/600 foot deep gorge, about 25 minutes' walk from Meiringen), and for the

Reichenbach Falls. Sherlock Holmes enthusiasts won't need reminding that Conan Doyle recounts in *The Final Problem* how the villainous Dr. Moriarty tried to fling the famous detective down these very falls. The faithful will also remember that it was at nearby Rosenlaui that Holmes spent the night before the fateful struggle. American author Sam Rosenberg, in a book about Holmes, has put forward the theory that Conan Doyle modeled Moriarty on the famous, but somewhat sinister, German philosopher Nietzsche. Part of the evidence for this comes from the hotel register at Rosenlaui, which shows that Nietzsche had a holiday there in 1877. It is also known that when, at the suggestion of Sir Henry Lunn (the father of winter sports in Switzerland), Conan Doyle visited the falls a few years later to see whether they would be suitable for the intended demise of Holmes, he also went to Rosenlaui, where he must have learned of Nietzsche's visit.

The Simmental and Gstaad

From Spiez, on Lake Thun, the highway leads southwest into the Simmental, or Simmen Valley. Weissenburgbad, a short distance north of Weissenburg on the main Simmen Valley road, is hidden in a romantic gorge. Its mineral water, famous since the 15th century, achieves excellent results in curing respiratory troubles. Higher up in the Simmen Valley, we reach Boltigen, just beyond which the Jaun Pass road leads off to the right. This is a most attractive and not unduly difficult side trip, although there are many hairpin bends up to the summit and on the descent. You'll be rewarded, too, just before you reach Bulle, by a splendid view of Gruyères, in the middle distance to the left, standing proudly on top of its rocky pinnacle.

Zweisimmen is the main town of the Simmen Valley, and although it is primarily important as a cattle market, it is also a winter sports resort, with a gondola cableway (said to be Europe's longest) to the splendid skiing slopes on Rinderberg (2,010 meters, 6,600 feet high). Pleasant short walks lead to the Mannenberg ruins and the Simmen Falls.

From Zweisimmen, still following the River Simme, we can reach Lenk by railway or secondary road. Lenk, situated at 1,096 meters (3,600 feet), is surrounded by wild glaciers and thundering waterfalls, and dominated by the mighty Wildstrübel mountain. From two glaciers, seven torrents rush down to the valley, which is popularly called Siebental ('Valley of the Seven'). Lenk is both a spa, founded on one of the strongest sulphurous springs in Europe, and a beautiful and popular winter sports resort. Being in a rather isolated position, it is comparatively cheap.

If, instead of turning at Zweisimmen up to Lenk, we had continued along the main road, passing the resorts of Saanenmöser and Schönried, we would have come to Saanen, a winter sports and summer resort. Spare a little time here to turn off the main road into the village, for its streets contain many particularly fine old wooden chalets. Some date from the 16th century and their projecting gables and facades are beautifully carved, ornamented and inscribed. At Saanen, the road forks. One branch goes along the beautiful Sarine Valley, through Château d'Oex and the Pays d'Enhaut, which we will look at in the chapter on the *Lake Geneva Region*. The other turns south to go through Gstaad and then over the Col du Pillon to Aigle, in the Rhône Valley.

In recent years, Gstaad has caught up with St. Moritz, Arosa and Davos as a popularity leader and is without doubt the most fashionable of the Bernese Oberland winter resorts. It has an impressive location, surrounded by forests, hills, glaciers and small mountain lakes well stocked with trout. There are golf and tennis tournaments every summer, and during the winter season the annual horse show and skijoring are among the main attractions. In addition, ice-hockey matches, ski-meetings, curling competitions and toboggan races are also organized. Chalet owners here include Prince Rainier and the Aga Khan. Yehudi Menuhin is a frequent visitor here, not least for the famous Menuhin Festival each August.

If we return once again to Spiez and this time head due south, either by road or by the wonderful Lötschberg Railway, we will pass the ruins of both Tellenberg Castle and a massive stone viaduct, before alighting at Blausee-Mitholz (974 meters, 3,200 feet), the station for Blausee. The lovely little lake here is, as its name suggests, a deep blue color. Algae and fossilized trees lie at the bottom of the lake and are clearly visible in the crystal clear water, as are the famous Blausee blue trout. The water is supposed to come underground from the Oeschinen Lake, and some scientists maintain that its extraordinary color is due to chemical effects of the minerals as it runs deep in the earth. An alternative suggestion is that it is due to the algae in the water.

Leaving Blausee-Mitholz, the train begins to traverse wilder and wilder regions; it goes on climbing and passing across many bridges and through long tunnels. Sometimes, as it twists and turns, you can see the tracks at three different levels. The next stop is Kandersteg, surrounded by mountains and scenery as magnificent as you can ever hope to see. Situated at a height of 1,173 meters (3,850 feet), it enjoys a rare advantage, being built on a plateau that extends for several kilometers. In consequence, visitors not keen on alpine climbing can spend their holiday on high ground and still be able to take pleasant walks on almost flat country. Those who wish to make longer excursions can

BERNE AND THE BERNESE OBERLAND

reach the famous and much admired Oeschinen Lake in about an hour and a half. This is a superb and romantic sight, with an amphitheater of rocks and glaciers in the background. The Kander Falls are also accessible. Kandersteg possesses the usual amenities for winter and summer holidays, including an indoor skating rink, which is now also open in July and August. This small resort, visited in the past by many celebrities, is nearly the most southerly point in the Bernese Oberland.

Walking in the Bernese Oberland

The Bernese Oberland is a rambler's paradise. Here are a few suggestions, arranged by districts, both for shorter and longer walks:

Eastern Oberland. *Meiringen—Brünig Pass—Lungern. Three and three-quarter hours.* On this route you pass the Alpbach Gorge, which is a remarkable wonder of nature. The Brünig Pass itself is one of the best-known and lowest passes in Switzerland. *Meiringen—Grosse Scheidegg—Grindelwald.* This is for the more ambitious rambler, as the walk takes six and a half hours. You will see the River Aare, you will be impressed by the mighty walls of the Wetterhorn, and have a magnificent view of the mountains encircling Grindelwald. Grindelwald itself is a world famous glacier village, with mild, green slopes on one side, and almost perpendicular mountains on the other.

Central Oberland. *Interlaken—Grünenbergpass—Inner Eriz. Six hours.* The route takes you amid rich and exotic rocks and wild forests. You pass the Seefeld and Tropfstein caves. Inside the caves are a maze of intersecting passages, and at the entrance you will be advised to unroll a ball of string, so that you will be able to find your way out again. In the Eriz region you will see the Zulg stream, which has many other streams and ditches running into it and gives the district a wild appearance. *Spiez—Rengglipass—Wilderswil. Eight hours.* On this route you reach the broad and high Aeschi chain with its widely scattered and picturesque wooden huts and houses. At Aeschi-Allmend there's a particularly beautiful view: to the north the lake and behind it chains of mountains. Between Wilderswil and Interlaken—if you continue—you will see the ruins of Unspunnen, restored.

West Oberland. *Goppenstein-Lötchenpass-Kandersteg. Nine and three-quarter hours.* The Gastern Valley is easily one of the greatest and finest of the high mountain valleys of the Alps. The easiest route is from the Goppenstein area, overnighting at the simple inn at Kummenalp above Wiler. There are a great many steep, rocky cliffs with thundering waterfalls, most particularly the snowy giants of the Valais. The Bietschhorn is the highest among the mountains: its glistening peaks, capped with glaciers, are an impressive and unforgettable sight. From Kandersteg, take the chair-lift to Oeschinensee for a spectacular view of this mountain lake.

PRACTICAL INFORMATION FOR BERNE

GETTING AROUND BERNE. By Bus and Tram. Berne has an extensive and inexpensive network of buses and trams, most of which start from the main station. Fares range from 80 centimes, for the shortest trips, to Fr. 1.20. Tourist cards for an unlimited number of rides are available for the whole network: 1-day Fr. 3, 2-day Fr. 5, 3-day Fr. 7. There is a 24-hour season ticket, good for the entire network, which costs Fr. 4. These tickets are available from the public transport ticket office in the subway leading down to the main station (take the escalator in front of Loeb's department store and turn right through the Christoffel Tower). Ordinary tickets are available at tram and bus stops; you should buy your ticket before boarding the tram or bus.

There is also a little railway (the only 'profitable' one in Switzerland) which runs from the Bundesterrasse (the terrace behind the Houses of Parliament) down to Marzili on the banks of the Aare. This is the Marzili cogwheel railway. It works on the water balance system. The track itself is only 105 meters (320 ft.) long, but during the one-minute trip, it climbs 32 meters (70 ft.). The one-way trip costs 50 centimes.

By Taxi. These are plentiful in Berne, but, as elsewhere, expensive.

By Bicycle. Available from the main rail station.

HOTELS. Nearly all the hotels that we include in our listings below have a wide range of rooms, a good many of which may well fall into a lower grading than that which we have given here. The best advice is always to check beforehand with the hotel (we have provided phone numbers to facilitate this). Note that, in the case of Berne, we have not included any Expensive-category hotels, though you should be able to find such rooms in both of the Deluxe establishments.

Deluxe

Bellevue Palace, Kochergasse 3–5 (tel. 224581). High above the River Aare with a superb view of the Alps; very much a hotel in the grand tradition; excellent restaurant.

Schweizerhof, Schweizerhoflaube 11 (tel. 224501). Another fine hotel; notable for its splendid decor and memorable cuisine; opposite the station.

Moderate

Alfa, Laupenstr. 15 (tel. 253866). A quiet hotel a few minutes from the station.

BERNE AND THE BERNESE OBERLAND

Bären, Schauplatzgasse 4 (tel. 223367). Large and plush with good, if expensive, restaurant.

Bern, Zeughausgasse 9 (tel. 211021). Berne's newest 200-bed hotel; in the city center.

Bristol, Schauplatzgasse 10 (tel. 220101). Breakfast only; spacious and comfortable. Partially renovated. Non-renovated part is quieter.

City-Mövenpick, Bubenbergplatz 7 (tel. 225377). Central with quiet rooms; facilities for the handicapped. Breakfast only; restaurant adjacent.

Metropole, Zeughausgasse 26–28 (tel. 225021). Comfortable modern hotel in the center of town. Good food in all three restaurants.

Savoy, Neuengasse 26 (tel. 224405). Breakfast only; central and with facilities for the handicapped.

Silvahof, Jubiläumsstr. 97 (tel. 431531). In own grounds and very quiet.

Wächter-Mövenpick, Genfergasse 4 (tel. 220866). Central and quiet family hotel near the station.

Inexpensive

Bahnhof-Süd, Bümplizstr. 189 (tel. 565111). Quiet; with skittle-alley.

Continental, Zeughausgasse 27 (tel. 222626). Near the Kornhausplatz. Good food in all its restaurants, but breakfast only in the hotel.

Goldener Adler, Gerechtigkeitsgasse 7 (tel. 221725). In historic building with facilities for children and the handicapped.

Hospiz z. Heimat, Gerechtigkeitsgasse 50 (tel. 220436). Atmospheric and central.

Jardin, Militarstr. 38 (tel. 416388). With easy access to city center.

Krebs, Genfergasse 8 (tel. 224942). Breakfast only; quiet rooms.

National, Hirschengraben 24 (tel. 251988). Central. Good restaurant.

Nydegg, Gerechtigkeitsgasse 1 (tel. 228686). In the old town; simple and very moderately priced.

Regina-Arabelle, Mittelstr. 6 (tel. 230305). In own grounds and quiet.

Touring, Eigerplatz (tel. 458666). Good family hotel.

Zum Goldenen Schlüssel, Rathausgasse 72 (tel. 220216). Historic building in the heart of the old town. Just renovated.

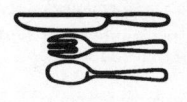

RESTAURANTS. The standard of Berne's cooking is high and there are a great many restaurants in all price categories. The city has a reputation for giving better than average value for money.

Expensive

Bären, Schauplatzgasse 4 (tel. 223367). First-class.

Bellevue Palace, Kochergasse (tel. 224581). Also Grill (E) and City Restaurant (I-M) in same establishment.

Commerce, Gerechtigkeitsgasse 74 (tel. 221161). Spanish cuisine.

Della Casa, Schauplatzgasse 16 (tel. 222142). Elegant and very good.

Du Théâtre, Theaterplatz 7 (tel. 227177). Excellent food. A bit high falutin'.

Ermitage, Amthausgasse 10 (tel. 223541). Tabatière, Bonbonnière, Carnotzet. Bar. Attractive atmosphere up- and downstairs.
Mistral, Kramgasse 42 (tel. 228277). Closed Sunday. Excellent lamb.
Räblus, Zeughausgasse 3 (tel. 225908). Outstanding. Bar pianist.
Schultheissenstube, in Schweizerhof hotel (see above). Outstanding; very expensive, but worth every franc.
Zum Rathaus, Rathausplatz 5 (tel. 226183). Very fine, expensive though.

Moderate

Hong Kong, Hodlerstr. 16 (tel. 222649). Chinese specialties. Recommended.
Kornhauskeller, Kornhausplatz 18 (tel. 221133). Cellar restaurant specializing in Swiss cuisine. Closed Monday.
Le Mazot, Bärenplatz 5 (tel. 227088). Swiss specialties.
Pinocchio, Aarbergergasse 6 (tel. 223362). Italian specialties.
Taverne Valaisanne, Neuengasse 40 (tel. 227766). Fondue, raclette, waferthin mountain-dried beef. Reader-recommended—go upstairs.

Inexpensive

EPA, Marktgasse 24. Department store restaurant.
Gfeller Rindlisbacher, Bärenplatz 21 (tel. 226944). All kinds of quiches and fruit tarts. Cheapest coffee in town but no alcohol.
The Greenhouse, Gurtengasse (tel. 221211). Very good value—cheapest dish Fr.5.50. No alcohol.
Loeb, Spitalgasse 47–57. On 2nd floor of department store.
McDonald's, Neuengasse 24, (tel. 222722).
Migrolino, in Marktgasse over Migros chainstore. Basic, self-service.
Mövenpick, branches at Aarbergergasse 30 (tel. 226414); Bubenbergplatz 5a (tel. 224713); Neuengasse 44 (tel. 220866); and Waisenhausplatz 28 (tel. 224563). All have more expensive menus as well. Marvellous seafood.
Vegetaris, Neuengasse 15. A first-floor restaurant where, surprisingly, you can eat outside in a quiet, first-floor garden. Sumptuous breakfasts are served Saturdays. Succulent salads and imaginative vegetarian food. No alcohol.
Wendy, Laupenstr. 1 (tel. 252414).

ENTERTAINMENT. Cinema. There are 21 cinemas in and around Berne. Most have four performances a day and show a wide range of films. English-language films almost always have French or German subtitles.

Discos and Clubs. The chances of finding nightlife in Berne are relatively limited, though it should still be possible to have a good night out. There are two places where jazz is generally played, *Mahoganny Hall* in Läuferplatz and *Café Shalimar* in Monbijoustrasse, 5 minutes' walk from the station. Behind these two in Wallgasse, there is a convincingly English pub, the *Mr. Pickwick*, which is open until after midnight. You can get a meal at a reasonable price.

There are few dance halls and discos: the *Cadillac* and *BaBaLu Action One* are near the station, *Hollywood 2000* and *Frisco* are in Neuengasse in the same

BERNE AND THE BERNESE OBERLAND

same building. The *Mocambo* is in Genfergasse and *Jaylin's* is at the Schweizerhof Hotel. Weekdays are very much less expensive than weekends. Drinks of all kinds are expensive; a Coke will cost upwards of Fr. 5 (that's around $2) and a whiskey will be at least Fr. 10 (around $5)—so go during the week and make a Coke last a long time.

Theaters. Most performances are in German, so unless you speak the language well you may find a visit to the theater rather a puzzling affair. The *Municipal Theater*, in Kornhausplatz, however, has a wide repertoire of operas, operettas, musicals and ballets. *Käfigturm Theater*, Spitalgasse 4, has ballet, pantomime, cabaret and recitations. *Kleintheater* (little Theater), Kramgasse 6, has modern German-language plays and outstanding acting. For details of what's on, see *This Week in Berne*, free from the tourist office.

Concerts. *Casino Concert Hall*, Casinoplatz. *Conservatoire*, Kramgasse 36 (closed during school holidays). *Radio-Studio Berne*, Schwartztorstrasse 21. *Französische Kirche* (French Church), Zeughausgasse 8. *Berne Cathedral* also presents evening concerts from June to September.

MUSEUMS. Opening hours vary so much and change so often that it's best to consult *This Week in Berne*, which gives full details on all museums. Entrance fees vary from Fr. 1 to 3. Some museums are free. All the principal museums can be reached on foot from the station in about 10 minutes. There's a lot to see, so spread your museum visits out a bit to give yourself time to digest them comfortably.

Art Museum (Kunstmuseum), Hodlerstrasse 12. Completely reconstructed. The collection includes works by Cézanne, Hodler, Braque, Picasso, and other artists of the 19th and 20th centuries as well as the important Klee collection.

Einstein House, Kramgasse 49. Einstein lived here for part of his 7-year stay in Berne (1902–9), working on his special theory of relativity and starting work on his general theory of relativity.

Historical Museum, Helvetiaplatz 5. Entrance free. One of Switzerland's most important historical museums with internationally renowned collections on Bernese history and prehistoric times, applied art, ethnology and coin and medal engraving. A major attraction is the fine collection of 15th-century tapestries from the heyday of Burgundian-Dutch culture.

Käfigturm (Prison Tower) **Museum.** Information and exhibition center devoted to the economic and cultural life of Berne. Permanent sound/slide show illustrating the Canton's history, tourism and cultural and economic aspects.

Municipal Art Gallery (Kunsthalle), Helvetiaplatz 1. Temporary exhibitions of national and international art.

Natural History Museum, Bernastrasse 15. One of Europe's major natural history museums. 220 dioramas showing Swiss and foreign mammals and birds. Extensive collection of minerals, crystals and precious stones from the Swiss

THE FACE OF SWITZERLAND

Alps. Most popular exhibit is the perfectly preserved St. Bernard rescue dog, Barry.

PTT Museum, Helvetiaplatz 4. Entrance free. Houses one of the most extensive collections of rare stamps open to the public in the world.

Swiss Alpine Museum, Helvetiaplatz 4 (see PTT Museum above; same address). Scenery and cultural life in the Swiss Alps, history of mountaineering, collection of reliefs, cartography.

SHOPPING. Berne's proud boast is that its 6 kilometers (3.75 miles) of arcades makes it Europe's largest all-weather Medieval shopping center! The focal points for good shopping lie between the main station and the Zytglogge Tower. You will find watchmakers' and jewelers', clothing stores, shops specializing in leather goods, embroidery and stationery, department stores, cafés-cum-cake-shops, etc. The shops all lie so close together that the best thing to do is walk right down the town under the arcades on one side and then up the other to be quite sure not to miss anything. The best stores for you to make for are *EPA* on the left half way down Marktgasse (toiletries, tights, food department in the basement), *ABM* and *Globus* in Spitalgasse, both on the right going down the town and *Migros* for literally everything, again on the left going down Marktgasse. Here you will find the food department on the ground floor and everything else in the basement. Sports equipment, books and the music department are on the first floor next to a discount market good for wines.

USEFUL ADDRESSES. *Official Tourist Office,* in the main railroad station, open May 1 to Oct. 1, Mon.-Sat. 8 AM to 8:30 PM, Sun. 10 to 8:30; Oct. to Apr., Mon. to Sat. 8 AM to 6:30 PM, Sun. 10 to 5. *American Express,* Marktgasse 37. *Cook's,* Bubenbergplatz 8. *American Embassy,* Jubiläumsstr 93. *British Embassy,* Thunstr. 50. *English-Swiss Association.* Amthausgasse 1, meets Thurs. 8:30 PM.

City Guides. Official guides to help you tour Berne are available at the Tourist Office. Rates: up to 2 hrs. about Fr. 45. Daily city tours by coach with English-speaking guides start from near the main station: price about Fr. 14.

Car Hire. *Avis,* Effingerstrasse 20. *Hertz,* Casinoplatz/Kochergasse 1. *Europcar,* Laupenstrasse 15. *Budget,* Seilerstr. 1.

HOTELS AND RESTAURANTS ELSEWHERE IN THE REGION

ADELBODEN. (All inclusive). *Huldi & Waldhaus* (L), tel. 731531. Quiet and comfortable. *Nevada Palace* (L), tel. 732131. Best in town with indoor pool, tennis, skating, curling and sauna, but pricey with it. *Parkhotel Bellevue* (L), tel. 731621. Quiet with indoor pool and sauna and facilities for children. *Alpenrose* (M), tel. 731161. Comfortable. *Kreuz* (M), tel. 732121.

BERNE AND THE BERNESE OBERLAND

AESCHI. *Baumgarten* (I), tel. 544121. Very quiet hotel in own grounds. *Niesen* (I), tel. 543626. Facilities for the handicapped.

BEATENBERG. *Favorita* (I), tel. 411204. Quiet and central; breakfast only. *Kurhaus Silberhorn* (I), tel. 411212. Very quiet hotel in own grounds with sauna. *Oberland* (I), tel. 411231. Medium-sized and quiet. Recommended.

BIEL (BIENNE). *Continental* (M), tel. 223255. Modern and centrally-located; quiet. *Elite* (M), tel. 225441. Comfortable and well-appointed. *Bären* (I), tel. 224573. Small and central. Breakfast only.
Restaurants. *Bielstube* (M), tel 226588. Excellent. *Buffet de la Gare* (M).

BÖNIGEN. (All inclusive). *Seiler au Lac* (L), tel. 223021. Splendid views from this quiet hotel. *Park-Hotel* (M), tel. 227106. Centrally located; by lake.

BRIENZ. *Bären* (I), tel. 512412. Quiet hotel by lake. *De La Gare* (I), tel. 512712. Small inexpensive hotel.

BURGDORF. *Touring-Bernerhof* (I), tel. 221652. Quiet and central with facilities for the handicapped. Very reasonable.

FAULENSEE. *Strandhotel Seeblick* (I), tel. 542321. Lakeside hotel and restaurant.

GRINDELWALD. *Grand Hotel Regina* (L), tel. 545455. Indoor and outdoor pools, tennis and sauna; dancing in the evenings. *Silberhorn* (E), tel. 532822. Quiet with facilities for children; kosher food. *Alpina* (M), tel. 533333. Comfortable and quiet. *Derby-Bahnhof* (M), tel. 545461. Centrally located family hotel. Bowling. *Parkhotel Schoenegg* (M), tel. 531853. Indoor pool, gymnasium and sauna; quiet hotel in own grounds. *Sport-Hotel Jungfrau* (M), tel. 531341. Tennis. *Lauberhorn* (I), tel. 531082. In own grounds with riding. *Schweizerheim* (I), tel. 531058. Simple and small but very reasonably priced.
Virtually all the restaurants are in the hotels.

GSTAAD. (All inclusive). *Alpina Grand Hotel* (L), tel. 45725. Comfortable; magnificent food. *Bellevue Grand Hotel* (L), tel. 43264. 2 restaurants; facilities for children and quiet location. *Palace* (L), tel. 83131. One of Switzerland's great hotels. Indoor and outdoor pools, sauna, dancing, gardens and all amenities. *Park Hotel Reuteler* (L), tel. 83377. Tennis and skating. *Alphorn* (E), tel. 44545. Quiet hotel with indoor pool and ideal for children. *Olden* (E), tel. 43444. Central; dancing in the evenings. *Posthotel Rössli* (E), tel. 43412. Atmospheric and attractive.
Again, virtually all the restaurants are in the hotels.

THE FACE OF SWITZERLAND

INTERLAKEN. *Metropole* (L), tel. 212151. 18-story building with superb views from top floor. *Victoria-Jungfrau Grand Hotel* (L), tel. 212171. Indoor pool, tennis; one of the great Swiss hotels. *Bellevue-Garden-Hotel* (E), tel. 224431. Quiet and comfortable. *Du Lac* (E), tel. 222922. Near Lake Brienz boat landing stage; recommended. *Royal-St.-Georges* (E), tel. 227575. *Stella* (E), tel. 228871. Exceptionally pleasant and highly recommended; indoor pool. *Chalet Oberland* (M), tel. 229431. Recommended. Excellent food. *Park-Hotel Mattenhof* (M), tel. 216121. Tennis, pool, facilities for children. *Alpina* (I), tel. 228031. Simple but inexpensive. *De la Paix* (I), tel. 227044. Superior hotel in this category; sauna. *Gasthof Hirschen* (I), tel. 221545. In historic and attractive building. No rooms with bath in *Alpina* or *Gasthof Hirschen*.

Restaurants. *La Terrasse* (M-E), at Victoria-Jungfrau Grand Hotel (see above). Very good food. *A la Fine Gueule* (I-M), in Carlton Hotel (tel. 223821). *Krebs* (I-M), tel. 227116. *Metropole* (I), in hotel of same name (see above). First class. *Schuh* is the best place in Interlaken for morning coffee and afternoon tea.

KANDERSTEG. (All inclusive). *Royal-Bellevue* (L), tel. 751212. Riding, tennis, water skiing, 2 pools; very quiet. *Victoria & Ritter* (E), tel. 751444. Indoor pool, tennis; ideal for children. *Alpenrose* (M), tel. 751170. Quiet and comfortable. *Parkhotel Gemmi* (M), tel. 751117. Indoor pool and attractive location. *Schweizerhof* (M), tel. 751241. Tennis. *Alpenblick* (I), tel. 751129. Breakfast only

KLEINE SCHEIDEGG. (All inclusive). *Scheidegg* (E), tel. 551212. Quiet, fine views.

LENK. *Kreuz* (L), tel. 31387. Indoor pool and sauna and facilities for the handicapped. *Kurhotel Lenkerhof* (L), tel. 31424. Tennis and cure facilities. *Waldrand* (E), tel. 33232. Quiet. Diet meals. Garden. *Sternen* (I), tel. 31509. Centrally located.

MEIRINGEN. *Du Sauvage* (M), tel. 714141. Good family hotel in quiet location with riding. *Sherlock Holmes* (M), tel. 714242. Indoor pool, gymnasium and sauna in this quiet hotel. *Tourist* (I), tel. 711044. Small and central.

MERLINGEN. *Beatus* (L), tel. 512121. Splendid lakeside location with waterskiing, indoor pool and sauna; very comfortable. *Du Lac* (I), tel. 511524. Lakeside hotel in own grounds with pool; very quiet.

MÜRREN. *Blumental* (E), tel. 551826. *Eiger* (L), tel. 551331. Indoor pool, gymnasium and sauna. *Jungfrau Lodge* (L), tel. 552824. Tennis; quiet hotel. *Alpenruhe* (M), tel. 552738. *Alpina* (M), tel. 551361. Tennis and marvelous views. *Mürren* (M), tel. 552424. Center of winter social life. *Sporthotel Edelweiss* (M), tel. 551312. *Touriste* (M), tel. 551327.

BERNE AND THE BERNESE OBERLAND

SAANENMÖSER. (All inclusive). *Hornberg* (L), tel. 44440. Indoor pool and sauna in this quiet and comfortable hotel. *Bahnhof* (E), tel. 41506. *Golf & Sport Hotel* (E), tel. 43222. Curling, tennis, skating and golf.

SPIEZ. *Belvédère Silence* (E), tel. 543333. Quiet hotel with marvelous views. *Bahnhof Terminus* (M), tel. 543121. Central. *Edenhotel* (M), tel. 541154. Pool and tennis. *Bellevue* (I), tel. 542314. Good views; quiet.
Restaurant. Welle (M), tel. 544043. Large terrace on edge of the lake beside the boat dock. Fish specialties. Perfect summer spot.

SUNDLAUENEN. *Interlaken Manor Farm Camping Estate* (tel. 222264). Camping and caravanning. All water sports. Hotel and restaurant *Neuhaus* (M) nearby. *Beatus* (I), tel. 411624. Modest but very reasonable.

THUN. *Freienhof* (M), tel. 224672. Much modernized 14th-century building in old town; quiet. *Holiday* (M), tel. 365757. Lakeside hotel. Swimming, bar and terrace. *Krone* (M), tel. 228282. Historic building with indoor pool and facilities for children. *Beau Rivage* (I), tel. 222236. Indoor pool.
Restaurants. Casa Barba (I-M), tel. 222227. Spanish specialties. *Simmenthalerhof* (I-M), tel. 222203. Very good. *Steinbock* (I-M), tel. 224051. Also very good.

WENGEN. (All inclusive). *Parkhotel Beausite* (L), tel. 552521. Indoor pool and sauna. *Regina* (L), tel. 551512. Splendid family hotel. *Silberhorn* (L), tel. 552241. Sauna and gymnasium. *Victoria Lauberhorn* (L), tel. 565151. Central, quiet rooms. *Alpenrose* (E), tel. 553216. Quiet. *Belvédère* (E), tel. 552412. Good family hotel. *Eiger* (E), tel. 551131. Central. Good restaurant. *Falken* (E), tel. 551431. Central and quiet. *Eden* (M), tel. 551634. *Bären* (I), tel. 551419. Breakfast only. Very reasonable. *Bristol* (I), tel. 551551. Good views.

WILDERSWIL. *Jungfrau* (M), tel. 223531. Quiet, well-appointed hotel in own grounds. *Bären* (I), tel. 223521. Comfortable and central. *Alpenblick* (I), tel. 221841. Quiet and comfortable; very reasonable.

ZWEISIMMEN. *Krone* (I), tel. 226226. Ideal family hotel. *Sonnegg* (I), tel. 22333. Diet meals. *Sport-Motel* (I), tel. 21431. Quiet; golf.

WINTER SPORTS. The Bernese Oberland is, of course, one of the world's most celebrated winter sports areas. A separate book would be required to do full justice to the winter activities of the resorts of the Oberland, but here is a brief rundown on the principal centers. Remember, every one of these resorts has its own tourist office; a postcard will bring you detailed information concerning any of them.

Berne, 550 meters (1,800 feet); 1 funicular railway, 2 km. of downhill runs, 1.2 km. of cross-country trails, tobogganing, skating, ski schools.

Biel, 450 meters (1,480 feet); 2 funicular railways, 4 lifts, 1.3 km. of downhill runs, 50 km. of cross-country trails; curling, ski schools.

Bönigen, 580 meters (1,900 feet); 5 km. of ski-hiking, 2 km. of prepared tobogganing; trails, skating.

Brienz, 580–2,025 meters (1,900–6,650 feet); 3 lifts, 15 km. of downhill runs, 5 km. of ski-hiking trails, ski schools.

Grindelwald, 1,030 meters (3,380 feet); 2 funicular railways, 1 cable car, 19 lifts, 120 km. of downhill runs, 25 km. of cross-country trails, 10 km. of ski-hiking trails, 7.5 km. of tobogganing trails, 10 km. of special ski bob runs; skating, curling, ski schools.

Gstaad, 1,110 meters (3,650 feet); 8 cable cars, 12 lifts, 220 km. of downhill runs, 21 km. of cross-country trails, 15 km. of ski-hiking trails, 6 km. of ski bob trails; skating, curling, ski schools.

Interlaken, 580 meters (1,900 feet); skating on either a natural or artificial ice rink.

Kandersteg, 1,090 meters (3,900 feet); 1 cable car, 5 lifts, 11 km. of downhill runs, 18 km. of cross-country trails, 36 km. of ski-hiking trails, tobogganing; skating, curling, ski schools.

Lenk, 1,110 meters (3,650 feet); 4 cable cars, 14 lifts, 40 km. of downhill runs, 46 km. of cross-country trails, 42 km. of ski-hiking trails; skating, ski bob, ski schools.

Meiringen, 609 meters (2,000 feet); 4 cable cars, 10 lifts, 50 km. of downhill runs, 40 km. of cross-country trails, 15 km. of ski-hiking trails, 21.5 km. of prepared tobogganing trails; skating, ski bob, ski schools.

Mürren, 1,110 meters (5,400 feet); 2 funicular railways, 4 cable cars, 7 lifts, 29 km. of downhill runs, 1.5 km. of cross-country trails, 3 km. of prepared tobogganing trails; curling, skating, ski schools.

Wengen, 1,310 meters (4,300 feet); 3 funicular railways, 3 cable cars, 16 lifts, 90 km. of downhill runs, 1.5 km. of prepared tobogganing trails; skating, curling, ski schools, 25 km. of ski bob trails.

Wilderswil, 580 meters (1,900 feet); skating and cross-country skiing (1.5 km. of trails) only.

Zweisimmen, 960 meters (3,150 feet); 3 cable cars, 5 lifts, 25 km. of downhill runs, 45 km. of cross-country trails, 26 km. of ski-hiking trails, 7 km. of toboggan trails; ski schools.

BASLE, BASEL-LAND AND THE NORTHWEST

Switzerland's Rhineland

Basle, on Switzerland's northern border, marks the northeastern end of the Swiss Jura and is within easy reach of the Black Forest in Germany and the French Vosges. As well as being at the center of Europe's road and rail network, the city, which lies on the river Rhine, is also a major inland port.

Six bridges span the Rhine as it turns majestically northwards through Basle, dividing the city into two parts. On the upper, or western bank, is Gross-Basel (Greater Basle), the commercial, cultural and intellectual center. Opposite, is Klein-Basel (Little Basle), center of the city's industry. An interesting landmark can be seen on the western end of the central bridge (Mittlere Brücke). This is the facsimile of the famous Lällen King's (Lällen König) head in the History Museum. It stares fiercely across the water, sticking out its tongue at the Klein-Baslers.

The city's history is long and distinguished. There had been primitive settlements on or near the present site for many years, when in 44 BC the Romans arrived. True to form their leader, Munatius Plancus, quickly recognized the strategic and commercial potential of the area and founded a town called Augusta Raurica, near Augst and about 10 kilometers from the present city. This town was subsequently destroyed in the 3rd century AD by the invading Alamanni, although the remains —including an 8,000-seat amphitheater—have now been excavated. The name Basilia appears for the first time in AD 374 in records of the late Roman historian Ammianus Marcellinus.

Shortly afterwards, the city became a bishop's see, its bishop-princes in the succeeding centuries gaining immense spiritual and temporal power. In 1226, the first stone bridge to cross the Rhine was constructed at Basle, by that time a city of trade and transit.

In 1471 the Basle merchant fairs were instituted, attracting the beautiful products of medieval craftsmanship. Ideally situated as a receiving and distributing center for goods, Basle lay open to the cross-currents of thought as well, and became a center, not only of commerce, but of ideas. Its university, the oldest in Switzerland, is said to have been founded in 1460 by Aeneas Silvius Piccolomini, who later became Pope Pius II. Early Renaissance and Reformation thinkers, including Paracelsus, gathered here; and many artists, including Konrad Witz, Urs Graf, Niklaus Manuel Deutsch, Tobias Stimmer, and Hans Holbein the Younger, have associations with the city. Crafts and skills prospered as Basle was carried forward on the crest of booming Renaissance trade.

In 1501, the wealthy city joined the confederate states of Switzerland. Nearly thirty years later, it formally adopted the teachings of the Reformation and subsequently became one of the leading centers of the movement in Switzerland. This event spelled the end of the restrictive powers of the bishop-princes of Basle.

Banking, Trade and Wealth

Basle is, above all, a city of trade and industry, and its name is known throughout the world as a center of international banking and insurance. In addition, it is the headquarters of Switzerland's international forwarding and shipping business, the center of the country's chemical industry, and the home of the nation's most important trade event, the Swiss Industries Fair, held annually in April.

BASLE, BASEL-LAND AND THE NORTHWEST

Not surprisingly there is an air of prosperity about the city, founded on centuries of successful enterprise. Nor is this confined just to a healthy industrial sector; the many beautiful houses on the edge of Basle testify to the individual wealth of the community. Indeed, it is commonly said that more than half of Switzerland's millionaires (and there are quite a number) are Baslers. But the signs of affluence are discreet; you will see few flashy houses or cars, and no ostentatious jewelry or clothes. Prosperity is enjoyed quietly and in private.

Exploring Basle

Basle is a city with an atmosphere entirely of its own, in which elements of tradition and medievalism are unexpectedly mingled with the modern. The best way to capture some of the feeling of the place is to sit in a terrace café beside the Rhine or stroll along the tree-lined Rheinweg, a pleasant riverside esplanade backed by old houses pressed one against the other. Either way, one looks across the fast-flowing water of this great river as it sweeps through the heart of the city. You'll sense a tang of the sea about this Swiss city for, although most of the river's traffic stops at the docks a mile or so downstream, you'll probably see some gigantic barges chugging past laboriously, perhaps to or from Rotterdam, 800 kilometers (500 miles) away. You'll notice the odd little gondola-like ferryboats, attached to a high wire, silently crossing from shore to shore with no power other than the river current itself. Silhouetting the skyline is Basle's cathedral, and behind and around it splendid old buildings and fine modern ones, a maze of quaint old lanes and busy streets, the old merging imperceptibly with the new.

The cathedral (or Münster), with its viewpoint terrace on a hillock overlooking the Rhine, has all the charm of Burgundian architecture. Of dark red sandstone, it was consecrated at the beginning of the 11th century. Three hundred years later, it was almost completely destroyed by an earthquake and then rebuilt in its present Romanesque-Gothic style. Inside you will find the 14th-century tomb of Queen Anne, wife of Rudolph of Habsburg, and that of Erasmus of Rotterdam. In front of the cathedral is the Münsterplatz, an exquisite square known throughout Europe for the perfection of its proportions. From here there is a pleasant walk down Augustinergasse past the Natural History Museum, (worth a visit only if you are interested in zoology, mineralogy, entomology or in relics of the prehistoric lake-dwellers), to the Martinsgasse. On the way to the 13th-century Martinskirche, Basle's oldest church, you will pass two magnificent baroque residences on the right side of the street, the Blue House and the White House, which are considered to be outstanding examples of patrician Basle homes. The Blue House has a splendid wrought-iron gate.

Now, go back to the Münsterplatz and take the picturesque Rittergasse as far as it goes, turning left to the Wettstein Bridge, where there is a marvelous panorama of the city on both sides of the Rhine. Retrace your steps once more and just beyond the Rittergasse junction, in St. Alben-Graben, you'll see the huge Kunstmuseum (Fine Arts Museum). One of the best in Europe, it features great works by late medieval and early Renaissance artists from Germany, Flanders, and Basle. Here you will find the world's largest collection of Holbein paintings, (Holbein the Younger came to Basle in 1515, at the age of eighteen). Virtually all the great masters are well represented and the museum's long galleries are studded with famous pictures, from the medieval Cranach and Grünewald to Rothko and today's exponents of minimal art. The Impressionists are marvelously covered and so are the Swiss painters Klee, Böcklin and Hodler.

To see most of the remainder of the places of interest in Gross-Basel, it is best to begin from the central railway station. If you feel in the mood to spend half a day at one of Europe's most delightful zoos, turn left as you leave the station, walk until you see the viaduct crossing the Birsig River, and follow the signs to the entrance.

Picture Gallery and Barefoot Square

From the zoo, follow the Birsig River and then along Steinentorstrasse to the Steinenberg, in which street you will find the Kunsthalle, or Picture Gallery. Whether or not you stop for a visit will depend upon your interest in what is being shown at the time. Close to the Kunsthalle is the Stadttheater and famous Tinguely fountain. On the opposite side of the road, beside the bustling Barfüsserplatz (Barefoot Square), there is the municipal casino with its elegant restaurant and concert halls. The old Franciscan church on Barfüsserplatz houses the Historical Museum.

A few paces farther on is Freiestrasse, Basle's fashionable shopping street, leading to the busy market square dominated by the colorful 16th-century town hall. It's worth going into the cool, quiet courtyard. If you sit down on one of the benches, you will see the red walls of the courtyard are covered with interesting, if somewhat crude murals, with three inscriptions—one being 'Freiheit ist über Silber und Gold' (Freedom is above silver and gold).

Just beyond the Town Hall is the fish market, where there is a Gothic fountain. From here, by climbing up narrow medieval streets, you arrive at St. Peter's Square (Peters-platz) and the New University, where the scholarly traditions of Erasmus, Paracelsus, the Bernoullis, Euler, the mathematician, and Burckhardt, the historian of the Renaissance, are still felt. In the immediate vicinity are the university library

BASLE, BASEL-LAND AND THE NORTHWEST

(over a million volumes) and the twin-towered 14th-century Spalen Gate (Spalentor).

Basle's busy port on the downstream side of the city warrants a visit. There, from the viewing platform on the tall red silo (reached by elevator), you can get a fine panorama of the port area, the city and the surrounding countryside—France, Germany and Switzerland. Not far from the silo is a prominent pylon on a jetty marking the point where the three frontiers join. All city tour buses stop there. Walk around it and in half a dozen steps you'll have been in three countries—without a passport.

Upstream to Lake Constance

Basle is the gateway to what is often called 'Switzerland's Rhineland', a beautiful region lying along the river between Basle and Lake Constance. The river is only navigable to Rheinfelden, to which point in the summer there are pleasant riverboat excursions. The departure point in Basle is near the Hotel Trois Rois/Drei Könige (journey time about two hours). A more accurate title would be 'Switzerland's Northern Rhineland', for the river goes far beyond the lake. Lake Constance is to the Rhine what Lake Geneva is to the Rhône—a vast, intermediate reservoir, a natural regulator of waterflow. At the eastern end of Lake Constance, the Rhine changes character abruptly, turns southward, past Austria and Liechtenstein, and then continues southwest to its sources high in the Gotthard mountains. These areas are covered in our chapter on Northeastern Switzerland.

Switzerland's Rhineland (we'll stick to that name) takes in the cantons of Aargau, Zurich, Thurgau, on the southern bank of the river, and the surprising enclave of Canton Schaffhausen on the northerly shore. It's a region of striking contrast: along the river are the delightful medieval towns of Laufenburg, Schaffhausen and Stein-am-Rhein; and the impressive Rhine Falls, Europe's biggest waterfall, which forms an effective navigational barrier. Above the falls, by the reed covered banks of Canton Thurgau, are pleasant little resorts and villages.

To the south of the river is a highly prosperous agricultural countryside, favored by fertile soil and a mild climate, as well as some important pockets of thriving industry, several spas and a sprinkling of castles.

Exploring Switzerland's Rhineland

To see both of the Swiss Rhineland's faces—the river itself and the country lying to the south—only two trips are necessary. One takes you in a broad sweep south of the river; the other follows the Rhine and leaves you in the Lake Constance area, ready for further explorations.

The first trip goes to Canton Aargau, and then back through Solothurn and the Baselbiet (Basel–land) to Basle. If you drive to Brugg—about 51 kilometers, 32 miles east of Basle—you'll be in what is known as Rübliland ('the carrot country'). This is one of the most fertile parts of Switzerland, and 95% of the land is under cultivation. Most of its best-known products are agricultural: the canned foods and jams of Lenzburg come from these parts, and the straw products of Freiamt, but also, a little disconcertingly, the cement of Wildegg. On the way to Brugg, before the road climbs over the Bözberg, the lowest pass of the Jura (underneath which the railway burrows in a mile-long tunnel), you'll go through the Fricktal and the little town of Frick, a paradise in spring when cherry trees are in blossom.

Brugg is a charming old town not far from the point where the Reuss, Lucerne's river, and the Limmat, coming from Zurich, flow into the Aare, the river of Berne. Many old castles bear witness to the importance of this part of the country in olden times. Habsburg, Brunegg, Wildegg, Auenstein, Lenzburg, Biberstein and Wildenstein castles are all within a dozen or so miles south of Brugg. Nine kilometers (six miles) to the east is Baden, a long-established spa known even to the Romans; not far away are the ruins of Roman Vindonissa, including a large amphitheater. Today, Baden is also a major center of the Swiss electrical industry. Bad Schinznach, a smaller spa (but, like Baden, renowned for its sulphur springs), is just over four kilometers (three miles) south of Brugg and boasts a golf course. Nearby is the little village of Birr, where Pestalozzi is buried.

If you drive eight kilometers (five miles) southeast from Lenzburg, with its 11th-century castle, turn left and keep to Highway 1 at the intersection, you'll soon come to Wohlen, a small town noted for its straw-work, and, a little farther on, to the picturesque old townlet of Bremgarten, with a delightful 11th-century covered bridge over the Reuss. Had you turned right at the intersection and driven for about 10 kilometers (around six miles), you would have reached Lake Hallwil, which has an 11th-century castle on an island at its northern end. From nearby Boniswil, picturesque roads lead south through Reinach and Menziken, the tobacco-processing centers of the Aargau, to Beromünster. The fine old Collegiate church here certainly rates a visit.

Doubling back (northwards) through Reinach, you will shortly reach Aarau, the capital of Canton Aargau. Famous throughout Switzerland for the bells it casts, it also manufactures electric light bulbs and high-quality telescopes. There is a fine view of the city and its splendid old houses from the bridge over the River Aare.

BASLE, BASEL-LAND AND THE NORTHWEST

Following the Aare upstream (south) you come to Schönenwerd, its past mirrored in its beautiful 12th-century church. Still on the river is Olten, an important railroad center, a favored setting for conventions, and consequently well provided with hotels and restaurants. Its modern bridge and business section are of today, but walk across the wooden bridge into the narrow streets of the old town, and you will think yourself in some ancient village.

Three miles south of Olten, just off our route, lies historic Aarburg, with its castle dating from the 11th century. We turn southwest, however, through Hägendorf, with its Devil's Gorge, Oensingen, with its castle, and the rock redoubt of Neu-Bechburg, to Solothurn (Soleure), capital of the canton of the same name. We have now left the Aargau, although not the River Aare.

To Solothurn and Liestal

Solothurn, with its rich cathedral, holds the record with Trier (Treves) in Germany for being the oldest Roman settlement north of the Alps. The city's fortifications, different sections dating from successive periods of Solothurn's long history, are of great interest. More recently, elegant homes with lovely gardens have contributed to the special charm of the town.

The Aare continues southwest, now through flat country planted with fruit trees, now between hills, and under aged covered bridges, but we leave it just beyond Solothurn, turning northwest along a secondary road for our journey back to Basle, through the Baselbiet. By a steep and narrow road we cross the Weissenstein, with its splendid alpine views, then turn east at Gänsbrunnen and head for Balsthal, near which are the impressive ruins of Neu-Falkenstein castle.

At Balsthal we have a choice. Northeast, through the hill country of the Baselbiet takes us first to Langenbruck, a holiday paradise in both winter and summer, next up a valley to Waldenburg, a watch-manufacturing town. From here a short journey will bring you finally to Liestal. This is the region's chief town, and its main attractions are St. Martin's church in the center; the late Gothic city hall; the Upper Gate; and the little back streets. From here, it is only 16 kilometers (10 miles) back to Basle.

The other route, less direct, is more interesting. From Balsthal you head north to Mümliswil and the Passwang Pass, which reaches an altitude of 1,000 meters (3,280 feet) and provides some fine views. Coming down again on the other side, via Erschwil, you come to Laufen, upstream from Basle on the River Birs. Laufen, still enclosed within its ancient walls, is the chief community in the Birs Valley, which winds northeast through Aesch towards Basle. The important castle of Angenstein, as well as several other castles and the cloister of Mariastein, lie to the west of Basle. Passing through Dornach, with the fantastic Goetheanum, world headquarters of the Rudolph Steiner Anthroposophical Society, and then through Arlesheim, with its fine 17th-century baroque Collegiate Church, we cross the Münchenstein Bridge and find ourselves in Basle again.

PRACTICAL INFORMATION FOR BASLE AND BASEL-LAND

GETTING TO TOWN FROM THE AIRPORT. Basle shares its airport with the French city of Mulhouse, and indeed the airport itself is actually in France. There is a regular bus service to and from the airport from the rail station in the center of town. This takes around 15 minutes and costs Frs. 4.60 per person. Customs formalities between France and Switzerland are minimal.

GETTING AROUND TOWN. By Bus and Tram. As with most Swiss cities, the public transport system is efficient and inexpensive. Buy your ticket at the machines at all stops (these also have maps of the transport network). You can also buy a 24-hour ticket which entitles you to unlimited travel on all bus and tram lines. These are available at only a few of the vending machines at stops, so check with the Tourist Office if you are uncertain where to obtain them.

HOTELS. Nearly all the hotels that we include in our listings below have a wide range of rooms, a good many of which may well fall into a lower grading than that which we have given here. The best advice is always to check beforehand with the hotel (we have provided phone numbers to facilitate this).

Deluxe

Basel Hilton, Aeschengraben 31 (tel. 226622). Near the rail station; with indoor pool, sauna, airconditioning and facilities for the handicapped.

Drei Könige am Rhein, Blumenrain 8 (tel. 255252). Historic building and very quiet. Its Rhine terrace is as famous as its cuisine.

Euler & Grand Hotel, Centralbahnplatz 1 (tel. 234500). Elegant luxury. Very central but quiet. Outstanding restaurant.

BASLE, BASEL-LAND AND THE NORTHWEST

International, Steinentorstr. 25 (tel. 221870). Sauna, indoor pool and airconditioning throughout.

Expensive

Alexander, Riechenring 85 (tel. 267000). Central and attractive; quiet, and with bowling.

Basel, Münzgasse 12 (tel. 252423). Recommended.

Moderate

Bristol, Centralbahnstr. 15 (tel. 223822). Central; and with facilities for the handicapped.

Cavalier, Reiterstr. 1 (tel. 392262). Attractive hotel in own grounds.

City-Hotel, Henric-Petristr 12 (tel. 237811). Very quiet but central; airconditioning.

Drachen, Aeschenvorstadt 24 (tel. 239090). Very quiet and centrally located with special facilities for children.

Gotthard-Terminus, Centralbahnstr. 13 (tel. 225250). Central; facilities for the handicapped.

Jura, Centralbahnplatz 11 (tel. 231800). Near the station; facilities for the handicapped.

Spalenbrunnen, Schützenmattstr. 2 (tel. 258233). Very centrally located.

Victoria am Bahnhof, Centralbahnplatz 3–4 (tel. 225566). Near the station but quiet rooms.

Inexpensive

Engel, Hauptstr. 46, Pratteln (tel. 817173). Small hotel, with bowling.

Engelhof, Stiftsgasse 1 (tel. 262220). Historic building; very quiet but central. Breakfast only.

Merkur, Theaterstr. 24 (tel. 233740). Medium-sized hotel; very quiet.

Rochat, Petersgraben 23 (tel. 258140). Very central.

Steinenschanze, Steinengraben 69 (tel. 235353). Very quiet; in own grounds; central. *Very* inexpensive.

Vogt-Flügelrad, Küchengasse 20 (tel. 234241). Central; quiet.

Restaurants

Expensive

Bruderholz, Bruderholzallee 4 (tel. 253369). One of Switzerland's most famous restaurants. French specialties. Closed Sun., Mon.

Cochon d' Or, Blumenrain 12. Excellent French cuisine.

La Marmite, Klybeckstr. 15. French food.

Schützenhaus, Schützenmatt 56 (tel. 236760). Excellent restaurant in historic building with fine regional specialties.

Moderate

Chez Donati, St. Johanns-Vorstadt 48 (tel. 570919). Italian food at its best. Closed Mon. and July.

Chez Pepino, Hammerstr. 87 (tel. 339415). Homemade pasta here.

Drachen, Aeschenvorstadt 24 (tel. 236920).
Escargot, at the main rail station (tel. 225333).
Pagode, Steinenvorstadt 32 (tel. 238077). Chinese specialties galore.

Inexpensive

Alexander, Riechenring 85 (tel. 267000). Recommended.
Brauner Mutz, Barfüsserplatz 10 (tel. 253369). Beer hall. Popular meat dishes.
Pfauen, St. Johanns-Vorstadt 13 (tel. 253267). Excellent fresh and salt water fish. Recommended.
Safran Zunft, Gerbergasse 11 (tel. 251959). Fondue 'Bacchus' with all the trimmings (all 14 of them).
St. Alban-Eck, St. Alban-Vorstadt 60 (tel. 230320). Excellent.

ENTERTAINMENT. The fine *Stadttheater* produces opera, operetta, musical comedy, ballet and drama; the *Komödie,* plays (in German). Cabaret at the *Théâtre Fauteuil.* The many nightspots range from dance bars and nightclubs with and without floorshows to striptease. Some stay open to 2 A.M. or later. You can check all entertainment in magazine *Basel aktuel* free from the tourist office.

MUSEUMS. Antiken-Museum, St. Albangraben 5. Opened in 1966, it is the only one of its kind in Switzerland, with Greek art 2,500—100 BC, Italian art 1,000 BC—AD 300.
Basler Papiermühle, St. Alban-Tal 35. Located in 15th-century papermill. Includes water driven stamping mill plus many exhibits on paper-making, typography and book-binding through the ages.
Ethnological Museum, Augustinerstrasse 2. Large and remarkable museum with some 100,000 exhibits from all corners of the globe; those from New Guinea and the South Seas are the pride and joy of the collection.
Kirschgarten, Elisabethenstrasse 27. Museum of 18th-century Basle life contained in an old house. Furniture, costume, clocks, porcelain, silver, toys, etc.
Kunstmuseum, St. Albangraben. Splendidly interesting museum, with an impressive collection of works beautifully displayed, from 13th-century triptychs to modern paintings.
Jewish Museum of Switzerland, Kornhausgasse 18. An appropriate collection; this is the city where Herzl organized the first Zionist congress in 1897.
Museum of Contemporary Art, St. Alban-Tal 2. Considerable collection of modern works by Ernst, Giacometti and Sutherland among others.

BASLE, BASEL-LAND AND THE NORTHWEST

SHOPPING. Shopping in Basle, or at any rate window-shopping, is inclined to center on elegant Freiestrasse. But don't miss the less famous streets (and their sometimes tiny side streets) which wind most of the way from the Fischmarkt area to the station.

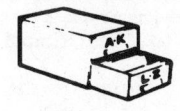

USEFUL ADDRESSES. *Basle Tourist Office,* Blumenrain 2, (tel. 061–253811). *British Rail,* Centralbahnplatz 9 (tel. 061–231404). *Swissair,* main rail station. *Wagon Lits Cook's,* Freiestrasse 3 (P.O. Box 41).

Car Hire. *Avis,* Münchensteinerstrasse 73; *Hertz,* Gartenstrasse 120; *Budget Rent-a-Car,* Bachlettenstr. 7; *Europcar,* Peter Merianstrasse 58; *City Autovermietung,* Birmannsgasse 28.

HOTELS AND RESTAURANTS ELSEWHERE IN THE REGION

Remember that all these hotels are likely to have a very wide range of room prices—with the (E) and (M) ones being able to provide accommodations at lower rates than their stated grades.

AARAU. *Aarauerhof* (I), tel. 245527. Large and very comfortable. *Anker* (I), tel. 227418. Historic and quiet with facilities for the handicapped.

BADEN. (All inclusive). *Staadhof* (L), tel. 225251. In- and outdoor thermal pools, beauty parlor, medical center. *Verenahof* (L), tel. 225251. (As Staadhof). Select and elegant. Thermal baths, resident physician. *Blume* (E), tel. 225569. Romantic family hotel built round an atrium, Roman style. Thermal baths, treatment on the premises.

BRUGG. *Rotes Haus* (I), tel. 411479. Well-appointed hotel. Skittles.

EGERKINGEN. *Motel AGIP* (I), tel. 612121. Very quiet in own grounds with facilities for the handicapped. *Rössli* (I), tel. 715858. Very reasonable.

LANGENBRUCK. *Landgasthof Bären* (M), tel. 601414. Historic hotel where Napoleon is reputed to have stayed. With sauna; excellent restaurant.

LAUFENBURG. *Adler* (I), tel. 641232. Surprisingly low prices.

LIESTAL. *Engel* (M), tel. 912511. Comfortable family hotel in attractive surroundings.

OLTEN. *Europe AG* (M), tel. 223355. *Schweizerhof* (I), tel. 214571. Central.

Restaurants. *Zollhaus* (I-E), tel. 213628. Closed after 9:30 Sunday evenings. Rated "very good". *Felsenburg* (I-M), tel. 212220. Also rated "very good". Closed Tuesday.

RHEINFELDEN. (All inclusive). *Eden Solbad* (L), tel. 875404. Quiet and with cure facilities. *Schwanen Solbad* (E), tel. 875344. Sauna, gymnasium, cure facilities. *Schiff am Rhein* (M), tel. 876087. Quiet rooms; bowling. *Schützen* (M), tel. 875004. Indoor pool, cure facilities. *Goldener Adler* (I), tel. 875332. Central, in historic building. No showers.

SEENGEN. *Schloss Brestenberg* (M), tel. 542212. 17th-century manor house overlooking lake. Due to reopen after renovation in 1986.

SOLOTHURN. *Krone* (M), tel. 224412. One of Switzerland's oldest inns, though much modernized now. *Astoria* (I), tel. 227571. Splendid view. *Roter Turm* (I), tel. 229621. Modern and bright. Good food. Recommended.
Restaurants. *Misteli-Gasche* (I-M), tel. 223281. Closed Sunday evening. *Chez Denon* (M), tel. 222531. *Tiger* (I), tel. 222412. Closed Wednesday.

WOHLEN. *Baren und Casino* (I), tel. 221135. Terrace, grill and bar.

ZOFINGEN. *Engel* (I), tel. 515050. Breakfast only. *Romerbad* (I), tel. 511293. No showers; very basic. *Zofingen* (I), tel. 500100. Central, terrace and grill.

ZURZACH. *Zurzacherhof* (E), tel. 490121. Quiet rooms. *Turmhotel* (M), tel. 492440. Pool and cure facilities.
Restaurant. *Ochsen* (I-M), tel. 492330. Fish, Chateaubriand.

THE JURA, NEUCHÂTEL AND FRIBOURG

Where 'East ist Ost' and 'West est Ouest'

Although the subtitle of this chapter is roughly correct, you will find there is no sharply defined geographical boundary with 'German' Switzerland on one side and 'French' on the other. However, for the sake of convenience, if you draw a line from Montreux to Fribourg, extending it to Neuchâtel, then up through Biel (Bienne) and due north to Delémont, you can say fairly confidently that the country is mainly French-speaking to the west and German-speaking to the east. The western half of the upper valley of the Rhône is also predominantly French-speaking but differs in character from the Jura and is described in a later chapter.

THE FACE OF SWITZERLAND

It is well to keep in mind that there exists a shaded area on either side of the 'language frontier', where French and German influences are rather delicately balanced. Along the imaginary line it is not unusual to hear towns referred to by either their French or German names: Bienne = Biel; Morat = Murten; Neuchâtel = Neuenburg; Soleure = Solothurn; and you may find your 'thank you' answered by a bilingual *Merci vielmal*.

One of the most unusual regions in Switzerland, this area includes the old walled university town of Fribourg, plunging to the river from its hilltop railroad station; the historic city of Neuchâtel, entrance to the region of watchmakers and a considerable university and educational center in its own right (with its lake for warm-weather pleasures); and the Jura region, little known to outside visitors but enjoyed by the Swiss who vacation here. The Jura is the horse country of Switzerland, with meadows, rolling hills and excellent bicycling routes through small rural villages. The region has particularly active hiking organizations. In the Canton of Neuchâtel alone there are 2,212 kilometers (1,375 miles) of marked footpaths, maintained by local organizations.

Fribourg's Unique Role

Between the rich pasturelands of the Swiss plateau and the alpine foothills, Fribourg exudes a feeling of happy satisfaction, produced by centuries of prosperity and the knowledge of its importance in the Catholic world. The city was founded in about 1156 when Berthold of Zähringen decided that the rocky cliffs of the twisting Sarine River exactly met his idea of security. The House of Zähringen died out in 1218, and Fribourg then passed first into the hands of the counts of Kyburg and next to Count Habsburg-Laufenburg, who sold it a few years later to his cousin Rudolph of Habsburg. In the first half of the 15th century the city saw many battles between Berne on the one side, and Savoy on the other, receiving little help in the process from the Habsburgs, who had other fish to fry. Eventually, in 1452, Fribourg came under Savoy's 'protection'.

During this time, however, the city had won many rights and liberties, and extended its territory, absorbing the estates of neighboring feudal lords. The Burgundian Wars, in which Fribourg supported the confederate states, brought further spoils in the form of more estates and municipalities. In 1481, thanks to the intervention of Nicholas of Flüe, Fribourg was admitted to the Confederation as a sovereign canton. Thereafter, skillful purchases brought Fribourg still more estates and municipalities while, externally, its history merged with that of the

THE JURA, NEUCHÂTEL AND FRIBOURG

Confederation. Its citizens resisted the Reformation, making their state a stronghold of Catholicism. This was further strengthened by the foundation of the Catholic College of St. Michael in 1584 and, three centuries later, of Switzerland's only bilingual Catholic university.

Six centuries of peace were broken when, on March 1st, 1798, French troops suddenly occupied the city, and the influence of the French Revolution ended the power of the patrician oligarchy that had held power for nearly two centuries. In 1814, with the loosening of France's grip on Switzerland, a patrician, or aristocratic, government was restored in Fribourg, only to be replaced once again in 1830 by a democratic regime.

Architecturally, Fribourg is a delight. The ancient patrician houses in the old quarter around the cathedral are treasured and well-preserved. The city hall has all the pristine glory of its 16th-century origin, and the picturesque Bernese-style fountains add a lighter note to the winding streets. It is a city of memorable views. From the Zähringen viaduct you can look down to the River Sarine far below, with the ancient covered wooden bridge of Berne, and the high-arched Gottéron Bridge beyond: and from the Gottéron Bridge itself, or from the Chapelle de Lorette, or the Milieu or St. Jean bridges, you will get a splendid view of the town.

A must for sightseers is the Cathedral of St. Nicholas, dating from the 13th century. It is a magnificent building, while its organ is famous throughout the world. The Church and Convent of the Cordeliers is an 18th-century building on the site of an earlier edifice. Its treasures include a 16th-century triptych on the high altar by the anonymous 'Nelkenmeisters' (two artists who signed their works only with a red and white carnation), a carved wood triptych believed to be Alsatian, a notable side altar, and a 16th-century retable by the Fribourg artist, Hans Fries. The Church of the Augustines possesses a magnificent 17th-century altar by Peter Spring, the sculptor-monk. In complete contrast to this are the modern university buildings in the new quarter, reached from the cathedral area by the rue de Romont and the rue de Lausanne.

Wednesday and Saturday are the market days, when you may find the farmers and their wives in national dress. For the men this means a white, shortsleeved shirt under a linen jacket, and a skull cap of embroidered velvet or straw. For women, a dainty blouse under a tight-waisted, sleeveless cotton dress, with full ankle length skirt ornamented by a colorful apron; the whole set off with a draped neck square and a wide-brimmed straw hat. This is weekday dress; Sunday costumes are more ornate.

Fribourg to Gruyères

The canton of Fribourg is bilingual because it straddles the language frontier. But as two-thirds of its inhabitants speak French and only one-third German, it may be considered French. Its lush pasturelands, particularly around Gruyères, are rich in milk and cream yielded by the plump little Fribourg cows, black and white like the cantonal coat of arms. Gruyère cheese, home-cured hams, bacon and sausage, *Vacherin* (a delicious creamy cheese made in Alpine pastures during the summer and preserved for winter in cherrywood boxes)—these are all products of Fribourg's agricultural hinterland. By the way, the town is spelled with a final "s", the region—and the cheese—without one.

Gruyères itself is one of the most picturesque villages in the whole of Europe. To reach it you can either take a train from Fribourg (changing at Bulle for the final stage of the journey), or take the longer route by car. In either case you will pass through Romont, a delightful, sleepy little township, surrounded by cool meadowlands. It is worth leaving the highway for a while to climb into this 13th-century town (composed of two broad streets) to enjoy the magnificent view from the castle terrace. This fortress was originally built by Peter II of Savoy, and its 13th-century ramparts completely surround the town forming a belvedere from which the Alps—from Mont Blanc to the Bernese Oberland—can be seen. In 1581 the government of Fribourg added a new wing to the castle, and today it houses the administration of the district of Glâne. From this high point you can see two other notable buildings in the town; the 12th-century Cistercian convent, and the 17th-century Capuchin monastery.

As you continue on to Gruyères look at the architecture of the farms and outbuildings; it is different from that of Berne and from the modified Bernese style of Vaud. Instead, Fribourg farmsteads are composed of two units; the stone-built living quarters and the wooden barns, both under the same roof. The eaves are wide and peaked, and shelter from the cold is provided by a lean-to on the windward side.

You will find Gruyères enchanting if you are here when bus tours are *not*. It stands high on a rocky crag, its medieval houses and single main street cozy within its ramparts. It is a perfect specimen of the medieval stronghold, and was once capital of the idyllic Alpine estates of the counts of Gruyères (whose crest bears a crane, from the French word *grue*), vassal lords of the Kingdom of Burgundy.

In all there were 19 counts, who from 1080 to 1554 fought, went on Crusades, and lorded it over their serfs. Michael of Gruyères, the last of them, was a lover of luxury and spent lavishly. Fribourg and Berne did not mind his extravagances, for when at last he fled from his

THE JURA, NEUCHÂTEL AND FRIBOURG

creditors, these two powerful cantons divided up his estates between them. Fribourg and Bernese bailiffs succeeded each other in the old castle until 1848, when the castle was bought by a wealthy Genevan family, whose members were patrons of the arts. One of their guests was Corot, and there are several panels by him in the drawing room.

The one real street in Gruyères is lined with Renaissance houses in perfect condition; their façades are 15th to 17th-century. From the ramparts and the castle terrace, the view extends to Broc, the place where Peter-Cailler-Kohler chocolate is made. Beyond is the artificial Lake of Gruyères, built to feed the powerful hydroelectric plants. In the town itself is a cheese dairy which is open to visitors.

A few miles southeast of Gruyères is one of Switzerland's newer resorts, Moléson-Village. From there, you can go by aerial cableway to Plan Francey (1,493 meters, 4,900 feet) and thence to Mount Moléson (2,010 meters, 6,600 feet) or to Vudella (1,645 meters, 5,400 feet). Moléson-Village offers several lifts, miles of marked ski-runs, and no less than four mountain restaurants seating a total of a thousand persons. There's a postal coach between Moléson-Village and Bulle.

There is now an historical museum (the Musée Gruérien) at Bulle, established near the castle in a new building. The collections include paintings (a number of Courbets among them), engravings, documents —all brought to life by an audio-visual show which illustrates the life and traditions of the Gruyère area.

Gruyères to Château d'Oex

From Gruyères it is a 25 minute train ride to Montbovon, where you change trains for the quarter-hour trip which follows the glorious Sarine River to Château d'Oex, the gateway to the Pays d'Enhaut ('the highlands'), one of the most scenic regions of southwestern Switzerland. Château d'Oex, actually in the Canton of Vaud, is a growing winter sports and summer resort. Within a few miles, there are a couple of dozen assorted lifts and cableways, the latter leading up to La Montagnette at 1,700 meters (5,600 feet). If you are interested in peasant handicrafts, a visit to the local museum will be worthwhile but, on a clear day, let nothing interfere with an hour's postal coach ride to the Col des Mosses. This will be one of your most unforgettable experiences in Switzerland. You will see the entire panorama of the Alps, extending into both France and Italy, and there will be no more doubt as to why this region is called the 'Pays d'Enhaut'. (See Château d'Oex under Alpes Vaudoises.)

An alternative excursion from Fribourg is north to the lovely lakeside town of Murten (or Morat), a half-hour by train. This bilingual town is in the canton of Fribourg; and it was here that in 1476 Charles the Bold suffered his second defeat at the hands of the Confederation.

Murten and Avenches

Murten has retained all its medieval charm. The modern highway enters and leaves the old part of the town through the 13th-century gates; and the houses and shops which line the broad main street (Hauptgasse) look out from under deep, vaulted arcades. The town was founded by the dukes of Zähringen in the 12th century, and became an Imperial city in the 13th before passing into the hands of Savoy, whose dukes built the imposing castle and ramparts. Its diminutive namesake lake is fed by the River Broye and its outflow goes into Lake Neuchâtel. The renovated town mill houses an historical museum, complete with two water–powered mill wheels. Also on view are prehistoric finds, ancient military exhibits, and trophies from the Burgundian Wars.

It is a pleasant 15-minute drive to the southwest, at first along the lakeside, to Avenches, the old Celtic capital of the Helvetians. Later, as Aventicum, it became an important Roman city of 40,000 (about 20 times its present population), until the Alamanni destroyed it in the 3rd century. You can still see the remains of a Roman amphitheater where 12,000 bloodthirsty spectators watched the games. The collection of Roman antiquities at the museum is noteworthy although the famous bust of Marcus Aurelius, unearthed at Avenches a few years ago, has been moved to Lausanne.

A bare 20 minutes on the smooth-running electrified Swiss Federal Railways mainline, or a 12 kilometer (eight miles) drive along the Lausanne road, will take you to Payerne. Here you should visit the carefully restored 11th-century Romanesque abbey church, one of the finest you will see anywhere, before returning to Fribourg, a half-hour's journey.

Neuchâtel

The story of Neuchâtel really begins in 1011, for in that year it is first mentioned in a deed of gift made by King Rudolph III of Burgundy to his wife Irmengarde. The township was then probably little more than a fortified village. In 1034, two years after the death of Rudolph, Neuchâtel was given by the German Emperor Conrad II in fief to a local lord whose descendants, using the title 'count', greatly developed their domains, encouraging both agriculture and industry. Three centuries later the direct line of the house died out, and thereafter Neuchâtel came under the rule of several dynasties, until in 1707 it passed to

THE JURA, NEUCHÂTEL AND FRIBOURG

Frederic I, Prussia's first king. But although in theory a Prussian principality, this made little difference to the life of the people because their sovereign left them to manage their own affairs. Neuchâtel retained its French culture, and the 18th century saw the rise of a new and lucrative craft—watchmaking. From 1806 Napoleon inevitably loomed into the picture, and for the next eight years the town was held by his Chief of Staff, Maréchal Berthier.

In 1815, Neuchâtel became a member of the Swiss Confederation, and a very odd member too. With the fall of Napoleon it had reverted to the King of Prussia and was, in consequence, the only non-Republican canton in a republican confederation. Its loyalties were therefore divided between the King of Prussia, Frédéric-Guillaume III and the Federal Parliament in Berne, who were themselves not wholly on speaking terms. The events which shook the great European powers at the beginning of 1848 allowed the people of Neuchâtel to become a republic without bloodshed, and in 1857 the king formally acknowledged Neuchâtel's independence.

Throughout the 18th century, watchmaking progressed rapidly from a home craft to the status of an industry, and a number of allied trades sprang up, absorbing the canton's labor. During the present century, watchmaking has become increasingly scientific, and the city has helped manufacturers by placing an observatory and an Institute for Horological Research at their service. Astronomical observations, research on metals, and improved manufacturing techniques have turned watchmaking from an industry into a science. Not everyone in this region is a watchmaker of course. There are also farmers and vintners along the sunny shore of the lake, but scientific horology is the main source of the canton's wealth.

Exploring Neuchâtel

Located at the foot of the Jura, flanked by vineyards and facing southeast, Neuchâtel is a belvedere from which can be viewed, across the lake and central plateau, the whole crowded range of the middle Alps, from the majestic mass of Mont-Blanc to the Bernese Oberland. It is a prosperous, although not a very large city, and possesses an air of almost tangible dignity. In the lower part of the town, bordering the placid lake, are broad avenues lined with imposing butter-colored sandstone buildings; giving an overall effect of unruffled but compact grandeur. The influence of Prussia has not left so much as a scratch on its culture and way of life, and it is one of the citizens' boasts that they speak 'the best French in Switzerland.' This in turn is one reason why so many finishing schools have been established here, and why Neuchâtel and its university (founded in 1838) have won such fame in educational circles.

Sightseeing in Neuchâtel should include the Collegiate Church—in the old quarter of the city—a handsome Romanesque and Gothic structure dating from the 12th century; and grouped around it the castle (mainly 15th and 16th centuries), ramparts, cloisters and a shady terrace. The influence of French architectural styles predominates in the city. In the Rue des Moulins for example, are two perfect specimens of the Louis XIII period; there is a fine Louis XIV house in the Market Square (Place des Halles), notable for its turreted 16th-century Maison des Halles. The Renaissance has left its mark at the Croix du Marché, while in the City Hall Square (Place de l'Hôtel de Ville) the 18th century prevails. There are several fine patrician houses, such as the mansion of Du Peyrou, the friend, protector, and publisher of Jean-Jacques Rousseau. But almost anywhere in the old town you will find picturesque buildings, and strolling among them is all the more enjoyable now that many of the streets are closed to traffic. Among the museums, that of Fine Arts and History has recently been renovated and much improved. If you get tired of walking you can relax in the shade of the trees lining Neuchâtel's lively, lengthy quays while looking across the water to the distant Alps. Here too, changes are taking place. A large sports area and small port are being built, and a landscaped lake-side walk linking the wine-growing village of Colombier with St. Blaise is planned.

La Tene at the eastern tip of the lake was the site of excavations whose finds gave their name to a whole period of European Iron Age culture. Today the finds can be seen in the town's Archeological Museum.

The Jura

Straddling the French frontier, from Geneva almost all the way to Basle, lie the Jura Mountains; an impressive range although one very different in character from the Alps. By alpine standards the mountains are relatively low, and few peaks exceed 1,500 meters (5,000 feet). It is a region of pine forests, lush pastures, and deeply cleft often craggy valleys where the farmers lived in relative isolation until the invasion of railways and roads. Nevertheless, in winter some parts of the Jura can be very cold. At La Brévine, a windswept hamlet between Le Locle and Les Verrières on the Franco-Swiss frontier, the temperature sometimes drops as low as minus 34 degrees Centigrade (minus 30 degrees Fahrenheit).

The Jura also has a number of thriving winter sports resorts, although most are comparatively small, with local rather than interna-

THE JURA, NEUCHÂTEL AND FRIBOURG

tional appeal. Surprisingly it is a region which is relatively uncluttered with tourists, since travelers usually by-pass it in favour of more famous places.

Strangely too, it has a number of pockets of industry. Occasionally, without warning and in the middle of nowhere, one comes to a large, white factory—probably bearing a world-famous name. If you look at your watch face you may well see the same name, for watchmaking—one of Switzerland's most important industries—has long been one of the principal occupations of the region.

The Jura is divided into several well-defined districts: Franches-Montagnes, with its chief town, Saignelégier; the French-speaking Bernese Jura, including St. Imier; Delémont, Porrentruy, the Ajoie area and the Neuchâtel Jura, with the great watchmaking centers of La Chaux-de-Fonds and Le Locle.

To La Chaux-de-Fonds and Ste-Croix

From Neuchâtel, take the main highway north to Valangin, where the beautiful mountain road known as the Vue des Alpes begins. As the highway rises, the view extends over Lake Neuchâtel towards the Savoy Alps and into the Bernese Oberland.

La Chaux-de-Fonds, which lies in a hollow, is not a picturesque town. Its straight, broad streets and avenues lie stiffly at right angles, and are bordered by stone houses. All the buildings are relatively new, since the old town was destroyed by fire at the end of the 19th century; and recently an ultramodern industrial and residential sector has sprung up among the pastures on the western side of La Chaux-de-Fonds. As you pass through the town you will see on the factories the names of many internationally famous makes of watches; and if you wish to learn more about the craft, the International Museum of Horology, 'Man and Time' is truly outstanding.

Leaving La Chaux-de-Fonds you should turn off southwest to reach Le Locle, another important watchmaking center. From here it is worth continuing on for a few kilometers to Col des Roches, and then through the tunnel—for on the other side you will have a magnificent view of France. From here you will be able to see the River Doubs as it runs through high cliffs, a small lake, and finally to a waterfall. Next, backtrack to Le Locle, turn right and continue through meadows and pine covered hills to Les Petits-Ponts. There, another right turn will take you to Fleurier along the Val de Travers; the winding gorges of this valley are extremely picturesque. Beyond Fleurier you climb up to Ste. Croix where, from the pine-covered ridge above the village (which, incidentally, makes music boxes) there's a splendid view. If you're a glutton for views, turn left here to Les Rasses—it's only a couple of kilometers—for another fine one. From Ste. Croix you drive down towards Yverdon and then return along the lake shore to Neuchâtel.

To Moutier and Delémont

From Neuchâtel, take the Vue des Alpes route to La Chaux-de-Fonds and bear northeast (right) along the pretty valley of St. Imier, a small watchmaking center which lies at the foot of Mont Soleil (1,219 meters, 4,200 feet) and faces Mont Chasseral (1,615 meters, 5,300 feet) the Jura's highest mountain. St. Imier is a modern town, but not blatantly so, and legend has it that it was founded by a holy hermit from Burgundy. A trip by funicular up Mont Soleil is worthwhile, especially if you have time to spend a night there to see the sunrise the following morning. On winter Sundays Mont Soleil is a favorite haunt of skiers from Basle.

From St. Imer it is about 40 kilometers (25 miles) to the medieval town of Moutier, which produces a special cheese called *Tête de Moine* (Monk's Head), the only reminder of the once renowned monastery of Bellelay. At Moutier, you turn north to Delémont, the chief town of the Bernese Jura, located in a wide picturesque valley. It has an ancient story and is first mentioned in history in AD 727. In the 11th century, Delémont was annexed by the bishop-princes of Basle, who often used it as a summer residence. At the beginning of the 18th century they built a castle for this purpose, but they had left things too late, for in 1793 the town was seized by France and later, in 1815, given to Berne under the Treaty of Vienna. Visitors will find that even today Delémont retains an 18th-century charm.

The round trip from Delémont northwest to Porrentruy and back is about 55 kilometers (35 miles) long, and is a beautiful run along part of the Corniche du I. If you have time for a side-trip, take the secondary road on the left just beyond Les Rangiers. After about six kilometers (four miles) you will come to the charming fortified town of St. Ursanne, where time seems to have stood still. At the far end of the narrow bridge there's a picturesque view of the old houses lining the side of the River Doubs. Porrentruy, at 425 meters (1,400 feet), has about 8,500 inhabitants and is the chief center of the Ajoie district. Its splendid castle, above the town, was yet another residence of the bishop-princes of Basle and it can boast several fine 18th-century buildings. Like many of the Jura towns, Porrentruy has an excellent watchmaking school where for generations skilled craftsmen have been trained; but thanks to the lovely surrounding countryside and excellent local food, the district is also a popular holiday center in summer. Year round, it organizes special horseback riding holidays, trekking from village to village in the region. At the local airfield, you can learn to fly or glide,

THE JURA, NEUCHÂTEL AND FRIBOURG 145

and if you aspire to be a balloonist you can make a trip over the Jura with an expert pilot.

Saignelégier to Bienne

From St. Ursanne, which we mentioned above, a delightful picturesque drive takes you along the secondary road which leads southwest into the Franches-Montagnes, past the villages of Soubey and Les Enfers, to Saignelégier.

Saignelégier is the center of a horse-breeding area, and also, on the second weekend in August, the scene of a fascinating horse show and market with races that attract large crowds. The Franches-Montagnes horse is used chiefly for military purposes and agriculture.

The district has typical Jura scenery: rolling hills, long valleys and pine-capped hummocks, although the grazing land is mostly poor. Peat is dug in certain areas, and the roots of the yellow gentian are used for making a powerful liqueur, said to have medicinal properties.

From Saignelégier continue to Le Noirmont, a typical Jura village, through La Chaux-de-Fonds, and so down again to Neuchâtel.

At Neuchâtel the vineyards begin. Their wines, chiefly white, are light, somewhat sparkling, and have a distinct bouquet. They are bottled before the second fermentation begins, so have a rather high carbonic acid content. These wines are exported, as well as consumed on the home market.

About six kilometers (4 miles) southwest of Neuchâtel, and well worth a visit, is the medieval village of Colombier. It lies just to the right of the main road and is approached through a massive stone gateway, beside the impressive 16th-century castle.

The lakeside village of Grandson (Vaud) is about 25 kilometers (16 miles) further on. It is said that a member of the Grandson family accompanied William of Normandy (better known as the Conqueror) to England in 1066, where he founded the English barony of Grandison. Otto I of Grandson took part in the Crusades, and one of his descendants, so legend has it, was a troubadour whose poems were praised by Chaucer. When the Burgundian Wars broke out in the late 15th century Grandson castle, much rebuilt in the 13th and 15th centuries, was in the hands of Charles of Burgundy. In 1475 the Swiss won it by siege, but early the next year their garrison was surprised by Duke Charles, and 418 of their men were captured and hanged from the apple trees in the castle orchard. A few days later the Swiss returned to Grandson and, after inflicting a crushing defeat on the Burgundians, retaliated by stringing their prisoners from the same apple trees. After being used for three centuries as a residence by the Bernese bailiffs, the castle was bought in 1875 by the de Blonay family, who restored it.

Just under five kilometers (three miles) beyond Grandson is the busy market and industrial town of Yverdon, also something of a spa. It was here that the famous Swiss educationalist Pestalozzi (born in 1746), opened an experimental school in the castle, an enterprise which attracted other reformers from both Germany and England, (one of his visitors was the poet Southey). The castle, built by Peter II of Savoy in the middle of the 13th century, has been restored and modernized, and in front of Yverdon's town hall, notable for its Louis XV façade, is a monument to commemorate Pestalozzi. From Yverdon you can return to Neuchâtel by the other side of the lake, the road passing alongside the mini-lake of Morat (Murtensee). On the way you will pass the ancient, lakeside townlet of Estavayer, almost every corner of which has some special charm of its own, not least of which is the well kept, moated castle.

Only about 11 kilometers (seven miles) from Lake Neuchâtel is Lake Bienne (Lac de Bienne or Bielersee), its smaller but sprightly neighbor. Projecting from the southern shore, like a long thin finger pointing to the city of Bienne at the other end of the lake, is the extraordinary St. Peter's Isle. On the island's lumpy wooded headland you will find an old monastery, now a small hotel, where Jean-Jacques Rousseau stayed for a time in 1765.

Bienne (or Biel) itself is a busy industrial and commercial city, which also has a tourist eye-opener—the well-preserved and restored 'old town'. This can best be seen by walking from the busy junction of the rue du Canal and rue de Nidau up rue du Bourg, past the fine Gothic town hall with its 17th-century fountain, and taking one of the streets on the right to the famous 'Ring', a medieval architectural gem. The focal point of ancient Bienne, the Ring is a picturesque little square with a 15th-century church, arcaded houses and, in the center, a fountain. Almost adjacent to the Ring is the High Street (Obergasse), again with lovely old arcaded buildings and, of course, the inevitable fountain.

Today (need you guess?), watchmaking is one of Bienne's main industries, but at the same time, the town has much to entertain the tourist, from theater to water sports, and it's a good excursion center with boat trips down the lake or up the River Aare to Solothurn. Both French and German are spoken with equal ease and, indeed, are often mixed together in conversation. Such is the language frontier of Switzerland.

PRACTICAL INFORMATION FOR FRIBOURG, NEUCHÂTEL AND JURA CANTONS

HOTELS AND RESTAURANTS. Nearly all the hotels that we include in our listings below have a wide range of rooms, a good many of which may well fall into a lower grading than that which we have given here. The best advice is always to check beforehand with the hotel (we have provided phone numbers to facilitate this).

BULLE. *Des Alpes & Terminus* (I), tel. 29292. *Le Rallye* (I), tel. 28498. Splendid view. *Du Tonnelier* (I), tel. 27745. Simple and central.
Restaurants. *Café de la Gare* (I-M), tel. 27688. Try the *fondue au Vacherin*. *De l'Hôtel de Ville* (I-M), tel. 27888. *Des XIII Cantons* (M), tel. 27731.

CHATEL-ST.-DENIS/LES-PACCOTS. *Corbetta* (I), tel. 567120. Quiet and attractive. No showers. *Ermitage* (I), tel. 567541. Indoor pool and bowling.
Restaurant. *Tivoli* (I-M), tel. 567039. *Fondue fribourgeoise.*

LA CHAUX-DE-FONDS. *Moreau* (M), tel. 232222. Good family hotel with facilities for the handicapped. *Fleur-de-Lys* (I), tel. 233731. Quiet.
Restaurants. *Aérogare* (M), tel. 268266. *La Provençale* (M), at Hotel de la Poste (tel. 222203). Very good. *Migros.* Self-service. Excellent choice. Salad buffet.

CRÉSUZ. *Vieux Chalet* (I), tel. 71286. Quiet and very small.

DELÉMONT. *City* (M), tel. 229444. Grill and restaurant. *National* (I), tel. 229622. Good restaurant, bar and terrace.

ESTAVAYER-LE-LAC. *Du Chateau* (I), tel. 631049. Very small but attractive and very reasonable. No showers. *Du Lac* (I), tel. 631343. Lakeside hotel.
Restaurants. *Du Lac* (I-E), tel. 631343. Excellent. *Hostellerie des Chevaliers* (I-E), tel. 61933. First class. *Hostellerie St. Georges* (I-M), tel. 62246. For *quiche gruyèrienne.* Also very good.

FRIBOURG. *Alpha* (M), rue du Simplon 13, tel. 227272. Gymnasium and quiet rooms. *Eurotel* (M), Grands Places, tel. 813131. Central with golf and indoor pool. *Elite* (I), rue du Criblet 7, tel. 223836. Recommended. Near railway station. Breakfast only. *Duc Bertold* (I), tel. 811121. In old town.

Restaurants. *Aigle Noir* (M-E), rue des Alpes 58, tel. 224977. *Duc Bertold* (M-E), rue Bouchers 112, tel. 811121. First class. *Restaurant Francois* (M-E), 1st floor of rail station, tel. 222816. Highly recommended. *De la Gérine* (M), Marly, tel. 461498. Recommended for its excellent fish, among other things. *Café du Midi* (I-M), rue de Romont 25, tel. 223133. All things cheesy; excellent. *Frascati* (I-M), rue de Romont 3, tel. 228256. Italian food. Good pizzas. *La Fleur de Lys* (I), rue des Forgerons 18 in the old town, tel. 227961. Cheap and good. Jazz some evenings.

GEMPENACH. *Motel Gempenach* (M), tel. 950838. Closed Jan.

GRUYÈRES. *Hostellerie des Chevaliers* (M), tel. 61933. Quiet. *Hostellerie St. Georges* (M), tel. 62246. *Hôtel de Ville* (I), tel. 62424. Historic building.

LE LOCLE. *Des Trois Rois* (M), tel. 316555. Has an excellent restaurant. *Café de la Poste* (I), tel. 312454.

Restaurants. *Chez Sandro* (M), tel. 314087. *Buffet de la Gare* (I), tel. 313038.

MORAT. *Schiff* (M), tel. 712644. Quiet and comfortable. Famous restaurant. *Weisses Kreuz* (M), tel. 712641. Bowling and facilities for the handicapped. *Krone* (I), tel. 715252. Central, but with quiet rooms.

MORAT-MEYRIEZ. *Le Vieux Manoir au Lac* (E), tel. 711283. Old house in charming setting with park and private harbor on the lake. Excellent but expensive grill room.

MUNTELIER. *Bonne Auberge des Bains* (I), tel. 712262. Excellent restaurant. (I-M).

NEUCHÂTEL. *Beaulac* (M), tel. 258822. Splendidly situated by the lake; quiet but central. *City* (M), tel. 255412. In the lower town. *Eurotel* (M), tel. 212121. Modern and a little antiseptic; indoor pool and sauna. *Touring* (I), tel. 255501. Quiet.

Restaurants. *Le Banneret* (E), tel. 252861. French specialties, but American beef too. *Le Café Suisse* (M), tel. 252425. *Cafe du Théâtre* (M), tel. 252977. *St. Honoré* (M), tel. 259595. For French cuisine. *Buffet de la Gare* (I), tel. 254853. First class.

At St. Blaise, 5 km. (3 miles) away is *Chez Norbert* (E), tel. 333680. Probably the best food in the district.

PORRENTRUY. *Belvédère* (I), tel. 662561. Small and budget value.

SAIGNELEGIER. *Bellevue* (I), tel. 511620. Sauna, stables, restaurant. *De la Gare du Parc* (I), tel. 511121. Good restaurant.

THE JURA, NEUCHATEL AND FRIBOURG 149

THIELLE. *Novotel Neuchâtel-Thielle* (I), tel. 335757. Quiet hotel with pool; 6 miles east of Neuchâtel.

USEFUL ADDRESSES. Bulle. *Office du Tourisme de la Gruyère,* av. de la Gare 4, tel. 029–28022. **Delémont.** *Office du Tourisme du Jura,* rte. de Bâle 25, tel. 066–229777. **Fribourg.** *Office du Tourisme,* Grands-Places 10, tel. 037–813175. *Wagons-Lits Tourisme,* rue de Romont 10, tel. 037–813161. **La Chaux-de-Fonds.** *Office du Tourisme,* rte. Neuve 11, tel. 039–281313. **Morat.** *Office du Tourisme,* Schlossgasse 5, tel. 037–715112. **Neuchâtel.** *Office du Tourisme,* pl. Numadroz 1, tel. 038–254242.

Car Hire. In Neuchâtel: *Hertz,* Station S.-Raeli, 15 rue de Neuchâtel; *Avis,* Garage Hirondelle, rue Pierre-à-Mazel 25.

WINTER SPORTS. Chatel-St Denis, 815 meters (2,680 feet); 10 lifts, 18 km. of downhill runs, 12 km. of cross-country trails, 8 km. of ski-hiking trails; ski schools.

La Chaux-de-Fonds, 1,120 meters (3,350 feet); 18 lifts, 27 km. of downhill runs, cross-country skiing, 2.5 km. of tobogganing trails; curling, ski bob, skating, ski schools.

Gruyères, 850–1,110 meters (2,800–3,650 feet); 2 cable cars, 4 lifts, 20 km. of downhill runs; ski bob, ski schools.

La Neuveville, 440 meters (1,450 feet); 3 lifts, 12 km. of downhill runs, 15 km. of cross-country trails; downhill ski school.

MUSEUMS. Bulle. *Musée Gruérien,* 19 rue de la Condémine. Extensive collection of local art and rustic furniture.

La Chaux-de-Fonds. *International Museum of Horology,* 'Man and Time,' 29 rue des Musées.

Fribourg. *Musée d'art et d'histoire,* 227 rue Pierre-Aeby. Outstanding collection of archeological and historical finds. Sculpture and paintings of 10th-18th century. Art exhibitions in newly reconstructed wing. *Musée d'histoire naturelle,* Pérolles. Collections cover geography, mineralogy, geology, paleontology and zoology. Don't miss the famous automatic dolls in the *History museum.* Constructed between 1719 and 1773 by Swiss watchmakers, they have toured Europe in their time, and will still write, draw and play for you. Demonstrations the first Sunday of each month at 2:30 P.M. For other performances, check with the Official Information Office.

Neuchâtel. *Musée d'art et d'histoire,* Quai Léopold-Robert, east of the port. Rich collection of art and history of the canton: clocks, watches, coins, ceramics, porcelain and glass. Includes the work of Swiss artists, the French Impressionists and 18th-20th century French artists. Frequent temporary exhibitions. *Musée d'ethnographie,* 4 rue Saint-Nicolas. Important Far-Eastern collection. Remarkable toys and musical instruments. *Musée cantonal d'archéologie,* 7 rue Du Peyrou. Rich collection of archeological finds from the canton.

LUCERNE AND CENTRAL SWITZERLAND

Historic Heart of a Nation

To enter Lucerne is to approach the heart of historic Switzerland, for the deeply indented shoreline of the Vierwaldstättersee ('Lake of the Four Forest Cantons')—better known as Lake Lucerne—was the cradle of the Swiss Confederation. To the Swiss, the names of Rütli, Brunnen, and Altdorf—all places near the lake—recall the pact signed in 1291 between the clans of Schwyz, Unterwalden and Uri.

This is also the area in which William Tell is said to have lived: and according to legend it was at Altdorf that the famous archer was forced by the Habsburg bailiff, Gessler, to shoot an apple from the top of his son's head with a crossbow. As with all good legends this one has little basis in fact; but that hardly seems to matter, and its hero has made

LUCERNE

a splendid subject for many plays and monuments, as well as an opera and countless souvenirs.

But Altdorf is by no means the only famous town in the area, and the charms of Rigi, Pilatus, Bürgenstock, and of course Lucerne itself, have been well known to visitors for over a century.

Initially (during the early Middle Ages), Lucerne's role was as a vassal city of the House of Habsburg, and at the outbreak of the conflict between the Swiss and the Austrians she was unwillingly forced to fight against her mountain neighbors. After the defeat of the Habsburg army at Morgarten in 1315, the city felt it necessary to maintain friendly relations with the Confederates, since she had a growing reputation as a marketing and trading center to protect. In consequence it was for economic reasons, as well as to assert their individual rights, that the citizens of Lucerne signed—in 1332—a pact of perpetual alliance with the founder members of the Confederation.

From that time on, although it did not shake off the final traces of Habsburg rule until after the victory at Sempach in 1386, Lucerne shared the martial fervor of the Swiss, participating in all their conflicts with the outside world. But although a free, and fairly prosperous city, Lucerne never acquired the same degree of power and wealth as her great allies; Basle, Berne, and Zurich. And until fairly recent times, the canton and its capital remained something of a quiet and relatively unknown backwater.

The town itself lies at the foot of the mountain slopes, and the natural charm of its surroundings is enhanced by the many 15th- and 16th-century buildings which still remain. Also worth seeing is the city hall, and of course the famous covered wooden bridges, with which Lucerne is so often associated. Lucerne has never had much in the way of industry, not even participating in the embroidery, spinning, weaving and wood and ivory carving that were, until some 40 years ago, the principal activities in much of the rest of Central Switzerland. As a result, the town depends chiefly on tourism for its not inconsiderable prosperity.

Exploring Lucerne

Like several Swiss cities, Lucerne is built at the end of a lake. To be more accurate, it is at the head of a large bay, for the Lake of Lucerne (or Vierwaldstättersee, as you will usually see it referred to locally) is so tortuous in outline that it is difficult to say where the end is. From the lake, the River Reuss flows through the town, before being joined on the far side by the River Emme. The two 14th- and 15th-century covered wooden bridges, the 17th-century town hall, and the delightful 'old' town, all help to create an atmosphere of medieval solidity. This impression is further enhanced by the picturesque Weinmarkt, the Fritschi fountain, and the ancient city walls topped by watch towers. In and around the old quarter is a maze of charming, narrow and traffic-free streets and little squares bordered by lovely old buildings. There are also plenty of enticing shops.

The Kapellbrücke (Chapel Bridge), the larger of the two covered bridges, crosses the river diagonally from the old St. Peter's Chapel, past the octagonal Wasserturm (water tower) to the southern bank. The paintings on the timber ceilings of this bridge represent scenes from Lucerne's history. Those on the other bridge, the Spreuerbrücke (or Mill Bridge), are typically medieval and illustrate a grim dance of death.

If you cross either of these two bridges, or the busy Seebrücke, you'll come to the 'new' town on the south side of the River Reuss. Here, close together, are the lake steamer landing stages, the railroad station, the Kunsthaus and, next to the Municipal Theater, the splendid Jesuit Church, a rococo masterpiece and one of the most beautiful churches in Switzerland. Around the corner from the Church in Pilatusstrasse is the city tourist office.

No visit to Lucerne is complete without a trip to the famous Lion Monument (Löwendenkmal). As much a Lucerne trademark as the Kapellbrücke, this is the much praised dying lion designed by Thorwaldsen and carved out of the living rock by Ahorn in 1820–1821. Dedicated to the Swiss Guards of Louis XVI who died after defending the Tuileries during the French Revolution in 1792, the thirty-foot lion, lying in a niche hewn out of the cliffside, forms a unique and surprisingly moving memorial. It is close to the Glacier Gardens, a remarkable natural phenomenon discovered in 1872 by geologists who literally unearthed huge potholes created by glacier water during the Ice Age as well as many fossils. There's an Alpine and Ice Age Museum.

As a contrast, there are the attractive lakeside gardens and quays, with their magnificent views which give visitors a foretaste of the mountain and lake scenery that lies in store for them.

As an excursion center Lucerne has few rivals. Among the shorter trips is a two-and-a-half-hour conducted coach tour of the town and its surroundings taking in the beautifully situated Richard Wagner Museum at Tribschen. There, souvenirs and relics of the great maestro have been reverently assembled, together with a fascinating collection of musical instruments. In the center of town, there is a small but excellent collection of Picassos in Am Rhyn-Haus, next to the Old Town Hall. And on the north side of the lake, a little outside the center, is the world-famous Swiss Transport Museum. Buses take the holidaymaker to Meggen or Horw. There is a fine Museum of Swiss Folk Costumes and Folklore at Utenberg.

LUCERNE

Then there are Lucerne's two neighboring mountains—Rigi (1,798 meters, 5,900 feet) to the east of the city and 2,100-meter (7,000 foot) Pilatus to the south. The summits of both can be reached easily.

Lucerne, indeed, presents the tourist with a problem: which to choose from an almost bewildering selection of day and half-day excursions by train or lake steamer. To pick, almost at random, a mere dozen places, there are—in alphabetical order—Altdorf (capital of Canton Uri and much involved in the William Tell legend); Brunnen (famed for the views from its lakeside promenades); Bürgenstock (from which you can look vertically down to the lake); Einsiedeln (pilgrimage center with its notable Abbey Church); the pleasant winter sports and summer resort of Engelberg; little Immensee on Lake Zug; Kleintitlis and its glacier, over 3,000 meters (9,900 feet) high; Klewinalp (high above Lake Lucerne); the historic field of Rütli; the little city of Schwyz (which guards Switzerland's priceless archives); Schönbüel (2,010 meters, 6,600 feet); and Zurich (Switzerland's largest city). High on your list, too, should be a slow boat journey down the lake, crisscrossing from place to place and presenting you with a panorama of constantly changing beauty. On the other hand, if you want to stay put and steep yourself in cultural activities, what better than Lucerne during its International Festival of Music? Then, every day for three weeks towards the end of August, there are performances by outstanding artists.

Lakes, Mountains and Legends

Everyone knows the story of William Tell, the apple on his son's head and the well-aimed arrow, and no visitor to central Switzerland will leave without hearing much more about him. But perhaps only a handful of the tourists who gaze respectfully up at his impressive statue in front of Altdorf's medieval tower have the vaguest idea whether he really existed. They can hardly be blamed, since most Swiss, to whom he is a national hero, don't know either.

Unfortunately it must be reported that most historians discount the Tell story as mere legend. They point out that although much has been written about it through the ages, the story is either contradictory or at variance with historical fact, and there are no valid records to prove the existence of Tell, his son, the apple, or even the tyrant Gessler. But take heart. Whether there is any truth in the legend or not, all are agreed that broadly speaking, a situation such as that described in *The Story of William Tell* by Friedrich Schiller did exist in central Switzerland during the 13th century. A proud and independent people were being oppressed by their Austrian overlords, and the spirit of rebellion was rife. All this contributed to the signing of a pact of perpetual

THE FACE OF SWITZERLAND

co-operation and mutual assistance in 1291, an event in which William Tell is popularly believed to have played a major part.

Thus, although there may be no more truth in this legend than in any other, it is a fair allegory of the times, and those visitors who go to Altdorf every year to pay tribute to the hero's memory are not making an empty gesture.

It is easy to see that the spirit of the hardy old archer lives on in the hearts of the people of this region. They're soft spoken, friendly and tolerant of the views of others, but at the same time carry themselves with a dignity that allows no doubt about their independence.

The William Tell country is the area of central Switzerland surrounding the Lake of Lucerne, and it is certainly one of the most beautiful summer holiday regions Switzerland has to offer. It has established a reputation for winter sports, the leading resorts being Andermatt, Stoos and Engelberg. From the top of Gemsstock, approached by cable car from Andermatt, it is said that you can see 600 alpine peaks.

Andermatt is near the meeting point of three alpine passes: the Gotthard, the Furka and the Oberalp, and is thus linked by road to the four points of the Swiss compass. The Furka-Oberalp railway also passes through here providing a fabulous journey between the Rhône Valley and the Grisons. Every day, summer and winter, there are through carriages all the way from Zermatt to St. Moritz, providing one of the world's most memorable rail journeys.

Smart white steamers—some of them beautifully kept and picturesque old paddle-steamers—ply the Lake of Lucerne and provide an ideal means of transport for exploring the region, assuming that you are not in too much of a hurry. The lake itself is the fifth largest in Switzerland, with a surface area of 113 sq. kms. (44 sq. miles), and a very long and varied coastline, so that a journey on board one of the slow-moving steamers takes some time. In fact, if you are going to explore all the little towns and resorts that are worth seeing, several days will be required. With this in mind, the transport companies of the region issue a Holiday Season Ticket (valid for 15 consecutive days) which allows five days of unlimited travel and half-price travel for ten more. It is issued only in summer, however.

Leading off Lake Lucerne in almost every direction are valleys, from most of which branch off yet more valleys, all with a charm of their own and all worth exploring if you have the time. You'll always be in the presence of mountains, and again and again you will come across lakes, sometimes tiny ones high in the mountains, sometimes larger ones like Lake Zug.

Exploring Central Switzerland

The greater part of central Switzerland can be explored from Lucerne. One of the most popular excursions is to Mount Pilatus, over 2,100 meters (7,000 feet), and the highest peak in the immediate vicinity. One route is to go by train or lake steamer to Alpnachstad and thence by the electric Pilatus Railway, claimed by its owners to be the steepest cogwheel railway in the world. Sometimes up gradients of nearly 1 in 2, the red trains take thirty minutes to climb the 1,693 meters (5,560 feet) to the summit station. The trains run only during the summer. Another way of getting to the top is to take a trolley bus from Lucerne to the suburb of Kriens and there join one of the procession of little, four-seat cable cars which take you over mountainside meadows and among trees on an eerily silent, half-hour trip to Fräkmüntegg (1,400 meters, 4,600 feet). There you change to a cable car, seating up to 40 people, for the final climb up the near vertical rock face to the summit. This service runs all year round.

If you wish, you can go by one route and return by the other, as the terminals of both the cable car and the Pilatus Railway are in the same building, which is perched giddily in a saddle between two of the Pilatus peaks. Above the terminals is the Bellevue Hotel, a modern circular structure which many visit to watch, from their bedrooms, the sunrise or sunset. Close by is the older, traditional style Pilatus-Kulm Hotel. It takes little more than ten minutes to climb from the terminals, up steep but well-prepared paths and steps, to the top of the two nearest peaks. From either, and from the various paths and tunnels cut out of the rock, there are magnificent views. To the north the view extends to the Black Forest in Germany; east to the Säntis range and Lake Constance; and southeast to the Grisons. In the south are the Alps, and to the northwest the Jura.

Pilatus owes its name, according to one legend, to Pontius Pilate, whose body, it is said, was brought there after the Crucifixion by the devil, and whose ghost, when disturbed, demonstrates displeasure by bringing storm and destruction to Lucerne. Not unnaturally, to avoid any such happening the town put a ban on anyone climbing the mountain. This lasted until after the Middle Ages. Unfortunately, historians of greater reliability aver that this is nonsense and that the name comes from *pileatus*, or 'hair covered', because of the way wisps of cloud often stream from the summit like wind-blown hair.

Certainly Pilatus was the cradle of mountain climbing. Ban or no ban, it has, for centuries, been climbed by a steadily increasing number of mountaineers. The first primitive inn was built at the top in 1856, and Queen Victoria rode to the summit of the mountain on muleback some twelve years later. You may not find a mule, but if you want to climb on foot the easiest route is from Hergiswil and it will take you about five hours to get to a well-deserved drink on the Kulm Hotel terrace.

After the trip to the top of Pilatus you should plan to go on the next clear day to Mount Rigi. You may ask what you can see from the top of Rigi that you can't from the top of old Hair Covered. In fact you'll find the two mountains have very different personalities. Pilatus is stern, forbidding and grandiose, with an enigmatic charm; while Rigi (despite its height of 1,798 meters, 5,900 feet) seems a friendly, homely little mountain. It has greensward on top, and the slopes are covered with trees and lush pastureland where in summer obviously contented cows graze to a cacophony of cowbells. You may not see as far from its summit, but the views are prettier.

The Top of Rigi

There are two electric rack-and-pinion railways leading up to the top of the Rigi. One runs from the pretty little resort of Vitznau on the northern shore of Lake Lucerne; the other from Arth-Goldau, around the other side of the mountain at the southern tip of Lake Zug. These railways were built by competing companies back in the 1870's, and it was a race to see which outfit would first get its line to the top and capture the lion's share of the lucrative tourist business. The Vitznau line won, but that from Arth-Goldau gets its fair share of trade as its lower terminal, on the main St. Gotthard railway, is more accessible. Vitznau can be reached only by steamer and road, although there is a cable car from Weggis up to Rigi-Kaltbad, where you can join the Vitznau train to the top.

Visitors who want to see everything can go up one way and down one of the others, but whichever route you take the view is equally impressive. If you're the athletic type and want to try it on foot, start from Küssnacht, which is at the end of the northern arm that protrudes from Lake Lucerne. It will take a good three hours and you will be puffing when you get to the top. But nobody will give you a medal for your pains, as the climb is considered strictly child's play in Switzerland. Mark Twain recounts in *A Tramp Abroad* how he labored up the path in the dark so as to be at the top of Rigi for the much vaunted sunrise, but was so tired when he got there that he fell asleep and didn't wake up until sunset. Not realizing how time had flown, he thought for a moment that the sun had changed direction. Even though he may only have seen the sunset, Twain describes the view in enthusiastic terms.

LUCERNE

At the top of Rigi is another Kulm hotel, with a restaurant and a terrace where, on summer afternoons, there may be a Swiss boy or girl yodeling and playing the accordion. Even if you don't normally care for yodelers, they make wonderful background music for the lovely view of the lake and distant Alps. Near the Rigi-Kaltbad-First station (1,432 meters, 4,700 feet), is the Hostellerie Rigi, an ultramodern hotel bristling with good and unusual ideas. Not surprisingly, they have a Mark Twain Bar. There is a host of trails winding down through the meadows and woods of the Rigi and its companion hills, and in winter these become ski-runs that are popular with beginners, if not exciting enough for advanced enthusiasts.

The Bürgenstock and Stans

Having taken in the views from the top of Pilatus and Rigi, you may consider you've had your fill of heights. If so, you are going to miss half the fun for we haven't yet been to Bürgenstock, to the Stanserhorn, or to Mount Titlis.

The Bürgenstock, a mountain ridge jutting out into Lake Lucerne, isn't particularly high but it rises so steeply from the water that the view of the lake and surrounding area from the top is strikingly beautiful—which probably explains why, for at least part of the year, many famous people, including film stars and world-famous musicians, live here. Although you can drive to Bürgenstock up a steep, narrow road from Stansstad, the most interesting and dramatic way is to make the thirty-minute steamer trip from Lucerne to Kehrsiten, where a funicular will take you 456 meters (1,500 feet) above the lake to a group of hotels. This may not surprise you since the Swiss have a habit of crowning their peaks with a hotel or two. But this is rather different, since there are five—with a nine-hole golf course thrown in! Even if you are not going to stay in any of them, it is worth glancing inside since they are decorated in a style which, even by Swiss standards, is luxurious.

Mr. Frey, the owner of the three largest hotels, has combed the world for artistic treasures to furnish his mountain palaces, and a stroll through the various salons and reception halls is much like visiting a fine museum or art gallery, except that the hospitality is better.

Afterwards, unless you've no head for heights, you should walk along the cliff path (about fifteen minutes) to the Hammetschwand electric lift, which, in next to no time, will waft you up the almost vertical cliff face to the summit, some 165 meters (540 feet) higher. From there, if the weather has been kind to you, you'll see most of Lake Lucerne, part of the Jura mountains, and a splendid selection of Alps.

Just to the south of Bürgenstock are Stans and the valley of the Engelberg Aa. Stans is rich in historical memories, and Engelberg is one of the country's outstanding resorts in both winter and summer. There are also two more mountains to climb—by funicular, of course. They are the Stanserhorn and Mount Titlis.

The journey to Stans from Lucerne is an easy one which can be completed via either the Engelberg railway, or by road. The town is the capital of the half-canton of Nidwalden, and is a pleasant little summer resort with an interesting early baroque church. From Stans you can take a funicular and cable car to the top of Stanserhorn (1,888 meters, 6,200 feet), for a fine view and the inevitable restaurant.

In the past the town has been associated with three of Switzerland's great heroes. The first is Arnold von Winkelried, who engineered the victory of the Confederates over Leopold II at the battle of Sempach in 1386. The Austrians, armed with long spears, formed a Roman square so that the Swiss, wielding axes and halberds, couldn't get in close enough to do any damage. Shouting 'Forward, Confederates, I will open a path!' von Winkelried threw himself on the spears, clasping as many of them as he could to his breast, thus effectively giving his compatriots an opening into the square. Early pictures of this original kamikaze action make him look like a human pincushion.

The next great name in Stans is that of a hermit, Nikolaus von Flüe, who was born in Flüeli, no more than ten miles to the south. It was just a century after Arnold von Winkelried had laid down his life for liberty that Nikolaus also saved the Confederation, although through wise counsel rather than soldierly sacrifice. When the Confederates fell to quarreling over the spoils of the Burgundian wars, he came to the town and mediated in their disputes at the Diet of Stans in 1481. He was canonized in 1947.

The third name to conjure with is that of Heinrich Pestalozzi, the father of modern education. Although he was not born here, it was in Stans, after nearly 2,000 of its inhabitants had been massacred by the French in 1798, that this great humanist gathered together the homeless children, practising the educational theories that are now famous.

Engelberg

The train journey from Lucerne to Engelberg takes about an hour; and after leaving the lakeside the track runs through orchards, meadows, and along the canyon of the River Aa, before finally reaching the wide valley in which the village lies. It is a quiet, unspoilt place, clustered around a Benedictine monastery (founded in 1120) whose library contains some rare manuscripts dating from the 11th century—and earlier. As a resort the village is popular in both summer—for those who want to get away from it all and relax—and winter. It boasts

LUCERNE

a fine selection of slopes, served by an efficient network of funiculars, cable cars, chairlifts, and skilifts.

Towering above Engelberg is the permanently snow-covered peak of Mount Titlis. At 3,200 meters (10,500 feet) high, it is central Switzerland's highest peak. A must for visitors—although the trip is not cheap—is the sensational ascent to Kleintitlis (3,017 meters, 9,900 feet), which is just below the summit. From Engelberg a funicular will take you up to the first of a series of three cable cars, the last stage going directly over the Titlis glacier and its apparently bottomless crevasses to the top station. There, from the sun terrace, the glass-enclosed viewing hall or the restaurant you'll see an Alpine panorama (if you have chosen a clear day) which will leave a lasting memory. The trip is not recommended, of course, for people with heart trouble; at 3,000 meters (10,000 feet) the air is pretty thin. But otherwise you need have no worry. The Swiss are a careful people and take safety precautions very seriously. For example, on the funiculars there are periodic inspections during which huge weights are put in the cars, which are hauled halfway up the incline; then the cable is loosened to see whether the brakes will hold. They have to be able to stop the car within a few feet. All of which is a comforting thought as your little train climbs up a railway as steep as a roof, or as your cable car creeps silently up a seemingly ridiculously thin cable slung between mountain peaks.

Around and About the Lake

Having climbed some of the more notable peaks in this area comfortably and without effort (there are others, with and without funiculars and cable cars, if you want them), you may now prefer to take a more normal view of things, such as going to Altdorf to see where William Tell is said to have shot his famous arrow; to Schwyz, the cradle of Switzerland; and of course, on a steamer trip down the lake.

There are three routes to Altdorf from Lucerne. The fastest is along the new highway, a journey of about half an hour. But you can also go by steamer all the way to Flüelen at the extreme end of the lake (it takes about three hours) and thence by bus for the short distance to Altdorf. The final route is via the Gotthard railway, about an hour's journey. From Lucerne the train follows the lake to the end of the Küssnacht basin, then goes along the southern shore of Lake Zug and next past the smaller Lake Lauerz before coming to Schwyz-Seewen, six minutes by bus from the historic town of Schwyz, to which we shall return in a moment. Less than five kilometers (three miles) beyond Schwyz-Seewen the train meets up again with Lake Lucerne at the resort of Brunnen and then follows the lake shore to Flüelen for Altdorf. Between Brunnen and Flüelen, and always close to the railway, is the remarkable Axenstrasse, a road cut out of the cliffs which, along this part of the lake, rise almost sheer from the water.

The Swiss have long had a reputation as outstanding engineers and road builders as the 19th-century Axenstrasse demonstrates. Their latest triumph is the St. Gotthard road tunnel, which opened in 1980. Over 14km. (9 miles) in length, it is the longest of its kind in the world, and is in all respects a technological marvel with first-rate safety facilities. What's more, it's toll free. But if it's scenery you want, take the old St. Gotthard pass.

Whether you go by train or lake steamer, or out one way and back the other, depends on time available. But if at all possible try to make at least one trip by steamer between Lucerne and Flüelen. And try, too, to stop off at the town of Schwyz—fifteen minutes by bus from the steamer landing stage at Brunnen, and much less from Schwyz-Seewen railroad station.

Historic Schwyz

Schwyz, capital of the canton of the same name, should be visited by everyone interested in Swiss history. A quiet, dignified little place, it seems conscious of the fact that it is one of the oldest and most historic towns in Switzerland, that it gave the country both its name and its flag, and that it is entrusted with Switzerland's most precious archives. It was here in the 14th century that the word Schweiz (German for Switzerland) was first recorded as the name of the mountain Confederacy which grew to become Switzerland.

Traces of an independent settlement at Schwyz have been found as far back as the Bronze Age (2,500–800 BC); but by the 13th century the inhabitants, like much of the rest of what is now central Switzerland, were under the rule of the House of Habsburg. Discontent was rife. In 1291 they joined with the folk of neighboring Uri and Unterwalden in the famous Oath of Eternal Alliance. You can see the beautifully scripted and sealed original of the documents, battle flags and paintings of the period in Schwyz's Bundesbrief-Archiv, an impressively simple concrete building completed in 1936.

Schwyz has several notable baroque churches and a large number of fine old patrician homes dating from the 17th and 18th centuries, not least being the Redinghaus, with its magnificent interior and fine stained glass. Curiously, many of these splendid houses owe their origin to the battlefield. The men of Schwyz had a reputation as fine soldiers and in the 16th and 17th centuries were in considerable demand in other countries as mercenaries. They went abroad, fought in the many battles of the period, collected what in those days was handsome pay, returned home, and with the money built many of the houses you can see today.

From Schwyz it is only a ten-minute bus ride to Schlattli. There, a funicular (said to be Switzerland's steepest) will take you to a height of 1,310 meters (4,300 feet), and to the hamlet of Stoos on a cozy mountain plateau. Boasting several lifts, some going up to over 1,800 meters (6,000 feet), Stoos in winter is a first-rate, although unsophisticated, winter sports resort. In summer it turns into a hideaway for those seeking peace and quiet (Stoos has no roads, no cars) among alpine meadows and wildflowers, and with magnificent scenery. Down in the Muotta valley, and not very far from Schlattli, are the ruins of the Suvorov Bridge, over which the French, under Masséna, and the Russians, under Suvorov, fought a major battle in 1799. Farther along the valley you can visit the vast Hölloch Caves. Already over 80km. (50 miles) of caves and corridors have been explored but they remain strangely unexploited although the public can go in for a couple of kilometers.

Einsiedeln, Sacred and Secular

From Schwyz it is a pleasant 29km. (18 mile) trip northward to Einsiedeln. On the way you can make a side trip to the small mountain lake of Aegeri; passing, near Sattel, the famous battlefield of Morgarten. There, in 1351, Swiss peasants were victorious against troops of Frederick of Austria, an event which helped create modern Switzerland.

Einsiedeln is both a summer and winter resort, but it is not from this that the town's real fame comes. Most notably it is the home of the Black Madonna of Einsiedeln, and therefore one of Europe's most important centers of pilgrimage. She is housed in the abbey church of the Benedictine monastery. Secondly, on September 14th every year the great Festival of the Miraculous Dedication takes place, complete with torchlight processions. Further celebrations take place once every five years, when *The Great World Theater,* a religious drama written by Don Pedro Calderón, is performed in front of the abbey church. Lastly, as if this was not enough to ensure Einsiedeln's reputation, Paracelsus, the eminent Renaissance physician, was born in the district.

The monastery of Einsiedeln was founded, like the Grossmünster in Zurich, during the time of Charlemagne. Meinrad, a Hohenzollern count and Benedictine monk, seeking to pursue his devotions in solitude, selected the site as being the most remote he could find. He built a little chapel for the image of the Virgin (which had been given to him by the abbess of Zurich), and since food was scarce in the region, two ravens kindly supplied him with the necessities of life. He lived for a while in peace, but some men who thought he possessed hidden treasures murdered him. The ravens followed the slayers to Zurich. Bent on justice being done, the birds attracted so much attention to the men by shrieking round their heads that they were detected and punished. The monastery was built over Meinrad's grave. When it was completed in the year 946 the Bishop of Constance was invited to consecrate it, but as he began the ceremony a voice was heard crying out in the chapel three times, 'Brother, desist: God Himself has consecrated this building'. A papal bull acknowledged the miracle and promised a special indulgence to pilgrims.

Through the ages the monastery of Einsiedeln has been destroyed by fire on several occasions, each time to be rebuilt, but always the Black Madonna has been saved. When the French Revolutionaries plundered the church, hoping to carry off the sacred image, it had already been taken to the Tyrol for safe keeping. Today the Madonna is housed in a black marble chapel just inside the west entrance to the church. Seen from a distance its color appears to be a rich bronze, not black, and there is something quaint and gentle about the figure, splendidly arrayed in jewels, which lends it a curious grace. The abbey church itself, built by Caspar Moosbrugger in 1735 and decorated by the famous brothers Egid Quirid and Cosmos Damian Asam, is one of the finest late-Baroque churches of its kind, the impressive simplicity and grace of the exterior contrasting vividly with the exuberance of its richly ornate interior. In front of the church is a huge square, the conspicuous centerpiece being a gilded statue of the Virgin surmounted by a large gilded crown. Round the base, water trickles from 14 spouts, and pilgrims, to be sure of good luck, traditionally drink from each one in turn.

It is in this square that, about every five years, Calderón's *The Great World Theater* is presented, with a cast of 700 performers, all amateurs living in Einsiedeln. The play, first performed before the Court of Spain in 1685, is a drama of life and the problems of man. For generations the monks of the monastery have coached these amateur actors for their parts in this and other religious plays.

Exploring the Lake by Steamer

If you decide to take the lake steamer from Lucerne one of the boat's first calls will be at Weggis, a town noted for its mild, almost subtropical climate. During 1897 Mark Twain stayed here. Behind the resort you'll notice the aerial cableway which goes up to Rigi-Kaltbad, and opposite it, on the other side of the lake you will see the Hammetschwand elevator going to the top of Bürgenstock. After stopping at Vitznau, lower terminal of the Rigi cogwheel railway, the steamer sails through the giant gateway formed by the promontories of Bürgenstock and Vitznauerstock to call at the resort of Beckenried on the other side of the lake. From here there's a cable car to Klewenalp (1,600 meters, 5,250 feet), a small winter sports and summer resort in a wonderful position overlooking the lake. The steamer again crosses the lake, this time to the little resort of Gersau, which, from 1332 to 1798, was an independent republic—the world's smallest. The boat's next port of call is Treib on the Seelisberg peninsula (look for the beautifully decorated chalet, still an inn, beside the jetty) before she returns to the northern shore and the resort of Brunnen, famed for the lovely views from its lakeside promenades. It is through the rocky mass of the Seelisberg that the new Seelisberg road tunnel (9.6 kilometers, 6 miles long) was driven, providing, together with the St. Gotthard road tunnel a swift new route across the Alps. At Brunnen the steamer turns south around the Seelisberg peninsula to enter the last basin of Lake Lucerne, the Urnersee, at the end of which is Flüelen. Now in succession come three points of major interest to those who revere the Tell saga and the Oath of Eternal Alliance—the Schillerstein (on the right as you pass the peninsula), the Rütli meadow (a little farther on, just above the Rütli landing stage), and Tellsplatte (on the other—eastern—side of the lake).

The Schillerstein, a natural rock obelisk sticking nearly 26 meters (85 feet) up out of the lake, bears the simple dedication 'To the author of *Wilhelm Tell,* Friedrich Schiller. 1859'. The Rütli meadow is where the Confederates of Schwyz, Unterwald and Uri are said to have met on the night of November 7, 1307, to renew the 1291 Oath of Eternal Alliance. Now it is a national shrine and every year, on August 1st, their Independence Day, Swiss citizens gather in the meadow in remembrance of the Oath—at night the sky glows with the light of hundreds of bonfires on the mountain tops. Tellsplatte, at the foot of the Axen mountain, is the rocky ledge onto which the rebellious archer leaped to escape from the boat in which the bailiff Gessler was taking him to prison, pushing the boat back into the stormy waves as he did so. The Tell Chapel, much rebuilt in 1881, contains four frescoes which show the taking of the oath on the Field of Rütli, Tell shooting the apple on his son's head, Tell's escape, and Gessler's death.

From Flüelen it is only a short distance to Altdorf where, in the town's main square, Tell is said to have replied to Gessler's challenge and performed his world famous feat of successfully shooting an apple from his small son's head. With true Swiss caution, he had a second arrow, reserved for the heart of the tyrant should the first miss its mark. The whole drama, as told by Schiller, is enacted every second or third summer in Altdorf's Wilhelm Tell Theater.

THE FACE OF SWITZERLAND

Before leaving central Switzerland let us return to our starting point, Lucerne, for a quick look at the second largest lake in the region, Lake Zug, less than two kilometers from the Küssnacht arm of Lake Lucerne. The Zugersee, to give it its Swiss name, is about 22 kilometers (14 miles) long, and lies on the edge of Switzerland's most steeply mountainous region. Unlike the other lakes in the area only its southern shore rises sharply; in the north it has no more than gently rising hills.

A road hugs the shore round most of the lake. In the northeast is the lakeside town of Zug, capital of its namesake canton (the smallest in the Confederation). Although with much modern development, it is an ancient walled city with a distinctly medieval air, enhanced by massive towers and by the delicate spires of the 15th to 16th-century church of St. Oswald. In the town hall, an early 16th-century building with Gothic carvings, there are exhibits of gold and silver work, embroideries, wood carvings, stained glass, paintings, and with the flag said to have been held aloft to the last by Wolfgang Kolin. He perished in 1422 in the battle of Arbedo, where 3,000 Swiss valiantly tried to hold off 24,000 Milanese soldiers. There's a fountain in his honor in Kolinplatz.

From the Zugerberg (974 meters, 3,200 feet) overlooking the town there is a famous view taking in the peaks of Jungfrau, Eiger, Mönch, Finsteraarhorn and, nearer at hand, Rigi and Pilatus. But if, after your tour, you are tired and have had enough of heights, you need go no farther than Zug's quayside promenades. The view there may not match up to Zugerberg's but it is still a pretty respectable one and you should be able to pick out several peaks which, earlier on in our tour of central Switzerland, appeared before you in wide-screen close-up.

PRACTICAL INFORMATION FOR LUCERNE AND CENTRAL SWITZERLAND

GETTING AROUND. By Boat. Lake Lucerne has a very good network of steamers with a couple of 'old timer' paddlesteamers still going strong. They connect virtually every community on the lakeside. The larger vessels have full restaurant facilities and even most of the smaller ones offer refreshments. As elsewhere in Switzerland they link, where practical, with both the train and post-bus services. In the off-peak season there is a much more limited service and you should check on availability when you arrive. The roundtrip/excursion tickets offer best value for money.

LUCERNE

By Train and Bus. The whole area has many railways, some part of the national system, others privately owned and also the numerous mountain and cable railways, plus funiculars. Add to this the excellent post-bus routes and the Lucerne city transport and there is no problem in getting about.

The Regional Holiday Season Ticket for the area is valid for 15 days of which five are for unlimited travel and the other 10 you get half fare. Ideal if you plan to do a lot of sightseeing—and we are sure you will.

By Car. The road network around the Lake of Lucerne is excellent, and there are motorways running the length of the southern side of the lake and extending north to Schwyz and Zug. All secondary roads are good, and many provide spectacular views. The remarkable Seelisberg and St. Gotthard road tunnels (9 km. and 15 km.—6 and 9 miles—long respectively) opened in 1980 and have enormously speeded up access across the Alps to southern Switzerland; there are no toll charges. But be warned that the roads do get very busy in the high season.

HOTELS. Lucerne has a positive surfeit of hotels in all price categories, and the visitor should have no difficulty in finding a room, even at the height of the summer. Nearly all the hotels in our listings have a wide range of rooms, a good many of which may well fall into a lower grading than that which we give here. The best advice is always to check beforehand with the hotel. Nearly all hotels have restaurants, and a number of the more expensive have two or three.

There is an accommodations office in the rail station, and the Tourist Office can also help in booking rooms. All hotels are obliged to give visitors a copy of the town's official tourist guide which, apart from giving details of restaurants, excursions, museums and the like, is good for reductions on some excursions and booking tennis courts.

Note that during the winter a number of hotels are closed and that many are given over to tour groups during the season.

Deluxe

Carlton Hotel Tivoli, tel. 513051. Lakeside hotel with considerable comfort; tennis and nightclub. Open April to Oct. only.

Grand Hotel National, tel. 501111. Superbly situated on the lakeshore; suites fit for a king, ordinary rooms for a crown prince; one of the country's very top hotels. Sauna and indoor pool; excellent food.

Palace, tel. 502222. Spacious hotel that faces the lake across a tree-lined promenade; famous and luxurious. Has excellent restaurant, the *Mignon*.

Schweizerhof, tel. 502211. Traditional elegance in this old hotel; very quiet and with facilities for children. Three restaurants, of which *Rotonde* is first class.

Expensive

Astoria, tel. 235323. Panoramic rooftop terrace and bar; facilities for the handicapped; highly recommended.

Balances & Bellevue, tel. 511851. Quiet, old-world hotel in atmospheric building; centrally located. Open April to Oct. only.

Château Gütsch, tel. 220272. Queen Victoria stayed in this historic hotel; very quiet with splendid views and outdoor pool.

Europe Grand Hotel, tel. 301111. Attractive view of the lake; quiet and comfortable. Open April to Oct. only.

Flora, tel. 244444. Central but quiet; good restaurant, nightclub.

Luzernerhof, tel. 514646. Central, with good restaurant and facilities for the handicapped.

Montana, tel. 516565. Situated on hillside with magnificent views and its own private cable car; quiet and highly recommended. Open April to Oct. only.

Moderate

Des Alpes, tel. 515825. Close to the river and with good restaurant; very quiet.

De la Paix, tel. 515253. Characteristic and very comfortable hotel in the old town near the Lion monument. Indoor pool, sauna and excellent restaurant, *Le Lapin*.

Johanniter, tel. 231855. Reader-recommended. Large for its category.

Park, tel. 239232. Central but quiet; close to the station. Very good, and inexpensive, restaurant.

Rebstock Hotel Garni, tel. 513581/2. Attractive building in the heart of the old town by the cathedral. Despite the name, has an excellent outdoor restaurant. Breakfast only.

Schiff, tel. 513851. Very superior hotel for this category; attractive building. Excellent, inexpensive restaurant.

Inexpensive

Alpina, tel. 230077. Basic, but conveniently located in the middle of town.
Bären, tel. 221063. No rooms with bath available; breakfast only.
Le Cachet, tel. 515546. Central; breakfast only.
Goldener Stern, tel. 230891. Central, with restaurant.
Kolping, tel. 512351. Quiet and central; restaurant.
Pickwick, tel. 515927. Central with terrace and bar.
Spatz, tel. 411075. Breakfast only.
SSR Touristenhotel, tel. 512474. No rooms with bath or shower available.
Steghof, tel. 444343. Bar and restaurant; all rooms with TV.
Villa Maria, tel. 312119. In own grounds and very quiet. Breakfast only.
Weinhof, tel. 511251. Central with restaurant.
Weisses Kreuz, tel. 516023. No rooms with bath or shower.

There is a **Youth Hostel** at Sedelstr. 13 with 206 beds in 39 rooms and two dormitories with 28 beds each. Take bus no. 2 from the rail station to the Schlossberg stop, from where it is a 15 minute walk.

LUCERNE

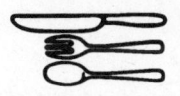

RESTAURANTS. Lucerne is something of a gourmet's paradise and the town fairly bristles with restaurants. The more expensive ones are as good as any you will find in Switzerland, while the less expensive offer extremely good value for money, frequently in highly atmospheric and always attractive surroundings. The food everywhere is excellent and our list is no more than a selection. The older part of the town in particular has many excellent, inexpensive spots.

Expensive

Arbalète French Restaurant, tel. 230864. Restaurant of the Hotel Monopol and Metropole in Pilatusstr. Very good indeed.

Chez Marianne, zum Raben, tel. 515135. Four excellent restaurants, all quite different in character and cuisine, in delightfully converted old building in the Kornmarkt by the Old Town Hall. Highly recommended; book ahead.

Le Manoir, tel. 232248. Splendid and atmospheric French restaurant in Bundesplatz, in the new part of town. Highly recommended.

Le Mignon, tel. 502222. Magnificent restaurant in the Palace Hotel. Best to book ahead.

Old Swiss House, tel. 516171. Near the Lion monument in converted house; recommended.

Le Rotonde, tel. 502211. Sophisticated restaurant of the Schweizerhof Hotel; delightful view of the lake.

Von-Pfyffer-Stube, tel. 501111. In the Grand Hotel National; first class.

Moderate

Le Lapin, tel. 515253. Characteristic and welcome restaurant in the Hotel de la Paix. Excellent food, but can be a little expensive.

Fritschi, Sternenpl. 5 tel. 511615. Reader-recommended. Upstairs.

Kunsthaus-Kongresshaus, Bahnhofplatz. Near the boat landing stage at the Strandbad; with attractive garden terrace.

Li Tai Pe, tel. 511023. Popular Chinese restaurant in Furrengasse.

Walliser Spycher, tel. 512976. *The* place for *fondue* and *raclette;* in Eisengasse in the heart of the Old Town close by the Kornmarkt.

Wilden Mann, tel. 23166. Lucerne's most famous restaurant, in business since 1517; Bahnhofstr. Also excellent (M–E) hotel.

Inexpensive

Hubertus, In the Old Town. Excellent Italian food; atmospheric and noisy.

Ilge, Pfistergasse 17. Good Swiss-German food.

Mövenpick. Two locations in town—opposite the Tourist Office in Pilatusstrasse, and in the old town in Grendelstrasse. Both provide traditionally reliable food expected of the chain, and also have more expensive menus.

Mostrose, Rathausquai 11. Excellent Swiss and Italian food; with a terrace overlooking the river Reuss.

Schiff, tel. 513851. In hotel of the same name; remarkable value, highly recommended.

Zunfthaus zu Pfistern, Kornmarkt, tel. 513650. Also has more expensive dishes.

ENTERTAINMENT. Surprisingly perhaps for a town as sober as Lucerne, the nightlife is pretty lively. Many of the more exotic spots are concentrated in the old town, an area similar to the Niederdorf in Zurich. Small discos and clubs are the norm, and, as there is little to distinguish one from another, the best bet is to walk around and see what takes your fancy. But among Lucerne's more long-lived and popular clubs are *San Francisco* on Haldenstrasse (along the north side of the lake by the cathedral), where there is a floor show and dancing. A successful disco is the *Disco Club* in the Flora hotel just off Pilatusstrasse, where they also present folklore shows (yodeling, accordions, and lots of thigh-slapping). The *Des Alpes* hotel on Rathausquai north of the river has a similar folklore restaurant. A more unusual folklore show is given on board the *Nightboat,* which, as its name suggests, is a lake boat. It leaves every evening in summer from the quay by the station.

However, the most sophisticated nightlife in Lucerne is to be found at the *Casino* on the northern shore of the lake. You can play *boule* in the Gambling Room, disco the night away in the *Black Jack* club, watch an international show in the *Red Rose* (i.e. watch a strip show) or have a meal in *Le Chalet* while watching a folklore display.

Tennis is available at Brüelmoos near the Lido, at the Spittelerquai and at Allemand. But demand for courts is great, and it is essential to book ahead. There is an 18-hole golf course at Allemand; but again it is best to call in advance. There is also an indoor pool at Allemand, and, of course, you can also swim in the lake at the Lido.

Full details of all these clubs and sports facilities are given in the official guide and are also available from the Tourist Office in Pilatusstrasse.

MUSEUMS. Electric Model Railway. At Dietschiberg outside town beyond the lion monument, and a must for train buffs. 1,000 m. (3,280 ft.) of track scaled down (1:10). Open June–Sept. (weather permitting).

Glacier Garden. Denkmalstrasse 4. Extraordinary evidence of the glaciers that once covered the whole of the Lucerne region. The attached museum has a world-famous relief of the Alps. By the lion monument.

Museum of Fine Art (Kunsthaus), Robert-Zünd-Strasse 1. Representative collection of pictures and sculptures from Central Switzerland from the Middle Ages to the present day. It also includes 19th-century Swiss landscape paintings and 19th- and 20th-century European paintings.

Museum of Natural History (Naturhistorischesmuseum), Kasernen-platz 6. Just by the southern end of the Spreurbrüche and the country's most attractive museum of its type. Geology, minerals, fossils, flora and fauna of Central Switzerland are carefully documented and displayed.

LUCERNE

Museum of Swiss National Costume and Folklore, Bruchstrasse 5. Colorful national costumes; in the same building as the archives of the Federal Yodelers' Club. Open Easter to Nov.

Panorama, Löwenplatz. An imposing painted panorama of scenes from the Franco-Prussian War of 1870-71. May not be to everyone's taste. Up by the Glacier Garden. Open mid-March to mid-Nov.

Richard Wagner Museum, Wagnerweg 27. Delightfully located villa on the south side of the lake where the maestro lived from 1866 to 1872. Now contains many momentoes of the composer and a collection of old instruments.

Swiss Transport Museum, Lidostrasse 5. On the north side of the lake and easily reached by public transport or on foot (about 30 minutes from the rail station). Outstandingly fine collection of rail locomotives and carriages, airplanes, cars and ships, as well as many working models. It also has Switzerland's first (and only) planetarium and a building for aerospace exhibits. Three restaurants and the Hans Erni Museum are attached.

SHOPPING. Lucerne is proud of the fact that it has one of the finest medieval shopping centers in Europe (a boast that Berne may even dispute!). The narrow, twisting, cobbled streets of the old town are traffic-free and ideal for window-shopping, whatever your taste. However, it must also be said that most of the souvenir shops are unattractive and much of what they sell is over-priced and tatty.

USEFUL ADDRESSES. Lucerne *Tourist Office,* Pilatusstrasse 14 (tel. 041–235252). *Central Switzerland Tourist Office,* Pilatusstrasse 14 (tel. 237045). *American Express,* Schweizerhofquai 4 (tel. 501177). *Cook's,* Denkmalstrasse 1. *English Church,* Haldenstrasse.

Car Hire. *Avis,* Zurichstrasse 35; *Europcar,* Löwenstrasse 20; *Hertz,* Maihofstrasse 101.

HOTELS AND RESTAURANTS ELSEWHERE IN THE REGION

ALTDORF. *Bahnhof* (I), tel. 21032. Central and very inexpensive. No rooms with bath or shower. *Goldener Schlüssel* (I), tel. 21002. Historic building in the heart of this historic town.
Restaurant. *Höfli* (I), tel. 22197. Closed Wednesday.

AMSTEG. *Stern und Post* (M), tel. 64440. One time Post House; atmospheric and good value.

ANDERMATT. *Krone* (M), tel. 67206. Sauna and gymnasium; central. *Monopol-Metropol* (M), tel. 67575. Indoor pool and facilities for the handicapped. *Bergidyll* (I), tel. 67455. Central. Diet meals; bar.

170 THE FACE OF SWITZERLAND

Restaurant. *Drei Könige* (M), tel. 67203. Lantern-lit grill room. Cheese, Chinese and Bourguignonne fondues.

BRUNNEN. *Seehotel Waldstätterhof* (E), tel. 331133. Lakeside location with tennis, good restaurant and extensive grounds; facilities for children. *Bellevue au Lac Kursaal* (M), tel. 3113318. On lakeside; quiet and comfortable. *Parkhotel Hellerbad* (M), tel. 311681. Cure facilities, tennis and gardens; central but quiet.
Restaurant. *Weisses Rössli* (I), tel. 311022. Indonesian rice specialties, fondues.

BUERGENSTOCK. *Grand Hotel* (L), tel. 641212. Golf, tennis, pool, bowling; on the expensive side. *Park Hotel* (E), tel. 641331. Many facilities; in own grounds. *Waldheim* (I), tel. 641306. In own grounds with pool and great view. Reader-recommended. Fitness and games rooms. Special food.

EINSIEDELN. *Drei Könige* (M), tel. 532441. Large but quiet hotel. *Pfauen am Klosterplatz* (I), tel. 534545. Centrally located. *Katharinahof* (I), tel. 532508. Central but very quiet hotel in own grounds; sauna. *St. Josef* (I), tel. 532151. Small and central. *Storchen* (I), tel. 533760. Central and quiet.

ENGELBERG. *Bellevue Terminus* (M), tel. 941213. Quiet, in own grounds with indoor tennis court. *Crystal* (M), tel. 942122. Central and quiet family hotel. *Ring-Hotel* (M), tel. 941822. Good family hotel in own grounds. *Alpenklub* (I), tel. 941243. Central and rather superior inexpensive hotel. Breakfast only.
Restaurant. *Hess* (I–M), tel. 941366. Recommended.

FLÜELEN. *Flüelerhof-Grill Rustico* (I), tel. 21149. Quiet and with great views. *Hostellerie Sternen* (I), tel. 21835. Central and quiet. *Tourist* (I), tel. 21591. Historic building.

GERSAU. *Beau-Rivage* (I), tel. 841223. Centrally-located with pool and gym. *Seehotel Schwert* (I), tel. 841134. Lakeside hotel with sailing and marvelous views; in own grounds and very quiet. Breakfast only.

HERGISWIL. *Pilatus am See* (E), tel. 951555. Large lakeside hotel with indoor pool and gym. *Belvedere AG am See* (M), tel. 951185. Very quiet lakeside hotel in own grounds.

KLEWENALP. (All inclusive). *Klewenalp Hotel* (M), tel. 642922. Fine location above the lake; special facilities for children; bowls.

KUSSNACHT AM RIGI. *Engel* (I), tel. 811057. Once the town hall (dates from 15th century) and meeting place of the local parliaments. *Seehotel Drei Konige* (I), tel. 811069. Very quiet; with tennis and sailing.

LUCERNE

MELCHSEE-FRUTT. (All inclusive). *Reinhard am See* (E), tel. 671275. Lakeside hotel with skating and curling in the winter. *Glogghuis* (M), tel. 671139. Tennis, indoor pool. Central, quiet; bar.

OBERIBERG. *Posthotel* (M), tel. 561172. Comfortable; in own grounds.

PILATUS. *Bellevue* (I), tel. 961255. Near the summit of the mountain at nearly 7,000 ft. so very quiet (as may be imagined). *Pilatus-Kulm* (I), tel. 961255. Less expensive hotel but almost as high up the mountain. No rooms with bath.

RIGI. *Rigi Kulm* (I), tel. 831312. At the summit (5,906 ft.).
At Rigi-Kaltbad: *Hostellerie Rigi* (E), tel. 831616. Indoor pool and sauna. *Bellevue* (M), tel. 831351. Less swanky but the same fantastic view.

SCHWYZ. *Wysses Rössli* (M), tel. 211922. Centrally-located; historic building. *Hirschen* (I), tel. 211276. Small and central.

SEELISBERG. *Bellevue* (I), tel. 311626. Very quiet hotel in own grounds with pool, tennis and special facilities for the handicapped.

STANS. *Regina* (I), tel. 613173. Central; breakfast only. *Stanserhof* (I), tel. 614122. Comfortable, well-equipped hotel; bowling.

STOOS. *Sporthotel Stoos* (E), tel. 211505. Indoor pool, tennis and ice rink. *Klingenstock* (I), tel. 2151212.

VITZNAU. *Park-Hotel* (L), tel. 831322. Lakeside hotel of considerable sophistication and comfort; with waterskiing, tennis, indoor pool and sauna. *Seehotel Vitznauerhof* (M), tel. 831315. Lakeside hotel in own grounds with tennis and facilities for the handicapped; very quiet. *Alpenrose* (I), tel. 831377. Lakeside hotel; comfortable and with bowls. *Schiff* (I), tel. 831357. Small; on the lake. No rooms with baths or shower.

WEGGIS. (All inclusive). *Albana* (E), tel. 932141. Ideal family hotel. *Beau-Rivage* (E), tel. 931422. Pool among the many facilities. Reader-recommended. *Park* (E), tel. 931313. Beautiful situation in lakeside park. Tennis, swimming, boating. *Central am See* (M), tel. 931252. Smack on lake. Heated pool. Excellent value. Editor-recommended. *Rigi am See* (M), tel. 932151. Comfortable hotel by lake. *Rössli* (M), tel. 931106. Central, but very quiet rooms.

ZUG. *City Hotel Ochsen* (E), tel. 213232. In the heart of town in an historic building. *Rosenberg* (M), tel. 214343. Quiet; in own grounds with good view.
Restaurants. *Aklin* (I–E), Am Zytturm (tel. 211866). Excellent. *Hirschen* (I–M), tel. 212930. *Rosenberg* (I–M), tel. 217171. Very good.

THE FACE OF SWITZERLAND

WINTER SPORTS. With the exception of Andermatt, Engelberg and Stoos, the ski resorts of central Switzerland attract relatively few foreign visitors. They are primarily nonfashionable, inexpensive resorts jammed at the weekend with Swiss from nearby Lucerne and Zurich. But during the week you can enjoy unbelievable freedom on the slopes and skilifts. However, beware Saturdays, Sundays and holidays unless skiing means so much that you are prepared to wait an hour or more for a cable car or lift. Because of relative lack of elevation, some resorts (Andermatt, Engelberg, Melchsee-Frutt and, possibly, Stoos excepted) have a fairly short winter season.

Andermatt, 1,450 meters (4,750 feet); 2 cable cars, 6 lifts, 43 km. of downhill runs, 20 km. of cross-country trails; tobogganing, curling, ski schools, skating.

Einsiedeln, 915 meters (3,000 feet); 6 lifts, 3.5 km. of downhill runs, 45 km. of cross-country trails, 16 km. of ski-hiking trails, 2 km. of tobogganing tracks; ski schools, curling.

Engelberg, 1,030 meters (3,380 feet); 2 funicular railways, 7 cable cars, 15 lifts, 45 km. of downhill runs, 23 km. of cross-country trails, 3.5 km. of toboggan runs; ski schools, skating.

Hoch-Ybrig, 1,050–2,200 meters (3,445–7,218 feet); 15 cable cars and lifts, 50 km. downhill runs, 30 km. cross-country trails, night skiing, ski school.

Hospental, 1,435 meters (4,715 feet); 1 lift, 8 km. of downhill runs, 16 km. of cross-country trails; ski school (downhill).

Lucerne, 450 meters (1,470 feet); a big center for sightseeing and nightlife, but limited to curling and skating as far as outdoor winter sports go.

Lungern, 725 meters (2,380 feet); 8 km. of downhill runs, 6 km. of cross-country trails; tobogganing, skating, ski schools, 2 cable cars, 2 ski lifts.

Melchsee, 1,920 meters (6,300 feet); 2 cable cars, 5 lifts, 32 km. of downhill runs, 18 km. of cross-country trails, 10 km. of ski-hiking trails; ski schools.

Oberiberg, 1,130 meters (3,700 feet); 3 lifts, 5 km. of downhill runs, 2 km. of cross-country trails, 15 km. of ski-hiking trails, 1 cable car.

Rigi, 1,310 meters (4,300 feet); 2 funicular railways, 2 cable cars, 5 lifts, 25 km. of downhill runs, 14 km. of cross-country trails, 5 km. of ski-hiking trails; curling, ski bob, ski schools.

Schwyz, 520 meters (1,700 feet); 3 cable cars, 9 lifts, 50 km. of downhill trails, 8 km. of cross-country tracks, 6 km. of ski-hiking trails; tobogganing, ski schools.

Sörenberg, 1,666 meters (5,465 feet); 2 cable cars, numerous ski lifts; 43 km. of downhill trails, 25 km. of cross-country tracks.

Stoos, 1,310 meters (4,300 feet); 1 cable car, 6 lifts, 15 km. of downhill trails, 8 km. of cross-country tracks, 3 km. of ski-hiking trails; curling, ski schools.

Wilen-Sarnen, 485 meters (1,600 feet); a cross-country ski center—15 km. of trails for both cross-country and ski-hiking; cross-country ski school.

Zug, 435 meters (1,430 feet); 2 lifts, 9 km. of cross-country trails, 17 km. of ski-hiking trails; curling, ski schools.

ZURICH

Prosperous and Protestant

To most people who have never been there, Zurich is thought of as the industrial heart of Switzerland, its Pittsburgh or Manchester. Thus, when on holiday, travelers tend to concentrate on Lucerne or Berne, giving Zurich the go-by. This is a mistake, for they would find Zurich a jewel set among rolling green hills, with one end of the long, crescent-shaped Lake of Zurich nosing inquisitively into the center of the town like a shimmering blue eel. The largest city in Switzerland (it has a population of about 370,000), Zurich is built around the northern tip of the lake and on the flanks of the surrounding wooded hills. Through its heart run the swift but shallow Limmat River and the smaller Sihl River, which rises in the nearby Sihl Lake and wanders down the western shore of Lake Zurich to join the Limmat in the center of town. There are factories (most of them in the industrial suburbs north of

Zurich), but there is no smoke; moreover, there are no slums. The industries run on electricity, and the buildings in which they are housed look more like sanatoria or colleges than factories. The Swiss don't live in drab streets or dirty houses, but in pretty little villas with flowers around the door, or in ultramodern apartment blocks. They can afford to, because they are among the highest paid workers in Europe.

Zurich is a Protestant city. Beside the Wasserkirche, overlooked by the Grossmünster—a church said to have been founded by Charlemagne—stands the statue of Ulrich Zwingli. As pastor in the Grossmünster he first preached the Reformation there on New Year's Day, 1519, and continued to do so with such effect that four years later almost to the day, after a great public debate, the city formally associated itself with the new faith. Until his death in battle in 1531 at the village of Kappel some fourteen miles south of Zurich, Zwingli defied the Pope and much of the Swiss Confederation in his fierce championship of the Reformation.

One has only to look at the bronze replica of his face to realize that this man took a stern view of life. It is as if the disapproving regard his statue directs towards Niederdorf (which happens to be the amusement center of the city) were meant to burn continually into the consciousness of every citizen, a constant reminder of the pitfalls of the pleasures of the flesh and idleness.

The good citizens of Zurich work hard, go to church and avoid self-indulgence. Are they, then, Puritans? Perhaps. But if so, a lot of good old Christian virtues, all too rare in the world today, go along with their Puritanism. They are scrupulously honest, fastidiously clean, and noted for their generosity and kindness.

The very Puritanism of the Zurichers has its engaging side. Although they live their own lives according to their lights, permitting themselves no foolishness, they don't expect other people to follow their example, and are, in fact, anxious to prove to others that they are broad-minded. Visitors to Zurich are constantly being reminded that the blue-laws don't apply to them, and this is done in an apologetic tone of voice that implies, 'Please bear with us. We can't help it if we don't know how to play'. In fact, they *do* know how to play. The Schauspielhaus (Playhouse), for example, handsomely supported by Zurich's upper crust, puts on all kinds of daring and avant garde entertainment.

The visitor will also find that nightlife in Zurich has become much more varied and exciting (not to mention 'liberated') than it was say ten years ago. Then, though you could find the odd spot that stayed open till about two in the morning, for the most part Zurich nightlife was a pretty staid affair. Nowadays, however, the visitor will have no difficulty finding almost any species of nightly entertainment.

A Bit of History

Zurich can trace its history as far back as any other Swiss city, and has some ancient buildings and monuments to prove it, but for the most part the Zurich that the visitor encounters today is a 19th-century city. And indeed the people of Zurich have made considerable efforts to ensure that the harmony of their 19th-century buildings remains unspoilt. There are strict building regulations, all designed to ensure that the homogeneity of the city is retained. You'll see, particularly in the old part of the city around Lindenhof-Platz, that they've done an excellent job in harmonizing the new with the old.

As long ago as 3,000 BC, there were human habitations on the site of what is now Zurich. During the Stone Age and towards the end of the Bronze Age, 1,000 BC, a dwelling existed on Lindenhof Hill. Certainly, during the Roman occupation (which started in the middle of the 1st century AD) a fort and a customs station were built on the Lindenhof, then known by the Latin name Turicum. In the 5th century, the Alamanni ousted the Romans. Charlemagne did much for Zurich in the 8th century and was probably responsible for founding what is now the Grossmünster. His grandson, Ludwig the German, founded the original Fraumünster, on the opposite bank of the Limmat, in 853, installing his daughter, Hildegarde, as abbess.

During the Middle Ages Zurich suffered as much from border disputes as any other part of Europe, and on one occasion the city was only saved from conquest by the Austrians by the action of its women. The Zurich army had fought valiantly on the approaches, but had been beaten and were falling back to within the city gates. The women donned armor, took up spears and swords, and marched to the Lindenhof in full battle array. The Austrians, seeing them from a distance, thought they had to do battle with a second Zurich army as tough as the first, and discreetly withdrew. A fountain and small statue on top of the hill commemorates this event.

Zurich became one of the Imperial cities of the German Empire in 1218, and joined the Swiss Confederation in 1351. In the 16th century, after the initial turmoil of the Reformation, the city started an era of great cultural activity and economic growth. The French Revolution brought a period of decline and confusion, but afterwards Zurich quickly got back into stride to become, as it is today, one of Europe's most important and prosperous commercial and industrial cities.

It is also a major cultural and educational center. The University of Zurich and the Federal Institute of Technology are famous. The city was the birthplace of Johann Pestalozzi, the great Swiss educator, and the poets C. F. Meyer and Gottfried Keller. More recently, Zurich has become a mecca for students in the field of psychological studies through the establishment of the C. G. Jung Institute for training and research work in analytical psychology.

Many famous people have lived and worked in Zurich, including Lenin, who used to study at the Sozialarchiv. James Joyce, who is buried in Zurich's Fluntern cemetery, wrote part of *Ulysses* in the city. Wagner composed much of *Tristan und Isolde* there, and it is also where Thornton Wilder wrote *Our Town*. And Dada, the anti-art, anti-bourgeois movement, first saw the light of day in Zurich during World War I under the guiding hand of its radical founder Tristan Tzara.

Exploring Zurich

Arriving at Zurich's splendid 19th-century Hauptbahnhof, you don't have to go far to start your sightseeing. Inside the station is the tourist office, and on the north side the Swiss National Museum.

At the other (south) side is Bahnhofplatz, hub of the city transport system. Once a moderately elegant square, it is now a conglomeration of shudderingly drab shelters for bus and tram passengers. You can avoid this eyesore by taking the escalator which burrows down to 'Shop-Ville', a vast, brilliantly lit mini-town of excellent shops beneath Bahnhofplatz itself. Up the other side is fashionable Bahnhofstrasse, which leads all the way to Bürkli-Platz on the shore of Lake Zurich. Bordered by lime trees, very expensive shops and opulent offices, most of Bahnhofstrasse is now a huge sidewalk free of all traffic except for the Holy Cows—as some Zurich citizens call their trams. Towards the end, on the right, is Parade-Platz, around which are clustered some of Europe's biggest banking houses and 'gnomeries.' On either side of Bürkli-Platz—a busy traffic junction—are attractive quays with lawns, flower beds, and trees which encircle the end of the lake. To the right is the Kongresshaus; capable of accommodating over 1,700 people in its halls, concert hall and restaurants. Also facing the lake are the offices of some of the big insurance companies, a reminder of Zurich's importance in the insurance world.

The left hand, or western, shore of Lake Zurich, including the suburbs of Enge, Wollishofen and Kilchberg, is a smart residential district. Each year, on December 6, Wollishofen puts on a rather eerie Christmas Parade. The young people dress up in white nightshirts and carry illuminated tiaras. Accompanied by Santa Claus, they march through the streets tooting horns and clanging cowbells in an effort to exorcise the Spirit of Winter. The custom is believed to date from the pre-Christian era.

ZURICH

Points of Interest

1. Centre Le Corbusier
2. Federal Institute of Technology
3. Fraumünster
4. Grossmünster
5. Hauptbahnhof (Central Station); Tourist Information Bureau
6. Kongresshaus
7. Kunsthaus (Zürich Art Museum)
8. Landesmuseum (National Museum); Kunstmuseum
9. Opernhaus
10. Peterskirche
11. Rathaus (Town Hall)
12. Rietberg Museum
13. Schauspielhaus
14. University of Zürich
15. Wasserkirche
16. Wohnkultur

Between Enge and Wollishofen is the lakeshore Strandbad, or public lido, and on the right shore of the lake stretches the long tree-shaded Utoquai, a lovely promenade where all of fashionable Zurich likes to stroll on Sunday afternoons. It is lined with boat harbors and bathing establishments. Farther down, on Seefeld-Quai, are more fine mansions and public gardens.

For leisurely sightseeing, with some unorthodox views, try the regular May to September motor launch service from the Central Station up the Limmat River and to the lake.

Nightlife and Sightseeing

From Bürkli-Platz a bridge crosses the River Limmat where it leaves the lake. At the far end is the Bellevue-Platz, with a host of cinemas, nightclubs, cabarets, restaurants, and cafés clustered around it. Due to the 2 AM closing time it is as well to start early if you wish to take in any of these places. Many are found along the Limmatquai, past the Grossmünster; others are in the narrow, winding streets of this section of the city. The aspect of the place is somewhat sinister at night because of the narrow streets, but that's just an illusion—there's nothing that dangerous or exciting to be found in the way of night life in Zurich.

The Limmatquai is lined with old guildhalls, including the Rüden, Saffran, Schmieden, Schneidern and Zimmerleuten, all with interesting façades. You'll find some good restaurants in these guildhalls, and elsewhere in the neighborhood, too.

The Grossmünster cathedral, towering above the Limmatquai, is dedicated to the saints Felix, Regula and Exuperantius, who converted the inhabitants of Turicum to Christianity in the 3rd century. Legend has it that they were beheaded by the town's governor—Decius—after having been scourged, plunged into boiling oil, and forced to drink molten lead in an effort to make them deny their faith. These intrepid saints not only underwent their ordeals without flinching, but after the headsman's axe had fallen they still had enough strength to pick up their heads and walk to a nearby hilltop, where they lay down to eternal rest in graves they dug themselves! The Great Seal of Zurich shows them carrying their heads jauntily under their arms. The cathedral itself is 12th-century Romanesque, though it also has two 15th-century Gothic towers, one bearing a statue of Charlemagne. Crossing the Münsterbrücke (cathedral bridge), we come to the Münsterhof, a charming old square notable for the Waag and Meise guildhalls and the Fraumünster.

Although founded around 853, the Fraumünster's present structure dates back only to the 13th century. The remains of the original cloisters have been incorporated in the adjacent Stadthaus. Just to the north

ZURICH

of the Fraumünster is the old parish church of Zurich, the Peterskirche, part of which dates from the 13th century. It has a massive tower surmounted by a large, golden-faced clock (it is in fact the largest in Europe). All around this church is another maze of narrow, winding streets leading up to Lindenhof-Platz, site of the old Roman fortress and the statue of the Women of Zurich. It is the most picturesque quarter of the town and also has many fine restaurants.

Crossing the river again, via the Rathausbrücke, the visitor comes to the old town hall, a fine building dating from the 17th century. It is now the seat of the city and cantonal parliaments. The old council chamber contains a splendid porcelain stove, presented to Zurich by the people of Winterthur when the town hall was built, and an elaborate tapestry. In another room is the Peace of Zurich, the document by which Austria ceded Lombardy to the house of Savoy in 1859.

Zurich from Above

If you now follow the Limmatquai down to the end, only about 350 meters (400 yards), you will come to the terminus of a curious old cable railway that, setting off through the back of an apartment house, leads up to Leonhardstrasse, near the campuses of the University of Zurich and the Federal Institute of Technology. From the latter, there is a fine view of the city.

Some clear day during your stay in Zurich, you should go to the little Selnau railroad station on the Sihl River and take the twenty-five-minute ride to Uetliberg, 850 meters (2,800 feet) up, on the heights above the city. It costs a few francs to reach this point, and from it you have a magnificent view over the lake to the snow-clad peaks beyond. In case the bracing air makes you hungry, there is a pleasant restaurant on a terrace where you can drink in the view while eating. Or bring your own lunch: there are plenty of picnic spots here.

From the same station, you can get a train along the valley of the Sihl to Gontenbach, with its deer park and zoo, to Sihlwald with its forest house, or Sihlbrugg, where there are beautiful walks.

On the northeastern fringe of Zurich, just over a kilometer from the railway station, is Zürichberg, a 600 meter (2,000 feet) high series of hills which can easily be reached by cable car or by tram. There, apart from the fine views and equally fine walks, you'll find the zoo, a large model railway, small golf course, a swimming pool with artificial waves, and in winter an ice rink.

Excursions Up the Lake

One of the many excellent excursions from the city takes the visitor on a pleasant steamboat voyage up the Lake of Zurich to the historic town of Rapperswil. It is an easy four-hour trip—the boat leaves from the landing stage at the end of the Bahnhofstrasse in Zurich. The lake is about 38km. (24 miles) long, and just under 5km. (3 miles) wide at the widest part. Although other Swiss lakes offer more grandiose scenery, none can present such a succession of charming views. The banks rise in gentle slopes, in the midst of which are numerous pretty villas and thriving villages. On the east side are lofty wooded hills, with the Alps forming a striking background.

Each town along the lake has its own character, and the entire area is rich in charm, even for a country as well stocked in this commodity as Switzerland. Most of the tourists making use of the excursion steamers on the Lake of Zurich are Swiss, which in itself is a fair recommendation to foreign visitors to become acquainted with the district.

The first stopping place of interest after leaving Zurich is Meilen, an idyllic little town with a 15th-century church. It was here, in the winter of 1853, when the lake was unusually low, that ethnologists discovered the traces of prehistoric lacustrian settlements that provided graphic evidence of the fact that there were human dwellings in the area as long ago as 3,000 years before Christ. Arrows, tools, bones of tame animals and other evidence of this long-ago civilization were discovered and can now be seen in Zurich's Swiss National Museum. The exact site where the traces were found is now underwater, but other evidence of pile-dwellings can be found several miles from Meilen at Wetzikon, where a former lake has become a peat moor.

Another town along the lake is Stäfa, once well-known as a producer of silk, but now engaged in making wine. Here Goethe stayed for a time in the year 1797 and wrote his play *Jery and Bately,* inspired by the Swiss scenery. Nearly opposite is the little island of Ufenau, which has a ruined church and the grave of Ulrich von Hutten, a friend of Luther's, who had fled to Zurich from his persecutors to seek the protection of Zwingli.

Rapperswil is seen long before the steamer reaches its snug little harbor, since it stands on a knoll above the lake, its monastery and castle outlined against the sky. The latter was built in 1229, and during the 14th century became a Habsburg stronghold. In 1350 it was here that the conspirators met to plot the Massacre of Zurich—the first in a series of feuds with the city at the other end of the lake. From 1870 until just before World War II, the castle became the repository for the national relics of Poland, during that country's long, and sadly still continuing, fight for freedom. The Rapperswil town hall has a carved Gothic portal and, inside, a colossal old wrought-iron stove. The monastery, built by the Capuchins, is fairly recent, but its tall spire adds to the quaintness of the little town, which has many fine old houses and a distinctly medieval appearance.

Winterthur, Town to the North

Finally, a look at Winterthur. With a population of about 90,000, Winterthur is considered an industrial center, but most visitors will see it more as a cultural center, with a distinguished history. The city's origins can be traced back to AD 294, and during the Middle Ages it became a mecca for craftsmen, before falling under the yoke of Zurich. Manuscripts, paintings, furniture, and everyday items which chronicle the city's development can be seen in the Heimatmuseum.

Today Winterthur boasts two art collections, the Oskar Reinhart Foundation and the Public Art Gallery, both of which have collections of Swiss, German and Austrian painting dating from the 18th century onwards. On the musical side, the town's symphony orchestra (founded over 330 years ago) is one of the best in Switzerland. Even the surrounding countryside seems to be dominated more by its four historic castles in the surrounding hills than by the modern industrial developments. The most notable of these fortresses is the Kyburg, which for several centuries was the seat of the counts of the same name, many of whom played prominent roles in Swiss history. Technorama, a museum devoted to technology, was opened recently on Frauenfeldstrasse, just outside Winterthur.

PRACTICAL INFORMATION FOR ZURICH

GETTING TO TOWN FROM THE AIRPORT. Zurich airport (Kloten), the country's principal international airport, has a main line rail station beneath its terminal buildings. There are regular and fast services into Zurich itself, all of which go to the main rail station, the Hauptbahnhof, in the center of town; the trip takes about 10 minutes. You can also get through trains from Kloten to Aarau, Baden, Berne, Bienne (Biel), Geneva, Lausanne, Lucerne, Olten, St. Gallen, Solothurn, Winterthur and Zug. But there are also easy connections via Zurich to cities all over the country. Trains run from around 6 AM to midnight. There is also a bus service into Zurich, which takes around 20 to 30 minutes. Taxis into town, at around Fr. 40, are unjustifiably expensive.

THE FACE OF SWITZERLAND

GETTING AROUND TOWN. By Bus and Tram. Buses and tram services are excellent. Most services start from the main rail station, the Hauptbahnhof, in the center of town. Buy tickets from the machine at the stop before boarding. There is a one-day season ticket which is good for all trips on the Zurich network. A free booklet with full details and maps (in English) is available from all city transit offices (VBZ).

By Taxi. Taxis are expensive and not recommended unless you are in a real hurry.

By Bicycle. Bicycles are available for hire at the rail station.

SPECIAL EVENTS. All the explosive forces that are bottled inside the staid, reserved Zurichers are released during the *Sechseläuten,* a continuous program of processions, bands, fireworks and general jollification on the third or fourth Sunday and Monday in Apr. The merrymaking culminates on Monday evening in the burning of *Böögg,* a huge cotton-wool snowman symbolizing winter.

The International June Festival is dedicated to all branches of the arts. If you are in the city during this period you will find music, theater, the fine arts, magnificent concerts featuring well-known orchestras and soloists, operas and plays in a variety of languages, folk music, and outstanding exhibitions of painting and sculpture.

But Zurich is an active city, so it's safe to say that whenever you go there will be something interesting going on. A useful source of information is the *Official Weekly Bulletin* (in English), which is obtainable from the Tourist Office, and lists current events, restaurants, cinemas, and other useful things.

HOTELS. If you want the best—and can afford it—Zurich offers a large choice of superb hotels. But the city also has a sizeable quantity of more moderately-priced establishments that still maintain the very highest standards. However, as Zurich is generally rather on the expensive side, there is unfortunately something of a lack of inexpensive hotels. Note, though, that nearly all the hotels that we include in our listings below have a wide range of rooms, a good many of which may well fall within a lower price category than that which we have given here. The best advice is always check beforehand with the hotel direct.

There is an accommodations office at the rail station that will certainly be able to find you a hotel if you arrive in town without reservations. They charge a small fee.

ZURICH

Deluxe

Atlantis Sheraton, Döltschiweg 234 (tel. 4630000). With indoor pool, sauna and considerable luxury; quiet location.

Baur au Lac, Talstr. 1 (tel. 2211650). Stands in its own lakeside minipark near the end of the Bahnhofstr; an elegant establishment.

Carlton Elite, Bahnhofstr 41 (tel. 2116560). In the heart of chic downtown Zurich.

Dolder Grand Hotel, Kurhaustr. 65 (tel. 2516231). Up among the pinewoods, but only about 10 minutes from the city center; outdoor pool and superb views.

Eden au Lac, Utoquai 45 (tel. 479404). Charming and popular with tranquil atmosphere and highly recommended restaurant; attractive view over the lake.

St. Gotthard, Bahnhofstr. 87 (tel. 2115500). Central and plush with an excellent restaurant.

Savoy Baur en Ville, Poststr. 12 (tel. 2115360). Situated in the middle of the exclusive shopping center on Bahnhofstr.

Schweizerhof, Bahnhofplatz 7 (tel. 2118640). Opposite the station; all rooms airconditioned.

Zum Storchen, Weinplatz 2 (tel. 2115510). Historic building in the heart of town; splendid view from the first class restaurant.

Zurich, Neumühlequai 42 (tel. 3636363). In the heart of the city by the river Limmat and only a few minutes' walk from the station; indoor pool.

Expensive

Ascot, Lavatertsr. 15 (tel. 2011800). Very central and very smart.

Continental, Stampfenbachstr. 60 (tel. 3633363). All rooms airconditioned; dancing; central.

Glärnischof, Claridenstr. 30 (tel. 2024747). Smart grill restaurant and all the expected comforts.

Nova-Park, Bedenerstr. 420 (tel. 542221). Indoor pool, gymnasium and sauna.

Rigihof, Univeritätstr. 101 (tel. 3611685). Suitable for children; recommended.

Schifflände, Schifflände 18 (tel. 694050). Fairly new but lacks nothing in plush comfort.

Moderate

Du Théâtre, Seilergraben 69 (tel. 2526062). Breakfast only; central.

Florhof, Florhofgasse 4 (tel. 474470). Central but quietly situated elegant mansion hotel.

Franziskaner, Stüssihofstatt 1 (tel. 2520120). Small and central.

Trümpy, Limmatstr. 5 (tel. 425400). Central, with good grill restaurant and TV in all rooms.

Inexpensive

Bahnpost, Reitergasse 6 (tel. 2413211). Central but quiet and very reasonably priced. No rooms with bath. Breakfast only but with restaurant.

Buchzelg, Buchzelgstr. 50 (tel. 538200). A rather superior hotel for this category; in own grounds.
Fischer, Schaffhauserstr. 520 (tel. 3012755).
Leonhard, Limmatquai 136 (tel. 2510550). In the heart of town.
Limmathof, Limmatquai 142 (tel. 474220). Simple, but central.
Spirgarten, Lindenplatz 5 (tel. 622400). With good restaurant and bowling.
Splendid, Rosengasse 5 (tel. 2525850). Central. No rooms with bath.

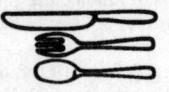

RESTAURANTS. Zurich is justifiably famous for its excellent food, but much of it, and certainly in all the best spots, is rather expensive. But at the same time, there are also many less expensive places where, if you study the menu carefully, it is possible to eat well without breaking the bank.

Expensive

Baur au Lac Grill, Talstr. 1 (tel. 2211650). In the hotel of the same name, but not to be confused with the main dining room of the Baur au Lac. The cuisine is French at its best, but with an excellent selection of regional dishes as well.

Fischstube Zürichhorn, Bellerivestr. 160 (tel. 552520). Built on piles over the lake and especially delightful on a warm evening. Excellent food.

Haus zum Rüden, Limmatquai 42 (tel. 479590). Attractive gothic restaurant of the Society of Noblemen. Atmospheric, and with excellent food.

Kronenhalle, Rämistr. 4 (tel. 2510256). The works by famous artists which adorn the walls here are all originals and match the restaurant's friendly atmosphere and memorable food. This was James Joyce's favorite restaurant and there's a portrait of the writer, inscribed to the then proprietor, above his favored table.

Florhof, Florhofgasse 4 (tel. 474470). Elegant and small restaurant in the hotel of the same name.

Rotisserie Cote d'Or, in the Goldenes Schwert. Excellent.

Veltliner Keller, Schlüsselgasse 8 (tel. 2213228). In the old part of the city, and rather difficult to find, this restaurant is a must, though it is very expensive. In a fine setting, you'll find superbly prepared regional specialties (fully described in English on the menu) together with excellent wines. Even if the food was not magnificent, it would be worth a visit just to see the splendid carved wood of the dining rooms.

Zunfthaus zur Schmieden, Marktgasse 20 (tel. 2515287). Guildhall restaurant of the blacksmiths; atmospheric.

Zunfthaus zur Zimmerleuten, Limmatquai 40 (tel. 2520834). Guildhall restaurant of the carpenters.

Moderate

Bauschänzli, Stadthausquai. Between the Fraumünster and the Quai Bridge. Garden restaurant on the river Limmat.

Blockhus, Schifflände 4. Rustic decor, with fondue the specialty of the house. The portions are so big, they can easily be split in two.

ZURICH

Bodega Espanola, Münstergasse 15. Spanish, of course, in decor and cuisine. The casual atmosphere and carefree waiters make a good change of pace from most other Swiss restaurants.

Le Dézaley Cave Vaudoise, Römergasse 7. Famous old landmark. Intimate and quiet with carefully prepared dishes.

Mövenpick. Many locations all over Switzerland. Check in phone book for nearest one. Swiss restaurant chain with wide price range. Seafood and other specialties can be much more than Moderate.

Inexpensive

Bahnhofbuffet. In the railway station. Somewhat noisy but with good food. This restaurant—like the trains—is divided into two classes, with the first considerably more expensive.

Café Select, Limmatquai 16. For the literati who like the leisurely chessplaying atmosphere and the low-priced *Tagesteller* (plat du jour).

Mensa, Rämistrasse 71, and **Mensa Polyterrasse,** Leonhardstrasse 34, are student places where you can get rockbottom prices with a student ID card.

Migros. 45 locations throughout Zürich. Cafeterias in economy-priced supermarket chain. Standup and sitdown sections, but sometimes it's cheaper if you stay on your feet.

Odeon, Limmatquai 2. Where the newspapermen and the actors go to swap good stories. Atmospheric. Good food.

Oepfelchammer, Rindermarkt 12. Mostly for the younger crowd who go for wine, women and song in a carved-wooden-table atmosphere.

Olivenbaum, Stadelhoferstrasse 10. One of four places operated by a temperance organization, serving plain but substantial food at very low prices.

Weisser Wind, Oberdorfstrasse 20. Features country atmosphere, excellent food and a gratifying tab.

Zeughauskeller, Bahnhofstr. 28a/Paradeplatz.

Zunfthaus zur Saffran, Limmatquai 54. The restaurant of the saffron merchants' guildhall, where you can eat inexpensively—and otherwise.

ENTERTAINMENT. Discos and Clubs. Zurich's nightspots are undistinguished for the most part and they tend to close soon after midnight. There is also very little that is not pretty pricey. There is a group of bars, some good, some bad, along the Niederdorfstrasse. Without wasting too much time, they can be classified as follows: striptease/hostess, *Maxim, La Puce* (in the small bar), *Terrasse* and *Red House.* Dancing, *Macotte, La Ferme* (rustic decor), *Bellerive.* There are also a number of discos, many of which are quite good. For jazz, try *Piccadilly* at Zähringerstrasse 33 and *Casa Bar* at Münstergasse 30.

Nightspots here are anything but permanent institutions, so check them beforehand with your hotel porter or at the tourist office. Remember also that many of them can be expensive, and that drinks are very expensive.

186 THE FACE OF SWITZERLAND

Theaters and Concerts. The *Opernhaus* (grand opera, light opera) although not up to Vienna or Milan standards, produces excellent performances for the annual June festival. The *Schauspielhaus* is one of the best serious theaters in Europe. If you have a special interest in the stage, you'll undoubtedly enjoy its classical and modern drama and comedy, even without understanding German. The *Bernhard Theater* plays more modern works; the small *Theater am Hechtplatz* is an experimental stage for all sorts of entertainment.

MUSEUMS. Centre Le Corbusier, Bellerivestrasse at Höschgasse. Last building designed by the great Swiss architect. It is devoted largely to his paintings, which, though not as well-known as his architectural work, are surprisingly good.

Kellenberger Watch and Clock Collection, Town Hall, Marktgasse 20.

Kunstmuseum (Art Gallery), Museumstr. 52. Important art collection. Includes the 'Münzkabinett'—an extensive coin collection.

Museum of Applied Arts (Kunstgewerbemuseum), Ausstellungstrasse 60. Graphic and applied arts; there is a fine library.

Museum der Zeitmessung (Museum of Time-Measurement), 31 Bahnhofstr., below the watchmaker's store. A rich and varied collection of watches, clocks and all manner of time-measuring devices dating back to pre-Christian times.

Puppenmuseum Sacha Morgenthaler (the Sacha Morgenthaler Dolls' Museum), Bärengasse 22, in the Bärengasse Wohnmuseum (Museum of Domestic Life). A fascinating collection of dolls made by Sacha Morgenthaler.

Rietberg Museum, Gablerstr. 15. Admirable collection of primitive and Oriental sculptures.

Swiss National Museum (Landesmuseum), Museumstrasse 2. Just behind the main rail station. Especially good for students of Swiss history.

Winterhur (about 20 miles northeast of Zurich). **Oskar Reinhart Foundation,** Stadthausstr. 6. One of Switzerland's three major art collections.

Winterthur Technorama der Schweiz, Frauenfelderstr. (outside town). Impressive display of all things technical and technological. Opened in 1981.

Wohnkultur, Bärengasse 20–22. Two marvelous patrician homes dating from 1650 and decorated in styles current between then and the mid-19th century.

Zurich Art Museum (Kunsthaus), Heimplatz. Small but outstanding permanent collection, especially strong on French moderns. Exhibitions here are often excellent.

SHOPPING. Leading south from the main railroad station and busy Bahnhofplatz (under which lies *Shop-Ville,* Zurich's subterranean shopping center) is the fashionable and elegant Bahnhofstrasse, which the Zurichers call 'the Fifth Avenue of Switzerland'. In this street and in those leading off to the right and left you'll find some of the handsomest shops and department

ZURICH

stores in Europe. Opening hours 8 or 9 AM until 6:30 PM (Sats. 4 PM). Though expensive, you'll find everything here from cameras, haute couture and leather goods through watches and sports equipment.

If you're after handcrafts and souvenirs, try one of the following: *Schweizer Heimatwerk,* Rudolf-Brun-Brücke, Bahnhofstrasse 2, Rennweg 14 and Zurich Airport; *'La Ticinella',* Fraumünsterstrasse 13; *Seiler Teddy's Souvenir Shop,* Limmatquai 34; *Franz Carl Weber,* Bahnhofstrasse 62.

USEFUL ADDRESSES. *Zurich Tourist Office,* situated in main railway station. *American Consulate,* Talacker 35. *British Consulate,* Dufourstrasse 56. *Swiss National Tourist Office,* Bellariastrasse 38. *American Express,* Bahnhofstrasse 20. *Cook's,* Talacker 42. *Swiss Friends of U.S.A.,* Zunfthaus zur Zimmerleuten, Limmatquai 40. *Swiss British Society,* Mythenquai 50–60. *Golf,* Zumikon Links (18 holes), 30 mins. by Forch tram from Stadelhofen station; Dolder Hotel, 9 holes. *Swimming,* Lido Beach on lake; Waidberg Woods pool; Dolder Hotel pool; Hallenschwimmbad, Sihlstrasse 71.

Car Hire. *Avis,* Stampfenbachstrasse 62, also Airport-Hilton hotel; *Hertz,* Lagerstrasse 33 and Hotels International, Nova-Park and Zurich; *Europcar,* Josefstrasse 53; *Budget Rent-a-Car,* Tödistrasse 9; *Tilden International,* Lindenstrasse 33, and *Winterhalder,* Gerbergasse 4. All also at Zurich airport.

WINTER SPORTS. Zurich, and surrounding areas, may not be exactly world famous when it comes to winter sports, and the season is certainly somewhat limited due to the relatively low altitudes, but a stay in Zurich doesn't necessarily mean having to forgo wintery pursuits.

Winterthur, 477 meters (1,565 feet); a skating center with an artificial lake. Lessons available.

Zurich, 411 meters (1,350 feet); provides some skiing, but the emphasis is on cross-country skiing (28 km. of trails) and ski-hiking (10 km. of trails). Three funicular railways operate in the area, and there is also skating, curling and tobogganing.

EASTERN SWITZERLAND

Charm and Creature Comforts

Eastern Switzerland is rich in variety, rich in tradition—and just plain rich! Yet despite the obvious prosperity, the region retains an air of other-worldliness. Everywhere you will see past and present interwoven. Houses—new as well as old—with frescoes and carved-wood balconies; turrets, roofs, and entire walls made of wood shingles so delicate that, when weathered, they look almost like fur.

But although the old customs are as much a part of life today as they were centuries ago, time in St. Gallen has not entirely stood still. The textile industry has introduced new technology into the town, and a variety of modern architectural styles can be seen in the new public buildings. But, many tourists have been slow to appreciate the attractions of eastern Switzerland, and as a result it has managed to retain much more of its regional personality than some of the more well-

EASTERN SWITZERLAND

developed areas. As a result, prices are often lower here than in the more famous parts of the country.

The region lies to the east of Zurich and comprises the cantons of Glarus, Schaffhausen, Thurgau, St. Gallen and—cocooned within the latter, and itself divided into two half-cantons (Inner and Outer Rhoden)—Appenzell. The Principality of Liechtenstein is also a part of the area administratively. However, as it is also a separate country in its own right, albeit a very tiny one, we have given it a chapter all of its own. This follows immediately after this chapter. Within this area, the landscape varies from the snowcapped peaks of Mount Säntis, almost 2,500 meters (8,200 feet) high, through the mountain valleys and the rolling hills of Appenzell, to the shores of Lake Constance. To the east and the north is the Rhine, separating Switzerland from Liechtenstein, Austria and Germany.

Towns range from the delightful St. Gallen to spas such as Bad Ragaz, and scores of summer and winter resorts. Some smaller towns, notably Appenzell, played a big part in forming the Swiss Confederation. In Appenzell itself, and in Glarus, the picturesque Landsgemeinde, or open-air parliament can still be seen.

Exploring St. Gallen

As well as being Switzerland's largest eastern city, St. Gallen is also an excellent center for tourists, since in addition to its own attractions, it provides easy access to Lake Constance, the Säntis mountains, and the Appenzell country. The town itself lies less than an hour from Zurich by train, and balances its role as an important, modern textile center with a medieval cultural heritage. Its origins date back to 612, when the Irish missionary Gallus laid the foundations of an abbey that was to become a major cultural center of medieval Europe. The abbey itself was largely destroyed during the Reformation, but in its magnificent rococo library (dating from the 18th century), containing over 100,000 volumes, visitors can see illuminated manuscripts which are over 1,000 years old.

The valley town of St. Gallen, which grew up in a semicircle around the abbey walls, owed allegiance to the abbot until the early-15th century when, by making an alliance with the farmers of Appenzell, the citizens gained political freedom. Religious freedom followed a century later with the Reformation, brought to the area by the humanist Vadin —whose statue can be seen in the market place. As a Protestant town St. Gallen then formed an independent miniature state surrounded by monastic territory. This lasted until the French Revolution, when the present canton was founded and the monasteries secularized. The abbot's former residence is now the seat of government and the local parliament.

The splendid twin-towered rococo cathedral, built in 1756, is the town's most imposing building; its superbly restored interior fairly scintillates with light and color. On the northern side of the cathedral lies the old quarter whose ancient houses are rich in oriel windows and frescoes. By way of contrast it is worth visiting the new Municipal Theater and University; both are almost stark in their simplicity, but conceived with great imagination. St. Gallen's long connection with textiles is traced in the Stickereimuseum (embroidery museum) in Vadianstrasse, which houses examples of lace and embroidery made in the town from the 16th century onwards. The collection includes many pieces worn by famous European courtiers, and some stunning examples of modern work. The town is also well provided with parks and gardens, and one of the most interesting is the Peter and Paul Deer Park, where you can see ibex, chamois, stags, marmots, deer, and wild boar; and of course wonderful alpine views.

About seventeen miles west of St. Gallen is Wil, a beautiful 700-year-old town, once part of the estates of the Abbey of St Gall. The massive 15th-century residence of the Bishop-Princes, the Hof zu Wil, still dominates the old Hofplatz but now houses the local museum. From the terrace of St. Nicolas church you may see the Vorarlberg, Säntis, Churfirsten and Glärnisch Alps.

A good half-day excursion from St. Gallen is to the cable car at Schwagalp, which lies about 32kms. (20 miles) south from the town. This will take you up Mount Säntis to within a few meters of the summit, and from there—weather permitting—you will have incredible views of the Swiss Alps, and far beyond. There is a restaurant and small hotel near the summit.

Resorts and Spas

A popular resort area in St. Gallen canton is the Toggenburg Valley, which runs in a great curve between Mount Säntis and the Walensee. In the fine alpine surroundings of the Upper Toggenburg, beside the River Thur, are the neighboring resorts of Wildhaus, Unterwasser and Alt-St. Johann, skiing centers in the winter and the starting points for excursions in the Churfirsten and Alpstein mountains in summer. Wildhaus is the birthplace of Swiss reformer Ulrich Zwingli, whose house can still be visited. Lower down the valley, also on the River Thur, are the adjacent resorts of Krummenau, Ebnat-Kappel, Nesslau and Neu-St. Johann. A secondary road leads eastwards from the latter, through the spa and winter sports resort of Rietbad, to Schwägalp.

EASTERN SWITZERLAND

The southern slopes of the Churfirsten mountains, across which there are no roads, drop steeply to become the northern shores of the lake of Walensee, a deep, 16 km.-long (10 miles) gash in the mountains. At the western end of the lake is Weesen, a quiet little resort noted for its mild climate. Four miles away, along the northern shore, is the winter sports center of Amden. Opposite, running along the southern shore, is a spectacular road which travels through a number of small resorts to the lakeside village of Unterterzen. This is the lower terminal for the cable railway which goes up to Tannenbodenalp, and the Flumserberg health resort and winter sports area, a picturesque region of mountain slopes which looks across the end of Walensee to the Churfirsten mountains. You can also reach it by steep roads that wind upwards from Flums, a small town situated in the valley that runs from the east end of Walensee to the Rhine, near Bad Ragaz. At Tannenbodenalp you can go on one of the world's longest cableways; over a distance of nearly two miles, a procession of little four-seater cabins climbs steadily up to Leist (2,056 metres, 6,750 feet).

Bad Ragaz, with its beautiful golf course, is a well-run and well-established resort in a quiet mountain setting beside the Rhine. As well as having a modern spa establishment, the town is also equipped as a winter resort, and there is a cablecar running up to Pardiel (1,630 metres, 5,350 feet), and a connecting lift to Laufboden (2,224 metres, 7,300 feet). An excellent range of hotels compliments these facilities.

From both Pardiel and (more particularly) Laufboden there are outstanding views, and in summer the latter is the starting point for the 'five lakes' walk, which takes in five beautiful mountain lakes. In complete contrast, the famous walk (you can now go by minibus part of the way) up the Tamina Gorge will give you a dramatic taste of a journey to the center of the earth. Deep down in the gorge a narrow path winds along under overhanging rock sides. In places they touch to form a natural bridge. It's best in May or June when the snows are melting and water roars down the gorge in a tumbling, tempestuous torrent. At the end of the path is the hot spring from which over a million gallons of healing waters a day come up, at over 32°C (90°F), to be piped down to the spa at Bad Ragaz. The healing properties of the waters were known many centuries ago. Then, it is said, luckless patients were lowered into the waters by a rope from the top of the chasm!

Appenzell

Another delightful trip from St. Gallen is to Appenzell, in its namesake canton. A narrow gauge railway takes you in about half an hour via the mountain village resorts of Teufen and Gais. Appenzell canton had until recent times almost no communications with the surrounding provinces, and so has retained many of its ancient customs. It is one of three cantons (including Glarus, Ob- and Nidwalden) where the Landsgemeinde is still held. This is an open air town-meeting where each male citizen votes personally on all the laws, budgets, and taxes imposed by his administrators. Those taking part can be distinguished by the sword which they carry, a symbol of the right to vote. It is one of the few surviving examples of direct (as opposed to representative) democracy.

The assembly takes place on the last Sunday in April in the towns of Appenzell (every year), Hundwil (years with odd numbers), and Trogen (years with even numbers). Trogen is also the home of Kinderdorf Pestalozzi, a group of houses in which more than 200 orphans from many European countries are educated together in an effort to bridge differences of language, religion and outlook.

The Appenzell countryside is rich, being covered with fruit trees and meadows and, as might be expected in such a fertile land, dairying is the major industry. In the spring, when the herds are driven up to the mountain pastures, picturesque festivals are held, and in the fall, when they come down to the valleys again the cow with the greatest milk-yield during the year is fêted and decked with flowers. Hand embroidery is also a specialty of the Appenzell, and few tourists leave without buying some. But don't expect to get a fantastic bargain, the local people are very well aware of the value of their work. In the town of Appenzell itself, the old town hall, dating from 1561, with its folklore museum, is worth seeing. A delightful side trip can be made up the Schwende Valley, by railway or road, to the resort of Wasserauen. From here it is only a short walk to the Seealpsee, one of the loveliest mountain lakes in Switzerland. From Wasserauen you can also take a cable car up the Ebenalp (1,645 metres, 5,400 feet), where there is a splendid viewing point. Similar, equally rewarding, trips can be taken to the summits of the Hoher Kasten, (1,800 metres, 6,000 feet) near Brülisau; and the Kronberg, (1,676 metres, 5,500 feet) at Jakobsbad.

You can return to St. Gallen from Appenzell by a different, slightly longer route, via the resort of Urnasch and Herisau—capital of the half-canton of Appenzell/Outer Rhoden.

Glarus

To the south of St. Gallen is the secluded canton of Glarus, which is marked on its southern border by Mount Tödi, 3,626 metres (11,900 feet) high. Shortly after leaving the lake of Walensee you will join the River Linth, which winds southwards through the canton in its own deep valley. Scattered along it you will find a series of small industrial towns, though they do not interfere with the beauty of the valley itself.

This provides a good foretaste of what you may expect throughout the rest of the canton: alpine pastures, snow-covered peaks, mountain lakes —from the diminutive Ober-See to the equally beautiful Klöntaler-See —figs, vineyards, chamois, and marmots; all wrapped in an aura of isolation.

All this can be found less than 20km. (13 miles) from Glarus, the cantonal capital. This is a small industrial town whose buildings almost all date from after 1861, the result of a disastrous fire. Here, in the disproportionately large Zaunplatz the citizens gather every year on the first Sunday in May, to take part in the Landsgemeinde, the open air parliament.

Schaffhausen

Schaffhausen, capital of the northernmost canton of Switzerland, is an easy train ride or drive from Zurich or St. Gallen. England's William Cox wrote of the local people, "Here, every person has the mien of content and satisfaction. The cleanliness of the homes and the people is peculiarly striking, and I can trace in all their manners, behavior and dress some strong outlines that distinguish this happy people from neighboring nations. Perhaps it may be prejudice, but I am the more pleased because their first appearance reminds me of my own countrymen, and I could think for a moment that I am in England." It is certainly true that the people of Schaffhausen are far less inhibited and more easy going than most Swiss. The reason they give is that they are not surrounded by mountains, which are said to have the tendency to make the mountain dweller introspective and silent. Another reason may be the fine red wines produced by the region!

A city of about 36,000 inhabitants, Schaffhausen has preserved, like most towns in this area, a medieval aspect. From the early Middle Ages, it was an important depot for river cargoes, as these had to be loaded and unloaded there because of the natural barrier created by the waterfall and rapids. The name Schaffhausen is probably derived from the 'skiffhouses' ranged along the river bank. Rising picturesquely from the water's edge, Schaffhausen, with its numerous oriel windows and fountains, has such an air of antiquity that it is sometimes called the Swiss Nuremberg.

The town is dominated by the 16th-century Munot Castle, perched on a hilltop seemingly made for the purpose. A covered passage links this formidable fortress to the rest of the town, and there is a fine view from its massive tower. In some of the winding streets of the older sections of the town, there are some interesting frescoed houses, notably the Haus Zum Ritter in the Vordergasse, with its 16th-century frescoes by Tobias Stimmer. The Münster, a Romanesque basilica dating from the 11th century, is, however, the chief architectural feature of Schaffhausen. In a small courtyard off the cloisters stands a famous old bell (cast in 1468) that inspired Schiller to write his *Lied von der Glocke*. The adjacent monastery of All Hallows (zu Allerheiligen) has been transformed into a national museum, one of the most important in Switzerland.

Neuhausen and the Falls

On the northern bank of the Rhine, Neuhausen and Schaffhausen, with a combined population of over 40,000, are for all practical purposes the same town, the former being the industrial section. Neuhausen's factories, which make among other things arms, railroad cars and aluminum products, derive at least part of their power from the famous Rhine falls on the southern fringe of the town. Probably the most impressive waterfall in central Europe, it is easy to understand how it inspired an enthusiastic description by John Ruskin. Just above the falls the river is around 150 metres (500 foot) wide, and the drop itself—taken in three giant leaps—measures almost 25 metres (80 feet). The flow of water can reach over 1,200 tons a second; and in the huge rock basin below the fall it seethes and boils angrily.

Probably the best view of the falls is from the grounds of Laufen Castle, almost directly above them on the southern shore. In the castle itself, there is a collection of Swiss carvings worth half an hour of the visitor's time. A path leads down from the castle to a small tunnel in the rock and on to Känzeli, a wooden platform beside the falls. Descending again, you enter through a massive doorway to the Fischetz, another platform overhanging the cascade. You'll need a raincoat here, for the spray is quite heavy. Alternatively, from the center of Schaffhausen a fifteen-minute trolley bus ride will take you to Neuhausen. There, a walk of a couple of hundred yards down a steep lane will bring you to a fine viewpoint on the northern side of the falls. Nearby there's a good restaurant, and a picturesque little Fischerstube, or fisherman's museum, where souvenirs of great salmon catches from the river are to be seen.

The falls are best viewed early on a sunny morning, when the rainbows are all around, or at sunset. On moonlit nights, the effects are exquisite, and often in summer the falls are illuminated to provide an eerie and quite different aspect.

En Route to Constance

From Schaffhausen, many visitors prefer to go on by river steamer to Constance and Kreuzlingen, a splendid trip scenically taking about four hours. There are boats two or three times a day, depending on the season. The train and highway both follow the same route and, of course, take less time.

Leaving Schaffhausen, the steamer passes the old convent of Paradies on the starboard side. Nearby, is the spot where the Austrian army under Archduke Charles is said to have crossed the Rhine in 1799; and farther on, near Diessenhofen, is the historic crossing point used by the French army in 1800, before the battle of Hohenlinden. The scenery along the river banks changes continually: forests and vineyards, trim little medieval villages, and stern old fortified castles. Diessenhofen, called Gunodorum by the Romans, has a lovely old clock tower and houses dating from the 16th and 17th centuries.

Stein-am-Rhein, where the river starts to widen out into the lower parts of Lake Constance, is one of the most picturesque medieval towns in Switzerland. Near the northern shore is the old hilltop castle of Hohenklingen, approached by a steep road. From the battlements, you can get a superb view of the river, the lake beyond, and the surrounding countryside, as well as the little gem of the town below. Lining the streets of Stein-am-Rhein, particularly the main street (Hauptgasse) and the town hall square (Rathausplatz), is an unrivaled collection of quaint houses rich in oriel windows and elaborate frescoes. The town hall has a museum of arms and stained glass, much from the 16th and 17th centuries, which is also well worth a visit.

The 15th-century Sonne, distinguished by a medieval emblem of the sun, provides delightful surroundings in which to enjoy a good dinner or simply a glass of white Steiner or red Rheinhalder wine, both native to the region. Immediately below is a fountain with a statue of a Swiss mercenary leaning on his pike, surrounded by beds of flowers. All the houses opposite are adorned by their owners' coats of arms painted in bright colors.

A short distance up the river, past the last bridge over the Rhine before Lake Constance, is the Benedictine monastery of St. George, built in 1005 and well-preserved. A curious old monument with a lovely cloister, it also has a small museum open to the public and featuring some fine examples of woodwork and old paintings. As the river widens into the Untersee—the southwestern branch of Lake Constance—the boat passes the Isle of Werd, on which you can see the beautiful old chapel of St. Othmar. Opposite lies the village of Eschenz, the castles of Freudenfels and Liebenfels, and the one-time monastery of Oehningen. On the Swiss side, at the foot of a chain of hills, picturesque villages succeed one another. Between Mammern and Steckborn, in a small bay, is the little summer resort of Glarisegg, located in the middle of a large natural park. Steckborn is dominated by the imposing Turmhof Castle, built in 1342, and has some fine old houses, including the Baronenhaus and the Gerichtshaus.

In the middle of the Untersee is the German island of Reichenau, about 3 km. (2 miles) long and 1.5 km. (1 mile) wide. Charles the Fat, great-grandson of Charlemagne, was buried there. The island has three small villages—Mittelzell, Unterzell and Oberzell—and there is an interesting Romanesque basilica at Niederzell. On the Swiss side of the lake, and behind the village of Mannenbach (nearly opposite Reichenau), is the castle of Arenenberg. There, from 1818, Hortense de Beauharnais, formerly Queen of Holland, lived with her son, who was later to become Emperor Napoleon III. After the fall of the Empire, Empress Eugénie stayed there for some time before giving it to the canton of Thurgau in 1906. Nowadays, it is a museum containing numerous souvenirs of the Second Empire. Nearby are two additional châteaux with Napoleonic memories. In Salenstein, which was at one time the traditional residence of the Abbot of Reichenau and which dates from the 12th century, the Duchess of Dino, a companion of Hortense de Beauharnais, went to live in 1817. Eugensberg Castle was built four years later by Eugène de Beauharnais, the son of the Empress Joséphine, and born before she married Napoleon.

Not far beyond Ermatingen, the Untersee quickly narrows to become, at Gottlieben, a riverlike channel which, on the other side of the German city of Constance, joins the main body of the lake. The Dominican monastery at Gottlieben is where the Protestant reformers John Huss and Jerome of Prague were imprisoned in the 15th century by order of the Emperor Sigismund and Pope John XXII. Pope John was himself confined in the same castle a few years later.

Constance—Over the German Border

The German city of Constance (population about 170,000), with its Swiss suburb of Kreuzlingen, dominates the straits. It is on the Swiss side of the lake, but in 1805 was ceded to Baden by the Treaty of Pressburg. In Roman days it was known as Constantia, and its name in German now is Konstanz. As a focal point for many of the main alpine passes into Italy it achieved early significance as a trading center, and has had a long and turbulent history. Together with the Gottlieben monastery, it is alive with memories of John Huss, burnt at the stake in 1415 by order of the Council of Constance. His house in the Hussenstrasse bears his effigy, and in the cathedral, visitors can see the spot on which he stood when the sentence was delivered. Kneeling before his accusers, he cried, 'Lord Jesus, forgive my enemies'. Those who revere his memory say that the stone on which he knelt always remains dry, even when those around it are damp. Protestantism having gained the upper hand only temporarily in the 16th century, Constance is now mainly Catholic.

The Münster, or cathedral, of Constance, was founded in 1052, but did not begin to assume its present form until the start of the 15th century. The Gothic tower at the west end was erected in 1850. From the platforms around the openwork spire, there is a magnificent view of the town, the lake, the valley of the Rhine and the Austrian mountains. The oak doors of the chief entrance are decorated with reliefs by Simon Haider, dating from 1470 and representing scenes in the life of Christ. The nave is supported by sixteen monolithic pillars, and the choir stalls are handsomely carved. The cathedral contains the tomb of Robert Hallam, Bishop of Salisbury, and in the ancient crypt, there is a representation in stone of the Holy Sepulcher.

Other points of interest in Constance include the Konzilgebäude, where the Council of Constance held its sittings; the Renaissance town hall (Rathaus), with historical frescoes on its façade; the Rosgarten Museum, notable for its prehistoric Roman and medieval collections; and the monument to Count Zeppelin, whose famous airships were built near Friedrichshafen on the other side of the lake. In the market square stands the house in front of which the Emperor Sigismund gave Frederick of Nuremberg the 'March' of Brandenburg in 1417. And another old house, inscribed with the words 'Curia Pacis', is said to be where peace was signed between Barbarossa and the Lombardy city-states in 1183. Outside the town is the Field of Bruhl, where John Huss was burned at the stake in 1415 and Jerome of Prague a year later. The spot is marked by a rough monument of stones.

Constance is a good center for excursions, with steamer services to many of the towns and resorts around Lake Constance itself and on Ueberlingensee, its northwestern branch. You can get steamers in the adjacent Swiss town of Kreuzlingen for excursions to the Untersee and down the Rhine to Schaffhausen.

If it were not for the frontier stations in the connecting streets, it would be difficult to know where the German city of Constance ends and Swiss Kreuzlingen begins. There is no difficulty in walking from one to the other, but a valid passport is necessary (although, in some cases, an identity card is accepted). Kreuzlingen, much smaller than Constance, has a picturesque old quarter. In what was formerly an Augustine priory, founded in the 10th century by Bishop Conrad of Constance, there is now a teachers' training college. The original building was destroyed during the Thirty Years' War and the present structure built shortly afterwards. In the chapel a magnificent piece of woodcarving, the Passion of Kreuzlingen, contains many hundreds of separate sculptured figures, all the work of one anonymous Tyrolean craftsman. Also on view is an embroidered vest, adorned with pearls, presented to a local dignitary by the medieval antipope Pope John XXIII, when he came to Constance in 1414.

Lake Constance

Called the Bodensee in German, Lake Constance is about 65km. (40 miles) long and 15km. (almost 10 miles) wide; making it second in size only to Lake Geneva. Since it is not protected by mountains it is turbulent in stormy weather and even on fine days is apt to be hazy. Thus it has a gloomy, brooding aspect, in contrast to the jewel-like quality of other Swiss lakes; but many visitors find that this makes it more romantic. Certainly it abounds in lore of a more lurid type than is usual in Switzerland—tales of smuggling and fleeing refugees, rather than poetry and William Tell. One of these stories relates that after the war a group of contraband runners were found to be operating a submarine in its waters, and running a highly profitable trade between Germany and Switzerland. The local geography favors this sort of thing, since the frontiers of three countries—Switzerland, Austria, and Germany—run down the middle of the lake.

Turning to more everyday activities, Constance provides excellent opportunities for fishing (either trout or whitefish), and is frequented by over 70 species of birds. From its shores can be seen both the Appenzell and the Vorarlberg Alps, the latter being in Austria.

The German island of Mainau, the former home of the Grand Duke of Baden and also the residence of Prince Lennart Bernadotte, (nephew of the late King Gustav VI Adolf of Sweden), is about 6km. (4 miles) north of Constance. Connected to the mainland by a bridge, it can be reached from Constance either through a wood or by lake steamer. It has a remarkable garden of subtropical vegetation, reminiscent of the most beautiful Italian gardens, a product of the exceptionally mild climate of the area.

On the opposite shore of Lake Constance, again in Germany, is the town of Friedrichshafen, a pleasant town with a population of around 53,000, a castle that was formerly the summer home of the Kings of Württemberg, and a notable exhibition of Zeppelin mementos in the municipal museum. Farther along the lake, still on the German side, is the splendidly situated little town of Lindau with some 25,000 inhabitants. Approached by rail over a causeway or by road over a long bridge, Lindau was once a powerful fortress, an Imperial city and, in ancient times, the site of a Roman fortification. Its town hall, although much restored in 1887, dated from the 15th century.

Back to Switzerland

After our brief excursion to some of the German parts of the lake, let us return once more to Switzerland, at Kreuzlingen. From here, as we proceed southeast along the shore of the lake, we come first to Bottighofen, and then to Münsterlingen, which has a former Benedictine convent, founded in the 10th century although rebuilt in the 18th. It is now a hospital for the canton of Thurgau. A little beyond it, on a hill overlooking the lake, is the pretty village of Altnau; then in rapid succession, Güttingen, Kesswil, Uttwil and, finally, Romanshorn. The latter is a small industrial town and an important ferry port for Friedrichshafen, but also a surprisingly pleasant place with fine views of the mountains of Switzerland and Austria.

Halfway to Rorschach, the town and resort of Arbon (known to the Romans as Arbor Felix) lies on a little promontory jutting out into the lake and surrounded by lovely meadows and orchards. It was a Celtic town before the Romans came in the year 60 BC and built military fortifications. There is a medieval château, which is now public property and so open to visitors. The St. Gallus church, with its fine stained-glass windows, and St. Martin's Church are both worth seeing. The latter is late Gothic and has an interesting collection of relics dating from the days of the Romans.

Rorschach

Rorschach, in the canton of St. Gallen and with 10,000 inhabitants, is the largest port on the Swiss side of the lake. It is on a small, well-protected bay at the foot of the Rorschacherberg, a beautiful 883 meters (2,900 foot) mountain covered with orchards, pine forests and little meadows. Rorschach carries on a thriving trade with Germany, and the imposing Kornhaus, built by the convent of St. Gallen in 1746, indicates what was for generations the nature of that trade. The building is in baroque style and has an interesting little folklore museum. The village church (1667) is also baroque. Near the town is the Dornier factory and Altenrhein, a small airport capable of accommodating both land-based planes and seaplanes.

One can make a number of scenic excursions from the town of Rorschach. On the surrounding hills, there are several old castles, and a good road leads to the ancient abbey of Mariaberg, built by the abbots of St. Gallen and now used as a school. Nearby is St. Anna Castle, long inhabited by the lords of Rorschach and restored during the early part of the last century. Although it is not open to visitors, the Duke of Parma's château of Wartegg, formerly the summer residence of the

Prince of Hohenzollern, is worth seeing from outside, and the ascent of the Rossbüchel, 959 meters (3,150 feet), is rewarded with an excellent view of the Rhätikon and Vorarlberg mountains.

There are two railroad stations in Rorschach, the main station and another smaller one, by the port in the town center, from which the cogwheel trains climb up to Heiden. Only 5.5km. (3.5 miles) long, the train's route ascends through lovely orchards, past old castles and over a number of viaducts, disclosing beautiful views of the valleys, mountains and the upper Rhine. Heiden itself is 790 meters (2,600 feet) high, and is situated on a sunlit terrace surrounded by meadows and nicely wooded hills. The village was almost entirely destroyed by fire in 1838 and was rebuilt to a uniform pattern (but in traditional style), so that it has a neat charm. It is a well-known health resort, with carbonic acid and brine baths, electrotherapy, massage and other treatments. It also has a famous Kursaal with frequent concerts. Henri Dunant, founder of the Red Cross, spent many years working in the local hospital.

Another interesting trip from Rorschach is to St. Margrethen, where, in 1900, the Swiss and Austrian governments undertook important engineering works to regulate the Rhine's flow. Two long cuts were made, one at St. Margrethen, and another, a little farther south, between Altstätten and Diepoldsau. These enable the river to flow straight into Lake Constance instead of winding around the countryside to join the lake at Altenrhein.

From Rorschach, the end of this tour, both rail and road links lead to Zurich, via St. Gallen, or through Bad Ragaz to the Grisons.

PRACTICAL INFORMATION FOR EASTERN SWITZERLAND

HOTELS AND RESTAURANTS. Nearly all the hotels that we include in our listings below have a wide range of rooms, a good many of which may well fall into a lower grading than that which we have given here. The best advice is always to check beforehand with the hotel (we have provided phone numbers to facilitate this).

APPENZELL. *Säntis* (M), tel. 872644. Historic building; riding. *Hecht* (I), tel. 871025. Central; skittles. *Taube* (I), tel. 871149. Small and inexpensive with sauna; central but quiet.

Restaurant. *Säntis* (I–M), in hotel (see above). Local specialties, river trout, Appenzell wine. Graded "excellent".

EASTERN SWITZERLAND

ARBON. *Metropol* (M), tel. 463535. Beside Lake Constance; with roof garden, outdoor pool and sailing school.

BAD RAGAZ. (All inclusive). *Grand Hotel Hof Ragaz* (L), tel. 90131. Cure facilities; comfortable. *Quellenhof* (L), tel. 90111. In park with cure facilities, golf and tennis. *Cristal* (E), tel. 92877. Indoor pool and sauna; near the station. *Ochsen* (M), tel. 91428. Central with gymnasium and TV in all rooms. *Park* (M), tel. 92244. *Quelle* (I) tel. 91113. Central. Garden, terrace. Diet meals. *Traube* (I), tel. 91460. Small hotel in own grounds; ideal for children.
Restaurant. *National* (M), tel. 91304. The veal soufflé is famous—and there's game during the open season.

BRAUNWALD. (All inclusive). *Bellevue* (E), tel. 843841. Tennis, sauna, indoor pool; good for children. *Alpina* (M), tel. 843284. Marvelous view from the restaurant; quiet. *Tödiblick* (M), tel. 841236. Quiet hotel in park.
Restaurants. *Alpenblick* (I–M), tel. 841544. Scampi, snails, frogs' legs à la provençale, porterhouse T-bone steak. *Rubschen* (I–M), tel. 841534. French cuisine.

FLUMSERBERG. (All inclusive). *Alpina* (M), tel. 31232. Quiet and in own grounds. *Gauenpark* (M), tel. 33131. Indoor pool and bowls.

GLARUS. *Glarnerhof* (I), tel. 614106. Historic building; central and quiet. *Stadthof* (I), tel. 616366. Central. Facilities for the handicapped.

HEIDEN. *Krone-Schweizerhof* (M), tel. 911127. Central hotel in own grounds with pool. *Linde* (I), tel. 911414. Central and quiet.

HORN. *Bad Horn* (M), tel. 415511. Lakeside hotel in own grounds.

KREUZLINGEN. *Elmont-Plaza* (M), tel. 726868. *Bahnhof-Post* (I), tel. 727972. *Emmishofen* (I), tel. 726060. A superior inexpensive hotel; quiet, and with skittle-alley.
Restaurants. *Gasthaus Burg* (I-M), tel. 751822. Closed Wednesday all day, Thursday to 5. *Schäfli* (I-M), tel. 722228. In town center; with a quiet garden.

NEUHAUSEN. *Bellevue* (M), tel. 22121. Overlooks the Rhine falls.

RAPPERSWIL. *Schwanen* (M), tel. 277777. Centrally located in historic building. *Schiff* (I), tel. 273888. Delightful small hotel in attractive building. *Speer* (I), tel. 271720. Small and quiet; atmospheric.
Restaurants. *Eden* (E), tel. 271221. Graded "excellent" in *Passeport Bleu*. Fish and meat specialties. Gastronomic menus Fr.60 to Fr.80. *Hirschen* (M), tel. 276624. Fillets of perch, *Hainanese Mah Mee*, soufflé Grand Marnier.

ROMANSHORN. *Parkhotel Inseli* (M), tel. 635353. Central but very quiet; in own grounds. *Seehotel* (I), tel. 634294. Lakeside location; quiet and in own grounds. Breakfast only.

RORSCHACH. *Waldau* (E), tel. 430180. Indoor tennis, two pools (indoor and outdoor), sauna and gym; very quiet and comfortable. *Anker* (I), tel. 414243. Lakeside hotel with waterskiing and sailing; central.
Restaurant. *Bahnhofbuffet* (M), terrace on lake; has own wines and fish specialties.

ST. GALLEN. *Hecht am Marktplatz* (E), tel. 226502. Attractive hotel with dancing and excellent restaurant; central. *Walhalla beim Bahnhof* (E), tel. 222922. Near the station; comfortable. *Continental* (M), tel. 278811. Central. *Dom* (M), tel. 232044. Breakfast only; comfortable and friendly hotel near the cathedral. *Ekkehard* (I), tel. 224714. Central; with bowling. *Sonne Rotmonten* (I), tel. 244342. Quiet and comfortable.
Restaurants. *Schnäggehüsli* (Snail Shell) (E), tel. 256525. Snail soup, salmon trout, homemade pâté. *Walhalla* (M), in hotel (see above). Graded "excellent" in *Passeport Bleu*. *Schwarzer Bären* (M), tel. 247497.

SCHAFFHAUSEN. *Kronenhof* (M), tel. 56631. Quiet and central. *Bahnhof* (I), tel. 54001. Quiet and central, with facilities for the handicapped. *Parkvilla* (I), tel. 52737. Central but very quiet; tennis.

TROGEN. *Krone* (I), tel. 941304. Small hotel in historic building.

UNTERWASSER. *Säntis* (E), tel. 52811. With indoor pool and sauna. *Sternen* (I), tel. 52424. Dancing in evenings. Facilities for the handicapped.

WEESEN. *Parkhotel Schwert* (I), tel. 431474. Quiet and central, with marvelous view from the restaurant.

WILDHAUS. (All inclusive). *Acker* (E), tel. 59111. Indoor pool, sauna and gymnasium; good for children. *Hirschen* (E), tel. 52252. Pool and sauna. *Toggenburg* (M), tel. 52323.

WIL. *Schwanen* (I), tel. 220155. Central. Grill and snack bar.

USEFUL ADDRESS. Tourist Information: Verkehrsverband Ostschweiz (VVO), Bahnhofplatz 1a, Postfach 475, St. Gallen 9001, (tel. 071–226262).

EASTERN SWITZERLAND

MUSEUMS. Rapperswil. *Heimatmuseum.* Brenyhaus, am Herrenberg. Important folklore-ethnic collection.

St. Gallen. *Historical Museum,* Museumstr. 50. Outstanding cultural and historical collection, arts sacred and profane, arms, flags, silverwork. *Textilmuseum,* Vadianstr. 2. Important textiles collection. European lace and embroidery.

Schaffhausen. *Museum Allerheiligen,* Klosterplatz 1. A major collection of the arts and crafts: manuscripts, paintings, painted glass, gold- and silverwork, costumes, arms, flags, uniforms.

WINTER SPORTS. Eastern Switzerland is dotted with resorts catering to downhill and cross-country skiers, as well as those who prefer tobogganing, skating and curling.

Appenzell, 820 meters (2,700 feet); 3 cable cars and 14 lifts, 30 km. of downhill runs, 99 km. of cross-country trails, 41 km. of ski-hiking; trails, ski schools.

Bad Ragaz, 517 meters (1,700 feet); 2 cable cars, 3 lifts, 12 km. of downhill runs, 3 km. of cross-country trails; ski schools.

Braunwald, 1,250 meters–1,460 meters (4,100–4,800 feet); 1 funicular railway, 1 cable car, 5 lifts, 20 km. of downhill runs, 6 km. of cross-country trails; curling, ski bob, ski schools.

Flumserberg, 1,005 meters–1,310 meters (3,300–4,300 feet); 2 cable cars, 14 lifts, 55 km. of downhill runs, 6 km. of cross-country trails, 17 km. of ski-hiking trails; skating, curling, ski bob, ski schools.

Glarus, 485 meters (1,600 feet); 1 lift, 1 km. of downhill runs, 8 km. of trails for cross-country skiing; skating.

Heiden, 820 meters (2,700 feet); 3 lifts, less than 1 km. of downhill ski runs but 18 km. of cross-country trails and 50 km. of ski-hiking trails; ski schools.

St. Gallen, 670 meters (2,200 feet); 13 km. of cross-country trails and 1.3 km. of tobogganing trails; ski bob, ski schools.

Schaffhausen, 410 meters (1,350 feet); 16 km. of cross-country trails, 30 km. of ski-hiking trails; skating, curling.

Unterwasser, 305 meters (3,000 feet); 1 funicular railway, 1 cable car, 3 lifts, 47 km. of downhill runs, 18 km. of cross-country trails, 15 km. of ski-hiking trails; ski bob, tobogganing, ski schools.

Wildhaus, 500 meters (3,650 feet); 1 funicular railway, 1 cable car, 13 lifts, 50 km. of downhill runs, 45 km. of cross-country trails, 30 km. of ski-hiking trails; skating, curling, ski schools.

LIECHTENSTEIN

Postage-Stamp Principality

Crossing over from the world's oldest living democracy into a monarchy that is the last remnant of the Holy Roman Empire is the easiest thing in the world for anyone driving along the Swiss Rhine valley, between Lake Constance and the Grisons. You turn east at the right moment, cross a bridge, and there you are, smack in the middle of the realm of His Highness, Franz Josef II, Maria Alois Alfred Karl Johann Heinrich Michael George Ignatius Benediktus Gerhardus Majella, Prince von und zu Liechtenstein, Duke of Troppau and Jaegerndorf, and last of the hundreds of reigning kings, princes, dukes, and counts who once populated the map of the Holy Roman Empire.

His Highness rules as a constitutional monarch over only 96 square kilometers (61 square miles) and about 26,000 loyal subjects, but don't let appearances fool you. Liechtenstein may look like nothing but an oversized Alpine resort, with its gentle wooded hills in the north, fertile Rhine valley in the west, and craggy mountains in the east. But actually Liechtenstein is a complete state, with a sound and diversified economy and a prosperous people who can easily afford their friendly smiles and easy going ways, considering their glowing state of affairs.

Liechtensteiners insist that their case is different from other miniature states. They are not just the product of rivalries from great powers, a buffer zone between France and Spain like Andorra; nor are they tolerated only for curiosity's sake, as San Marino is by Italy; neither are they in danger of being swallowed by a bigger power if they lose their ruler, as in Monaco. They could depose their prince any day and continue as a free republic. But they won't because the house of Liechtenstein has proved a lucky charm.

A Hobby for the Man Who Has Everything

It all started at the end of the 17th century, when a wealthy Austrian prince, Johann Adam von Liechtenstein, bought up two bankrupt counts in the Rhine valley, united their lands, and in 1719 obtained an imperial deed, creating the Principality of Liechtenstein. In January 1969, Liechtenstein celebrated its 250th anniversary.

At that time the Liechtenstein family was already a power in the Holy Roman Empire. From the time of Hugo of Liechtenstein, a knight in the 12th century with a modest castle near Vienna, their wealth and power had grown consistently. In 1608 they were elevated to Princes of the empire, and when Johann Adam bought his new lands in the Rhine valley, he was already one of the richest men in Europe. The new principality was but a small fraction of the land all over the Austro-Hungarian Empire that belonged to the Liechtenstein family. Yet it suited his purpose to have a moderate-sized territory and thus qualify for a vote in the Diet of the Princes.

The new principality became the hobby of the wealthy Liechtenstein family. Although they spent most of their time at the glittering imperial court of Vienna or on their estates in Austria, Bohemia, Moravia, and Hungary, they spent most of their money on Liechtenstein. For many decades the rulers played the same role for their principality that the Monte Carlo gambling casino did for Monaco. If something went wrong with the budget, the prince took out his checkbook and asked, 'How much?'.

The champion spender was probably Prince Johann II, who reigned for a full 71 years (almost a record) until his death in 1929. He gave away the equivalent of about 75 million Swiss francs of his private fortune, some to charity, but most of it to make Liechtenstein a better place to live in. None of this huge amount came out of Liechtenstein's taxes.

Speaking of money, contrary to the popular impression Liechtensteiners do pay taxes, but these are moderate by international standards and are one of the reasons for Liechtenstein's economic boom in the last three decades. The principality has little difficulty finding capital for investments and has become the seat of numerous international holding and finance corporations. The new income from the economic boom is amply sufficient to make up for the former large subsidies from the private fortune of the princes.

The old saying that the Liechtenstein family may have a Principality on the Rhine, but a kingdom in Bohemia, is no longer true. World War I threatened misfortune in view of Liechtenstein's close links with the crumbling Austro-Hungarian Empire, but the little country bailed out just in time in 1918 and started the drift towards Switzerland that ended in the complete customs and monetary union of 1924. The Liechtenstein family recovered most of its fortune, then scattered over the new states that succeeded the Austro-Hungarian monarchy. From land, castles, jewelry, and the fabulous Liechtenstein gallery (probably the most valuable private collection of paintings in the world) they diversified their holdings into industry and blue-chip stocks.

The situation looked much gloomier after World War II when communist Czechoslovakia and Hungary expropriated the land holdings of the prince and offered a 'final settlement' of only about 6 or 7 percent of the actual value. Prince Franz Josef II, who had succeeded his childless uncle Franz I in 1938, proudly declined to sell what he regarded as his inalienable rights for some ready cash. But the Liechtenstein family is by no means impoverished. They still own large estates in Austria, the choicest vineyards in Liechtenstein, their art gallery, and a bank at their capital, Vaduz, which is doing brisk business with all the foreign corporations in town.

The Prince and His Family

Under these circumstances, nobody will doubt the sincerity of the prayers and congratulations that echoed through Liechtenstein in the summer of 1956, when 15,000 persons, almost as much as the official population at that time, gathered twice at Vaduz. First they celebrated the 50th birthday of their ruler (he was born on August 16th 1906, at one of the family's Austrian castles, Frauenthal in Styria,) and then the 150th anniversary of Liechtenstein's sovereign independence. This first came in 1806 when Austria's Emperor Franz II gave up his Imperial Crown, thus dissolving the Holy Roman Empire, to which Liechtenstein had previously owed allegiance. In 1815 Liechtenstein joined the

German Confederation but once again, in 1866, it regained the full sovereign independence which it still enjoys to this day.

Although Liechtensteiners could be sure of continuing as an independent state (and a prosperous one) even without a prince, they have no wish to do so and are understandably eager to leave things as they are. Fortunately they are spared one headache, the question of succession. The Liechtensteins are a prolific stock, and history knows no instance when His Highness' loyal subjects were worried about being left with a vacant throne. In the few cases of childless reigning princes there were always plenty of brothers or nephews around.

One of those nephews is the present ruling prince—Franz Josef II. In the tradition of his house he was the eldest of eight children and is the doting father of four sons and a daughter: Hereditary Prince Johann Adam Pius, Prince Philipp Erasmus, Prince Nikolaus Ferdinand, Prince Franz Josef Wenzel and Princess Nora Elisabeth. Their father has been careful to educate them in the democratic ways proper to the constitutional monarch of a small, freedom-loving country. The children were sent to the public elementary school at Vaduz, together with other Liechtensteiners. The boys then went on to Vienna's Catholic 'Schotten Gymnasium', Franz Josef's own prep school, where many generations of Liechtensteiners were educated by the learned padres of the Scottish Brothers order.

Sending the boys to Vienna for schooling was also useful in making them familiar with Austria, where the family still owns large estates and where they have hundreds of relatives by blood and by marriage in the Viennese aristocracy. For in spite of their democratic ways the Liechtensteiners are bluebloods indeed. The mother of the reigning prince was a Habsburg archduchess; a half-sister of that unfortunate heir to the Austrian throne, Archduke Franz Ferdinand, whose murder in 1914 was one of the incidents that touched off World War I.

In July 1967, during a week of nation-wide festivity, Liechtenstein saw a dazzling array of aristocratic Europe, when some 800 official guests—and many thousands of unofficial visitors—invaded the country to see the wedding (on Sunday July 30th in Vaduz Church) of Crown Prince Johann Adam to Countess Kinsky, member of an old Bohemian family now living in Bavaria.

Vaduz and Its Castle

Objectively speaking, Vaduz castle, although outwardly a jewel of medieval architecture, was at one time anything but an inviting place to live in. Starting in 1905 the gloomy, thick-walled fortress on a cliff overlooking Vaduz was completely renovated, and today it really is fit for a prince, lavishly furnished with costly antiques, tapestries, and valuable works of art. The famous Gothic bedroom contains furniture already antique when Columbus sailed for America.

But with all the money and care that went into redecorating the castle, Franz Josef II was the first reigning prince to take up permanent residence there. When Franz Josef succeeded his uncle in 1938, he was 32 and still unmarried, but the Liechtensteiners relaxed and rejoiced with him when their new ruler met the Countess Georgina Wilczek in Vienna. The phlegmatic, taciturn prince was properly impressed by vivacious 'Gina', one of the reigning belles of Viennese aristocracy. Legend has it that he first met her in a modern version of Andersen's fairytale about the princess and the swineherd; when she was pressed into the Nazi labor service during the war and had to work on a farm. In any case, they were married on March 3rd 1943, and to all appearances have lived happily ever after.

The prince leaves the ruling of his country to a democratically elected diet of 15 men, but works away at increasing his country's fortune and his own. Friends say he would have made an excellent investment banker, and he knows quite a lot about agriculture and forestry too, holding a university degree as a forestry engineer.

At the same time Princess Gina has given Liechtenstein a court, an institution that was sorely missed for many decades. The princess completed the new regime that started with the redecoration of the castle by making it the center of Liechtenstein's life. A continuous stream of guests from Liechtenstein and abroad and frequent return visits of members of the royal family to the homes of local notables have given tiny Vaduz a taste of society and have forged strong bonds between the people and their ruler.

There is still a considerable difference between Vaduz and most other courts, even certain small ones. The prince dislikes pomp. Donning a fancy uniform with gold braid or playing with crown and scepter would seem perfectly ghastly to him. Even the jubilee stamps, issued on the occasion of his 50th birthday, show him with only an ermine-collared cape and a heavy gold chain as signs of his office, over a simple white tie and tails . . . there is no sign of the crown.

The royal family follows an unostentatious style, shunning Cadillacs and Rolls-Royces and preferring cars of medium size. This kind of life strikes just the right note with Liechtenstein's hardworking, soberminded citizens. They have much of the democratic 'no-nonsense' attitude of the neighboring Swiss, but they gladly combine it with a little sparkle from the faint imperial glitter that still hangs over their other neighbor, Austria.

The Role of Switzerland

The political marriage of the principality with republican Switzerland has proved advantageous in every way. Except for Swiss economic policy, which extends to Liechtenstein more or less automatically by way of the customs union, there is absolutely no Swiss interference in Liechtenstein's politics and Liechtenstein is perfectly free to dissolve the customs, monetary, and postal union any time. Switzerland also represents Liechtenstein abroad; the only Liechtenstein minister accredited to a foreign government is the one at the Swiss capital, Bern. But the Swiss can act only with Liechtenstein's consent. They cannot enter into any agreement affecting Liechtenstein against that country's will.

Military service was abolished as long ago as 1868. Liechtenstein's present armed might consists of three dozen regular police and some three dozen men in an auxiliary police force. In those dangerous years before and during World War II, when Hitler annexed Austria and wanted to unite all German-speaking countries into one Reich, Swiss influence, along with the Prince's own urgent diplomatic efforts, succeeded in keeping Liechtenstein out of the conflict, but there was no attempt to press Liechtenstein into reintroducing military service.

During the last three and a half decades Liechtenstein has also participated in Switzerland's economic boom. The farm population has shrunk from 60 percent of the total 30 years ago to 3 percent now. Today, the Liechtenstein government is even a little wary of new investments because there are no longer sufficient Liechtensteiners to fill all jobs, and the high percentage of foreign workers employed has created serious problems. Another problem was the protection of the landscape. The government has succeeded there. The factories (their products range from calculating machines to false teeth) are tucked away unobtrusively, and with their clean white-and-glass facades look more like modernistic hotels.

So the Liechtensteiners continue to get the best of two worlds, a democratic freedom, peace, and prosperity like their Swiss neighbors, and a feeling of security from a dignified Prince, a heartening symbol of their independence, who gives much to his country and seeks little in return. Visiting Liechtenstein for its scenery is pleasant, but even more rewarding is the experience of being among people who have found a secure balance in a world of imbalance, a formula for taking the best of old worlds and new alike and making it into a way of life that is today all too rare.

Exploring Liechtenstein

Like ancient Gaul, Liechtenstein is divided into three parts: first the so-called lowlands, about 16 square kilometers (10 square miles) of wooded hills in the north; next, the flat Rhine valley in the southwest with its eastern slope rising towards the first ridge of mountains; and lastly the mountainous area between the first ridge and the second one which forms a natural border with Austria.

Exploring Liechtenstein, you should start at the capital, Vaduz, about halfway between the northern and southern extremities of the country. Vaduz is the political and natural center of the flat, fertile country along the Rhine. About three-quarters of Liechtenstein's population live in the five communal districts from Schaan, where road and railroad cross the Rhine from Switzerland, to Balzers in the south, where you can cross back into Switzerland via a bridge or via the scenic Luziensteig road on the eastern bank.

The 14 kilometers (nine miles) of road from Schaan to Mäls, the southernmost hamlet, are Liechtenstein's economic showcase. Neat farms, inns, houses, old churches and new schools line the road. Through the gaps on one side you can see the Rhine flats with their rich fields and orchards; on the other, creeping up the wooded slopes, are vineyards and the villas of the wealthy.

The villa quarter of Vaduz is growing steadily. Low taxes make the principality a pleasant dwelling place for people who have or earn good money without being bound to a certain spot by their jobs. Successful novelists and playwrights form a strong group among the 'new Liechtensteiners'.

The castle of Vaduz completely dominates the town. Perched on a cliff about 90 meters (300 feet) high, it can easily be reached either by car along the road which climbs up from the northern end of Vaduz towards the mountains, or in half an hour by foot. Normally the interior of the castle is out of bounds for tourists, since it is occupied by the royal family and an almost continuous stream of guests. But even if you cannot enter the castle, a visit is worth the trouble. Originally built in the 13th century it was burned down in the Swabian Wars of 1499 and partly rebuilt in the following centuries, until a complete overhaul that started in 1905 gave it its present form. There is another medieval building about ten minutes on foot from the center of town, the Rotes Haus, once a fortress for bailiffs of a Benedictine monastery in Switzerland.

For pleasant walks off the main road try one of the paths down to the Rhine, about half an hour, and then along the river on one of the two levees. Alternatively if you go in the opposite direction, a 40-

LIECHTENSTEIN

minute climb up the hill will bring you to a romantic ruin tucked away in the forest, the Wildschloss, once the seat of robber-barons. Cutting across the slope horizontally you reach the village of Schaan via the scenic Fürstenweg (Prince's Path) in less than an hour.

Schaan, about three kilometers (two miles) north of Vaduz, offers the same choice of walks down to the Rhine and up the mountains, and so does Triesen, also three kilometers from Vaduz, but to the south. Overlooking Triesen is the old St. Mamertus Chapel with quite an extensive view. Between Balzers and Mäls, the two southernmost villages, rises a steep hill bearing Gutenberg Castle, another splendid example of a medieval fortress. Unfortunately, like Vaduz it can be admired only from the outside, being privately owned.

From Vaduz (456 meters, 1,500 feet high) two good but sometimes narrow roads twist and climb steeply up into the mountains past the solidly romantic Vaduz castle (where there's a roadside parking place) and a succession of splendid views across the Rhine valley. At about 883 meters (2,900 feet) you pass the little town of Triesenberg. Beyond the town the road continues to wind upwards and after a couple of kilometers a side road sheers off to the left towards the mountain hotels of Masescha, at 1,250 meters (4,100 feet) and Gaflei. Masescha, Gaflei, nearby Silum and Triesenberg, all clinging to the steep side of the Rhine valley, are unpretentious, do-it-yourself skiing centers in winter and lovely centers for walks in summer.

Gaflei, at 1,460 meters (4,800 feet) is the starting point of the Fürstensteig, a path along the highest ridge between the Rhine and the Samina valley. Winding among and around several peaks which are between 1,800 and 2,000 meters high, it provides a relatively comfortable way of feeling like Sherpa Tenzing without doing any really dangerous climbing. A pair of good shoes is all you need, but don't try the Fürstensteig if you're apt to feel giddy looking down a sheer drop of a couple of thousand feet or so.

Back at the road junction above Triesenberg, if you now drive on towards the mountains you'll shortly pass through a kilometer tunnel under the first mountain ridge and emerge near the village of Steg (1,800 meters, 4,200 feet). Situated in a completely different setting—a high alpine valley, wild, impressive and with rushing mountain streams —Steg in winter is a simple, no-frills skiing center. In summer it becomes an excellent starting point for a wide choice of not-overstrenuous mountain hikes. One is the hike following the Samina river downstream (northwards) and then turning right up the Valorsch valley to Malbun, a roughly simi-circular excursion. Another is up the Samina valley to the Bettlerjoch pass (1,950 meters, 6,400 feet) along a tolerable track, broad enough for jeeps to take provisions up to the Joch alpine shelter, but forbidden to all other motor vehicles.

At the upper end of the Samina Valley experienced climbers can try one of Liechtenstein's highest peaks, the Grauspitz, Schwarzhorn or Naafkopf, each about 2,560 meters (8,400 feet) high.

If you now take the excellent new road which goes eastwards up easy grades beyond Steg you will find that in little more than a couple of miles it ends abruptly at Malbun (1,580 meters, 5,200 feet) a rapidly expanding, higgledy-piggledy village nestling on the floor of a huge mountain bowl. Hitherto little known outside Liechtenstein, in the last few years Malbun has begun to make modest impact on the international winter sports scene thanks to the splendid variety of slopes and the generous network of chairlifts and skilifts which serve them. For beginners it is outstanding, and it was here that the Prince of Wales and Princess Anne learned to ski while they were staying with the princely family at Vaduz castle. Winter finished, Malbun turns into an unpretentious summer resort for those who want complete rest or healthy exercise, plenty of fresh air, and comfortable quarters at a realistic price.

Incidentally, the only way to visit Austria from Liechtenstein via the mountains, without too much climbing, is provided by the path from Malbun to Sareiserjoch (1,860 meters, 6,100 feet) the border pass. If you're a glutton for exercise you'll find it takes about two hours on foot.

There's a regular bus service between Vaduz and Malbun but, if possible go by car—especially in summer. The return journey can take well under two hours including brief viewing stops en route, but leave more time if you can. Provided the weather's good, you'll want to linger.

The part of Liechtenstein least known to tourists is the 'lowland' area in the north, which, despite its name, has some fair-sized and very attractive hills. It's worth driving up to the Schellenberg hills, almost 1,000 meters (3,000 feet) high, where you can get fine views of the broad, flat valley of the Rhine with its steep sides, and gaze at an almost uninterrupted panorama of peaks—the mountains of Liechtenstein, Switzerland and Austria. From your viewpoints you will be able to see most of the little Principality we have just visited.

PRACTICAL INFORMATION FOR LIECHTENSTEIN

GETTING TO LIECHTENSTEIN. By Train. Although a number of European expresses cross Liechtenstein, none actually stops here. The best way to get here then is via the little station at Buchs in St. Gallen Canton or Sargens a little further away and then take the excellent, connecting post buses

LIECHTENSTEIN

into Vaduz. Taxis are available from both Buchs and Sargens, but they are very much more expensive. The bus from Buchs takes about 15 minutes, the bus from Sargens about 45 minutes. If you are coming from Austria, there is a good train service to Feldkirch on the Austrian border. Once you have crossed into Liechtenstein there are similarly good post bus services into Liechtenstein.

By Car. The N13 motorway runs along the Rhine frontier of Liechtenstein and this extends all the way up to Lake Constance in the north and south past Chur. To the west, motorways go most of the way to Zurich, Berne and Basle.

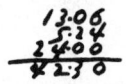

WHAT WILL IT COST. Generally speaking, most prices are on a par with, or sometimes a little lower than, Switzerland. In hotels, full pension with private bathroom (bed, breakfast, two meals, and tips) costs between Fr. 40 to 90 a day per person; in about three hotels slightly more; in a few, even less. Lunch or dinner is about Fr. 16 to 30 in Vaduz, but less in country inns.

FORMALITIES. None, if you enter Liechtenstein from Switzerland. There are no checks. All travel documents valid for Switzerland are also valid for Liechtenstein. For entering Liechtenstein from Austria, the formalities are the same as for entering Switzerland. Swiss customs officials and border police do the checking at the Liechtenstein-Austrian border.

MONEY. The Swiss franc is Liechtenstein's legal tender. Swiss currency regulations and rates of exchange also apply to Liechtenstein.

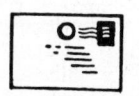

MAIL, TELEPHONE. The Swiss postal system extends to Liechtenstein, with one exception: mail posted in Liechtenstein must bear Liechtenstein stamps. Leichtenstein is famous for finely engraved stamps and frequent new issues. If you have philatelists among your friends, heavy correspondence is indicated. The mail, telegram, and telephone rates are, of course, the same as in Switzerland. Liechtenstein belongs to the automatic Swiss phone system. Any Swiss phone can be reached by simple dialing without the aid of the operator. In the same way you can phone any Liechtenstein number from Switzerland by dialing 075 (the Liechtenstein phone district) and then the listed number.

HOTELS. Nearly all the hotels included in our listings below have a wide range of rooms, a good many of which may well fall into a lower grading than that which we have given. The best advice is always to check with the hotel beforehand. There are no deluxe hotels in Liechtenstein, and most of the best ones are in Vaduz and along the Rhine valley. A Liechtenstein specialty are the mountain inns, all at least 4,000 ft up and all accessible by road.

Although, with one or two exceptions, unpretentious, they are recommended to anyone seeking peace, quiet, and fresh air. Prices for full board are applicable for a stay of three days of more. Most of the hotels and mountain inns are modern and have central heating, and also garages. There are camping grounds at Bendern, Triesen and Vaduz.

BALZERS. *Post* (I), tel. 41208. Small, with bowling and garden. *Römerhof* (I), tel. 41960. Small and inexpensive.

BENDERN. *Deutscher-Rhein* (I), tel. 31347.

ESCHEN. *Brühlhof* (I), tel. 31566. *Eintracht* (I), tel. 31356.

GAMPRIN. *Hotel Waldeck* (I), tel. 31462.

MALBUN. (All inclusive). *Gorfion* (M), tel. 24307. Garden. *Alpenhotel Malbun* (I), tel. 21181. Indoor pool; facilities for children. *Malbunerhof* (I), tel. 22944. Medium-sized hotel with indoor pool, sauna and bowling. *Montana* (I), tel. 27333. Small and central; skittles. *Walserhof* (I), tel. 23396. Small family hotel.

MASESCHA. *Berggasthof Massescha* (I), tel. 22337. 4 rooms only; quiet.

NENDELN. *Engel* (I), tel. 31260. *Landhaus* (I), tel. 32011. Country-style inn.

SCHAAN. *Dux* (I), tel. 21727. Garden; special facilities for children and the handicapped. *Linde* (I), tel. 21704. Quiet and central. *Schaanerhof* (I), tel. 21877. With indoor pool and sauna.

SILUM. *Berggasthof Silum* (I), tel. 21951.

STEG. *AlpenHotel Steg* (I), tel. 22146. Medium-sized hotel; very reasonably priced.

TRIESEN. *Landgasthof Schatzmann* (I), tel. 29070. Recommended.

TRIESENBERG. *Kulm* (I), tel. 28777. Good family hotel. *Martha Büler* (I), tel. 25777. 8 rooms only.

VADUZ. *Park-Hotel Sonnenhof* (E), tel. 21192. Quiet hotel with sauna and indoor pool 5 minutes from town; fine gardens and superb view. *Landhaus Prasch* (I), tel. 24663. Sauna and indoor pool. *Meierhof* (I), tel. 21836. With camping site. *Real* (I–E), tel. 22222. Central and small and highly recommended; excellent food. *Schlössle* (M–E), tel. 25621. Quiet; with skittles. *Engel* (I), tel. 21057. Good inexpensive hotel.

LIECHTENSTEIN 215

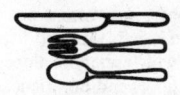

RESTAURANTS. The cuisine is Swiss with Austrian overtones. There are *quite* a few restaurants. In Vaduz, barely 5 minutes' walk from the center, try the *Torkel* restaurant, owned by the prince and surrounded by his vineyards. A good place to sample Vaduzer, the potent local red wine. Food at the *Engel* is highly thought of. Also atmospheric are *The Old Castle Inn* and *Linde*, the latter for a reasonably priced meal. *Café Wolf*, snacks only. Avoid the restaurants in the immediate vicinity of the castle as they are mostly very expensive. In Balzers: *Engel* and *Schlosshof-Gutenberg*. Also, *Post* in Hotel Post, very good and very cheap; and *Roxy*, a snack bar with dancing, no entrance fee, and very reasonable prices. In Triesenberg: *Sanina* and *Edelweiss*. In Malbun: *Scesaplana*. In Eschen: the *Haldenruh* and *Pinocchio*. In Triesen: both the *Linde* and the restaurant in the *Hotel Schäfle* are good. *Maschlina*, has disco dancing and a bar. A good lunch or dinner ranges from about 12 francs in an unsophisticated spot to around 40 or so in the best.

ENTERTAINMENT. There are movie houses at Vaduz and Schaan. There is dancing at the *Vaduzerhof* and *Engel* hotels in Vaduz, *Engel* and *Landhaus,* Nendeln, *Römerhof* at Balzers, and *Waldeck* at Gamprin, as well as at Malbun's *Gorfion, Galina* and *Turna*. Liechtenstein is not much of a place for nightlife.

SHOPPING. Due to the customs union, prices are the same as in Switzerland and you get the same goods. Apart from the usual souvenirs (there are attractive dolls with local costumes) and, of course, the Liechtenstein postage stamps, there is little to tempt you.

MUSEUMS. Largely as a result of the Prince's decision to allow part of his world-famous private collection to be on public display, visitors to Vaduz can always enjoy art exhibitions unmatched by any other community of similar size. Currently occupying the whole top floor of the National Gallery, above the Tourist Office, and beautifully lit and displayed, is a superb collection of the Prince's paintings by Rubens (the highlight of which is a superb cycle of nine huge pictures illustrating the *History of the Roman Consul Publius Decius Meus* and which also includes the same painter's splendid *Toilet of Venus* and the *Little Girl* portrait). The collection is expected to be on display for some time. On the floor below are important loan exhibitions. Admission covering both galleries is approximately Fr. 3.50.

The Historical Museum and Postal Museum are also worth a visit.

SPORTS. There are indoor swimming pools at the Sonnenhof and Landhaus Vaduzerhof hotels in Vaduz, a sauna-massage at the Schlössle and a pool at the Schaanerhof at Schaan, Krone at Schellenberg, the Alpenhotel, Malbunerhof, Gorfion and Turna hotels in Malbun, and at the Tourotel, Gaflei.

Although relatively unknown, Malbun is ideal for winter sports and has a near certainty of good snow. An excellent network of reasonably priced lifts, rarely congested except at high season weekends, serves a wide variety of slopes. The beginners' slopes are unusually good. There are ski schools and experienced guides are available for longer excursions.

Liechtenstein also has some good fishing (trout) streams.

USEFUL ADDRESSES. *Vaduz Tourist Office,* Engländerbau, 9490 Vaduz (tel. 075 21443); *Malbun Tourist Office,* 9497 Malbun-Triesenberg (tel. 075 26577); *Liechtenstein National Tourist Office,* POB 139, 9490 Vaduz (tel. 075 66288).

THE GRISONS AND ENGADINE

Winter Playground of the World

The canton of Grisons rivals the Bernese Oberland as the Swiss region most familiar to winter sports lovers. Here you will find famous resorts such as Arosa, Davos, Flims, Klosters, Lenzerheide, Pontresina, Scuol-Tarasp-Vulpera, and the vast conglomeration of St. Moritz and its satellites. Here the Engadine, the mountain-bordered valley of the River Inn and its chain of lovely lakes, cuts a 25-mile-long swath across the southern part of the Grisons. A land of contrasts, the Grisons has a rich cultural tradition and a vivid history, as well as scenic wonders that leave the visitor groping for superlatives. It has some of the highest and most rugged mountain chains in Europe, a host of silvery Alpine lakes, trout-filled rivers, and no fewer than 150 valleys sheltering a race of hardy peasant folk who are as independent and proud as they are hospitable.

Covering about 7,250 sq. km. (2,800 sq. miles), the canton of the Grisons is the largest in Switzerland and takes in more than one-sixth of the country. Originally the people were known as the 'gray confederates', and it is from this that the Swiss-German name for the canton—Graubünden—is taken. A little more than half the population of 160,000 speak Schwytzerdütsch, a third use Romansch, and the remainder an Italian dialect.

The recorded history of the area goes back as far as 600 BC, when an Etruscan prince named Rhaetus invaded the area and re-named it, unsurprisingly, Rhaetia. It became a Roman province, Rhaetia Prima, in 15 BC, and graves of Rhaetians who fought in the Roman armies have been found as far away as Libya. During the Thirty Years' War, the Grisons were invaded at various times by the armies of Austria, Spain, and France; all of whom sought to control the strategically important passes leading to Italy. From the 15th century onwards the people allied themselves with the Swiss, although it was not until 1803 that they officially entered the Swiss confederation and became the eighteenth Swiss canton.

The principal language of the area is German, but most of the local people have at least a working knowledge of French, Italian, and Romansch. The latter is Switzerland's fourth national language, and it is spoken only in this region. It sounds rather like Portuguese, with a little German thrown in.

The region's economy rests mainly on cattle, wood, and tourism, with the tourists playing the most important role. Internationally it owes its reputation to a few, highly sophisticated, winter playgrounds, patronized by the rich and famous. However, there are over a hundred holiday resorts throughout the region, which cater to all types of interests and budgets.

Exploring the Grisons

The canton is served by the highly efficient Swiss road system, and public transport is provided by the bright yellow post buses. In addition there is a rail network, centering on the Rhaetian narrow gauge line. This fascinating little railway runs for 386 km. (240 miles), using some 480 bridges and 117 tunnels. It is possible to combine a trip on this line—using some bus connections—with a circular tour of the canton. Alternatively the trip can be completed by car.

Begin by traveling north on the Rhaetian Railroad, from the provincial capital of Chur to Landquart, and then east to Klosters and Davos. From Davos take the Flüela Pass road to Susch, and then travel

THE GRISONS AND ENGADINE

northeast, by either bus or train, to Scuol. From here you can take a diversion, again by bus, to the castle of Tarasp. From Scuol head southwest to St. Moritz, where there is another possible side trip, to Muottas Muragl. Back on the main route take the bus north to Tiefencastel, traveling via the Julier Pass. Here, rejoining the Rhaetian Railway, you loop westwards to Thusis and Reichenau, and back to Chur.

This tour takes a good twelve hours' traveling time, so that with stopovers it should be undertaken only if the traveler can devote at least two full days to it. However, by eliminating the trip from Susch to Scuol and Tarasp, and returning directly to Chur from St. Moritz via the Albula Pass, the tour could at a pinch be shortened to a one-day jaunt. But by rushing hell-bent through the Grisons you will miss much of the region's fascination and get only a superficial glance at its fabulous scenery, something for which you may find it hard to forgive yourself when you return home.

Chur

Chur, the capital city of the Grisons, is generally considered to be the oldest continuously settled site in Switzerland; there are traces of habitation as far back as 2,500–3,000 BC. The Romans had a settlement here too which they founded in 15 BC and called Curia Raetorum. It was used to protect the Alpine routes leading to Lake Constance in the north. This camp was situated on the rocky terrace in the portion of the town south of the river. From about the 4th century, Chur was ruled by the Catholic bishops, who, in 1170, were raised to the status of bishop-princes. But in the 15th century, the irate inhabitants forced the ruling bishop-prince to give up much of his political power over the town. This process continued through the decades until, by 1526, Chur had become a city free from temporal domination of the bishops and subject only to the emperor.

Today Chur is a modern, well-developed city, with a population of around 37,000. It lies at the entrance to the Schanfigg Valley, within a ring of wooded mountains; and the River Plessur runs through the town before joining the Rhine a mile and a half downstream. From here a road and rail network extends in all directions, making Chur a good starting point for any day trips into the Grisons.

Much of the city still retains its medieval character. Narrow streets, cobble-stoned alleys, hidden courtyards, quaint and ancient buildings abound, punctuated by massive structures such as the 12th-century cathedral with its splendid, 14th-century high altar, the 15th-century St. Martin's church notable for its stained glass, the Rathaus and the Bishop's Palace. Red or green footprints painted on the sidewalks lead the visitor on two itineraries (described in the city's free brochure) which take in most of the sights. Each walk lasts about an hour; more if you linger.

From Chur, the route follows the fertile Rhine Valley downstream through vineyards, wheat fields and orchards. At Landquart we leave the Rhine, go through the dramatic Chlus gorge and follow the River Landquart upstream. After a long, winding but gentle ascent past a number of resort villages, including Saas and Mezzaselva (with Spa Serneus down in the valley to the right), we come to Klosters-Dorf and Klosters.

Klosters

Klosters, once a group of hamlets, is now a small town in a valley bordered by mountains. With some 3,500 inhabitants, it is a typical Grisons village, which has achieved special popularity as a well-equipped summer and winter sports resort. With Davos, it shares access to the long Parsenn slopes that are said to provide some of the best ski runs in the world. Tobogganing is believed to have originated here. It also has a heated outdoor swimming pool.

Named for the cloisters of a now extinct monastery, Klosters also has a pretty church with a clock tower. It is decorated with the coat of arms of the Grisons, showing a wild man pulling a fir tree out of the ground on one side, and a complacent apple tree on the other.

Klosters attracts young people who take their winter sports seriously, perhaps because it is smaller and has a more intimate atmosphere than its sister resort, Davos. The excellence of its children's ski school draws many families who rent chalets or flats during the holidays. The starting point for the best of the Klosters-Parsenn ski-runs is the Weissfluhjoch, reached by cable car from the town to the Gotschnagrat and then, after a short ski-run, by another cable car. The run back to Klosters is almost 10 km. (over 6 miles) long; with a change in altitude of around 1,500 meters, (5,000 feet). The variety of runs from the Weissfluhjoch and Gotschnagrat is almost unlimited, but the best-known are the ones that lead north to Küblis or south to Wolfgang. The Madrisa ski slopes, reached by the Albeina gondolas, are popular with both skiers (there are several well-placed lifts) and sunbathers.

The railway to Davos crosses the Landquart River by a lofty bridge, climbs through some stately pine forests, and then through Wolfgang, a skiing center, before dropping down again to the Davosersee and the town of Davos itself. Sir Arthur Conan Doyle put in a good deal of time in Davos, and Robert Louis Stevenson finished *Treasure Island* here in 1881.

THE GRISONS AND THE ENGADINE

Probably the most famous name among Swiss winter resorts is still that of St. Moritz, to which we shall come presently, but Davos—like Arosa and Gstaad—is pushing it hard.

Davos

Davos—in reality Davos-Dorf, with its indistinguishable Siamese-twin resort of Davos-Platz—owes its fame to the rise of skiing as the sport *à la mode* among the smart set in all western countries. Fanatic skiers supposedly find in Davos the world's most perfect terrain—the Parsenn run.

Davos lies at one end of the Davos Valley, running parallel to and northwest of the upper Engadine, and separated from it by the Albula chain of mountains, some of which are over 3,000 metres (10,000 feet) high. On the opposite side of the valley is the Strela chain, dominated by the Weissfluhjoch. The open, sunbathed slopes of this range provide the magnificent skiing that attracts devotees of the sport from all over the world. The Parsenn funicular railway takes skiers from Davos up to Weissfluhjoch, over 2,700 metres (9,000 feet) high, and the upper end of the Parsenn run. From there they can ski down over vast, open snowfields to the town, a drop of around 1,000 metres (3,500 feet). Or, striking off to the northeast, they come to Davos' neighboring resort, which we have already visited—Klosters. Another funicular, combined with a gondola, goes to Strela. There's a lift to Rinerhorn (2,286 metres, 7,500 feet), and a couple of dozen other mountain railways, cable cars and assorted lifts. Nearby is the well-equipped Brämabüel-Jakobshorn ski area, reached by cable car and lift.

Long before the skiing craze gave Davos international fame the place had a considerable vogue as a health resort. Robert Louis Stevenson stayed at the Hotel Belvédère. Its ideal situation from the standpoint of altitude and climate attracted tuberculosis sufferers as early as 1865, and it still has several of the finest sanatoria in Switzerland. With 12,000 inhabitants, Davos is even larger than St. Moritz, and it has more hotels and pensions, not counting the rest homes, health clinics and indoor swimming pools.

In addition to its unrivaled ski-runs, Davos also boasts a truly magnificent ice-rink on which hockey matches and exhibitions of international caliber are staged throughout the winter. It is overlooked by a vast and well appointed terrace. There are two fine ski schools in Davos, either one eminently capable of instilling in the novice sufficient skill to accomplish a fair sized schuss within a few days. As in some other Swiss resorts, the runs are constantly patrolled by guards who will set him right side up if he happens to do a nosedive into a snowdrift. Furthermore, the mountainsides are dotted with little inns and taverns, where toes can be thawed out and courage fortified with a jigger of Kirsch. English speaking visitors who mistrust such foreign concoctions will even find their favorite brands of whisky at most of these places (though at a steep price). It is also the Mecca of cross-country skiers. Over 70 km. (45 miles) of prepared trails across stunning landscapes make up a varying and ideal terrain for cross-country skiers.

In summer, Davos is pleasant, but no more so than dozens of other Swiss resorts, and it is considerably less picturesque than a great many of them. It offers sailing and swimming in the Lake of Davos, trout fishing in either the lake or the Landwasser River and its tributaries, mountain climbing with experienced guides, golf on an eighteen hole course, and skating, from June to October, on the open air ice rink.

The resort is dominated by the steeple of a pretty, late Gothic church, and the city hall, part of which dates from the 17th century, has some interesting stained-glass windows and coats of armor. There is a medical institute where much effective research has been carried out by Swiss scientists into the problems of tuberculosis, and on top of the Weissfluh another group of scientists has established an institute for the study of snow conditions and avalanches.

From Davos, the road leads over the Flüela Pass to Susch in the Engadine, a distance of eighteen miles. It's a relatively easy drive, as Alpine passes go, with no gradient steeper than 1 in 10, and comparatively few hairpin bends. Although the highway reaches an altitude of 2,377 meters (7,800 feet), it is normally open to traffic in winter.

At first the road climbs gently. As it rises dense larch forests give way first to pine trees, then to firs, and finally, above the timber line, to a rocky, desolate waste of boulders and jutting cliffs, much of it snow covered except in summer. It's impressive rather than beautiful scenery. Ahead, on the left, are the rocky slopes of Weisshorn, (3,078 meters, 10,100 feet), with Schwarzhorn, (3,139 meters, 10,300 feet), to the right, perennial snowcapped guardians of the pass. Towards the summit, even in August, the traveler may find himself driving through a light snowstorm. He will pass between two small lakes known as Schottensee and Schwarzsee.

At the summit itself is the Flüela Hospiz, a picturesque wooden chalet with a windmill, offering refreshments and a night's lodging at reasonable rates, though few tourists would care to spend much time in this barren, formidable spot.

The descent takes the motorist through a narrow valley crossing the Susasca, in sight of the 3,180 meter (10,600 feet) Piz Vadret, to the base of the great Grialetsch Glacier, a spectacular mass of ice and snow that serves as a reminder that this entire country was, long ago, hidden under a vast sheet of ice. The road winds downward, crossing the

THE GRISONS AND ENGADINE

torrential Fless River, and finally reaches Susch (or Süs) on the River En. The En, which eventually flows into the Danube, gives its name to this beautiful valley, the Engadine, 'The narrow place of the En'. Because of its chain of popular resorts, to many people the name of the Engadine is more familiar than that of the Grisons, the canton of which it is only a constituent (but important) part.

The Lower Engadine

One need only enter an Engadine house to be acutely conscious of its atmosphere and the almost painful state of cleanliness that exists within. The simple but solid façades, with their wonderful lattices and balconies, always prove attractive to foreigners, and their owners spare nothing to make them more picturesque. The deep windows are rich with flowers—geraniums, begonias and carnations—and flowering vines climb over the latticework. In winter, tiny bags of suet for the birds hang beside the windows.

The people of the Engadine are a proud lot. There is a story about a queen, traveling incognito, who once tried to buy a copper kettle that took her fancy as she was visiting the home of an Engadine peasant. The man didn't want to sell, and an aide drew him aside to tell him that the lady was a ruling queen, not accustomed to having her wishes denied. 'Very well', said the peasant, with a haughty gesture even the queen could not match; 'I'll *give* her the kettle. But it is not for sale'.

Susch, where the Flüela Pass road joins the main highway traversing the Engadine, is a quaint little place. The homes and other buildings here are all modern in construction if not in style, for the part of the village that lies on the left bank of the En was destroyed by fire in 1925, only the Evangelical Church being saved. Despite the latter's Roman tower, most of it is comparatively new, dating from 1515. During a restoration in 1742, the late Gothic style of its windows was changed, but in 1933, on the evidence of recently discovered fragments, they were restored to their original form. Susch is sheltered by the magnificent Piz d'Arpiglias, towering above it like a sentinel.

From Susch, our route follows the River En northeast to Scuol, a portion of the trip that can be made by road or rail. It passes through several rocky gorges, through which the En tumbles in turbulent fashion, and then emerges into flower-filled plains with a pleasant chain of attractive hamlets: Lavin, Guarda, Ardez, and the quaintly named Ftan.

Guarda, a beautiful village, is under federal protection, to ensure that the peasant dwellings with their two-tone, etched ornamentation, called *sgraffiti,* shall remain unchanged. A narrow lane from Guarda leads through Bos-cha to Ardez. In Ardez, dominated by the ruins of

Steinsberg Castle, are more of the graceful *sgraffiti* wall decorations, as well as some fine Italian ironwork, imported from Venice. Ftan, on a secondary road running higher up the hill, but parallel to the main highway, has a colorful old tower with a copper steeple. You'll get a good view, too, of Tarasp Castle, which is on the other side of the River En.

Scuol and Tarasp-Vulpera

Scuol, Vulpera, and Tarasp, three villages with a combined population of 2,000, form what is effectively one holiday and health resort complex; whose waters are reputed to be highly beneficial to sufferers from liver complaints. Most of the visitors are Swiss or German, but an increasing amount of British and Americans are arriving every year. Beautifully located in the open valley of the River En whose grass covered and wooded sides are backed by mountains, Scuol-Tarasp-Vulpera have hitherto been highly popular summer resorts. Now, thanks to a network of gondola cars and skilifts, and unobstructed south facing slopes, they are taking on a new role as winter sports resorts as well.

From Scuol and Vulpera, a bus goes up to the historic Tarasp Castle in half an hour, or the trip makes a nice hike of about an hour and a half. It is a real dream castle, pure white, perched on top of a sheer cliff some 152 meters (500 feet) above the valley. Notice the Austrian coats of arms, slit windows, painted shields and double walls. The main tower and chapel date from the 11th century, when it was the stronghold of the knights of Tarasp. Long a source of discord between the powerful Bishop of Chur and the Count of Tyrol, it became the seat of the Austrian governors until the last century, when the Grisons joined the Swiss Confederation. Some years ago, it was sold to a toothpaste manufacturer who spent three million Swiss francs (over a million dollars) restoring it and then gave it to the Prince of Hesse.

The Swiss National Park

At Tarasp, we have to return along the road to Susch, but instead of turning to go over the Flüela Pass again, we continue up the valley, along the banks of the River En, to St. Mortiz. Four miles past Susch is the village of Zernez. Close by is the entrance to the Swiss National Park. Patterned after the national parks in the United States, this was created in 1914 by a federal decree stating that 'an island of untouched primitive natural existence is to develop here in the midst of the seething waves of civilization'. The phraseology seems a bit extreme in view of the tranquility of the surroundings, for here the waves of

THE GRISONS AND ENGADINE

civilization don't seethe very hard. Within the limits of the seventy-square-mile park there is absolute protection for plants and animals; no shot can be fired, no flower picked, no tree cut down, and it is forbidden to camp or light fires. There is not even the sound of a cowbell since cattle can't be pastured in the park. Herds of chamois roam over the rocks, roebuck feed under the larch trees, deer drink from the transparent, icy streams. The ibex, historic emblem of the Grisons, is also to be seen.

The park lies in a mountainous region, the cleft of the Ofen Pass dividing it in two. But although the highest peak is little more than 3,150 meters (10,330 feet), the mountains are extremely rugged, and the valleys, filled with rocky debris, are among the wildest in the Alps. There are numerous hanging glaciers. Nevertheless, walking about the park is a delight, if a hilly one, for there are prepared paths, clearly marked, and visitors must follow them. The season lasts from about the middle of June, after the snow has melted, until it falls again in the autumn.

The park is the richest district in all the Alps for flowers because of its great differences in altitude, its varying rock types and formations, and its position astride the boundary between eastern and western Alpine flora. You'll see many rare plants that are to be found nowhere else in Switzerland as well as alpenroses, edelweiss, dwarf roses, valerian, mountain poppies, primroses, Alpine grasses, shrubs, and almost every variety of meadow flower and Alpine tree. The flowers are normally at their best in the second half of June. Then, although this may vary slightly according to the severity and timing of the preceding winter, the place is a riot of color: gentian, fiery red catchfly, violets of every shade, saxifrage, white Pyrenean and Alpine ranunculus, and a host of other flowers forming a kaleidoscope of bright color in the most superb natural setting.

But the Swiss National Park is not a solitary, floral oasis. Almost wherever you go in the Engadine, you'll find an abundance of wild flowers, and by mid-May, unless it is a late winter, the valleys will be covered with millions of crocuses and soldanella. They are followed by anemones, and, as these fade, the blue gentians start to bloom. Towards the end of June, when the haymaking begins, the beauty of the lower meadows is somewhat spoiled, but the flowers of the high pastures and the mountains remain throughout the summer with a coloring far more intense than anything at the lower altitudes. Remember though, that all except the commonest wild flowers are protected by strict cantonal laws. It is forbidden to pick or remove them in large quantities—'large quantities' being officially defined as more than ten specimens.

All the way from Scuol, our road has been closely following the River En, as it has done since it crossed the Austrian frontier (24 km.,

THE FACE OF SWITZERLAND

15 miles the other side of Scuol) to enter the lower Engadine. And it continues to do so through the upper Engadine and past St. Moritz, to the river's source near Maloja. It's a lovely ride, the road climbing and twisting gently but steadily, with peaks, often snow-capped, to either side, and the river gushing in foaming torrents below. The villages are all lovely, and there are many old churches and, not least, some splendid examples of Engadine houses.

The Upper Engadine

After Zernez, the road passes the castle of Rietberg, owned by the Planta family. The Planta crest, a bear's paw, is a familiar sight in the Grisons, and members of the family still live there. They rose to importance subsequent to 1295, when they were named hereditary bailiffs to the bishops of Chur.

Just beyond Zernez, near Brail, you will pass from the lower to the upper Engadine, then through the surprisingly named little resort of S-chanf to Zuoz. Spare a short while here, for Zuoz, a small winter sports and summer resort as well as an education center, is noted for its Engadine houses, many of which were constructed for the Planta family, this village being their home. Indeed, you'll see the family emblem on top of the fountain in the main square. The Planta bear's paw is also a frequent decoration in the little church with its tall tower and needle-like spire.

Samedan and Celerina

A few miles farther on, you'll come to Samedan and Celerina, two charming Engadine villages that, if it were not for their vast difference in character, might be called suburbs of St. Moritz. From Samedan you have a magnificent view of the Bernina chain of mountains: Piz Bernina, 4,050 metres (13,300 feet); Piz Palü and Piz Roseg at 3,900 metres (12,900 feet); Piz Morteratsch, 3,750 metres (12,300 feet); Piz Tschierva, 3,500 metres (11,700 feet); Piz Corvatsch, 3,440 metres (11,300 feet); Piz Rosatsch, 3,100 metres (10,200 feet); and many others. Samedan also has a golf course and is close to the Upper Engadine airport.

The trip up to Muottas Muragl should not be missed, since it provides a superb view over the lovely valley of the En. A funicular goes in fifteen minutes from Punt Muragl, between Samedan and Pontresina, to the summit; reaching an altitude of 2,450 metres (8,050 feet)—700 metres (2,300 feet) above the valley floor. From the top you will get an eagle's eye view of St. Moritz, the nearby watershed of Piz Lunghin, and the chain of lakes which stretches almost 16 km. (10 miles) towards Maloja. Within about 450 meters you will also find the

THE GRISONS AND ENGADINE

sources of the River Mera, flowing southwest to Lake Como and the Adriatic: the River En, which runs through the Engadine to meet the Danube and the Black Sea; and a stream which winds north into the River Julier, and so to the Rhine and the North Sea. Understandably the Engadine is called the 'roof of Europe.'

The mountain panorama forms a full semicircle, between Piz Languard in the southeast and Piz Kesch in the northwest. In the south, near the white peak of the famed Piz Palü, the highest mountains in the Bernina group may be seen, including Piz Bernina itself, above the dark mass of Piz Chalchagn. The wide ridge of Piz Tschierva and the pointed Piz Roseg follow and then the glacier world of the Sella group, above the cleft of the Roseg Valley. In the foreground, one sees the massive blocks of Piz Rosatsch and Surlej, and farther behind the lovely Piz La Margna, while the peaks of the Bergell mountains loom over the Maloja Pass. The west side of the valley is bounded by Piz Lagrev, flanked by Piz Julier and Piz Albana, which in turn give way to Piz Nair and the wild and rocky tower of Piz Ot. Deep down on the left, just out of sight, is Pontresina, where the Bernina and Roseg valleys meet, and to the right, in the En valley, is Celerina.

Celerina, St. Moritz's little brother, is a first-rate ski resort in its own right with the additional advantage of easy access to all the winter sports facilities of its more celebrated neighbor. The renowned Cresta run, mecca for bobsledders, ends here.

Among the main attractions of the upper Engadine are the many mountain railroads and cableways. Whether it's for a climbing excursion or just for an afternoon's walk, you can go from St. Moritz to Corviglia by funicular and from there by cableway to Piz Nair, a wonderful 3,000 metres (10,000 foot) mountaintop viewpoint that has a restaurant and café. On the terrace you can admire the fabulous view while sunbathing in a deckchair with a glass of your favorite potion close at hand. You can go from Celerina by cableway to Val Saluver or, as we have seen, by funicular to Muottas Muragl; from Pontresina by chairlift to Alp Languard; from Bernina by cableway to Diavolezza or to Piz Lagalb; from Surlej, between Lakes Champfèr and Silvaplana, to Piz Corvatsch (over 3,300 metres, 10,800 feet); and from Sils to Furtschellas.

St. Moritz

What eastern Switzerland lacks in large cities is made up for with places bearing world-famous names. Foremost among them is a little village whose natural beauties and health giving baths have caused it to grow into one of Europe's most famous resorts—St. Moritz. The average visitor thinks of St. Moritz, the site of the 1928 and 1948

Winter Olympics and the setting for dozens of films, as something of a world capital. If he goes there during either the winter or summer season, when the plush hotels are crowded with what remains of European nobility, statesmen, film stars and Arab oil sheiks, he will not be disappointed. But in summer the town does lose some of its glitter, and prices are appreciably less than in winter. Many people consider that St. Moritz is at its best during this relatively low season—the end of June and beginning of July—since the mountains and pastures are covered with spring flowers.

It has been fashionable for quite some time. Bronze relics uncovered in 1907 and now on view in the Engadine Museum at St. Moritz indicate that the healing qualities of its waters were known at least 3,000 years ago, long before Rome was founded. The Romans had a settlement there, and later—exactly when is not known—a church was founded on the site and dedicated to Mauritius, one of the early Christian martyrs. The first historical reference to the town was in 1139; and in 1537 Paracelsus, the great Renaissance physician, described in detail the health-giving properties of the St. Moritz springs. It is said that toward the end of the 17th century the Duke of Parma led a retinue of twenty-five persons over the mountain passes to take the waters; the first of a still-continuing parade of royal visitors seeking to rejuvenate their jaded livers by drinking from the bubbling fount of Piz Rosatsch. In 1747, a description of the town speaks of the presence of the mineral water itself, from which the town's fame originally came. It was vividly described by a German visitor in 1793. 'It puckers lips and tongue like the sharpest vinegar, goes to the head, and is like champagne in the nose.'

St. Moritz grew into a major tourist resort in the last century after the bed of the En was altered to prevent the river from destroying the mineral spring. This early engineering feat was carried out by subterfuge. The elders of the village were opposed to the 'new-fangled' development, so, when they were all away at a cattle market in Tirano, the younger men voted for the project in a town meeting and had it started by the time they returned. Then the first of the big luxury hotels was built, and by 1859 *Il Fögl Ladin,* the Romansch-language newspaper now published in Samedan, proudly announced that 'the unheard-of number of 450 visitors' had come during the year. A half century later, in 1910, the same newspaper more calmly recorded that 10,000 people had visited St. Moritz.

The elders apparently learned their lesson, for ever since they have devoted themselves to improving the resort and its facilities. After Edison had displayed his electric light at the Paris Exhibition of 1878, it was introduced in St. Moritz by Johannes Badrutt, one of Switzerland's great hoteliers, and a man who did as much as anyone to make

THE GRISONS AND ENGADINE

St. Moritz into a fashionable winter sports resort. Six years later, St. Moritz pioneered in winter sports with the construction of the first toboggan run—the Cresta—which, as it happened, started on Badrutt's own grounds. Then, in 1895, Philipp Mark, president of the local tourist bureau, gave one of the first ski-jumping exhibitions on a jump he had built himself in St. Moritz. The Olympic jump, with a height of 141 meters (465 feet) from takeoff to landing run, was made for the second-ever Winter Olympics, held here in 1928—an era when winter sports were regarded as a somewhat curious activity indulged in by the eccentric few with time to spare for a winter holiday and purses big enough to pay for it.

Twenty years later—1948—when the Winter Olympics were again held in St. Moritz, the resort became the first one to have staged them twice. Undoubtedly these two events were partially responsible for the superb facilities which have made St. Moritz synonymous with winter sports.

The town itself is located at an altitude of 1,856 meters (6,090 feet), in the upper Engadine valley on the shores of the lovely sky-blue Lake of St. Moritz. The latter is the northernmost of a chain of four lakes around which are scattered a number of resorts that give the upper Engadine much of its charm. The other three are Lakes Champfer, Silvaplana and Sils. Through all of them flows the En, here an infant river which rises nearby. The valley is enclosed by parallel mountain ranges, the Bernina chain on the southeast and the Julier chain to the northwest.

The resort is in three parts—St. Moritz-Dorf, situated on a mountain terrace 60 metres (200 feet) above the lake; St. Moritz-Bad charmingly located at the end of the lake; and Champfer-Suvretta. When, towards the end of the 19th century, the fashion for spas began to wane, St. Moritz-Bad began to take a back seat to St. Moritz-Dorf, the sparkling winter resort. But in recent years St. Moritz-Bad has staged a comeback by laying heavy emphasis on skiing and other winter sports. In 1973 it started a new direct aerial cableway to Signal, feeding the Plateau Nair lift, and in 1976 a splendid spa complex was opened. Unfortunately one of the side effects of this growth has been a rash of unsympathetic modern building, much of which has little architectural merit. The charming little lakeside resort is beginning to look like a Costa Moritza, but its popularity is assured.

As a town, St. Moritz-Dorf has only minor attractions. There is a leaning tower, all that remains of an old village church built in 1573, and the Segantini Museum, which contains some important works by Giovanni Segantini, the 19th-century Italian artist who settled in the Grisons and became a distinguished painter of Alpine life and scenery. Outside is the Olympic Stone listing all the medal winners at the St.

Moritz Winter Olympics. The Engadine Museum, in addition to the relics of prehistoric times previously mentioned, has an interesting collection of Engadine furniture. On the modern side, the town has some of the most fashionable shops in Switzerland.

Distractions at St. Moritz are virtually unlimited for the active sportsman, in either winter or summer. It is a skier's paradise, of course, and also offers wonderful ice skating, bobsledding, and riding and horse racing on the frozen lake. In summer, there's swimming, skating, summer skiing, sailing, riding, mountain-climbing, golf, tennis and, in the River En and the 25 lakes, some of the best fishing in Switzerland. Serious connoisseurs of night life and gambling may be a little bored, although in a modest way both are available. The ice rink is open all year.

On Lake Silvaplana, barely 6 km. (4 miles) from St. Moritz, is the Engadine village of Silvaplana, the first of the unspoiled village resorts outside the St. Moritz complex. Next comes Sils-Baselgia, little more than a couple of excellent hotels, and the tiny village of Sils-Maria, where Nietzsche wrote *Thus Spake Zarathustra*. Peace, quiet and good hotels are keynotes at Maria. Its summer highspots are horse-drawn bus excursions up the beautiful Fex Valley, or gentle mountain hiking amid breathtaking scenery. In winter its attraction is skiing without queueing via the Furtschellas cable car; and always the life and amenities of St. Moritz can be reached easily and quickly.

Pontresina

Half a dozen miles east of St. Moritz, and below our earlier viewpoint on Muottas Muragl, is another famous summer and winter resort, Pontresina; one of whose greatest assets is its altitude, since at about 1,828 metres (6,000 feet), it is only marginally lower than St. Moritz itself. Amply provided with fine hotels, Pontresina has everything the holidaymaker could desire. It stands at the center of a network of 200 km. (124 miles) of well-kept paths, some of them passing spectacularly alongside the glaciers that descend from the snowcovered mountains above. If walking is too tame for you, there are plenty of guides to take you mountaineering. Or you can sit under the shaggy pines of the Tais woods and listen to the morning concerts given daily from June through September. There is golf at the nearby eighteen-hole golf course, tennis, swimming in a splendid indoor pool, trout fishing in streams and lakes, two of which are free, a gymnasium, summer skiing and horse riding. The most popular excursion is by horse-drawn bus up the Val Roseg, a really lovely high Alpine valley. It takes about an hour each way, and there's a good restaurant at the terminus.

THE GRISONS AND ENGADINE

In winter, Pontresina turns to skiing. Just behind the village is the Alp Languard lift; the first level being for beginners, the second recommended only for moderately good skiers. At Bernina, about five miles up the valley by train or bus, are the high rise cable cars to Diavolezza and Lagalb, but the latter's for piste-bashers only. Pontresina is a major ski-touring center with 50 mapped-out tours. It's got a modern cross-country skiing center, skating, curling and, for those who don't ski, special routes kept open for winter walking. From Pontresina, too, it is easy to get to any of the various cable cars, mountain railways and lifts in the Upper Engadine.

From Pontresina, the Bernina Railway follows the old Bernina post road over the pass to Tirano, in Italy. It runs through magnificent countryside; wild and somewhat grim on the north side of the summit, quickly changing to lush meadows and trees on the southern descent—an indication of the warmer, Italian-type climate.

Although our itinerary at the start of this chapter planned a return from St. Moritz to Chur by post bus over the Julier Pass, there is an alternative, and a very attractive one, too. For you can go back by the Rhaetian Railway through the Albula tunnel and down the Albula valley via Filisur, Tiefencastel and Thusis—a fantastic journey in which the gallant little train twists and weaves its way among outstandingly fine mountain scenery well matched by the engineering skill of the railway's constructors. But our planned route is by road over the Julier Pass, which, incidentally, is kept open throughout the winter. From St. Moritz the road goes southwest through Champfèr to Silvaplana, where the Julier road branches northward. If you miss the turning you'll be on the road which goes all the way to Lake Como; very nice, but not what we have in mind.

The Julier Route

The Julier route is one of the three great Alpine passes (the Great St. Bernard and the Splügen are the other two) that are known to have been used by the Romans and, even in those days, the Julier was favored because of its immunity from avalanches. The present road, built between 1820 and 1826, is dominated by three mountains, Piz Julier, Piz Albana, and Piz Polaschin, and near the top it is marked by two pillars, around 1.5 meters (5 feet) high, which are said to be the remains of a Roman temple. Initially the climb is steep, giving a fine view of the Upper Engadine lakes, but it levels out before reaching the summit at 2,286 meters (7,500 feet). Here there is a souvenir shop and parking place, and the Julier Hospice, where refreshments can be obtained.

232 THE FACE OF SWITZERLAND

The first village of any importance after leaving Silvaplana is Bivio, which is about 8 km. (5) miles beyond the summit, at an altitude of 1,780 metres (5,850 feet). A former Roman settlement named Stabulum Bivio, it is called Bivio in Italian, Stalla in German, and Beiva in Romansch, and those who live here speak all three languages. The village itself is the entrance to the beautiful Val d'Err. From here our road follows the banks of the turbulent Julia River through splendid rocky gorges and over tempestuous cascades to Mulegns and Savognin, passing the artificial Lake of Marmorera, built to store water for hydroelectric power stations. Savognin is an unpretentious winter sports resort with sunny slopes served by a good network of gondola cars and lifts going up to 2,700 metres (8,900 feet). It's got a fine indoor pool and a dozen or more surprisingly good hotels from first class down. In summer there are splendid signposted mountain walks, gondola cars and lifts giving easy access to the higher ones. For several years Savognin was the residence of the celebrated painter Segantini. The district and its people are well represented in his works which you'll see everywhere—but only reproductions; originals are very expensive.

Six miles farther on we come to Tiefencastel, called Casti in Romansch, which is where the River Julia flows into the Albula. The village was entirely destroyed by fire in 1890, but above the 'new' one the tall white church of St. Ambrosius still stands out beautifully against the background of fir trees that cover the encroaching hills. A short distance from Tiefencastel is Vazerol, where there is a monument commemorating the oath of eternal union sworn by the 'Free Leagues' in 1471.

At Tiefencastel one can either take the direct road to Chur via Lenzerheide and Churwalden, or go on a more circuitous route by Thusis.

Lenzerheide, which almost adjoins Valbella, is a charming winter and summer resort at an altitude of 1,524 meters (5,000 feet), which enjoys long hours of sunshine and is virtually free of fog because of its situation in a high valley open to the south. It has two seasons, June-September (mountain climbers prefer the latter month) and December 15 to April.

Although the Lenzerheide-Valbella area is specially good for the intermediate grade skier, one of its principal attractions is the number of practice slopes which nature has thoughtfully provided for beginners. Another is the unusually good assortment of cable cars and lifts, including of course the cable car which runs up to Parpaner Rothorn, an altitude of 2,860 meters (9,400 feet).

The range of facilities provided at this resort is nothing if not comprehensive. It has a eighteen-hole golf course, seven tennis courts with instructors, horses for riding, swimming and rowing on Lake Lenzer-

THE GRISONS AND ENGADINE

heide, fishing in the Julia and Albula rivers, and a good indoor swimming pool at the Posthotel Valbella. Guided mountain trips are organized every week during July and August, and free botanic excursions start one month earlier. If you want to explore the countryside on foot, a map of the various routes is available at the resort.

But if you have not made too many stops since leaving St. Moritz, the day will still be young and the longer route by way of Thusis and Reichenau will prove inviting. You can go by train, bus or car.

Tiefencastel to Flims

The rail trip from Tiefencastel to Thusis is particularly interesting from an engineering point of view, since this section of the Rhaetian Railway passes through sixteen tunnels, one of them over three and a half miles long. There are also twenty-seven bridges or viaducts. One of these is the celebrated Solis Viaduct, the center arch of which is 41 metres (137 feet) across, and 89 metres (293 feet) high. The route is wonderfully scenic, threading through spectacular gorges and canyons, interspersed with peaceful valleys and pine forests for contrast.

Thusis, easily the most important town of the Domleschg Valley with about 1,700 inhabitants, is surrounded by high mountains and thick forests. It has a late Gothic church, dating from 1506, and in the center of the woods, an open air lido. The town is the starting point for climbers seeking to conquer the Piz Beverin, the Piz Curver, or the Stätzerhorn. Here the Albula River joins the Hinterrhein (or Upper Rhine). Perched on the rocky heights guarding the entrance to the Via Mala are the ruins of the old Hohenrhaetien Castle. The famous Via Mala, an ancient and dramatic road writhing along the bottom of a deep ravine, has now been replaced by a fine new one that eliminates the old bottlenecks. The route runs south through Andeer to the Splügen and San Bernardino passes, the latter of which has now been bypassed by a tunnel. The town of San Bernardino is a small winter resort.

From Thusis, we enter the fertile Domleschg Valley, through which flows the Upper Rhine to join the Lower Rhine (Vorderrhein) at Reichenau. This valley is one of the most scenic of the area, with numerous old castles, charming villages, blossoming orchards, and the stately Stätzerhorn towering above it to the east like a sentinel. Houses seen here are typical of the entire Grisons area; high, stuccoed structures with red-tiled roofs and small-paned windows set deep into the thick walls as protection against the cold. There is frequently a wooden balcony-porch running around the house at the second story, with gracefully carved railings invariably bordered with masses of flowers.

Rothenbrunnen, which comes next, means mineral waters containing iron. The town has a children's home, and there are old castles all over the place. In the triangle formed by the junction of the Upper Rhine and the Lower Rhine lies Reichenau Castle, which has a long and fascinating history. Built in the 14th century, it was in 1793 the refuge of the then-exiled future King of France, Louis-Philippe. He lived there under the name of Professor Chabaud. Later it passed into the hands of the Plantas, the family which owned so many of the castles in the Grisons.

From Reichenau-Tamins—a twin village lying on both banks of the river—it is only 9.5 km. (6 miles) to Chur, our starting point, via the attractive village of Ems. However, if you have time it is well worthwhile making a detour westward to Flims, a summer and winter resort in the Grisons Oberland. This region extends from Reichenau along the Vorderrhein (or Lower Rhine), and runs as far as Oberalp—near Andermatt.

Located at an altitude of 1,127 metres (3,700 feet) is Flims, set on a south-facing terrace overlooking the Rhine Valley. The town itself is in two adjacent sections: Flims-Dorf, which consists mostly of villas built among the meadows; and Flims-Waldhaus, in the pine trees and containing most of the hotels. Perhaps the greatest summer asset of Flims is the Caumasee, a small lake fed by warm springs that make it possible to swim there as early as June. In winter, aerial cableways to Cassonsgrat (2,636 metres, 8,650 feet) and Grauberg (2,224 metres, 7,300 feet), as well as several skilifts serve the broad snowfields above the village. A mile or so down the road from Waldhaus is Laax, a nice little village with a couple of small lakes. More important, it's a relatively new but up-and-coming skiing center with some excellent top medium grade and first class hotels. Close to Laax are the cable cars to Crap Sogn Gion (2,209 metres, 7,250 feet), and Crap Masegu (2,483 metres, 8,150 feet), with a well-planned system of linking skilifts.

Chur to Fashionable Arosa

From Chur one can strike east by rail or road towards the center of the circle we have just completed. It's a dead-end route, both rail and road stopping at the third of the three major resorts of the Grisons—Arosa. It's an idyllic high-altitude village about 1,800 metres (6,000 feet) above sea level. Aside from the invigorating atmosphere and clean, crystal-clear air that this altitude guarantees, Arosa has gained the reputation of being an unusually friendly resort. The largest of its many hotels is moderately sized so there is none of the chilling formality or impersonal efficiency sometimes found in mammoth establishments.

THE GRISONS AND ENGADINE

The accent is on freedom. It's not compulsorily dressy, nor deliberately fashionable, but it can be smart if one wants it that way. In the top hotels a few men may wear dinner jackets, but if they do it's because they want to, not because they have to. It follows that Arosa has fallen heir to some of those who find the winter elegance, ostentation, and glitter of St. Moritz just a trifle overbearing.

One of Arosa's specialties is a sport that has always appealed to the upper crust—horseracing. But here it is on snow and ice, and in winter. For although Arosa is an excellent summer resort like St. Moritz, it is more fashionable in winter, and more popular. This is hardly surprising, since the ski runs are among the best in Switzerland for beginners, intermediates and experts. There is always enough snow and, unlike many resorts, one can ski back right down into the village. With over 25 km. (15 miles) of runs, cross-country skiing has also become popular in recent years. Arosa has over seventy hotels and pensions. These can accommodate about 6,000 visitors. Over 6,000 more guests (mostly families) can be lodged in furnished apartments and chalets.

It would be hard to say whether Arosa offers the visitor more in summer or winter. In the former, there is the bathing beach on the little lake, with a swimming instructor at hand, and some of the hotels which open in summer have indoor pools. There are several tennis courts, tennis halls, an artificial ice rink (ice hall), and a 9-hole golf course, as well as fishing on either of two lakes, and boats for hire. And there are concerts, dances and a seemingly endless program of varied entertainment and sporting events.

In winter, the broad skiing fields above the tree line are made accessible to everyone by a good network of cleverly located skilifts and linking runs. There is also a well-known cable car running to Weisshorn, (2,650 meters, 8,700 feet); and gondola cars will take you to Hörnli (2,500 meters, 8,200 feet). The resort claims to have over 70 km. (47 miles) of piste, and the ski school, which has over 100 instructors, is one of Switzerland's largest. Curling, skating and ice hockey take place on several rinks (natural and artificial), the Obersee Ice Stadium having a roofed grandstand for spectators. For non-skiers (and 50% of Arosa's winter visitors are just that) there are many miles of carefully prepared paths for winter walking, and if you hanker after something different you can take the popular Arlenwald Road sleigh ride. And winter and summer you have a wide selection of entertainment and can enjoy magnificent mountain scenery which is as elegant as the resort itself.

PRACTICAL INFORMATION FOR THE GRISONS AND ENGADINE

HOTELS AND RESTAURANTS. Nearly all the hotels that we include in our listings below have a wide range of rooms, a good many of which may well fall into a lower grading than that which we have given here. The best advice is always to check beforehand with the hotel (we have provided phone numbers to facilitate this).

AROSA. (All inclusive). *Alexandra Palace Arosa* (L), tel. 310111. Modern and extremely smart. *Arosa Kulm Hotel* (L), tel. 310131. At the top end of town and well placed for Hörnli gondolas and Carmenna lift. *Des Alpes* (L), tel. 311851. Quiet and central. *Bellavista* (L), tel. 312421. Superior hotel with indoor pool. *Eden* (L), tel. 311877. Very comfortable. *Excelsior* (L), tel. 311661. With indoor pool. *Golfhotel Hof Maran* (L), tel. 310185. Every sporting facility; including golf as the name suggests. *Park-Hotel* (L), tel. 310165. Grand and comfortable. *Raetia* (L), tel. 310241. Very comfortable and modern. *Savoy* (L), tel. 310211. Indoor pool. *Tschuggen Grand Hotel* (L), 310221. All facilities at this luxurious spot. *Waldhotel National* (L), tel. 311351. Very quiet, in own garden; indoor pool and sauna. *Alpensonne* (E), tel. 311547. *Alpina* (E), tel. 311658. *Belvédère-Tanneck* (E), tel. 311335. Quiet and central. *Streiff* (E), tel. 311117. In garden. *Vetter* (E), tel. 311702. *Belri* (M), tel. 311237. In quiet location. *Ramoz* (M), tel. 311063. Modest. Skittles and terrace.

Restaurant. *Central* (I–M), tel. 311513. Try the Scampi Maison or the rack of lamb *à la Sarladaise*.

CELERINA. (All inclusive). *Cresta Palace* (L), tel. 33564. Indoor pool and many winter sports facilities. *Cresta Kulm* (E), tel. 33373. Quiet location. *Misani* (E), tel. 33314. With good restaurant. *Posthaus* (M), tel. 32222. Modest.

CHUR. *Chur* (I), tel. 222161. Sauna and dancing. *Drëi Könige* (I), tel. 221725. Central. *Duc de Rohan* (I), tel. 221022. Indoor pool and elegant restaurant; best in town. *Freieck* (I), tel. 221792. Quiet and central. *Posthotel* (I), tel. 226844. Centrally located. *Romantik Hotel Stern* (I), tel. 223555. Atmospheric historic building with good restaurant; central. *Zunfthaus zur Rebleuten* (I), tel. 221713. Atmospheric restaurant. Diet meals. Historic building.

Restaurants. There are several (E) restaurants in the *Duc de Rohan* hotel (see above). Specialties include *Crevettes Pisani*, veal kidneys *à la Palmir*. They also serve a Graubünder Rhine wine.

THE GRISONS AND ENGADINE

DAVOS. (All inclusive). In Davos Platz: *Central Sporthotel* (L), tel. 36522. *Morosani's Posthotel* (L), tel. 21161. *Steigenberger Belvédère* (L), tel. 36412. All facilities in this luxurious spot. *Sunstar Park* (L), tel. 21241. Quiet and comfortable. *Bellavista Sporthotel* (E), tel. 54252. In garden. *Alte Post* (M), tel. 35403. Central, restaurant. *Brauerei* (M), tel. 51488. Very quiet, terrace, diet meals. *Albana Pizzeria* (I), tel. 35841. Central; breakfast only. *Belmont* (I), tel. 35032. Very quiet; own grounds. Breakfast only. No showers.

In Davos Dorf: *Derby* (L), tel. 61166. Comfortable and quiet. *Fluela* (L), tel. 61221. Extremely grand with every amenity. *Montana Sporthotel* (L), tel. 53444. *Parsenn* (L), tel. 53232. Central location; bowling. *Sporthotel Meierhof* (L), tel. 74363. Central, in own grounds; facilities for the handicapped. *Meisser* (E), tel. 52333. Central, but very quiet, in own grounds. *Brauerei* (I), tel. 51488. In own grounds. *Sporthotel Hermann* (I), tel. 51737. Central.

There are few hotels in Davos that can be described as Inexpensive.

Restaurants. In Davos Dorf: *Meierhof* (I–M), tel. 61285. In Davos Laret: *Tschiery's Landhaus* (E), tel. 52121. Try the Menu Campagnard—country fare at its expensive best!

FLIMS. (All inclusive). *Adula* (L), tel. 390161. Indoor pool, gardens and good restaurant. *Parkhotel* (L), tel. 391181. In beautiful grounds with many sports facilities and all comforts. *Schweizerhof* (L), tel. 391212. Sporting facilities and attractive grounds. *Aparthotel des Alpes* (E), tel. 390101. *Schlosshotel* (E), tel. 391245. Central with good restaurant. *National* (M), tel. 391224. Comfortable and central. *Cresta* (I), tel. 391302. Central but quiet location.

Restaurants. In Flims Dorf: *Stiva,* with an open fireplace, and *Las Valettas* (both M–E, both in Hotel Crap Ner, tel. 392626). *Albana Sporthotel* (I): three restaurants, plus pizzeria, terrace and pub, near ski lifts and cableways; tel. 392333.

KLOSTERS. (All inclusive). *Pardenn* (L), tel. 41141. Indoor pool, sauna and bowling among the many facilities. *Silvretta* (L), tel. 41353. Grill restaurant. *Vereina* (L), tel. 41161. Tennis in grounds; indoor pool and sauna. *Kurhotel Bad Serneus* (E), tel. 41444. Cure facilities; quiet location. *Büel* (M), tel. 42669. Simple but central. *Silvapina* (M), tel. 41468. In own garden; ideal for children. With (I) rooms.

Restaurants. *Steinbock* (M), tel. 41636. *Rufinis* (I), tel. 41371. *Surval* (I), tel. 41121.

LAAX. (All inclusive). *Crap Sogn Gion* (E), tel. 392192. Indoor pool, sauna and bowling. *Happy Rancho Sporthotel* (E), tel. 390131. Exceptionally well equipped with 2 pools, tennis, sauna and solarium. *Sporthotel Signina* (E), tel. 390151. Indoor pool and tennis; in- and outdoor dancing. *Sporthotel Larisch* (M), tel. 22126. Indoor pool and sauna nearby.

Restaurant. *Sporthotel Larisch* (M), in hotel of same name (see above). Large rustic restaurant and Bündnerstube, garden terrace. Fondues, *Larisch-Topi,* fresh trout.

LENZERHEIDE. (All inclusive). *Grand Hotel Kurhaus* (L), tel. 341134. Comfortable and smart; central. *Guarda Val* (L), tel. 342214. Great rustic charm. *Schweizerhof* (L), tel. 341181. Smart and expensive. *Sunstar* (L), tel. 342491. Central with all comforts. *Lenzerhorn* (M), tel. 341105. Central with gardens.

At Lenzerheide-Valbella: *Post-Hotel Valbella* (L), tel. 341212. Tennis, indoor pool and sauna. *Valbella-Inn* (L), tel. 343663. Curling, tennis, sauna and indoor pool; facilities for children. *Kulm* (M), tel. 341180. Central, but in own grounds; facilities for children.

Restaurant. *Guarda-Val* (M), in hotel (see above). Atmospheric.

MALOJA. (All inclusive). *Maloja Kulm* (M–E), tel. 43105. Historic building at summit of the pass; very quiet.

PONTRESINA. (All inclusive). *Kronenhof-Bellavista* (L), tel. 66333. Expensive and grand; good restaurant. *Rosatsch* (L), tel. 66351. Sauna; centrally located. *Schweizerhof* (L), tel. 66412. *Walther* (L), tel. 66471. Ice rink, tennis and sauna among the facilities. *Bernina* (E), tel. 66221. Central; in own grounds with good restaurant. *Sporthotel Pontresina* (E), tel. 66331. *Bahnhof-Chesa Briotta* (M), tel. 66242. Simple hotel. No rooms with bath. With (I) rooms.

ST. MORITZ. (All inclusive). *Badrutt's Palace Hotel* (L), tel. 21101. Central, but with spacious grounds and marvelous views at the back; very expensive. *Carlton Hotel* (L), tel. 21141. Long famed for its quiet elegance and service; very expensive. *Chantarella* (L), tel. 21185. Good for children; in own grounds. *Crystal* (L), tel. 21165. Central; with sauna. *Kulm* (L), tel. 21151. A little out of the center with incredible views and price tags. *Schweizerhof* (L), tel. 22171. Gymnasium among the many facilities. *Steffani* (L), tel. 22101. Central; with bowling. *Suvretta House* (L), tel. 21121. About a mile out of town in marvelous grounds; very pricey. *Bellevue* (E), tel. 22161. Riding and sauna. *Soldanella* (E), tel. 33651. In own grounds; reasonable hotel. *Sporthotel Bären* (E), tel. 33656. Indoor pool; quiet location in own grounds. Breakfast only. *National* (M), tel. 33274. *Granita* (I), tel. 33629. Simple inexpensive hotel.

Restaurants. *Rôtisserie des Chevaliers* (M–E), tel. 21151. Graded "excellent" in the *Passeport Bleu* Swiss gastronomic guide. In St. Moritz Bad: *Steinbock* (I), tel. 36035. Specialties include French onion soup *au gratin*, lamb chops *à l'estragon*, Risotto Capuccino.

SAMEDAN. (All inclusive). *Bernina* (L), tel. 65421. Tennis and dancing. *Quadratscha* (E–L), tel. 64257. Indoor pool. *Des Alpes* (M), tel. 65262. *Donatz* (M), tel. 64666. Golf, ice rink and curling among the facilities *Hirschen* (I–M), tel. 65274. In historic building in the center of town. *Sporthotel* (I–M), tel. 65333. In own grounds.

Restaurant. *Le Pavillon* (M), in Bernina hotel (see above). Boletus mushrooms prepared at the table, fresh homemade goose liver pâté, calves' liver *à la Veneziana*.

THE GRISONS AND ENGADINE

SAVOGNIN. *Cresta* (E), tel. 741755. Large hotel with indoor and outdoor tennis, indoor pool, sauna and bowling. *Danilo* (M), tel. 741466. Central; with nightclub. *Piz Mitgel* (M), tel. 741161. Central; restaurant serving Swiss specialties. *Pianta* (I), tel. 741105. Central; popular restaurant. No showers.

S-CHANF. (All inclusive). *Park-Hotel Aurora* (M), tel. 71264. Quiet hotel in own grounds, with facilities for children and bowling. *Scaletta* (I), tel. 71271. Quiet and central, with bowling.

SCUOL. (All inclusive). *Belvedere Kurhotel* (L), tel. 91041. Comfortable and quiet. *Guardaval* (E), tel. 91321. Historic and atmospheric building; central but quiet. *Bellaval* (I–M), tel. 91481. Good family hotel. *La Staila* (I), tel. 91483. Ideal for children.
  Restaurant. *Filli* (I–M), tel. 99927.

SILS-MARIA, BASEGLIA. (All inclusive). At Sils-Maria: *Waldhaus* (L), tel. 45331. Indoor pool and tennis; quiet. *Maria* (E), tel. 45317. Sailing school as well as ice rink and curling. *Privata* (E), tel. 54247. Central; good for children. *Schweizerhof* (M), tel. 45252.
  At Siis-Baselgia: *Margna* (E), tel. 45306. Many facilities but rather expensive. *Chesa Randolina* (M), tel. 45224. Quiet. *Chasté* (I), tel. 45312. Small and simple inexpensive hotel.

SILVAPLANA. (All inclusive). *Albana* (L), tel. 49292. Sauna and gymnasium. *Chesa Guardalej* (L), tel. 23121. Swimming pool, sauna, solarium, squash, fitness room, tennis, curling, congress hall. *Julier* (E), tel. 48186. Adequate. *Sonne* (E), tel. 48152. Sailing, skating and dancing in quiet surroundings. *Arlas* (M), tel. 48148. Small hotel. *Chesa Grusaida* (M), tel. 48292.

SPLÜGEN. *Posthotel Bodenhaus* (M), tel. 621121. Notable 250-year-old building in this mountain village where Queen Victoria, Napoleon and Tolstoy, among others, are said to have stayed.

TARASP-VULPERA. (All inclusive). *Schweizerhof* (L). All facilities; open summer and winter. Reader-recommended. *Waldhaus* (L), tel. 91112. Cure facilities, tennis, golf and pool in this quiet, but expensive, hotel. Closed in winter. *Villa Silvana* (M), tel. 91354. Sports and cure facilities. *Tarasp* (I–M), tel. 91445. Ice rink; central but quiet.
  Restaurant. *Chastè* (M), tel. 91775. Rated in *Passeport Bleu* as "excellent". Try the sole fillets *à la Champs Elysées*.

ZUOZ. (All inclusive). *Engiadina* (E), tel. 71021. Curling, tennis, pool, sauna and dancing among the facilities in this centrally-located hotel. *Crusch-Alva* (M–E), tel. 71319. Small and central.

USEFUL ADDRESSES. Tourist Information: Verkehrsverein fuer Graubuenden (VVGR), Alexanderstr. 24, Postfach, 7001 Chur (tel. 081-221360). **Car Hire:** *Avis,* at Grabenstrasse 5, Chur; Flüelastr. 2, Davos; and Plazza da Scoula, St. Moritz. *Hertz* at Kasernenstr. 92, Chur; Dischmastr. 39A, Davos; Landstr. 142, Klosters; Via Maistra 46, St. Moritz. *Europcar,* Talstrasse 30, Davos.

WINTER SPORTS. The Grisons and Engadine are a veritable paradise for winter sports enthusiasts. Many of the resorts here number among the best, and most famous, in the whole world. Facilities everywhere are excellent.

Arosa, 1,800 meters (5,906 feet); 3 cable cars, 13 lifts, 70 km. of downhill runs, 35 km. of cross-country tracks; facilities for ski-hiking, skating, curling and ski bob. Schools for skiing (downhill and cross-country) and skating.

Celernia, 1,740 meters (5,700 feet); 2 funicular railways, 3 cable cars, 18 lifts, 60 km. of downhill runs, 15 km. of prepared cross-country tracks; ski schools.

Chur, 609 meters (2,000 feet); 3 cable cars, 3 lifts, 18 km. of trails for downhill skiers and 3 km. of trails for cross-country enthusiasts; tobogganing, skating and ski schools.

Davos, 1,615 meters (5,300 feet); 3 funicular railways, 8 cable cars, 29 lifts. This famous and well-equipped resort has 320 km. of downhill trails and 70 km. of cross-country tracks; skating rinks, toboggan trails and prepared runs, curling and ski schools.

Flims, 1,095 meters (3,600 feet); 6 cable cars, 25 lifts, 220 km. of downhill trails, 45 km. of cross-country tracks; tobogganing, ski bob, curling and ski schools.

Klosters, 1,220 meters (4,000 feet); 2 funicular railways, 1 cable car, 20 lifts, 160 km. of downhill runs, 35 km. of cross-country trails; skating, curling, ski schools.

Laax, 1,125 meters (3,400 feet); 6 cable cars, 25 lifts, 220 km. of downhill runs; highest starting point—3,050 meters (10,000 feet), 62 km. of cross-country tracks; tobogganing, skating, ski schools.

Lenzerheide, 1,510 meters (4,950 feet); 3 cable cars, 34 lifts, 155 km. of downhill runs, 42 km. of cross-country tracks, 30 km. of signalled ski-hiking trails; tobogganing, skating, curling, ski schools.

Maloja, 1,830 meters (6,000 feet); 2 lifts and 12 km. of downhill runs but the emphasis is on cross-country skiing (58 km. of prepared trails); skating, curling, ski schools.

Pontresina, 1,820 meters (5,970 feet); 1 funicular railway, 2 cable cars, 11 lifts, 87 km. of downhill runs, 120 km. of cross-country trails, 38 km. of ski-hiking trails, 9 open curling rinks; ski bob, ski schools.

St. Moritz, 1,875 meters (6,150 feet); 2 funicular railways, 6 cable cars and 47 lifts combine to transport over 50,000 people every hour in this legendary

THE GRISONS AND ENGADINE

ski resort; 400 km. of downhill runs, 150 km. of cross-country trails, 20 km. of special ski bob runs; tobogganing, curling, skating, ski schools.

Samedan, 1,765 meters (5,800 feet); 1 funicular railway, 3 lifts, 16 km. of downhill runs overshadowed by 120 km. of cross-country trails and 17 km. of ski-hiking trails; cross-country and downhill ski schools.

Savognin, 1,220 meters (4,000 feet); 2 cable cars, 14 lifts, 80 km. of downhill runs, 20 km. of cross-country trails, 4 km. of tobogganing runs; curling, ski schools.

S-chanf, 1,700 meters (5,578 feet); a small resort with the emphasis on cross-country skiing (60 km. of trails), 1 lift and 3 km. of runs for downhill skiers.

Silvaplana, 1,830 meters (6,000 feet); 2 cable cars, 7 lifts, 36 km. of downhill runs, 120 km. of cross-country trails, 20 km. of ski-hiking trails; 14 curling rinks, ski bob, downhill ski school.

Splügen, 1,465 meters (4,810 feet); 7 lifts, 22 km. of downhill runs, 30 km. of cross-country tracks; skating, ski schools.

Zuoz, 1,725 meters (5,660 feet); 3 lifts, 20 km. of downhill and cross-country trails, 17.5 km. of ski-hiking trails; tobogganing, ski schools.

THE VALAIS AND THE ALPES VALAISANNES

A Journey Up the Rhône

Extending along the valley of the upper Rhône from Lake Geneva to the river's source, the scenic canton of Valais (Wallis in German) is one of the most magnificent regions in Europe. The river valley itself is roughly L-shaped, with the angle resting on the town of Martigny, where the Val d'Entremont branches off to lead to the Great St. Bernard Pass. It is the right, or long, leg of the L that is the most characteristic and imposing part of the region.

But the Valais is far more than the riverbed of the Rhône and its cliff-like walls. It is an alpine network with a score or more of narrow valleys that wind left and right into even more remote areas. Mark Twain wrote in *A Tramp Abroad* of meeting British tourists in Zermatt

THE VALAIS AND THE ALPES VALAISANNES

at the end of one of the side valleys—they had made the journey by mule—but with a few hardy exceptions, such encounters used to be rare. Until quite recent times, only the feet of the mountain folk and their animals could negotiate the precipitous hillsides. Even today some of the more remote districts rarely see a tourist.

As in all Swiss areas, the Valais enjoys the freedom of choice in which language to use, and here both German and French are spoken.

Exploring the Valais

From Geneva the most direct route by road to the Valais leads along the precipitous southern shore of Lake Geneva which cuts across a corner of France. It is about 88 kilometers (55 miles) to St. Maurice, the real beginning of the Rhône Valley. The usual route, however, remains entirely in Switzerland and goes along the gentler northern shore. This road is about a third longer, but most of it is covered by a fast motorway.

Assuming you have elected to drive along the northern shore, you leave Lake Geneva at Villeneuve, a couple of kilometers beyond Montreux and the Castle of Chillon, and turn inland to drive southeastwards up the Rhône, at this point still in the canton of Vaud. The valley here is broad and alluvial, but by the time you reach Aigle (about 11 kilometers, seven miles away), the mountains are already beginning to crowd in on either side.

Still in the Vaud is Leysin, a popular all-year resort that lies at an altitude of 1,432 meters (4,200 feet), facing south (see under Lake Geneva Region and the Alpes Vaudoises). It can be reached by turning off the main highway to the left, and following a winding road for about 16 kilometers (10 miles). Alternatively take the cogwheel railway from Aigle.

Back in the valley, just beyond Aigle, another road leads to the left, or north. Follow this for 12 kilometers (8 miles) and you will come to Chesières and immediately afterwards, at 1,279 meters (4,200 feet), to Villars, one of the region's better-known summer and winter resorts, with splendid views and a nine-hole golf course. From Villars a mountain railway climbs up to Bretaye (1,858 meters, 6,100 feet), at the foot of Chamossaire, from which lifts fan out in all directions to the surrounding heights, where you can find wonderful ski-runs in winter and fine walks in summer. There is also a cable car to Roc d'Orsay at 2,010 meters (6,600 feet).

If you have made this detour, instead of returning to Aigle, you can continue beyond Villars. Almost immediately, the road (recently widened) begins its long winding descent, offering a succession of glorious views and passing through several picturesque villages before bringing you back to the main highway at Bex, just under 10 kilometers (six miles) beyond Aigle. The whole detour from Aigle to Bex will take rather less than an hour of gentle, if hilly, driving. But try to allow more. It's difficult to resist stopping to admire views, inspect villages, particularly on the downward run, and explore Villars. At Bex you will find a complete contrast because, thanks to its sheltered position on the valley floor this long-established brine spa enjoys a very mild climate—pomegranates, figs and grapes grow here.

Champéry and the Val d'Illiez

Another detour, this time to the southwest, starts from Bex. Don't miss it. You cross the River Rhône (passing out of the Vaud into the Valais), go through the industrial center of Monthey, five kilometers (three miles) west, and then turn up the valley which opens before you. After a couple of kilometers a sharp right fork leads up to Morgins, a small mountain and skiing resort at 1,400 meters (4,600 feet) that is virtually on the French border. Just before you reach Martigny, 14 kilometers (nine miles) further up the river, and Dents du Midi, the final escarpment of the Mont Blanc range, you will arrive at Champéry, an all-year resort perched 1,066 meters (3,500 feet) up in the Val d'Illiez. It has an ideal camping ground a short distance from the village, and is an excellent center for skiing and walking excursions. A cable car swings you a good kilometer higher to Planachaux at 1,767 meters (5,800 feet), where a collection of lifts gives access to some splendid runs. From Champéry it's about 20 kilometers (12 miles) back down to the Rhône and St. Maurice.

St. Maurice is where the two main roads from Lake Geneva, which have hugged each side of the wide Rhône Valley plane, converge; and it is here that both valley and river begin to change character. The mountains have closed in. The Rhône, although still a king-sized river, gradually loses its placidity, giving a foretaste of the mountain torrent it will become as we get nearer its source. St. Maurice owes its name, according to tradition, to Maurice, the leader of the Theban Legion who, with most of his men, was massacred here in AD 302 for refusing to acknowledge the pagan gods of Rome. To commemorate the martyrdom, an abbey was built; and it rapidly grew in importance and wealth. Recent excavations near the abbey church, mostly 17th-century but partly dating from the 11th, have revealed the foundations of the original building. An outstandingly rich collection of treasures has been discovered, and these are certainly worth a visit.

Just before you reach Martigny, 14 kilometers (nine miles) further up the Rhône, another mountainous side trip beckons from the valley floor. A right-hand fork will take you west and then south along a

THE VALAIS AND THE ALPES VALAISANNES

narrow military road (dating from World War II) that weaves through the gorges of the Trient River.

Salvan is the first village in this remote valley. Frequented as a summer resort by Swiss families who rent chalets for the season, it has been so isolated for years that many old traditions survive. On festival days the women have a beautiful and distinctive dress topped by an intricate type of ruching (45 meters per hat) now made only by the older generation. On the evening of August 1, villagers in costume dance to the sound of lively fiddles. The next village, Les Marécottes, is little more than a cluster of chalets and hotels in the pinewoods. Here the road ends, although a railway continues up the valley and eventually into France and Chamonix.

Martigny in ages past was a Roman camp called Octodorum. Today, as you've doubtless noted, it sits squarely astride a historic crossroads at the sharp angle of the River Rhône, the pivot of the L we were imagining. From the town roads go over the Great St. Bernard Pass to Italy, the Forclaz Pass to France, along the upper Rhône to the Simplon Pass and beyond, and down the Rhône Valley to Lake Geneva.

The Great St. Bernard Pass

The Great St. Bernard Pass is the oldest and possibly the most famous of the Swiss crossings. Known and used by the Celts and Romans centuries before the birth of Christ, it has watched an endless stream of emperors, knights and simple travelers. In the 11th century Frederick Barbarossa, the German king and Roman emperor, became almost a commuter over the pass as he went from one country to another to settle the problems which constantly beset him. Napoleon took an army of 40,000 across it en route to Marengo, where he defeated the Austrians in 1800. In somewhat greater comfort than Frederick or Napoleon, you will almost certainly want to explore the pass to the summit, either by car or, better still (because you can watch the scenery while someone else does the driving), by the Swiss postal buses that run to the famous hospice several times a day in summer.

Almost immediately after leaving Martigny, the road to the Grand St. Bernard Pass starts to climb up the valley of the Drance to the village of Sembrancher. Here, a road branches off to the left up the Bagnes Valley to the modern, exceptionally well-equipped resort of Verbier, which lies at 1,490 meters (4,900 feet). Verbier is very popular both with the Swiss and French, thanks largely to the excellent ski-runs served by over 30 assorted lifts and cable cars, one of which goes as far as Mount Gelé at over 3,000 meters (9,900 feet).

At Sembrancher, the St. Bernard Pass road enters the valley of Entremont, and about six kilometers (four miles) further on you will come to Orsières, from where a road to the right leads up the Ferret Valley. It then forks right again to Champex, a small winter sports resort which, due to its lakeside setting is also extremely beautiful in summer. It has a lift to La Breya at 2,190 meters (7,200 feet). You can also reach Champex from Les Vallettes, near Martigny, but this is via a difficult road.

From Orsières, you begin to appreciate the formidable character of the Great St. Bernard. Rocks and mountains close in on all sides as you reach Bourg-St. Pierre, whose inn was patronized by Napoleon (the chair he is said to have used is on display). Except when the winters are unusually severe, the road is kept open to this point so that postal buses can continue to bring mail and food supplies for the monastery at the top of the pass. From here, whenever the pass is blocked with winter snows, the lay brothers and monks have to carry everything up to the hospice on their backs.

But for travelers today the romantic but formidable old pass, which for centuries has been impassable for more than half of each year, has lost much of its fear. For the splendidly engineered new road, which you have seen branching off the old one on which we traveled, is the approach to the new five-and-a-half-kilometer (three and a half miles) St. Bernard Tunnel. This burrows through the mountain to emerge in Italy, thus enabling road traffic to use this important international route all the year round.

The hospice itself, bypassed by the new tunnel, is a gaunt block of grey stone which stands at the highest point on the old road (2,468 meters, 8,100 feet), since its founder wanted to make sure that it could be seen from a distance. For centuries it was a stopping-off point for pilgrims and weary travelers who were offered accommodations without charge, whether for one night or many. (Now you are directed to a nearby hotel—the Grand St. Bernard.)

There is an interesting story about the foundation of the hospice. In the year 1048 Bernard of Menthon, who was Bishop of Aosta, in answer to a request by Hugues of Provence, set out to clear the Mons Jovis—as the St. Bernard was then called—of brigands and highway robbers. It is said that on reaching the summit of the pass the good bishop found a pagan temple, over which he threw his chasuble. The shrine immediately crumbled to dust and, by the same power, the bandits were utterly defeated. Then Bernard, with the help of the canons of his diocese, established the hospice.

The service rendered to travelers by the canons of St. Bernard through the Middle Ages is incalculable. Kings and princes rewarded the hospice by showering estates upon the order. By the 12th century

THE VALAIS AND THE ALPES VALAISANNES

it owned 79 estates in England and elsewhere, among which were Priors Inn and the site of the present Savoy Hotel in London, as well as the Hospice of St. Nicholas and St. Bernard at Hornchurch (Essex).

The canons of St. Bernard are splendid athletes. Their training covers a period of seven years and includes not only the study of theology but also intensive physical preparation, for the priests must pass the official examinations for mountain guides, climbers, and professional skiers.

The St. Bernard dogs have for centuries been the surefooted helpers of the order. In 1949, after two years' travel on foot in Tibet, Canon Détry, of the St. Bernard Hospice, brought back proof that these dogs originated from Central Asia. The canon believes that in Greek and Roman times, Tibetan dogs were brought to Asia Minor with the silk caravans and used by the Romans as war dogs. When the Romans crossed the Alps the dogs found their natural climate, and those that escaped from the Roman armies reverted to their original state.

From near the hospice there is a lift—said to be one of the highest in the world—which will take you to La Chenalette at 2,800 meters (9,200 feet), from which, if you are lucky with the weather, you will have a view that includes no less than 27 glaciers.

Beyond the hospice you will quickly come to the customs post, and from there the road winds down into the Great St. Bernard Valley where it joins up once more with the tunnel route. Before Aosta (Italy) is reached, you will notice that the vegetation is distinctly Mediterranean in character, and you will find it difficult to imagine that in winter the hospice from which you have just come becomes utterly isolated from the world, with snow drifts that rise over three meters (12 feet), as high as the second story of the building.

Isérables and Sion

After allowing your senses to recover from the remarkable trip and sobering views of the St. Bernard, continue up the Rhône Valley, with terraced vineyards on its northern slopes and apricot trees in the middle. About 14 kilometers (nine miles) from Martigny you'll come to the village of Riddes, the terminus of a cable car. A road now links Riddes and Isérables.

This is an unforgettable excursion. The cable car rises in a straight line high above the meadows, depositing you on a platform at the entrance to the village, which is built out of the sheer rock like an eyrie, at a height of 1,035 meters (3,400 feet). A single rough street, lined with flower-decked chalets, leads to a venerable Romanesque church. The *mazots,* or barns, are raised on mushroom shaped blocks to discourage

THE FACE OF SWITZERLAND

mice from marauding among the winter food supplies and to ensure good air circulation.

The inhabitants of this ancient village have long had the curious nickname 'Bedjuis'. Some say it is derived from Bedouins and that the people are descended from the Saracen hordes who, after the battle of Poitiers in 732, overran some of the high alpine valleys. Certainly the people here seem different from many of those in Canton Valais, being stocky, swarthy, and dark eyed.

Back at Riddes on the valley floor, another 14 kilometers (nine miles) will take you to Sion, the capital of the Valais. The town is marked by two rocky hills that materialize in front of you like a fairytale landscape. Crowning the first, Tourbillon, you'll see a ruined castle; on the other, Valère, there is a church. Both indicate the age and ecclesiastical importance of Sion which has been a bishopric for nearly 1,500 years. Valère's church of Notre Dame, looking more like a fortified castle, dates from the 11th century, or even earlier. The ruins on Tourbillon are those of a bishop's residence built in the 13th century. From either hill there is a splendid view of the city below. Don't miss Sion's late Gothic cathedral, notable for its 9th-century Romanesque tower, nor the 17th-century town hall, with its gracious carved doors and ancient clock, and the early 16th-century Supersaxo house. The latter is a superb example of deliberately ostentatious luxury carried out with impeccable taste.

Sion's ancient streets once rang with the echoes of pageantry and ecclesiastical pomp. But the town today is a market center, sharing with nearby Sierre the task of collecting the produce of a prosperous agricultural region where fruit, vegetables and the vine provide a lucrative income. Valais strawberries and asparagus are flown to markets in London and Paris, and the canton produces some of the best wines in Switzerland. In April the mass of blossom in the orchards is not only a beautiful sight, but gives some indication of the immense amount of fruit to come.

The Valais, however, is not all fertile, and it has its share of rocks, mountain torrents and remote valleys; all of which are difficult to cultivate. Many of the women wear a functional version of the national costume: a long-sleeved black dress with a tight bodice and full skirt, a white blouse, black shoes and stockings, a colorful apron, and a black straw hat trimmed with velvet.

Just north of Sion you can see a resort in the making. At Anzère, on what used to be a bare but sunny mountainside plateau, the Swiss have built a carefully planned, deluxe holiday center with hotels, chalets, apartment blocks, skating rink, shops, a large underground car park, and all the necessary trappings, including a cable car to Pas-de-Maimbré at 2,176 meters (7,800 feet) and seven lifts. To the southwest

THE VALAIS AND THE ALPES VALAISANNES

on the opposite side of the Rhône valley lies Haute Nendaz, a mountainside hamlet turned smart mini-resort; above which is Super-Nendaz, at 1,584 meters (5,200 feet).

Up the Val d'Hérens to Evolène

From Sion a good road strikes south up the beautiful Val d'Hérens, past the curious, boulder-capped 'pyramides' of Euseigne, to Evolène and Les Haudères. Before the road was built the people of this valley had to be almost self-supporting and life was frugal. They developed a special local craft—the spinning and weaving of wool. Nowadays Evolène homespun, coarse and warm, is popular throughout Switzerland as knitting wool.

Evolène's charm lies not only in its scenic beauty but also in the old brown chalets and the national costume of the women. From here, the valley and road continue via Les Haudères, its picturesque old chalets overshadowed by the heights of the Dents du Veisivi, to tiny Arolla, which at 2,010 meters (6,600 feet) is one of the highest resorts in the Valais, making it popular with mountaineers.

Excursions from Sierre

If you continue up the valley of the Rhône for about 16 kilometers (10 miles) beyond Sion you will reach Sierre, which boasts of being the sunniest place in what is Switzerland's driest region. It is a busy market town which has thrived on the adjacent aluminum plant at Chippis, and this modern influence can be seen in the buildings, particularly around the station and the terminal of the funicular that runs to Montana. From the town there are three attractive side trips.

The first leads up the northern slope to the adjoining, sophisticated resort complex of Crans-Montana, most attractively perched over 1,500 meters (5,000 feet) up on a spacious sunny plateau among woods, grassland and small lakes. Film stars (including Gina Lollobrigida), tycoons and other celebrities are two-a-penny in the excellent hotels, ultramodern apartment blocks and fashionable shops. There is a golf course, casino, several cable cars and a whole assortment of chairlifts and skilifts. Among the trees on the surrounding mountain slopes are several large hospitals, where various Swiss cantons and cities send their patients to recuperate—an indication of the health-giving properties of the region. The approach to Montana from Sierre is either by funicular or by an excellent road. But if you prefer, you can turn off the main Rhône highway just beyond St. Leonard (about eight kilometers, five miles, from Sierre) to visit Montana and Crans, and then drop down into Sierre without any backtracking.

The second side trip leads northeast to Leukerbad (Loèche-les-Bains), an important health spa and winter sports resort set in a huge amphitheater of mountains at an altitude of 1,400 meters (4,600 feet). It boasts the hottest springs in Switzerland. From here there are cable cars to Gemmi and Torrent at 2,300 meters (7,600 feet), where there are wonderful alpine views and, especially at Gemmi, a famous selection of mountain hikes.

The third excursion is of a very different character. You turn south from Sierre and plunge into the high alpine valley of Anniviers. Here live perhaps the only remaining nomadic people of Europe, the name of the valley being derived from the Latin 'anni viatores' (year-round travelers).

The year of wandering starts in the spring when men, women, and children leave their headquarters in the villages, taking with them their priest and schoolmaster. Only one man is left in each hamlet—as the firewatcher. The migrants first descend to the slopes of the valley around Niouc, where they stay a few weeks, living in barns, and mazots, to till communal land and plant wheat, maize, and potatoes. This done, they move down the valley to Sierre where they cultivate collectively owned vineyards under an almost feudal statute-labor system: every man resident in the commune is obliged to put in so many days' work. The work in the vineyards is done to the accompaniment of fife and drum (usually six players), which roll out tuneless little airs all day long. In late summer the nomads move back up the high valley to gather in the crops and then go down again for the grape harvest. When the year's work on the land is over, they return to their mountain villages and remain there, snowed in all the winter.

Things have changed, however, in the picturesquely sited old village of Zinal, at the head of the valley, once only accessible over a very bad road. Now, with a fine new road kept open throughout the winter it has become a small, carefully planned all-year resort with a cableway to Serebois at 2,430 meters (8,000 feet). But the charming, rustic character of the village, with its ancient barns and chalets, has been retained since all the new structures have, by law, to blend in with the old.

About halfway between Sion and Zinal, at the mountainside village of Vissoie with its strategically placed old tower, a road branches off to Grimentz, a simple little winter sports and summer resort notable for its particularly picturesque old chalets. On the other side of Vissoie a short road climbs steeply up to the ski resort of St. Luc, which has one of the longest skilifts in Switzerland.

Zermatt and the Matterhorn

From Sierre, the Rhône road continues for 29 kilometers (18 miles) up to Visp. At the halfway point, just beyond Gampel-Steg, it passes a left-hand turnoff to the beautiful Lötschen Valley. Visp is the junction for the spectacular railway which, helped by rack-and-pinion, climbs up gradients as steep as 1 in 8 on its one-and-a-half-hour journey to Zermatt. Past picturesque mountain pastures, across rushing torrents, and through steep-sided narrow valleys, it curves and climbs up into the realm of snowy peaks and glaciers. When opened in 1891, it was considered one of the major engineering feats of the time, and even today it is a railway marvel. There is no road to Zermatt but from Visp you can drive as far as Täsch (vast car park at the station). There you have to take one of the frequent electric trains for the remaining five kilometers (three miles) to Zermatt itself—where no private cars are allowed.

Despite world fame, Zermatt is a pint sized town with barely 3,600 inhabitants; a little place with a lot of personality and an absolute ban on automobiles. Strolling down Bahnhofstrasse, Zermatt's principal street, the only dangers are the silent, electric mini-trucks which carry baggage between the station and the hotels, a few horse cabs, and a herd of about 80 goats which trot ceremoniously through the town, their bells clanging loudly, at 8.30 each morning.

At an altitude of 1,615 meters (5,300 feet), Zermatt is set in a hollow of meadows and trees ringed by mighty mountains, which include the unmistakable triangular mass of Matterhorn (4,477 meters, 14,690 feet), or Mont Cervin, as the French-speaking Swiss prefer to call it. In winter skiing is the great attraction, lasting until April on the more accessible runs and right through the summer in the Theodul Pass area. There are cable cars, lifts galore, nearly a score of skating and curling rinks, and every possible facility for mountain climbing. Indeed, the name Zermatt is synonymous with mountaineering. Over the last 100 years or more, Zermatt's guides have become world famous and have accompanied expeditions to the Himalayas and other great mountain ranges of the world.

At 5.30 A.M. on Friday July 13 1865, in the tiny hamlet of Zermatt, a certain Alexander Seiler stood at the door of his newly acquired hotel waving goodbye to a party of seven men starting off on a dangerous and historic climb. They were Edward Whymper, the Rev. Charles Hudson, Douglas Hadow, Lord Francis Douglas, and three guides, two Swiss—Peter Taugwalder and his son—and one French, Michel Croz. The next day, at 1.40 P.M., Whymper and his party achieved their objective by becoming the first people ever to set foot on the summit of the Matterhorn. But disaster followed: on the way down, Hadow slipped, a rope broke, and all except Whymper and the Taugwalders were killed by falling over 1,200 meters (4,000 feet) down the North Wall.

Alexander Seiler, the man who waved farewell to the ill-fated party, also had a distinguished, if less glamorous, career. He was new to Zermatt, having just purchased the tiny village's original hotel—Lauber's Inn—which he renamed Monte Rosa Hotel. He proved to be a born hotelier and the Monte Rosa became merely the first of the famous Seiler group of hotels.

From Zermatt to Gornergrat runs one of the highest cogwheel railways in Europe. Gornergrat has inspired so many grandiloquent descriptions that it is enough to say that among all your memories of Switzerland one of the most vivid will be of standing here at an altitude of over 3,100 meters (10,200 feet), gazing across glistening glaciers to Monte Rosa (the mountain, not the hotel!), the Matterhorn, and about 50 almost equally majestic peaks; as well as a grand total of 32 glaciers.

Another excellent excursion from Zermatt, this time a three-stage one, starts by taking the lift to Sunnega at 2,285 meters (7,500 feet), the gondola car to Blauherd (2,590 meters, 8,500 feet), and finally the cable car for the final climb of 217 meters (1,700 feet) to Findeln Rothorn, where once again—if you're lucky with the weather—the view will make you forget the cost. You can also go to Schwarzsee, nearly 2,600 meters (8,500 feet) high, by cableway. From there the awe-inspiring Matterhorn seems almost near enough to touch. Or you can take the cable car to Trockener Steg and Klein-Matterhorn (2,956 meters, 9,700 feet), where there's the largest summer skiing area in the Alps.

Saas-Fee and Grächen

Zermatt is at the head of one of the two valleys that lead south from Visp. In the other (the road forks at Stalden) at a height of nearly 1,800 meters (5,900 feet) is the important winter and summer resort of Saas-Fee; another car-free town. Besides a number of lifts there are cable cars to Längfluh, a good starting point for skiing and walking tours which lies at the foot of the Dom (a peak even higher than the Matterhorn); and to Felskinn (2,986 meters, 9,800 feet). There are also gondola cars to Hannig (2,376 meters, 7,800 feet) and Plattjen (2,529 meters, 8,300 feet). From Saas-Fee you can usually ski until mid-July at Felskinn.

Another fine holiday resort is at Grächen, a sunny village which lies on a magnificent mountain terrace 1,615 meters (5,300 feet) above sea level. You can reach it by car or postal bus from St. Niklaus Station.

THE VALAIS AND THE ALPES VALAISANNES

It has all the facilities for a summer and winter resort, with an aerial cableway that brings the tourists up to the splendid skiing fields on the Hannigalp. So much new has been built here in recent years that it is difficult to find the old heart of town.

Brig and the Simplon Pass

Back at Visp, if you continue up the Rhône Valley, you come quickly to the important rail and road junction of Brig. This small town has for centuries been a center of trade with Italy, for not only does it guard the Simplon route, but it also lies at the foot of the high valley of the Rhône. The latter leads past the Aletsch Glacier to Gletsch and the Grimsel Pass (for the route north to Meiringen and the Bernese Oberland) or the Furka Pass (towards Andermatt and central Switzerland).

Brig has one particularly interesting and curious feature—the Stockalper Castle, Switzerland's largest private residence. It was built between 1658 and 1678 for Gaspard Stockalper, a 17th-century Swiss tycoon who was the first to recognize the importance of the Simplon Pass for trade with Italy, and who amassed immense wealth by exploiting it to the full. But he also made much money from salt and other monopolies, and from a host of shrewd enterprises and deals. Likeable as well as rich, and speaking five languages, Stockalper was apparently quite a character and was welcomed at the courts of kings, the palaces of popes, and the salons of international society. He not only made money in vast quantities, but poured it in the same way into his fabulous new home—the Stockalperpalast. But the people of the Valais gradually came to resent their uncrowned king and his wealth. Eventually, and rather tragically, he had to flee in disguise to Italy over the very pass which had brought him much of his wealth. After six years of exile he returned, only to die shortly afterwards in his palatial home. This huge structure, instantly recognizable by its trio of onion-topped towers, has a gigantic central courtyard surrounded by elegant cloisters, and is certainly worth a visit. Nearby is Brigerbad, where there is a very pleasant open-air thermal bath.

Just above the eastern outskirts of Brig is the entrance to the twin Simplon Tunnels, through which famous international trains disappear into dank darkness to emerge almost 20 kilometers (12 miles, 500 yards) later into Italian daylight on the southern side of the Alps. The first of the twin tunnels—the world's longest railway tunnels—was started in 1898 and took six years to complete.

The Simplon Pass road also begins just outside Brig, meandering through deep gorges and wide, barren, rock-strewn pastures, and across the mountains' flanks. As the highway slowly rises, there are glimpses of Brig in the Rhône Valley below, giving an excellent view of these grim historic routes: at one point the Aletsch Glacier can be seen shimmering in the distance.

At the top of the pass stands the Simplon-Kulm Hotel (2,010 meters, 6,600 feet) and, just beyond it, the Simplon Hospice of the monks of St. Bernard, built 150 years ago at Napoleon's request. A little farther on, cupped in a hollow to the right of the main road, is the Alter Spital. A square, tall building with a church-like bell tower, this hospice was built in the 17th century by our friend, Gaspard Stockalper. Beside it you can still see parts of the old road of the merchant princes and Napoleon, and it is easy to imagine the hardships which travelers of those times had to bear in crossing the pass. The road drops rapidly from the summit, passing through Simplon village and then Gondo, the last village in Switzerland.

The Simplon Pass is an impressive gateway to Italy, with a succession of splendid views and lots of stopping places from which to admire them. It is a well-surfaced road (making it one of the easier of the major alpine passes), and the recent addition of extensive new tunnels and snow galleries means that it is now open throughout the year. If, however, exceptionally heavy snowfalls temporarily close the road your car can be taken by train through the rail tunnel between Brig and Iselle (the first village on the Italian side).

From Brig up the Rhône to Gletsch

We should not leave the neighborhood of Brig without mentioning one of the most remarkable trains in Europe, the *Glacier Express*. Starting from Zermatt, it runs through Brig, up the Rhône Valley, through the Furka Tunnel, past Andermatt, over the Oberalp Pass, and then down through Disentis and Chur in the Grisons to terminate in St. Moritz. From Andermatt onwards it carries a restaurant car. This famous train struggles across the backbone of Europe, running through places where a mountain goat would be hard pressed to find a footing. For miles it toils up gradients so severe that cogwheels are necessary and goes round curves so sharp that it seems in danger of tying a knot in itself. Much of the time it is above the timber line. Unfortunately, the most spectacular mountain section of the line over the Furka Pass via Gletsch has been closed. So no longer can you view the magnificent Rhône Glacier from the train. However, sights of a feat of nature have been replaced by the experience of a feat of man—the longest meter gauge railroad tunnel in the world, from Oberwald to Realp, at some 15.4 kilometers. This masterpiece of engineering provides a direct all-year connection between the resorts of the Valais, Central Switzerland and the Grisons.

THE VALAIS AND THE ALPES VALAISANNES

From Brig, closely following the route taken by the Glacier Express, the main road continues up the valley of the Rhône, before going underground at Oberwald, as we have mentioned above. To the north of the turbulent river is the great mass of the Bernese Oberland, with some of the highest mountains in Europe—Aletschhorn, Jungfrau, Mönch, Eiger, Schreckhorn, Finsteraarhorn and many others. Life in this part of the valley is especially hard, the soil poor and the road approach to Gletsch blocked by snow from November until about June. But it is a journey well worthwhile, one in which grimness, beauty and grandeur combine in a superb and powerful symphony, a fitting farewell to the Valais.

PRACTICAL INFORMATION FOR THE VALAIS AND ALPES VALAISANNES

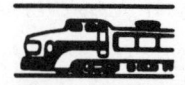

GETTING AROUND. By Train and Bus. The Valais is bisected from east to west by the main line coming from the Simplon Tunnel down the Rhône Valley to Lake Geneva. At Brig the spectacular Furka-Oberalp Railway runs east climbing up to Oberwald, then through the Furka Tunnel and on to Andermatt. To view the Rhône Glacier, take a post bus from Brig. Also from Brig the Berne, Lötschberg and Simplon Railway (usually known by its initials BLS) goes north to central Switzerland—another spectacular route. Again, also from Brig goes the even more scenic route via Visp and up the Mattertal to the famous resort of Zermatt at the foot of the Matterhorn. Indeed you can only reach Zermatt by train—cars are banned.

In addition most of the valleys in the region are served by postal coaches connecting with the main line trains. One of the best of these routes is to the resort of Saas Fee.

There is no single Regional Ticket covering the whole of the Valais. But those for Montreux/Vevey and the Chablais Region give good coverage of the western part of the canton, while the Bernese Oberland card covers the north, including Brig and Zermatt. Postal coach weekly season tickets effectively cover the central Rhône Valley, being available for the districts of Sion and Sierre. However, your best bet is—as usual—the superb-value Swiss Holiday Card, which includes everything!

HOTELS AND RESTAURANTS. Nearly all the hotels that we include in our listings below have a wide range of rooms, a good many of which may well fall into a lower grading than that which we have given here. The best advice is always to check beforehand with the hotel (we have provided phone numbers to facilitate this).

ANZÈRE. *Des Masques* (M), tel. 382651. *Grand Roc* (I), tel. 383535.

BOURG-SAINT-PIERRE. *Du Vieux Moulin* (I), tel. 49169. Small, with restaurant. Very reasonable.

BRIG. *Alpina-Volkshaus* (M), tel. 237636. With bowling. *Gliserallee* (I), tel. 231195. Very small and inexpensive. *Schlosshotel* (I), tel. 236455. Breakfast only; quiet and with facilities for the handicapped. *Victoria* (I), tel. 231503.
Restaurant. *Schlosskeller* (I–M), tel. 233352.

CHAMPÉRY. *De Champéry* (E), tel. 791711. Quiet and with bowling. *Beau-Séjour Vieux Chalet* (M), tel. 791701. Quiet. *Rose des Alpes* (I), tel. 791218.
Restaurant. *Des Alpes* (M–I), tel. 84222. Excellent.

CHAMPEX. *Des Alpes et Lac* (M), tel. 41151. Tennis and facilities for children. *Auberge de la Forêt* (I), tel. 41278. Small. *Du Glacier Sporting* (I), tel. 41207. Quiet and ideal for children.

CHARRAT. *De la Gare* (I), tel. 53698. Small, with restaurant.
Restaurant. *Mon Moulin* (E), tel. 53292. Excellent.

CRANS. *Alpine et Savoy* (L), tel. 412142. Gymnasium, indoor pool and sauna. *Beauséjour* (L), tel. 412446. Indoor pool and sauna. *De l'Etrier* (L), tel. 411515. 2 pools, riding and sauna. *Du Golf et des Sports* (L), tel. 414242. Tennis, indoor pool and sauna; very expensive. *Excelsior* (E–L), tel. 413821. Quiet and comfortable. *Elite* (E), tel. 414301. Pool and facilities for the handicapped; ideal for children. *Belmont* (M), tel. 411171. Quiet rooms. *Etoile* (M), tel. 411671. Central. *Les Mélèzes* (M), tel. 431812. Quiet hotel in own grounds. *Tourist* (M), tel. 413256. Breakfast only; central and in own grounds. *Centrale* (I), tel. 413767. Central. *Du Téléférique* (I), tel. 413367. Small.
Restaurant. *Rôtisserie de la Channe* (M–E), tel. 411258.

EVOLÈNE. *D'Evoléne* (I), tel. 831202. Tennis and pool; ideal for children. *Hermitage* (I), tel. 831232. Quiet.

GRÄCHEN. (All inclusive). *Elite* (M), tel. 561612. Quiet rooms. *Hannigalp & Valaisia* (M), tel. 562555. Indoor pool, gymnasium and sauna. *Waldheim* (M), tel. 561948. Quiet family hotel with gymnasium and sauna. *Walliserhof* (I–M), tel. 561122. With skittle alley. *Alpina* (I), tel. 562626. Central, but quiet rooms.

THE VALAIS AND THE ALPES VALAISANNES 257

GRIMENTZ. *La Cordée* (I), tel. 651246. Comfortable and very quiet with magnificent views. *De Moiry* (I), tel. 651144. Inexpensive and quiet. *Marenda* (I), tel. 651171. Large hotel in own grounds with excellent food; very quiet.

GRIMSEL. *Grimselblick* (I), tel. 731126. Small and with restaurant. *Grimsel-Hospiz* (I), tel. 731231. Very quiet and with superb views.

HAUTE-NENDAZ. *Mont-Calme* (I), tel, 882240. In own grounds. *Sourire* (I), tel. 882616. Central and quiet.

LEUKERBAD. (All inclusive). *Badehotel Bristol* (L), tel. 611833. Riding, tennis, indoor pool and gymnasium as well as cure facilities. *Badehotel des Alpes* (E–L), tel. 612651. Spa hotel; tennis and indoor pool; central. *Badehotel Grand-Bain* (E–L), tel. 611112. Spa hotel; tennis. *Escher* (M), tel. 611431. *Walliserhof* (M), tel. 611424. Centrally located and with facilities for the handicapped. *Zayetta* (M), tel 611646. Central and quiet and with sauna. *Chamois* (I), tel. 611357. Breakfast only; small, simple and inexpensive. *Dala* (I), tel. 611213. Breakfast only; central; facilities for the handicapped.

LES MARECOTTES. *Aux Milles Etoiles* (E), tel. 81547. Ideal family hotel with indoor pool, gym and sauna; very quiet. *Joli-Mont* (I), tel. 81470. Skating, tennis and outdoor pool; central and in own grounds.

MARTIGNY. *Du Rhône* (M), tel. 21717. Central with very quiet rooms and facilities for the handicapped. *De la Poste* (I), tel. 21444. Central and with quiet rooms. Breakfast only. *Du Grand St-Bernard* (I), tel. 22612. With restaurant.

MONTANA. *Curling* (E), tel. 411242. Pool and sauna; very quiet rooms. *De la Fôret* (E), tel. 413608. Indoor pool and sauna in this well-appointed hotel. *Mirabeau* (E), tel. 412912. Superior hotel with bowling; central. *St-Georges* (E), tel. 412414. Very quiet but central hotel in own grounds; pool. *Du Lac* (M), tel. 413414. Very quiet and in own grounds. *Forest* (M), tel. 411698. Medium-sized hotel in own grounds; quiet. *Cisalpin* (I), tel. 412425. *Weisshorn* (I), tel. 412152. Very small and very quiet hotel in own grounds. Very reasonable.

MORGINS. *Bellevue* (E), tel. 772771. Superior hotel with facilities for children, indoor pool and sauna. *Beau Site* (I), tel. 771138. Good value, Breakfast only. No rooms with bath.

SAAS-FEE. (All inclusive). *Beau-Site* (L), tel. 571122. Central; with indoor pool and sauna. *Grand Hotel* (L), tel. 571001. Comfortable and luxurious: pool and tennis. *Saaserhof* (L), tel. 571551. Facilities for the handicapped along with sauna and quiet rooms in this the smartest hotel in town. *Allalin* (E), tel. 571815. Central and quiet with marvelous view. *Burgener* (E), tel. 571522. Central but quiet and with superb view. *Dom* (M–E), tel. 591101. Quiet; sauna. *Britannia*

(I), tel. 571616. Sauna. *Sonnenhof* (M), tel. 572693. Quiet and good. *Des Alpes* (I), tel. 571555. Quiet rooms; sauna. Breakfast only.

SIMPLON. *Bellevue* (I), tel. 291331. Quiet rooms; restaurant. *Simplon-Blick* (I), tel. 291113. Quiet rooms; restaurant. No rooms with bath.

SION. *De la Gare* (I), tel. 232821. Airconditioned; near the station. *Touring* (I), tel. 231551. Facilities for the handicapped and quiet rooms.

Restaurants. *Caves de Tous Vents* (M–E), tel. 224684. Very good. *Big Ben Pub* (I–M), tel. 227977.

VERBIER. (All inclusive). *Rhodania* (L), tel. 70121. Comfortable and central. *Farinet* (E), tel. 76626. *Grand-Combin* (E), tel. 75515. Central and quiet and with facilities for the handicapped. *Le Mazot* (E), tel. 76812. Sauna. *Catogne* (M), tel. 75105. *Rosa-Blanche* (M), tel. 74472. Reasonable.

Restaurant. *Rosalp* (M–E), tel. 76323. Outstanding.

ZERMATT. (All inclusive). *Grand Hotel Zermatterhof* (L), tel. 661101. Tennis, indoor pool, sauna and gymnasium in this desirable hotel. *Mont Cervin-Seilerhaus* (L), tel. 661121. Famous and luxurious; tennis, indoor pool, sauna; central. *Monte Rosa* (L), tel. 671922. Atmospheric and comfortable. *Pollux* (L), tel. 671946. Quiet; sauna. *Alphubel* (E), tel. 673003. Central and quiet. *Butterfly* (E), tel. 673721. Central and quiet. *Carina* (E), tel. 671767. In own grounds; sauna. *Tannenhof* (I), tel. 673188. Breakfast only; reasonable. *Touring* (I–M), tel. 671177. Quiet.

Restaurants. *Seilerhaus & Otto-Furrer-Stube* (M–E), tel. 661121. *Tenne* (M–E), tel. 671801. Excellent. *Nicoletta* (I–M), tel. 671174. First class.

USEFUL ADDRESS. Tourist Information: Union valaisanne du tourisme (UVT), 6 rue de Lausanne, Case postale, 1951 Sion (tel. 027-222898).

WINTER SPORTS. The Valais is home to many of Switzerland's finest and best equipped winter sports resorts. In both numbers and facilities, they rival those of the Bernese Oberland and the Grisons. The following is a list of the major resorts.

Anzère, 1,525 meters (5,000 feet); 1 cable car, 9 lifts, 14 km. of downhill runs, 10 km. of cross-country trails; skating, ski bob, ski schools.

Bettmeralp, 1,956 meters (6,435 feet); 1 cable car, 6 lifts, 10 km. of ski-hiking trails, 5 km. of cross-country trails, tennis, minigolf, riding, heated indoor pool, ski school.

Brig, 690 meters (2,260 feet); 1 cable car, 4 lifts, 80 km. of downhill runs, 5 km. of cross-country trails; skating; ski schools.

Champéry, 1,035 meters (3,400 feet); 3 cable cars, 5 lifts, 35 km. of downhill runs, 6 km. of cross-country trails; ski bob, skating, tobogganing.

THE VALAIS AND THE ALPES VALAISANNES

Champex-Lac, 1,470 meters (4,823 feet); 4 lifts, 21 km. of downhill runs, 20 km. of cross-country trails, 3 km. of ski-hiking trails; skating, ski schools.

Crans, 1,525 meters (5,000 feet); 1 funicular railway, 8 cable cars, 25 lifts, 120 km. of downhill runs, 30 km. of cross-country trails, 15 km. of ski-hiking trails; ski bob, curling, ski schools.

Crans-Montana, offers all the facilities to be found in Crans plus a world-famous alpine golf course.

Evolène, 1,370 meters (4,500 feet); 4 lifts, 5 km. of downhill runs, 10 km. of cross-country trails, 8 km. of ski-hiking trails; curling, ski schools.

Graechen, 1,635 meters (5,360 feet); 1 cable car, 10 lifts, 7 km. of downhill runs, 32 km. of cross-country trails; curling, ski schools.

Grimentz, 1,600 meters (5,250 feet); 8 lifts, 50 km. of downhill runs, 5 km. of cross-country trails, 6 km. of ski-hiking trails, 5 km. of tobogganing runs; curling, ski schools.

Haute Nendaz, 1,310 meters (4,300 feet); 1 cable car, 18 lifts, 60 km. of down-hill runs, 15 km. of cross-country trails; curling, ski bob, ski schools.

Leukerbad, 1,415 meters (4,650 feet); 4 cable cars, 10 lifts, 30 km. of downhill runs, 25 km. of cross-country trails, 20 km. of ski-hiking trails; skating, curling, ski schools.

Les Marécottes, 1,110 meters (3,650 feet); 1 funicular railway, 1 cable car, 4 lifts, 21 km. of downhill runs, 2.5 km. of cross-country trails; tobogganing, ski bob, ski school.

Morgins, 1,430 meters (4,700 feet); 1 cable car, 18 lifts, 50 km. of downhill runs, 39 km. of ski-hiking, 0.4 km. of prepared toboggan runs; ski bob, ski school.

Riederalp, 1,200–2,000 meters (3,935–6,560 feet); 8 lifts, 10 km. of ski-hiking trails, 2 km. of cross-country trails, tennis, minigolf, heated indoor pool, ski school. Bettmeralp and Riederalp are linked and have a common season ticket for the lifts.

Saas Fee, 1,820 meters (5,980 feet); 5 cable cars, 17 lifts, 50 km. of downhill runs, 8 km. of cross-country trails, 3.5 km. of prepared toboggan runs; curling, ski schools.

Simplon, 1,495 meters (4,900 feet); 3 lifts, 8 km. of downhill runs, 8 km. of cross-country trails.

Verbier, 1,525 meters (5,000 feet); 9 cable cars, 27 lifts, 150 km. of downhill runs, 18 km. of cross-country trails, 1.1 km. of toboggan runs; curling, ski bob, ski school.

Zermatt, 1,635 meters (5,360 feet); 2 funicular railways, 12 cable cars, 19 lifts, 130 km. of downhill runs, 22 km. of cross-country trails, 46 km. of ski-hiking trails; curling, ski schools.

Zinal, 1,685 meters (5,530 feet); 1 cable car, 7 lifts, 60 km. of downhill runs, 10 km. of cross-country trails; skating, ski schools.

THE LAKE GENEVA REGION

Lausanne, Vevey and Montreux

One of the joys of Lake Geneva is that when you travel along the northern (Swiss) side the road never strays far from the shore and provides an unending succession of lovely views of the lake, mountains and vine-covered hillsides. But if you are in a hurry and take the motorway, which runs all the way from Geneva to Bex at the eastern end of the lake, the other drivers rather than the view will claim your attention.

From Geneva to Rolle, the shore road is bordered by fine parklands and estates strikingly reminiscent of the English countryside, a likeness which is more than mere coincidence. In the late 18th century the sons of wealthy Genevan and Vaud families often became tutors in prosperous English families. They returned with money in the bank and new ideas, planning their gardens in the style they had admired in England.

THE LAKE GENEVA REGION

At Coppet, 12 kilometers (eight miles) from Geneva, is the lovely old Château where the remarkable Madame de Staël spent many years in exile. She was the daughter of Suzanne Curchod, whose father was a Vaud parson. Suzanne had been jilted by the youthful Edward Gibbon in 1756 and, on the rebound, did very well for herself by accepting the hand of Jacques Necker, a Genevan banker who later became financial adviser to Louis XVI. The far-sighted Necker bought the mansion at Coppet as a retreat, and he was glad to take refuge there when the French Revolution broke out. At the château, Madame de Staël established an intellectual court whose literary salons were attended by giants of the early romantic period: Byron, Benjamin Constant, Sismondi, August Schlegel, the faithless Edward Gibbon, and others. The château, still kept as it was in Madame's time, may be visited every day except Monday. The regional museum of Vieux Coppet has just opened over the "Copétane" in the Grand-Rue.

Nyon, some eight kilometers (five miles) from Coppet, was founded by Julius Caesar in about 56 BC as a camp for war veterans. The Romans called it Noviodunum and the splendid Basilica they built there today houses an impressive museum with many remains from the Roman period. The castle was built by Louis, first Baron of Vaud, and taken over by the Bernese in 1570 as residence for their bailiffs. Today it houses a museum noted for its collection of Nyon china. In the 17th and 18th centuries Nyon was the center of a flourishing chinaware craft; its flowersprigged tea sets, vases, and bowls were in great demand and today are still sought by collectors. Nyon motifs are now used by Swiss manufacturers and for hand painted craftwork. If you leave the road to visit the town center you'll find one good view from the gardens and another from the castle. Down by the shore, with its delightful promenade, the Lac Léman museum features models of the lake's boats through the ages.

Further along the shore is Rolle, a pleasant, small town with a castle by the water's edge. If you have time it is worth turning left at Allaman —about five kilometers (three miles) beyond Rolle—to visit Aubonne, for much of the village has remained virtually unchanged since the 16th century. The 12th-century castle in Rolle was bought in 1670 by the eccentric J. B. Tavernier, a great French traveler who visited the courts of Persia and Turkey and wrote entertaining accounts of his journeys.

Morges, about 12 kilometers (eight miles) from Rolle, is a peaceful little lake port, popular among sailing enthusiasts. It too has a castle, in this instance built by the Duke of Savoy in about 1286 as a defense against the bishop-princes of Lausanne. Morges is one of the Vaud's principal wine-producing centers, and has an exuberant and joyful wine festival every year on the last weekend of September. It lasts for three days and the whole town throws itself into the merry making with floats, parties and, naturally, more than a little serious wine tasting. However, the festival has become very popular so if you want to join in the fun book your hotel well in advance.

La Côte

The district between Coppet and Morges is known as La Côte, the sunny slopes providing excellent conditions for vine-growing. La Côte vintages are light, white wines, mostly consumed on the home market.
About six kilometers (four miles) from Lausanne you'll come to St. Sulpice where, from May onwards, the owners of countless weekend houses move in for the summer enjoyment of Lake Geneva. St. Sulpice is also the proud possessor of the best preserved 11th-century Romanesque church in Switzerland, a charming little building. It was built by monks from the famous Cluny Abbey in Burgundy. Three original apses remain, although the nave has disappeared. The short bell tower is built of small stone blocks that were probably brought from the ruined Roman township at nearby Vidy. The adjoining priory was converted into a private residence during the 16th century.

Lausanne

The story of Lausanne, two-thirds of the way along the north shore of Lac Léman, is possibly less illustrious than that of Geneva, although just as ancient. Traces of prehistoric man have been found in and around the city, and when Julius Caesar arrived at the end of the first century BC he found settlements of lake dwellers and a primitive stronghold. The Romans established a military camp and relay point by the lake at Vidy, on the western fringe of present-day Lausanne (or 'Lousonna', as they called it) and the place became an important junction of routes into Gaul and over the Great St. Bernard Pass into Italy. Four centuries later the Alemanni, a German tribe, burned the township, and its citizens took refuge at another smaller settlement already established a bit higher up the hill. To this refuge came Bishop Maire (or Marius) fleeing from his burnt-out see of Aventicum (now the town of Avenches), near the eastern shore of Lake Neuchâtel. A church was built and trade began, merchants climbing with their pack mules to the developing town on the hill.

In the 12th century Italian, Flemish and French architects, with the encouragement of Pope Innocent IV, set about building a cathedral. By 1275, this beautiful Burgundian Gothic edifice—today considered one of the finest medieval churches in Switzerland—was ready for consecration. Another Pope, Gregory X, came expressly to perform the ceremony. To mark the occasion, the ubiquitous Rudolph of Habsburg brought his wife, eight children, seven cardinals, five archbishops, seventeen bishops, four dukes, fifteen counts, and a multitude of lesser lords, spiritual and temporal; for the Pope was to make it a double event by crowning him Emperor of Germany and the Holy Roman Empire.

With such a flying start, Lausanne's Cathedral of Notre Dame could not fail to become a pilgrimage center—and so it did. Merchants, traders and innkeepers thrived, their houses spreading down the hillside and into the two rocky valleys surrounding the crag on which the cathedral stood. The bishops in their palace-fortress waxed powerful and wealthy, building themselves a summer island-castle at Ouchy, the growing town's lake port and fishing village. Although the House of Savoy owned most of the neighboring territory, Lausanne itself was ruled firmly by the bishops.

Towards the end of the 15th century tension between the citizens of Lausanne and the all-powerful bishop mounted, with the result that in 1525, in order to assert its right of franchise, the city council concluded a treaty of 'fellow burgership' with the powerful cantons of Berne and Fribourg. Berne proved a fickle friend however, and in the summer of 1536 she declared war on Savoy and invaded the Pays de Vaud, the region around Lausanne which was a vassal territory of Savoy. Then, claiming that Sebastian of Montfaucon, the Bishop of Lausanne, was a partisan of Savoy, Berne also marched into this city, where the invading army was greeted as a liberator. But the conquering force chose to treat both Vaud and Lausanne as occupied territory, putting a bailiff in the bishop's castle and reducing the power of the city fathers to zero. That August, the city council felt compelled to renounce Catholicism and accept the reformed faith. Catholic churches were ransacked and the cathedral's treasures sent to fill Bernese coffers.

However, the culture of Lausanne remained intact and, despite the stern glances of Bernese society in the 18th century, grew particularly brilliant. The élite of the district offered warm-hearted hospitality to the cream of European society and intellect. From many countries aristocrats and literary celebrities, such as the historian Edward Gibbon, the Duke of Württemberg and Voltaire, were drawn to Lausanne and caught up in a social whirl of parties, amateur theatricals, whist and picnics. But revolt seethed behind this glittering facade, and it erupted in January 1798 when the Liberal Party, led by Fréderic César de la Harpe, proclaimed the independence of the Vaud and threw out the Bernese. Years of bickering followed until, in 1803, Napoleon Bonaparte introduced the Act of Mediation. Among other things this document, which for the first time in history used the word 'Switzerland' as the name of the whole country, created the independent Canton of Vaud, making Lausanne its capital.

The Modern City

As a prosperous market town, renowned as a center of culture, and with a romantic attraction for English travelers and residents, Lausanne began to take itself seriously towards the end of the 19th century. Construction of roads, avenues and bridges went on apace.

Lausanne today is as nearly picturesque as a modern, bustling city can be. Rising in tiers from the lakeside at Ouchy (360 meters, 1,200 feet above sea level) to over 600 meters (2,000 feet), it is situated on three hills. Two small rivers used to flow through gorges between the hills, but they are now entirely covered over and the valleys spanned by several handsome bridges carrying the flow of modern traffic high over the streets and houses beneath.

In the last 15 or 20 years this civic-minded community has become the business center of western Switzerland, adopting the title of 'capital city of the Léman region.' Not only does it lie on the major international rail routes, it is also an important national junction; and in consequence both the surrounding agricultural land and the expanding industrial towns of the canton (Yverdon, Cossonay, and Sainte-Croix) have to channel their trade through Lausanne.

Over the years Lausanne has become the home of many royal families, either reigning, deposed, or abidcated; but the general tone of the city owes much more to the hard-headed and humorous country people, from whom even some of the 'best' families have sprung. Moreover, many of the leading business families are descended from 17th-century French Huguenots. There has never been an oligarchy in Lausanne as in Fribourg, Geneva or Neuchâtel; and as a result less stress is laid on the quality of the family tree. An old farmstead or winegrower's vault is almost equal to a castle in terms of importance as a family seat.

Exploring Lausanne

Lausanne, a splendid excursion center and long popular with tourists, is a cosmopolitan city; one with an air of youthful vitality, stimulated by the great number of young people who attend its famous university and many educational establishments. Since 1945 the city has been enjoying a building spree. Old houses and whole quarters have been pulled down to make way for shining new office blocks and apartments; and garden suburbs are expanding to meet the housing shortage, caused by the growth of new industry.

Architectural exuberance has given Lausanne a rather lopsided air. A hillside skyscraper (seventeen stories on one side and fifteen on the other) contrasts brutally with the beautiful proportions of the cathedral

THE LAKE GENEVA REGION

rising in majesty on the crest of its hill. Atmospheric, although possibly unhygienic, alleys and narrow streets have been ruthlessly demolished but the old cité clustered around Notre Dame has been painstakingly and attractively restored and refurbished.

Most of the shopping and sightseeing in Lausanne can be done within 550 meters (600 yards) of the place St. François, the hub of the city and a traffic maelstrom. North of the place and close to the cathedral of Notre Dame, a fine example of Burgundian Gothic (carefully restored since the vandalism of Reformation days) is the 15th-century castle of St. Maire, formerly the bishop's palace; and the university (Palais de Rumine) with its fine museums. To the left, on the way from the Place to the cathedral, is the charming 17th-century City Hall, its clock tower looking down onto the bustling, colorful market in the place de la Palud. To the west of St. François, beyond the terminal of the funicular (which goes all the way down to Ouchy), are the 19th-century Law Courts. To the east, in the Park of Mon Repos are the handsome, modern buildings of the Federal Palace of Justice, Switzerland's Supreme Court of Appeal.

But almost any walk around the hilly streets, steep alleys and stairways is rewarding for it will take you past a succession of charming old buildings and incongruous, often impressive, new ones. You will get a hundred different views of the lake across rooftops, between buildings, or from the gardens. (But remember: in Lausanne it is 'Lac Léman'—none of that silly 'Lake Geneva' nonsense!) Perhaps the two finest views in Lausanne are from the Park of Montriond, a short walk from the station down avenue W. Fraisse, and from Le Signal, a justly famed viewpoint 640 meters (2,100 feet) high, which lies just over a kilometer north of the cathedral.

For those who enjoy walking, there are innumerable day and half-day trips to be made in the wooded hills of Jorat, about 820 meters (2,700 feet) high, above the city. A little lower, at Sauvabelin, just beyond Le Signal, there is a fine park, a charming little lake and a restaurant. Down by the waterside is Ouchy, with its long, elegant, tree-lined promenades that offer splendid views of both lake and mountains. You will also find colorful gardens and a wide range of hotels, including a number in the super-deluxe class. Ouchy is Lausanne's port, although it is far from being a conventional one. True, it's quite a busy spot, but its activity is mainly with the smart white steamers; more call here than at any other place on the lake. So it makes a fine starting point for excursions as well as being an international resort.

The Lavaux Region

On the eastern side of Lausanne is the Lavaux, a remarkably beautiful region of vineyards, which rise up the hillsides all the way from Pully, on the outskirts of Lausanne, to Montreux—a distance of around 24 kilometers (15 miles). Brown-roofed stone villages in the Savoy style, old defense towers and small baronial castles stud the green and brown landscape. The vineyards, enclosed within low stone walls, slope so steeply that all the work there has to be done by hand. Insecticides, fungicides, manures, and even soil washed down by summer storms are carried in baskets and containers strapped to men's backs. No wonder harvest in mid-October is a period for rejoicing! The grapes, picked by cheerful looking girls and women, are carried down by the men to the nearest road, emptied into vats and taken by horse or tractor to the nearest press. Some Lavaux vintages are excellent and in great demand, but unfortunately the yield is small.

At Cully, about eight kilometers (five miles) east of Lausanne, the motorist has a choice of roads just before entering the village. Straight on will take you along the main coastal road to Vevey. If instead you fork right, you will eventually come to the beautiful Corniche Road leading to Chexbres, a spick-and-span summer resort around 600 meters (2,000 feet) above sea level. Winding high above the lake through delightful, narrow-streeted villages among steeply-sloping vineyards, the Corniche Road offers a succession of fabulous views across the lake. But this magnificent detour is best savored in early summer or autumn when traffic is light, for the road is often narrow, and parking places few. From Chexbres, the Corniche Road winds down through the Dézaley (whose vineyards produce a light white wine) to rejoin the lake highway just before it enters Vevey.

Vevey to Montreux

Vevey needs no introduction to globetrotters. Together with neighboring Montreux it has been a popular resort with the British since the early 19th century. Charlie Chaplin lived just outside the town for many years. Facing the lofty Dent d'Oche peak across the lake, its romantic outlook exercises a great attraction. It's also the center of an important wine-producing region which, four or five times a century, celebrates the fact with a prodigious, world-famous 'Fêtes des Vignerons' (winegrowers' fair). The last one was held 30 July to 14 August 1977; there will probably not be another before the year 2000. However, you can get just a little of the feel of the great festival during the

THE LAKE GENEVA REGION

summer when a delightful market is held in the main square every Saturday morning. Wine tasters will not be disappointed.

On the heights above Vevey and Montreux lie several delightfully quiet summer or winter resorts accessible by road or rail: Les Pléiades, Les Avants, Mont-Pèlerin, and Blonay. Between Blonay and Chamby there is a railway, worked by 50-year-old steam locomotives, which runs for around five kilometers (three miles) through delightful countryside during summer weekends. The neighboring mountain slopes and valleys, particularly at Les Avants, are famous for the wonderful spring display of wild narcissi and daffodils, usually in bloom from about mid-May to mid-June.

At the eastern end of Vevey's lakeside promenade is La Tour-de-Peilz, named after a castle built here in 1280 by Peter of Savoy.

Exploring Montreux

Montreux, one of Europe's most beautifully situated resorts and the most popular in the Lake Geneva region, is a French-style Edwardian town, that caters almost exclusively to foreign visitors. It enjoys a remarkably mild climate thanks to mountains which protect it from cold north and east winds. Mulberries, magnolias and palm trees grow in its lush, well-tended gardens. Yet, despite the sheltering mountains, Montreux has a fine open situation, looking across the vast expanse of the lake, and eastwards up the wide Rhône Valley to a magnificent background of snowcapped peaks.

On the main Simplon railway line, Montreux is also the terminus of several mountain railways, not least the scenically splendid Montreux Oberland Bahn, whose comfortable little trains will take you on a winding journey among the mountains of the Bernese Oberland to Saanenmöser, Gstaad, Zweisimmen, and the Simmen valley.

While at Montreux, a trip by mountain railroad (the trains leave from the main station) to the Rochers de Naye is imperative. There, at 1,040 meters (6,700 feet) above sea level, you can enjoy the splendid view of Lake Geneva, the Savoy, and the Swiss Alps; and ski between December and April.

Another lovely trip from Montreux is the drive to Glion and Caux, both also accessible by train. At the top of the winding road is a memorable view, and the vast 'Mountain House' (Caux), former Palace Hotel and now the international conference center of the Moral Rearmament movement.

About two and a half kilometers (one and a half miles) from Montreux is the castle of Chillon. Although only a few meters from the shore the castle forms an island, and the romantic atmosphere is enhanced by the deep blue-green water which reflects it. Nearby the modern highway and the overhead cables of the electric railway provide a strange contrast.

As it stands today, Chillon was built under the direction of Duke Peter of Savoy in the 13th century with, it is said, the help of military architects from Plantaganet England. For a long period it served as a state prison, and one of the many unfortunate 'guests' was François Bonivard. As Prior of St. Victor in Geneva he had supported the Reformation, an act which infuriated the Catholic Duke of Savoy. To ponder on the error of his ways Bonivard was sent to Chillon, where he spent six gloomy years, much of the time chained to a pillar in the dungeon, before being released by the Bernese in 1536. Up to the 17th century, Chillon was the scene of many trials for such things as sorcery, the wretched victims coming to a gruesome end in the castle courtyard.

When he was in Clarens, on the other side of Montreux, in 1816, the poet Byron visited Chillon. He learned of Bonivard's incarceration and wrote his famous poem, *The Prisoner of Chillon*. If you visit the castle, usually open from mid-morning to late afternoon or early evening, you will see that Byron, like a true tourist, carved his name on a pillar in Bonivard's dungeon. You will also be able to see the great hall and torture chamber, and a fine collection of medieval furnishings and decorations.

Beyond Chillon the road curves round the end of the lake to the small town of Villeneuve, guarding the estuary of the River Rhône and the long narrow plain which lies beyond. Until 1940, most of this area was considered unsuitable for agriculture. It was covered with reeds and horsegrass and was swampy, but wartime food problems provided the spur to drastic action. Drainage and irrigation were undertaken by private enterprise, and vast areas of land were reclaimed.

Return to Geneva

At Villeneuve, your tour of the Swiss playground along Lake Geneva is almost ended, but if you wish, you can return to Geneva along the southern (French) shore. Just over six kilometers (four miles) from Villeneuve the road crosses the Rhône, here a muddy river which discolors the water where it enters the lake. A right turn soon after the bridge will bring you quickly to the lakeside village of St. Gingolph, half Swiss, half French.

The first large township in France is the popular resort and spa of Evian-les-Bains, which the Swiss often visit; crossing the lake on one of the busy little steamers to spend an afternoon shopping or, more likely, an evening trying their luck at the casino. Thonon, about nine kilometers (six miles) beyond Evian, is not only an important agricultural center but like Evian, another popular lakeside resort and spa. At

THE LAKE GENEVA REGION

Sciez, a further nine kilometers beyond Thonon, you can either go straight along the direct main road to Geneva or turn right for the more interesting secondary road along the lake through the little resort of Yvoire, crossing the frontier to re-enter Switzerland at Hermance, 14 kilometers (nine miles) from Geneva.

There are several interesting side-trips from the road along the northern shore of Lake Geneva. The first is from Nyon, where the northwestern exit from the town will bring you to Highway 90. This rises steeply into the Jura, winding and twisting up to St. Cergue at 1,035 meters (3,400 feet), a winter and summer sports resort noted for its bracing climate and outstanding views.

From St. Cergue, a secondary road cuts away to the northeast, passing through Bassins and St. George, and then over the Marchairuz Pass, closed in winter (1,447 meters), to Le Brassus, a watchmaking center in the Vaud Jura.

In a cleft of the straight Valley of Joux, so typical of Jura scenery, lies the Lake of Joux, ideal for sailing and windsurfing. You can drive along either shore, for both roads converge at Le Pont at the far end of the lake. The road then climbs over the Mollendruz Pass, 1,066 meters (3,500 feet) high. Halfway down the other side there is a magnificent panoramic view of Lake Geneva, with Lausanne in the foreground. From L'Isle, a village at the bottom, you can return to Nyon through Apples, Aubonne and Rolle.

Another pleasant little sidetrip—one you can complete in an afternoon—leads northwards from Lausanne or Morges, both roads joining up at the village of Cossonay. A few kilometers beyond Cossonay is La Sarraz, whose castle, on a rocky promontory, was originally built in the 11th century by the Burgundian kings. Reconstructed in the 13th century, it was destroyed by the Confederates in 1475 and once again rebuilt. Its last owner, Henri de Mandrot, gave the Castle of La Sarraz to the Canton of Vaud in 1920. Today, it is a national monument and houses a splendid furniture collection.

About six kilometers (four miles) from La Sarraz on the Vallorbe road is Croy, and if you take the left fork here you will quickly come to the charming old Jura village of Romainmotier, noted for its 11th-century Romanesque church. Returning through Croy it is only eight kilometers (five miles) to Orbe, once the Roman town of Urba. Quaint rather than beautiful, Orbe was later an important focal point in Charlemagne's Europe; and it was here that the Emperor's sons met to divide his estates. According to legend the cruel Queen Brunhilda of Burgundy also held court in Urba during the 9th century.

Roman ruins

At Bossaye, about two kilometers from Orbe along the road to Yverdon, are the ruins of several Roman villas from the 1st and 2nd centuries. Apart from Zofingen, near Olten, this is the only place in Switzerland where Roman mosaics can be viewed on their original sites. From here, you can either return via La Sarraz or go on to Yverdon and back via Echallens.

Any of the roads which lead up into the hills and valleys behind Vevey or Montreux are worth exploring. In only a few minutes they will bring you to splendid views and, in the late spring or early summer, to fields of wild flowers.

Quite different but equally lovely views can be seen from the fleet of smart, white paddle-steamers, diesel motor boats and even a 45-mph hydrofoil, which ply busily around and across the lake, calling frequently at all the towns and many of the lakeside villages.

PRACTICAL INFORMATION FOR LAUSANNE

GETTING INTO TOWN FROM THE AIRPORT. While Lausanne does not have its own airport, there are regular bus services (some 10 daily) from Geneva (Cointrin) airport to Ouchy, on the lakeside. The trip takes about one hour. However, you can also get to Lausanne from Geneva rail station, taking the bus from the airport to the station there before catching the train to Lausanne.

HOTELS. The hotels of Lausanne are renowned for their quiet elegance, air of luxury (even in the moderately-priced ones), huge size and, above all, courteous service. Be sure to book well in advance, particularly in the summer. Nearly all the hotels that we include in our listings below have a wide range of rooms, a good many of which may well fall into a lower grading than that which we have given here. The best advice is always to check before hand with the hotel. There is an accommodations office in the Tourist Office which will certainly be able to find you a hotel, however, if you arrive without reservations.

Deluxe

Beau Rivage, tel. 263831. Stands in its own grounds facing the lake at Ouchy; this is one of the great hotels of Europe. The many faciiities include sauna, tennis and indoor pool.

Lausanne Palace, tel. 203711. In the city center beside pleasant gardens and with a superb view from the terrace restaurant. All facilities.

Expensive

Alpha Palmiers, tel. 230131. In the city center with two good restaurants; quiet rooms.
Bellerive, tel. 296633. Down the hill between the city center and Ouchy; quiet and with facilities for the handicapped.
Continental, tel. 201551. Near the station; quiet and good; many facilities.
À la Gare Transit, tel. 279252. Small, quiet, family hotel.
Mirabeau, tel. 206231. Quiet and central; in own grounds.
De la Paix, tel. 207171. Quiet, central hotel; well-appointed and comfortable.
Parking Hôtel Motor Inn, tel. 271211. Very quiet but central, and with facilities for the handicapped.
La Résidence, tel. 277711. By the lake at Ouchy; tennis, gym, pool and sauna.
Royal Savoy, tel. 264201. Comfortable and well-appointed lakeside hotel at Ouchy.
Victoria, tel. 205771. Large hotel near the station; comfortable if a little faded.

Moderate

Angleterre, tel. 264145. Quiet hotel overlooking the lake.
City, tel. 202141. Central and well-appointed, with facilities for the handicapped.
Elite, tel. 202361. In the city center but quiet; in own grounds. Breakfast only.
De Lausanne, tel. 207841. Near the station.
Rex, tel. 32512 With bar and snack bar.
Des Voyageurs, tel. 231902. Central with bar.

Inexpensive

Des Fleurettes, tel. 269081. Small hotel in own grounds; very quiet.
De La Fôret, tel. 379211. Small; good restaurant.
Pres-Lac, tel. 284901. At Pully, on the eastern fringe of the city.
Regina, tel. 202441. Breakfast only; central but quiet.
Villereuse, tel. 263191. Small hotel at Ouchy.

Restaurants

Expensive

Le Beaujolais, tel. 201551. Restaurant of the Hotel Continental; extremely good.
Carnotzet du Petit-Chêne, tel. 230301. Typical Swiss cellar restaurant; in the Hotel Alpha-Palmiers. Boasts of having fed the likes of King Juan Carlos and Princess Grace. The fondue *bourguignonne* is superb.
La Grappe d' Or, tel. 230760. Excellent French cuisine.
Du Mont d' Or, tel. 267460. Fine French food.

Le Relais, tel. 203711. Restaurant of the Lausanne Palace hotel; excellent.
Le Richelieu, tel. 263235. Restaurant of the Hotel Carlton and generally considered one of the very best in town.
Aux 3 Tonneaux, tel. 220266. Very good, if not the absolute tops.

Moderate

Café de Jorat, tel. 202261. Unpretentious spot with excellent food.
Chaumière, tel. 235364. Rustic setting; American specialties.
Chez Godio, tel. 223934. Good Italian specialties.
Chez Pitch, tel. 282743. Steak and fish specialties on attractive outdoor terrace; at Pully at the eastern end of the city.
Il Grottino, tel. 227658. Italian specialties.
Voile d' Or, tel. 278011. Lakeside restaurant where you can dine in the excellent grill room (marvelous view), eat at the more moderately-priced snack bar or spend the whole day sunbathing, swimming or dancing.
White Horse Pub, tel. 267575. Try this place for surprisingly good steaks; relaxed atmosphere.

Inexpensive

Le Chalet Suisse, tel. 222312.
Du Theatre, tel. 233827.
Le Mandarin, tel. 237484. Good inexpensive Chinese specialties.

ENTERTAINMENT. The *Beaulieu* and the *Municipal* theaters present opera, operetta, concerts, plays, etc., all year round. International festival of music and ballet in May and June. The *Théâtres des Faux-Nez* (120 seats only) gives avant-garde plays in French.

The *Tabaris* is one of the most modern nightclubs in Switzerland and also about the most expensive. The *Brummell* in the Palace Hotel's building is also a first-class nightclub.

Good places to dance are the *Scotch-Bar, Johnnie's,* the *Paddock* in Victoria Hotel, the *Château d'Ouchy,* and the *Voile d'Or* down by the lakeside.

MUSEUMS. 'Art Brut' Collection, Château de Beaulieu, 11 av. des Bergières. Bequeathed to the town by Jean Dubuffet. Non-institutional art by people outside arts circles, even outside society—recluses, eccentrics, prison and asylum inmates. Reader-recommended as fascinating.

Rumine Palace. Large neo-Renaissance building housing the University, Library and three museums: *Fine Arts Museum,* with a fairly good collection of pictures by local artists, predominantly of the 19th century and likely to interest only a few, as well as a number of good European Old Masters and Impressionists and post-Impressionists; *Natural History Museum,* with exhibits chiefly on alpine wildlife and alpine geology; *Archeological and Historical Museum,* prehistorical exhibits from the region as well as Roman and medieval treasures.

THE LAKE GENEVA REGION

Historical Museum of the Old Bishop's Palace, exhibits on Lausanne from prehistorical times to the 17th century plus special changing exhibitions.
Museum of Decorative Arts, interesting exhibits of applied arts.

SHOPPING. As a shopping center, Lausanne is first-rate. Luxury stores are to be found in the rue de Bourg and rue St. François, also on the north side of the place St.-François. A cheaper shopping quarter is around the west (Geneva) side of the Grand Pont.

USEFUL ADDRESSES. Local, regional information and hotel booking office: *Lausanne Tourist Office,* 60 avenue d'Ouchy, tel. 021–277321. *American Express,* 14 avenue Mon Repos, and 5 chemin de Roseneck, Ouchy. *Wagons-Lits/Cook,* rue Centrale 6.

Car Hire. *Avis,* 50 avenue de la Gare; *Europcar,* place Riponne 12. *Hertz,* ch. de Mornex 34.

PRACTICAL INFORMATION FOR THE REST OF THE REGION

Hotels and Restaurants

CHATEAU d'OEX. *Beau-Séjour et Taverne* (M), tel. 47423. Central but very quiet. *De l' Ours* (M), tel. 46337. Quiet and central. *Hostellerie du Bon Accueil* (M), tel. 46320. Quiet family hotel in historic building in own grounds. *La Rocaille* (M), tel. 46215. Very comfortable hotel in own grounds. *La Printanière* (I), tel. 46113. Small hotel in own grounds; very quiet. No rooms with bath.
Restaurant. *Ermitage* (E), tel. 46003. *Bon Acceuil* (M), tel. 46320.

CHEXBRES. *Du Signal* (E), tel. 562525. Quiet with splendid view, tennis and pool. *Cécil* (I), tel. 561292. Pool. Both with good restaurants.

COPPET. *Du Lac* (E), tel. 761521. Good with restaurants. *Orange* (I), tel. 761037. Also with restaurant.
Restaurant. *La Petite Marmite* (I–M), tel. 761854. Hot and cold buffet and lots of it.

CRISSIER. Restaurant. *Girardet* (E), tel. 341514. Switzerland's best restaurant. Count on at least Fr. 100 per person and book a month in advance. An unforgettable experience. The food is *superb.*

LE BRASSUS. *De la Lande* (M), tel. 854441. Very comfortable. Sauna.

LES BIOUX. *Des Trois Suisses* (I). Lakeside family hotel. Excellent food. Recommended. Very reasonable.

LES DIABLERETS. *Eurotel* (E), tel. 531721. Indoor pool and sauna. *Grand Hôtel et Résidence Meurice* (E), tel. 531551. Sauna, gymnasium and indoor pool. *Mon Abri* (M), tel. 531481. Comfortable and quiet. *Les Lilas* (I), 531134. Small.

GLION. *Victoria* (E), tel. 625121. Gracious and appropriately Victorian; with pool and excellent food. *Des Alpes Vaudoises* (M), tel. 612787. Medium-sized hotel in own grounds; pool. *Mont Fleuri* (I), tel. 623887. *Placida* (I), tel. 612787. Pool.
Restaurant. *Jaman* (M). Friendly bar and restaurant with tasty food and an exceptional stock of Belgian beers.

LEYSIN. *Central-Résidence* (E), tel. 341211. Large and superior hotel with indoor pool, sauna, gym and tennis. *Le Relais* (E), tel. 342421. Well-appointed and central. *Mont Riant* (I), tel. 341235. Quiet hotel in own grounds. *Les Orchidées* (I), tel. 341421. Very quiet and good value. *Universitaire* (I), tel. 341191. Large; with sauna. No rooms with bath. Very reasonable.

MONTREUX. *Excelsior* (L), tel. 613305. Sauna, pool, beauty treatments, water sports. Chinese restaurant, health-food restaurant, French restaurant, and snack-bar. *Le Montreux Palace* (L), tel. 613231. Vast hotel with golf, tennis and outdoor pool. *Bonivard* (E–L), tel. 613358. Quiet. *Eden au Lac* (E), tel. 612601. Quiet; with pool. *Eurotel* (E), tel. 622951. Lakeside hotel with indoor pool; kitchenette in every room. *Hyatt Continental* (E), tel. 635131. Highly recommended. *National* (E), tel. 622511. Golf and outdoor pool and fine view from elevated gardens. *Suisse et Majestic* (E), tel. 612331. Sauna and gymnasium; facilities for children. *Bon Accueil* (M), tel. 620551. Breakfast only; central. *Helvétie* (M), tel. 614455. Central. *Masson* (I), tel. 612759. Facilities for children; quiet.
Restaurant. *Brasserie Bavaria* (I–M), av. du Casino 27 (tel. 612548). All the hotels listed above have good restaurants.

MORGES. *Du Mont-Blanc au Lac* (M), tel. 716371. Recommended.
Restaurant. *Du Léman* (M), tel. 712188. Excellent.

NYON. *Du Clos de Sadex* (E), tel. 612831. Small hotel on the lake; quiet and with waterskiing. *Beau Rivage* (M–E), tel. 613231. Splendid view.
Restaurants. *Le Léman* (M–E), tel. 612241. Excellent. Fish and nouvelle cuisine. *XVI Siècle* (M–E), tel. 612441. Spit-roast beef. *Maître Jacques* (M), tel. 612834. Fish, *entrecôte au gros poivre et aux bolets.*

ROCHERS DE NAYE. *Rochers de Naye* (I), tel. 615547. Simple and very inexpensive hotel beside the summit station, some 3,000 meters up; a spectacular location. No rooms with bath.

THE LAKE GENEVA REGION

ROLLE. *Rivesrolle* (E), tel. 753491. Recommended. *La Tête Noire* (I), tel. 752251. In own grounds; central. *Hostellerie du Château* (I), tel. 751661. Recommended.

Restaurants. *La Tête Noir* and *L'Hostellerie du Château* (see hotels above) recommended. *Cercele de la Côte* (M), tel. 752196. Various flambés.

VEVEY. *Trois Couronnes* (L), tel. 513005. Somewhat Victorian interior but much character and comfort; open air restaurant overlooking lake. *Du Lac* (E), tel. 511041. With swimming pool; lakeside location. *De Famille* (I), tel. 513931. Indoor pool and sauna; central.

Restaurants. *Du Raisin* (M–E), tel. 511028. Known as "chez Pierre" to the regulars. First class. *Le Chandelier* (I–M), tel. 528837.

VILLARS. *Eurotel* (L), tel. 353131. Central with indoor pool and sauna. *Grand Hôtel du Parc* (L), tel. 352121. Quiet with indoor pool and tennis, ideal for children. *Du Golf et Marie-Louise* (M), tel. 352477. Quiet and central; tennis. *Chalet Henriette* (I), tel. 352163. Facilities for the handicapped.

VILLENEUVE. *Byron* (E), tel. 601061. Comfortable lakeside hotel in own grounds with fine views. *Le Château* (I), tel. 601357.

USEFUL ADDRESS. Office du Tourisme du Canton de Vaud (OTV), 10 ave. de la Gare, Case Postale, 1002 Lausanne (tel. 021–227782).

WINTER SPORTS. Even if winter sports do not top the list of activities in the Lake Geneva Region there are, nonetheless, a few outstanding skiing resorts here and worth listing.

Chateau-d'Oex, 3,330 feet; 2 cable cars, 10 lifts, 35 km of downhill runs, 40 km. of cross-country trails, skating, 6 km. of ski bob trails, ski schools.

Les Diablerets, 1,220 meters (4,000 feet); 6 cable cars, 14 lifts, 60 km. of downhill runs, 15 km. of cross-country trails, 8 km. of prepared tobogganing trails; skating, curling, ski schools.

Leysin, 1,275 meters (4,185 feet); more than 48 km. of sign-posted and highly varied ski-runs served by 30 lifts, all inter-linked, and including a fast shuttle train service and 2 cable cars. Indoor and heated outdoor pools, skating, curling, ski bob, golf, hiking and indoor games.

Villars, 1,398/1,450 meters (4,585/4,755 feet); 60 km. downhill runs, 15 km. cross-country trails, 30 km. ski-hiking trails (vast skiing area for all levels). 19 lifts. Curling, swimming, tennis, golf, fishing, hiking (180 km. of marked paths). Skittles.

GENEVA

Cosmopolitan Corner of the Lake

The motorist who enters Switzerland from Lyon and the southwest, or from Grenoble and the south, rolls smoothly into Geneva through Chancy or St. Julien. If he comes via the impressive Mont Blanc tunnel, he will cross the frontier in the French town of Annemasse. By air, the traveler to Geneva is deposited at Cointrin airport. Whatever the approach, the sweep of the Lake of Geneva (Lac Leman) fills the eye.

The third largest city in Switzerland, Geneva faces northeast, crowded round the lower end of the lake, with attractive parks and avenues making a fine setting for the outflowing waters of the River Rhône in its rush from the alpine glaciers to the warmth of the Mediterranean.

Although today it is very much a city of the 20th century, it is nonetheless an ancient place, with a history that fades back into the mists of time. The crest of the hill on which the Cathedral of St. Peter

GENEVA

now stands offered an excellent strategic position, first for primitive tribes; next for the Romans, who stayed there for 500 years (until AD 443); and then for the early Burgundians and their later kings. In the first part of the 5th century Geneva became a bishopric, and by the end of the 11th century its prince-bishops had developed a See both rich and powerful. But they had to fight hard to defend it against the territorially greedy house of Savoy, and the conflicts between the two rumbled on through the 12th and the 14th centuries. In the meantime, the merchant classes were gradually gaining in wealth and power, building up their independence by freeing themselves whenever possible from the feudal lordship of the bishops.

This prosperity was given a boost at the beginning of the 15th century by a close commercial alliance between Geneva and the cloth-manufacturing town of Fribourg, about 100 miles to the northeast. Fribourg textiles found a ready market at Geneva's fairs, the medieval city's greatest source of trade and revenue. But in 1462 Louis XI of France and his nephew, the Duke of Savoy, put a stop to that by forbidding French merchants to attend the fairs, and at the same time switching the dates of the Lyon fairs to coincide with those at Geneva; steps which virtually brought an end to the city's prosperity.

Commercially almost ruined, torn by internal strife and threatened continually by the increasingly aggressive new Duke of Savoy, Geneva at last appealed for aid to the Swiss Confederation. The Swiss army intervened and in 1530 the Duke of Savoy signed a treaty by which, in effect, he agreed to trouble the city no longer. Geneva then concluded an alliance with the cantons of Fribourg and Berne and began to rebuild its economic stability.

But along with this newly found independence came William Farel —a fervent disciple of Zurich's great reformer Zwingli—and with him he brought from Berne all the constricting religious zeal of the Reformation. By 1536, the city had enthusiastically switched from Catholicism to the Protestant faith, said goodbye to the last of the Catholic prince-bishops, and was already under the influence of John Calvin, a French refugee who came to visit Farel and stayed to eclipse him.

Calvin turned Geneva from a lively city into one where theaters were closed, entertainment frowned upon, dancing forbidden, and food and drink regarded only as necessities of life to be taken without indulgence or enjoyment. Banquets, the wearing of jewels, and all forms of finery were forbidden by the Sumptuary Laws. But despite all this Geneva owes a lot to Calvin, for he also made it into a center of French learning, the academy he founded in 1599 being today's university. He also did much to restore the city's commercial prosperity.

All this time, the Duke of Savoy was still coveting Geneva and hoping to restore Catholicism. On the night of December 11th-12th,

1602, he made a surprise attack on the city, in an operation known as the Escalade, since his men attempted to scale the city walls with ladders. They were ignominiously defeated, an event commemorated on this date every year since by the Festival of the Escalade, with a costume parade and high jinks.

Although many left the city to escape the austerity and bigotry of Calvinism, far more English, French, and Italian refugees came in, giving Geneva a taste of the cosmopolitan atmosphere she has today and bringing with them new crafts and trades as well as a keen sense of business. Since the 16th century, Geneva has been one of Europe's leading watchmaking and jewelry centers, and the Reformation (which left citizens few leisure activities and little on which to spend their money) allowed for concentration on work and an accumulation of wealth. The city also became one of the main intellectual centers of Europe, but it was steadily getting less democratic and the government was passing into the hands of a few wealthy aristocrats.

All this received a severe check in 1798, when this rich but melancholy city was annexed by France during the revolution, to become the capital of the French Department of Léman. It remained in French hands until 1814, after the fall of Napoleon; and in the following year the city was admitted to the Swiss Confederation as a canton in its own right.

Since then most of the major landmarks in Geneva's history have been connected with international affairs. In 1863 the Red Cross was founded. 1864 saw the first Geneva Convention for the care of war casualties. The city became the home of the League of Nations and the International Labor Office in 1919. In 1946 the United Nations moved its European center into the Palais des Nations. Now the city hosts the World Health Organization, the International Boy Scouts, the World Meteorological Organization, the Ecumenical Council of Churches and many more. This high concentration of international involvement means that Geneva is far more cosmopolitan than typically Swiss.

Exploring Geneva

You can see a considerable part of Geneva's attractions in a single walk by starting off along the broad Rue du Mont-Blanc from the railroad station to the lake. Here you will be rewarded with a lovely view which, if you are lucky with the weather, includes a distant glimpse of Mont Blanc. It's visible from Geneva about one day out of three. Directly ahead of you, if you are there at the right time, the Jet d'Eau rises like a gigantic plume from a jetty thrusting out into the lake. On a sunny day this towering stream of water, over 130 meters (400

GENEVA

like a gigantic plume from a jetty thrusting out into the lake. On a sunny day this towering stream of water, over 130 meters (400 feet) high, can be seen for miles. Weather permitting it plays daily from May until September.

A right turn takes you along the Quai des Bergues, beside the Rhône, which leaves the lake at this point. Beneath the water alongside the opposite bank is a four-story, electronically controlled car park capable of taking 1,500 cars. In the center of the river is Rousseau Island, with a statue of the French philosopher Jean-Jacques Rousseau, who was born in Geneva. Just beyond you will pass the Pont de la Machine. Here the crystal-clear Rhône, its waters having lost the mud they carried when entering the eastern end of the lake, tumbles in a tumult of foam over the dam which regulates the level of the lake. By crossing the river at the next bridge, the Pont de l'Isle, you will pass the Tour de l'Isle, a one-time prison dating from the epoch of the Bishopric and where the Geneva Tourist Office is now located. Today it is almost swallowed up by more modern buildings on either side.

This brings you to the place Bel-Air, in the center of the banking and business district. If you cross the place you can follow the rue de la Corraterie to the place Neuve, which is the site of the Grand Théâtre, the Rath Art Gallery, and the Conservatory of Music. Just in front of you is the entrance to a park and on your left, bordering the square, is a high wall (part of the ancient ramparts) above which is a row of fine old buildings. Enter the park, which contains the university, and keep to your left.

Almost immediately, at the foot of the ramparts, you will come to Geneva's most famous monument, the international memorial to the Reformation. Built between 1909 and 1917, the Reformation Monument is a gigantic wall, over 90 meters (300 feet) long, which is as impressive for its simplicity and clean lines as for its sheer size. It is worth sitting down on the terrace steps—made of Mont–Blanc granite—which face the wall, since it is full of interest. The central group consists of four statues of the great leaders of the Reformation—Bèze, Calvin, Farel, and John Knox—each over 4.5 meters (15 feet) high. On either side of these giants are smaller statues (a mere 2.7 meters, 9 feet tall) of other personalities, such as Oliver Cromwell. Between the smaller figures are bas reliefs and inscriptions which tell the story of important events connected with the Reformation. Carved in the wall to the right of Cromwell, you'll see the presentation by the Houses of Parliament of the Bill of Rights to King William II, in 1689. Above it, in English, are listed the Bill's main features—the guiding principles of democracy. To the left of Cromwell is a bas relief of the Pilgrim Fathers praying on the deck of the *Mayflower* before signing the May-

THE FACE OF SWITZERLAND

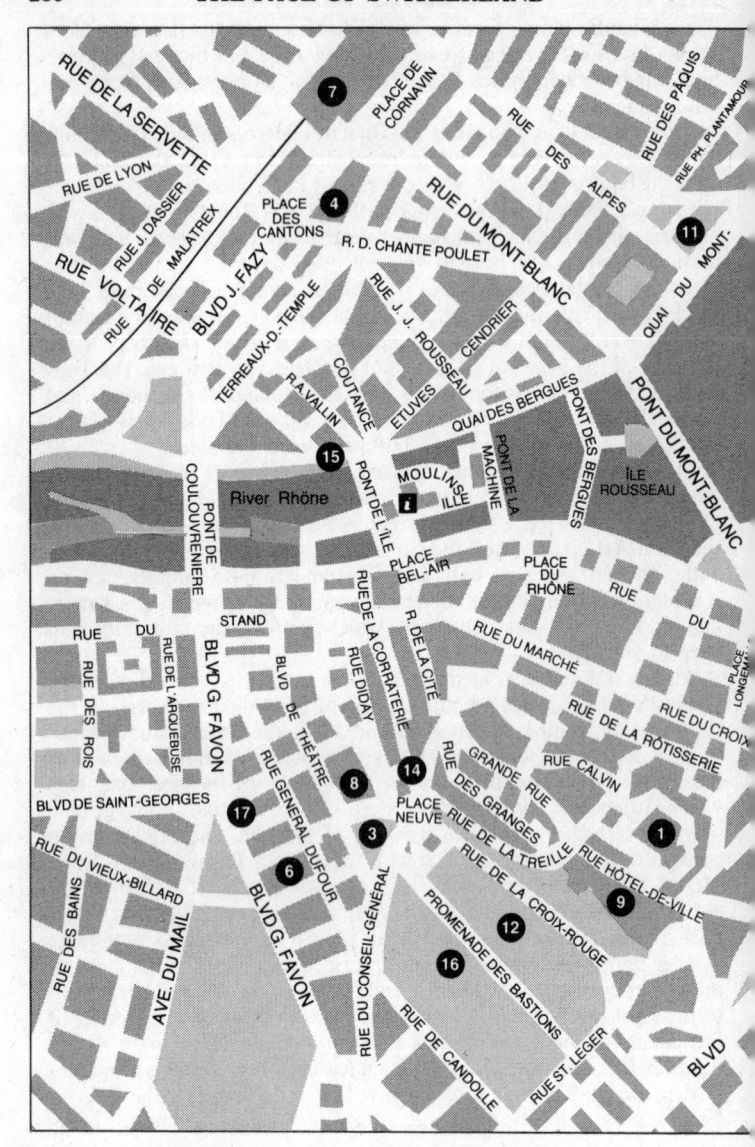

GENEVA

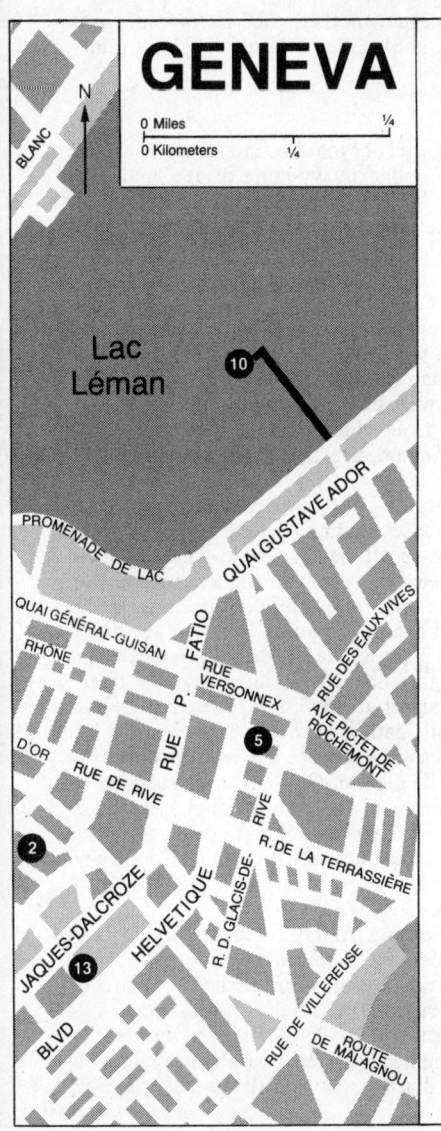

Points of Interest

1. Cathédrale de St. Pierre
2. Collège Calvin
3. Conservatoire de Musique
4. Église de Notre Dame
5. Église de St. Joseph
6. Église du Sacre Coeur
7. Gare de Cornavin (rail station)
8. Grand Théâtre
9. Hôtel de Ville (City Hall)
10. Jet d'Eau
11. Monument Brunswick
12. Monument de la Reformation
13. Musée d'Art et d'Histoire; Russian Church
14. Musée Rath
15. Tour de l'Île
16. Université
17. Victoria Hall

■ Tourist Information

flower Compact; and further left again another relief shows John Knox preaching with obvious passion in St. Giles Cathedral, Edinburgh.

St. Peter's and City Hall

If you leave the park by the gate just beyond the monument and turn left into rue St. Léger, passing under an ivy-hung bridge, and then climb up the winding street, you'll come to the charming place Bourg-de-Four. This dreamy little place was once the crossroads of some important routes which led to southern France via Annecy and Lyon, to Italy, to the Chablais, and elsewhere. Before that it served as a Roman Forum and as a cattle and wheat market. If, in the place, you turn right down rue des Chaudronniers you'll find, not far away on the left, Calvin's College, sponsored by the stern reformer himself in 1559 and now the Cantonal Grammar (High) School. Straight on down Chaudronniers it's only a short walk to the somewhat formal Art and History Museum and the Baur Collection, while on the left, looking like a part of Moscow's Red Square, are the golden, onion shaped cupolas of the Russian Church.

But staying in the place Bourg-de-Four turn left along any of the narrow streets, ramps, and staircases leading up to St. Peter's, whose stubby stone towers and green spire will be your guide. The interior of the cathedral has undergone extensive restoration and was reopened in November 1981. Climb up the north tower and admire the splendid view. Architecturally, perhaps the most intriguing feature of the building is the extraordinary contrast between the façade, a stern and rather beautiful classical portico, and the splendid Gothic of the rest of the building—a startling juxtaposition of architectural styles that is quite unique. Opposite, the City Hall, dating from the 16th century but restored and enlarged in later years, houses the famous Alabama Hall where, on August 22nd 1864, the Geneva Convention was signed by 16 countries, laying the foundation of the International Red Cross. Eight years later in 1872, a court of arbitration was convened in this same room to settle the Alabama dispute between Great Britain and the United States, easing the latter's unhappiness over British support to Confederate ships during the Civil War.

The winding, cobbled streets leading from the cathedral to the modern city are picturesque and pleasing. Rue Calvin has a number of 18th-century *hôtels,* the town residences of noble families; No. 11 is on the site of Calvin's house. In rue du Puits-Saint-Pierre, No. 6 is a 12th-century building. The Grand rue is the oldest street in Geneva. The rue Hôtel-de-Ville, once the headquarters of Italian religious refugees, is lined by 17th-century dwellings built with the craftsmanship typical of their former owners.

GENEVA

Rhône, du Croix d'Or, and rue du Marché, where superb shops, fashionable boutiques and the dazzling window displays of jewelers are an irresistible magnet for even the most budget conscious tourist. But don't neglect the side streets, where the prices are often noticeably lower. Antique lovers will also find it worthwhile, if expensive, to stroll along the narrow streets which tumble down from the old quarter which we have just visited.

For a glimpse of the international community at work you should take either a taxi or a bus (O) from the rail station to the place des Nations. A combined stroll through the attractive grounds of the international complex and visits to some of the buildings will take several interesting hours. Apart from the main buildings of such organizations as WHO, ICRC (Red Cross), UNO (with a cafe-restaurant looking onto its park), there are two museums—the Ariana, in a lovely 19th-century house with a collection mainly consisting of porcelain and ceramics, and the Château de Penthes, the Museum of the Swiss Abroad, also with a cafe-restaurant and a magnificent park.

PRACTICAL INFORMATION FOR GENEVA

GETTING TO TOWN FROM THE AIRPORT. There is a regular bus service from Geneva airport (Cointrin) to the rail station in the center of town. The service also runs from the station to the airport. It operates every 20 minutes from 7 A.M. to 11 P.M. and costs Fr. 6 per person for a single journey. The trip takes 15–20 minutes. There are lots of excellent taxis available, small and large, but the short journey isn't cheap.

GETTING AROUND GENEVA. By Bus and Tram. Services cover the city. Fares are as follows: Fr. 0.70 for adults for a maximum of three stops; Fr. 1.20 for the town network; Fr. 5 for a day pass valid on the entire network; Fr. 0.60 half tariff for children (from 6 to 12 years). You must buy your tickets at the machines at all stops before boarding vehicles.

By Taxi. These are easily available, but, as ever in Switzerland, are expensive. For radio cabs call 212223, 947111 or simply 141.

By Bicycle. Bicycles may be hired at the rail station.

THE FACE OF SWITZERLAND

SPECIAL EVENTS. From the visitor's standpoint, Geneva is a summer city when, of course, it is inevitably crowded. The four-day 'Fêtes of Geneva', with fireworks, street dancing, parades of flower-covered floats, etc., occurs in the middle of Aug., and naturally Geneva, like all Swiss communities, celebrates the national holiday, August 1. There is also much merrymaking during the festival of Escalade, Dec. 11–12. To check what's on, get a copy of the *Guide officiel de l'Office du Tourisme de Genève* or *How to see Geneva*.

HOTELS. Hotel rooms are at a premium all year round in Geneva. The press of events centered on the many international agencies in the city keeps the flow of foreign guests coming. Book in advance if you possibly can or you may well find yourself in difficulties.

Nearly all the hotels that we include in our listings below have a wide range of rooms, a good many of which may well fall into a lower grading than that which we have given here. The best advice is always to check beforehand with the hotel. Hotel reservations can be made through the automatic booking machines at the main entrance of the station (free of charge).

Deluxe

Beau Rivage, 13 quai du Mont Blanc (tel. 310221). Fine grill room and famous terrace; airconditioning throughout. One of the world's great hotels.

Des Bergues, 33 quai des Bergues (tel. 315050). A decidedly distinguished atmosphere pervades this luxury spot.

Bristol, 10 rue du Mont Blanc (tel. 324400). Plush and luxurious; health club; fine restaurant.

De la Paix, 11 quai Mont Blanc (tel. 326150). Small but attractive.

Président, 47 quai Wilson (tel. 311000). Delightfully decorated; airconditioning throughout.

La Réserve, 301 route de Lausanne (tel. 741741). In pleasant park with lakeside terrace and outdoor pool; quiet, elegant and luxurious.

Du Rhône, quai Turrettini (tel. 319831). Brisk service but pleasant hotel nonetheless; overlooks river.

Le Richemond, Jardin Brunswick (tel. 311400). Famous family-run hotel overlooking river.

Expensive

Grand-Pré, 35 rue du Grand-Pré (tel. 339150). Quiet and central.

Intercontinental 7–9 petit Saconnex (tel. 346091). With private suites, pool, sauna and smart shops; 18 storys and 400 rooms.

P.L.M. Rotary, 18–20 rue du Cendrier (tel. 315200).

Ramada Renaissance, 19 rue de Zurich (tel. 310241). Large modern hotel; central.

Rex, 44 av. Wendt (tel. 457150). Medium-sized hotel; central.

GENEVA

Royal, 41 rue de Lausanne (tel. 313600). Ask for a quiet room. Near the station; good restaurant.

Suisse, 10 pl. Cornavin (tel, 326630). Breakfast only; near the station.

Moderate

Amat-Carlton, 22 rue Amat (tel. 316850). TV in all rooms.

Athénée, 6 route de Malagnou (tel. 463933). Good value; central.

California, 1 rue Gevray (tel. 315550). Breakfast only; central but quiet.

Cornavin, 33 blvd. James-Fazy (tel. 322100). Breakfast only; central and close to the station—as the name implies—and quiet for its location.

Eden, 135 rue de Lausanne (tel. 326540). Near the Palais des Nations.

La Vendée, 28 ch. de la Vendée (tel. 920411). Reasonable.

Inexpensive

Ariana, 7 rue J.R. Chouet (tel. 339950). Breakfast only.

Astoria, 6 place Cornavin (tel. 321025). Breakfast only; handy for the station.

Bernina, 22 place Cornavin (tel. 314950). Good value. Recommended.

Drake, 32 rue Rothschild (tel. 316750). Quiet and central.

Epoque, 10 rue Voltaire (tel. 452550). Near the station; reasonable.

International et Terminus, 20 rue des Alpes (tel. 328095). With good grill restaurant.

Lido, 8 rue Chantepoulet (tel. 315530). Breakfast only; centrally located but quiet.

Mon Repos, 131 rue de Lausanne (tel. 328010). Quiet with good restaurant.

Rivoli, 6 rue des Pâquis (tel. 318550). Breakfast only; central, well-managed, comfortable. Studios with kitchenette. Garden. 2 mins. from main station. Recommended.

Union, 34 rue de Lausanne (tel. 320540). Simple but adequate.

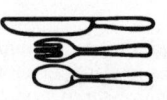

RESTAURANTS. Geneva is full of good restaurants, with French cooking dominant, though there are plenty of places that provide the mixed Swiss cuisine. Once more we advise you to stick to the daily *menu,* which can mean a moderately-priced meal even in an expensive restaurant.

Expensive

Au Boeuf Rouge, rue des Pâquis 7 (tel. 327537). Recommended.

Au Fin Bec, rue de Berne 55 (tel. 322919). One of Geneva's finest restaurants. Closed Sun.

Le Béarn, quai de la Poste 4 (tel. 210028). Classic French cuisine. Closed Sat. lunch and Sun.

Le Duc, quai Mont-Blanc 7 (tel. 317330). Outstanding seafood. Closed Sun. and Mon.

Entre Nous, 2 rue de la Zone, Ambilly (50 – 383585). In the suburb of Annemasse, just over the French border. An elegant, friendly little restaurant, well worth the short excursion for the excellent cooking. Closed Sun. even. and Mon.

Le Gentilhomme, in Le Richemond hotel (see above).

La Jonque d'Or, rue de Carouge 29 (tel. 293257). Authentic Vietnamese cuisine. Resident-recommended.

Le Neptune, in Du Rhône hotel (see above). Fine local dishes and seafood. Closed Sat. and Sun.

La Perle du Lac, 128 rue de Lausanne (tel. 513504). Celebrated dining, mainly French and seafood. A must in summer. Closed Mon. and over Xmas.

Tse-Fung, Hotel La Réserve (tel. 741736). Best Chinese food in town. Highly recommended.

Moderate

Le Bateau, an old paddle-steamer moored off the pont du Mont-Blanc, Jardin des Anglais. Also good for a light meal. Closed Jan. and Feb.

Buffet de la Gare des Eaux-Vives, tel. 361965. Nasi Goreng and other goodies. Recommended. (Not licensed.)

Les Philosophes, rue Goetz-Monin 2 (tel. 290657). Highly recommended bistro-type restaurant. Closed Sun.

Inexpensive

Al Cavalieri, 7 rue Cherbuliez (tel. 350956). Said to be Geneva's oldest eating place. Closed Mon. and July.

Chez Bouby, 1 rue Grenus (tel. 310927). Reader-recommended. Closed Sat. even. and Sun.

Coop-City, 5 rue du Commerce, on 6th floor of department store.

Migros, chain store cafeterias—a good bet for inexpensive meals. All over town.

Mövenpick, on place de la Fusterie, and a big branch on the Right Bank. Also has a more expensive part.

Restaurant Universitaire, 2 av. du Mail.

ENTERTAINMENT. Discos and Clubs. There are considerably more lively nightspots in Geneva than for example in Zurich. Most are fairly reasonably priced. The Vielle Ville (Old Town) is the area for a good part of Geneva's nightlife, and there are a number of attractive outdoor cafes around the Place Molard.

The best spot in town is *Maxim's* on pl. des Alpes. Probably the liveliest spot is *Ba-Ta-Clan,* which features a strip show, at 15 rue de la Fontaine (tel. 296498). The best disco is probably the *Hit Club* at 3 rue du Marche (tel. 212831). *Brasserie Landolt,* 2 rue de la Candolle, is a popular student hangout, with an outside terrace—which years agos was Lenin's favorite cafe in Geneva. Since nightspots are anything but permanent institutions and can change their character, it is best to check at your hotel before going.

Theaters and Concerts. The City Tourist Office produces an exhaustive *List of Events* every two months.

GENEVA

Concert halls include *Victoria Hall,* rue Général Dufour, where the fine *Orchestre de la Suisse Romande* gives its symphonic concerts; *Conservatoire de Musique,* place Neuve; *Salle de la Reformation,* 65 rue du Rhone; *Radio Geneva,* 66 Boulevard Carl-Vogt.

The *Grand Théâtre* and the *Comédie* produce opera, operetta and drama. Experimental productions are notable at the *Théâtre de Poche,* and there is a *marionette theater* at 4 rue Constantin. In summer, the openair *Théâtre de Verdure* features dance companies, classic and folkloric, and there are occasional plays and concerts in the lovely courtyard of the *Hôtel de Ville.*

In summer, along the quais there are free openair concerts; and Thursday and Saturday evenings the CGN steamer company runs dance cruises on the lake.

MUSEUMS. The most important collections are listed below. There are over thirty art galleries that have interesting temporary shows. To check on them, see *La Semaine à Genève* (This Week in Geneva).

Art and History, rue Charles-Galland. Fine permanent collection of archeological objects, painting and sculpture; particularly strong in decorative art. Open 10–5, closed Mon.

Barbier-Müller Collection, 4 rue Ecole-de-Chimie, museum of primitive arts. Tues. to Sat., 2.30–5.30.

Baur Collection, rue Munier-Romilly 8, not far from the Art and History Museum. In a former private house, a fine collection of Chinese and Japanese ceramics, jades, prints, etc. Open 2–6, closed Mon.

Ethnographic, 65–67 boulevard Carl-Vogt. Open 10–12, 2–5, closed Mon. and Tues.

History of Science Museum, 128 rue de Lausanne; good display of scientific instruments.

Watch, Clock and Enamels Museum, 15 route de Malagnou (beside Natural History Museum). Fine collection of timepieces and enamels. Open 10–12, 2–6, closed Mon. morn.

Museum of Old Musical Instruments, 23 rue Lefort. Opening times vary.

Natural History, 11 route de Malagnou. Splendidly arranged collection in new building. There is also a Botanical Museum and Conservatory near the United Nations buildings. Open 10–5, closed Mon. Cafeteria.

Palais des Nations, Parc de l'Ariana; European Office of the United Nations. Guided tours of the building are frequent—consult *How to see Geneva.*

Palais Wilson, 51 quai Wilson. 9–12, 2–6, free. Educational exhibition of the International Education Bureau.

Petit Palais, 2 terrasse Saint-Victor, has modern art from 19th century onwards, and also loan exhibitions. Open 10–12, 2–6, closed Mon. morn.

Rath, place Neuve. For temporary shows, frequently extremely good, often with exhibits from other countries. Open 10–12, 2–6; Wed. evenings 8–10; Closed Mon. morn.

Voltaire, 25 rue des Délices. Exhibits on Voltaire and his times—portraits, busts, furniture, etc.

THE FACE OF SWITZERLAND

SHOPPING. When you see the array of jewelry in the shops along the rue du Rhône, du Marché and rue de la Croix d'Or, or look at the many haute couture boutiques in the rue du Rhône, you'll know that Calvin's sumptuary laws are a dead letter in this town today. If you're looking for antiques, you'll have a field day in those little narrow streets that tumble down from the old quarters clustered around the cathedral, but the prices are not for the squeamish.

SPORTS. You can go swimming in the heart of the city at the Pâquis jetty, an artificial swimming take-off point built out from the quai du Mont-Blanc, but you'll probably enjoy it more if you go out a little way by No. 2 or 9 bus to Geneva Plage, near the yacht harbor, on the eastern fringe of the city, or on the other side of the free Reposoir beach, a little more than a mile from the center on the Lausanne road. If you want a heated, undercover pool of Olympic dimensions, try the new municipal swimming bath at quai des Vernets. You can hire boats at either the quai du Mont-Blanc or the quai Gustave-Ador, on the other bank.

The *Geneva Golf Club* (18 holes; 6,835 yards) is at Château Bessinge, route de la Capite, Cologny (Bus A from Rive to Chemin de Fraidieux); also at *Casino de Divonne,* 15 minutes from Geneva; prior appointment necessary. Tennis can be played at the *International Tennis Club,* chemin Rigot, upon prior appointment.

For horseback riding, mounts may be hired at the *Manège de Meyrin,* 31 chemin Golette, the *Manège d'Onex,* 111 rte. de Chancy, Onex, or the *Manàge de la Pallenterie,* rte. de Capite, Vésenaz.

USEFUL ADDRESSES: Local information and advice: *Office du Tourisme,* 1 rue Tour de l'Ile (tel. 022–287-233). *British Consulate,* 37/39 rue de Vermont. *American Express,* 7 rue du Mont-Blanc; 12 chemin de Rieu; 41 ave. Giuseppe Motta. *Cook's,* 4 rue du Mont-Blanc. *Money exchange* outside banking hours, Cornavin railway station Mon.–Fri. 5.15 A.M.–10.45 P.M.; Sat/Sun. 5.15 A.M.–8.45 P.M. Cointrin airport, open 6 A.M.–11 P.M.

THE TICINO

Canton of Contrasts

If you go to Ticino the chances are that you will cross the St. Gotthard massif, 3,000 meters (10,000 feet) high, which forms part of the Canton's northern boundary. Whether you drive through the longest motorway tunnel in the world, the St. Gotthard (16.8 km.), or take the train which emerges at Airolo, or, in summer, drive over the pass road (with a fine section that cuts out the top 25 hairpin bends) you'll have the same sensation—that this is Switzerland with a difference.

As the canton slopes southwards from the St. Gotthard heights to the shores of lakes Maggiore and Lugano, you will notice that both the climate and the scenery gradually become more Mediterranean than alpine. The buildings are also different, with chalets slowly giving way to cottages of dark, rough-hewn stone, and later to color-washed houses with orange-tiled roofs, interspersed with Italianate churches.

At the lower levels you will notice flourishing palm trees, and exotic flowers and shrubs of a most un-alpine appearance. You will also quickly realize that you have entered an Italian-speaking canton; the only one in Switzerland.

Projecting like a spearhead into Italy, it is hardly surprising that the Ticino has a distinctly Italian flavor. This is true not only of its food and wine, but also in its buildings, people, atmosphere and, perhaps above all, its climate. In the lake district December and January can be alternately mild and chilly, but the rest of the year is normally blissfully warm and sunny apart from occasional stormy spells—sometimes spectacular although usually shortlived—and summer can be downright hot.

But don't be fooled by Ticino's Italian appearance; you are still very much in Switzerland! Like many other Swiss cantons it has winter sports, alpine scenery, lakes, and plenty of mountain transport as well as typical Swiss efficiency and hospitality. But as an exclusive free offer Ticino throws in an almost Mediterranean climate at lower levels, and three world-famous resorts—Lugano, Locarno and Ascona.

Lugano, deep-set among steep-sided mountains by the lake of the same name is large, bustling, and perhaps a little brash. Locarno, slightly to the north on Lake Maggiore, is quieter, more sophisticated and rather more open; while neighboring Ascona is quaint, colorful and brimming with slightly self-conscious charm.

Just as the three resorts have their distinctive personalities, so do Ticino's many valleys, each vying with the others for scenery and charm; valleys which are almost always quiet and secluded, and occasionally primitive. Like many other unsung attractions in Ticino, these lovely valleys are missed by most tourists although a fine network of public transport makes nearly all easy to reach. In fact the canton is something of a motorist's paradise, since excellent, if sometimes narrow, roads lead everywhere, in several cases almost to the summit of fair-sized mountains.

Proof of the enduring appeal of this canton of contrast, which is fourth in size but tenth in population and has more than its fair share of attractions, is that it is visited by tourists of many countries despite the fact that it is somewhat remote from the main tourist centers.

Lugano

Because of its picturesque setting, Lugano is dubbed by some guide books and brochures as 'Queen of Ceresio', Lago di Ceresio being the Italian name for Lake Lugano. Lugano itself will leave an indelible imprint on your memory. Set in a large bay, with the green heights of

THE TICINO

Monte Brè and Monte San Salvatore standing like sentinels at each end, this Italianate city fully justifies the superlatives used to describe it.

It's a splendid, self-contained resort with a fine assortment of almost everything the visitor could want—hotels, restaurants, cafés, entertainment, culture, sport, tantalizing shops, beautiful lake and mountain surroundings; and a mild, sunny climate unexpected of a mountainous region. Less well-known is that like Locarno and Ascona, it is an exceptionally good center for day and half-day excursions by car, coach, train, steamer, cable car, lift, cogwheel railway, or even on foot. It lies in the middle of a region called the Sottoceneri, which extends southwards to the Italian frontier at Chiasso. It is an area which contains a wide range of scenery, from lakes, lush meadows, and mountains with magnificent views, to myriad valleys and villages; often so charming and unspoiled that it is difficult to believe that the bustle of Lugano can be so close.

The region has long been inhabited. It is known that the Liguri were here at least four centuries before Christ. About two centuries later the Romans arrived, bringing with them their culture and civilization. By the end of the Middle Ages the region was under the influence of nearby Como. Thereafter, but not always happily, it gradually came under the domination of the Swiss Confederation. But it was not until 1803 that the Lugano region joined with Bellinzona and Locarno to become a fully-fledged Swiss canton—that of Ticino. Half a century later the first trickle of tourists began to arrive. Lugano sits on the most important north–south rail and road arteries in Europe. There are regular daily connections from Agno Airport to Zurich, Berne, Geneva and Venice.

Exploring Lugano

The hub of Lugano is the lakeside Piazza Riforma with its neoclassical Municipio, or town hall, constructed in 1844. Around the Municipio and up the hill towards the cathedral lies the old town, a maze of winding, arcaded streets, sometimes steep and narrow. But outside this central area with its old-world charm and obvious Italian influence, Lugano at once becomes more modern and international with elegant shops, imposing buildings, and fine hotels.

It's a short but steep climb to the cathedral of San Lorenzo, which is not the most important of ecclesiastical edifices. But it is worth a visit, firstly for its 16th-century, early Renaissance façade, and secondly for the fine view of the city and lake from its terrace.

Of much greater importance is the Franciscan church of Santa Maria degli Angioli in Piazza Luini, where the arcaded Via Nassa—Lugano's principal shopping street—joins the lakeside promenade. Here, facing you as you enter the church, is the gigantic *Crucifixion* fresco painted by Bernardino Luini in 1529, unquestionably his greatest work. The lighting is poor, so to savor the color and detail go there on a bright day. In the church you'll also see the *Last Supper* and several other works by Luini.

On a more secular level, and a must for art lovers, is the Villa Favorita in Castagnola, a trolley-bus ride from the town center. From the entrance gates a ten-minute walk through lovely gardens beside the lake will bring you to the Pinacoteca. Here is the art collection formed by the late Baron Heinrich von Thyssen, generally regarded as one of the best private collections in Europe. It is still being added to by the present Baron. In over 20 superbly arranged and cleverly lit salons are displayed masterpieces from the Middle Ages to the 18th century including such treasures as J. van Eyck's *Annunciation* and Dürer's *Jesus among the Scribes.* But it is open only from Easter to October on Friday, Saturday and Sunday.

Closer to the town center is Lugano's beautifully cared-for municipal park, the lakeside Parco Civico. Here in summer, weather permitting, you can sit and listen to the frequent concerts in a setting of lawns, flower beds and majestic trees. Located in the park is the Villa Ciani, an art gallery which also has important exhibitions.

On the Cassarate side of the park is Lugano's vast lido with several swimming pools, lawns for sunbathing, restaurants, etc. Pollution has unfortunately meant that it is no longer possible to bathe from the lido itself, though the rest of the lake is now perfectly safe for swimming. Just outside the park on the other side is the Kursaal, a large entertainment center with nightclub, theater, cinema, gaming room (boule only) and restaurant, where there is almost always something going on.

One of Lugano's joys is just walking along the two-and-a-half-kilometer (one and a half miles) tree-shaded lakeside promenade; a rather unexpected sight along this walk is a bust of George Washington, in a little Greek rotunda. It does *not* commemorate a visit to Lugano by the president, but was sculpted by Angelo Brunere in 1859, at the request of a Swiss civil engineer who had made his fortune in the Americas.

Excursions

Probably the best way of getting your bearings and an idea of the excursion delights in store is to take the funicular trip from Paradiso to Monte San Salvatore (912 meters, 2,995 feet) or from Cassarate to Monte Brè 930 meters (3,052 feet) high. From either you will get an eagle's-eye view of Lugano, its irregularly shaped lake, and the hills, mountains and valleys of the region. Choose a good day, and go before the clouds have begun to gather around the mountain tops, as they so often do around midday. Even better is the ascent of Monte Generoso,

1,700 meters (5,590 feet) high. Take the steamer to Capolago at the southern end of the lake (about 50 minutes from Lugano) where, beside the landing stage, the little red cogwheel-train will be waiting to take you on its gallant 40-minute climb to the top station. The grassy summit is some 75 meters (250 feet) higher, but you don't need to be a mountaineer or a goat to reach it. There's a prepared path, steep and rough but not too difficult. From the summit on a clear day you'll see the Po Valley and the Apennines in the south, the snow capped Alps to the north, and much of Ticino in between.

To the Collina d'Oro

Projecting southwards from Lugano is an eight-kilometer-long (five miles) peninsula with twin parallel ridges. To the west, forming one side of the bay of Agno, is the Collina d'Oro (Golden Hill), the smaller but perhaps the prettier of the two. Longer, higher, more spectacular, and with even finer views is the eastern ridge starting at Monte San Salvatore and ending at Morcote on the southern tip of the peninsula, the village of Carona being in the center.

The road to the Collina d'Oro leads from Sorengo, on the outskirts of Lugano, past the mini-lake of Muzzano, to Gentilino with its cypress-surrounded church of Sant'Abbondio. In the cemetery are buried Bruno Walter the conductor, and the Nobel prizewinner and poet Hermann Hesse. Hesse lived in Montagnola, the next village, where you will get a fine view of Lugano. The last village along the Collina d'Oro ridge, and almost the end of the road, is Agra. From here, as from other villages, well-marked paths lead over the ridge and also down to the lake shore.

To Carona and the Malcantone

You can reach Carona and the easternmost ridge on foot from the top of Monte San Salvatore, by cable car from Melide, or—the best way—as part of a car tour of the whole peninsula. From Paradiso the road twists steeply up around Monte San Salvatore and then follows the crest of the ridge to go through a narrow archway under part of the church of Carona of Romanesque origin (it contains the *Death of John the Baptist* by Solari, a villager who was a pupil of Leonardo da Vinci). You need go no farther than the car park just through the arch to enjoy one of the most spectacular of many fine views on the tour. Have a look too, at the pretty and ancient frescoed houses in the village itself.

Beyond Carona the road passes the charming village of Vico Morcote before diving through the woods in a steep, winding descent to the old waterside townlet of Morcote. Spare time here (and pray for parking space) to wander among its lovely old decorated houses and arcades. As you will see from the work prominently displayed in shops, Morcote has a small art colony.

From Morcote you can take the lakeside road round the peninsula, turning right for Lugano, if you are in a hurry, at either Figino or Agnuzzo. Better still, continue round the lake to Ponte Tresa. Don't cross the bridge unless you have a passport; the other side is Italy. Turn right before the bridge and follow the River Tresa—by which Lake Lugano drains into Lake Maggiore—to Monteggio-Fornasette. At either place, if you bear right you'll head into the Malcantone, a region of wooded hills, green valleys, and quiet villages with a choice of some half-dozen different ways of getting back to Lugano.

To the Valleys North of Lugano

North of Lugano, and almost on the city's doorstep, lie several quiet and charming valleys easily reached by car or bus. They offer the visitor any number of memorable walks or drives among beautiful mountains and valleys, sometimes wooded, sometimes with lush pastures colored with wild flowers, and dotted with minuscule, sleepy villages; an area with hundreds of undiscovered picnic spots. The roads are good although usually narrow and often steep, but the traffic is surprisingly light.

Of many drives, one of the best is along Val Colla starting from Tesserete, eight kilometers (five miles) north of Lugano. Take the road which weaves along the mountainside through Bidogno to Bogno at the head of the valley. There it backtracks to return, often along the valley floor, to Lugano through Sonvico, with its 15th- and 16th-century church of San Giovanni Battista; and Dino with a church dating from the 12th century.

Alternatively from Tesserete you can go north up Val Capriasca, or west to the village of Ponte Capriasca, where there's a good fresco copy of Leonardo's *Last Supper* in the church of Sant'Ambrogio. If you look carefully you may notice several differences from the original, and also that two scenes—Christ on the Mount of Olives and the Sacrifice of Abraham—have been added by the artist, believed to have been Francesco Melzi.

Campione and its Casino

If you want to fritter away your fortune and find you can't do so quickly enough in Lugano's Kursaal with its five-franc limit, Campione d'Italia is a mere 20 minutes away. Almost directly across the lake from

THE TICINO

Lugano, Campione is a tiny bit of Italy entirely surrounded by Switzerland, and is mainly a large, glamorous, glittering casino where you can play Roulette, Baccara, Trente et quarante, Chemin de fer, Black Jack, Tout-va and what-have-you with almost unlimited stakes. There is a restaurant with an orchestra and floor show.

It was during the 8th century that Campione, then an imperial fief, was presented to the Monastery of San Ambrogio in Milan. Despite all the political upheavals in the region in the centuries which followed, Campione—except for a brief period—remained Italian and is so today. But if you go there you'll find no frontier post, no customs examination. The money used is Swiss. The postal services are Swiss, too.

Apart from its casino and anomalous international position, Campione has another claim to fame. In the late Middle Ages many of its citizens became builders, masons and sculptors, emigrating to Milan, where they founded the influential Campione school of stonework.

To Lake Como and Italy

Menaggio on Lake Como is only about 27 kilometers (17 miles) from Lugano. The trip can be made by road throughout, or by steamer as far as Porlezza, at the Italian end of Lake Lugano, and then by road.

The first village beyond Castagnola in the direction of Menaggio is Gandria. By any standards the place is picturesque, with charming houses rising in tiers from the water's edge, flights of steps, and alleys—too steep and narrow for motor vehicles. True, Gandria is touristy and well-equipped with souvenir shops; and there are other, equally appealing villages in the region, but none is so easily and pleasantly reached by the motor vessels which sail frequently from Lugano. If, after exploring the village and fortifying yourself at a café overlooking the lake, you are going back to Lugano it is worth while walking along the lakeside path (it will take about 40 minutes) to Castagnola, where you can complete your journey in a trolley-bus.

Just beyond Gandria, along the road which runs above the village, you enter Italy, and it is interesting to observe the many subtle differences which add up to a slight but unmistakable change in character.

It's best to make the trip to Lake Como about the end of April or the beginning of May, for then the azaleas are in bloom and at the height of the season there is a riot of color along the way. The azaleas are particularly fine in the formal gardens of the beautiful Villa Carlotta (open to the public), which is about five kilometers (three miles) south of Menaggio. Eight kilometers (five miles) farther on is Ospedaletto, with the minute, wooded island of Comacina a stone's throw from the shore. Be sure to go over to the island for a meal in the moderately priced restaurant, or even a picnic near the little chapel in the center.

A motor launch will soon come to fetch you if you stand on one of the quays.

The open-air markets in most Italian frontier towns during the week offer excellent buys in woolen and leather goods. Local residents loudly defend the advantages of one market over another, but whether you visit Como, Ponte Tresa, Luino, or Cannobio on market day (the day varies from town to town) the merchants are nearly always the same—they simply pack their trucks and move on to the next market the next day.

To Mendrisio and Chiasso

Across the Melide causeway, beside the excellent new motorway leading to the frontier town of Chiasso, is the village of Bissone. Here Francesco Borromini, part-architect of the Barberini Palace in Rome, was born, as was Carpoforo Tencalla (1623–1685), who founded a school of painting and architecture in Vienna before returning to his home town. The Tencalla House in Bissone is now open to the public from April to October. A lovely Italian Renaissance building acquired by the Ticino Craftsmen and Artists Society, it is furnished in the local style of the 17th century. You can also see Tencalla's frescoes in the Church of San Carpoforo in the village.

Ligornetto, the birthplace of Vicenza Vela, now houses the Vela Museum (open daily). Famous in 19th-century Italy, Vela's sculptures are to be found not only in Italian cities but also in Paris, Lisbon and Istanbul. *Spartacus,* in Lugano's Municipio, is also by him. Much of his work has been gathered together in a museum in his former villa, which was presented to the Swiss Confederation by his son, a talented painter.

The town of Mendrisio—also the name of the surrounding district—was involved in the great medieval power struggle between the Guelphs and Ghibellines, roughly representing the Pope and Emperor. Ruled by the Torriani family (Guelph partisans), the town was frequently oppressed by the Ghibelline viscounts. The Torrianis finally came out on top, but not until there had been a great deal of violence. Today Mendrisio has a peculiar charm that induces many a traveler to linger, and a visit to some of the historic monuments, such as the Chiesa di San Giovanni or the Palazzo Torriani-Fontana may help to work the spell. Mendrisio is also well-known for its elaborate evening processions on Maundy Thursday and Good Friday.

The oldest building in all Ticino stands in Riva San Vitale on the southeastern corner of Lake Lugano. The village, which proclaimed itself a republic in 1798 (and lost its independence after 16 days!)

contains a baptistry dating from about the 5th century, and a large stone baptismal font (for baptism by immersion) from the 5th century.

Locarno

Locarno's magnetism stems from the same sources as that of Lugano, yet its atmosphere is very different. Like Lugano it enjoys a subtropical climate, romantic lakeside setting, and Ticino's happy fusion of Italian grace with Swiss efficiency; and naturally enough it has become a popular international resort. But there the likeness ends. For Locarno, a smaller place on a larger lake, is less townlike and more leisurely and informal.

The town has had a dramatic and often disastrous history—particularly during the 16th century when nearly 60 of her illustrious families, rather than acknowledge the Roman Catholic Church, fled to Zurich (where, incidentally, they were instrumental in starting the silk industry). Next came a series of devastating floods followed, in 1576 by the Great Plague, of which Saint Carlo wrote in 1584 'only 700 out of the 4,800 who inhabited the town were left.'

It was not until 1925 that Locarno came into her own. In that year the little, unknown resort suddenly hit world headlines when Briand, Stresemann, Mussolini and Chamberlain met there to sign the Locarno Pact. The story goes that Lucerne was the favored location, but the French minister's girlfriend, who was fascinated by Locarno, persuaded him to insist upon holding the conference there. A more recent boost to the city's economy has been the establishment of the Locarno Film Festival. Held each year in the autumn it provides an international film market for Switzerland and has become an event of increasing artistic importance. It brings film people from many countries to Locarno and adds an important facet to the town's cultural life.

Exploring Locarno

Despite all the attractions of a top-class resort, Locarno has a quiet, rather dignified air. Interesting old streets converge on the delightful Piazza Grande where a fine sweep of Italian houses rises above arcaded shops. Locarno's shops, specializing in fashion, antiques, art and local handicrafts, are highly selective and sophisticated, so that even window-shopping is fun. Along the tree-shaded waterfront with its posh hotels, wisteria, orange blossom and magnolias bloom; and in early summer you may see a priest holding services outside the houses of little first communicants.

Locarno has some outstanding Romanesque and baroque churches. Most unusual is the beautiful basilical church, San Vittore, started around the 11th century; the back (the oldest part) and partially restored crypt are particularly fine. A bas-relief of the saint, sculpted in 1462 by Martino Berazone and now adorning the recently completed tower, was found on the ruined castle of the Muralti close by. Part of this castle was restored in 1926 and is now an important museum. Concerts are held in San Francesco church, reputedly founded by St. Anthony of Padua but rebuilt in 1538 and given an imposing Renaissance façade with emblems depicting Locarno's early class distinctions: an eagle representing noblemen, an ox the citizens, and a lamb the cultivators! For uninhibited baroque extravaganza the 17th-century Chiesa Nuova is hard to beat, with its giant stucco statue of St. Christopher outside and froth of superbly stuccoed angels within. The chancel of Santa Maria in Selva has exquisite frescoes, painted in 1400 and extremely moving in their simplicity. La Collegiate di Sant'Antonio Abate is worth visiting for the illusionistic painting, *The Dead Christ*, by the Orelli brothers.

The Madonna del Sasso sanctuary, crowning a rock—where Brother Bartolomeo da Ivrea saw a vision of the Virgin in 1480—is reached by funicular. The sanctuary, begun in 1487 and enlarged by stages, contains some lovely 15th-century paintings, including two by Bernadino de Conti and Bramantino's *Flight into Egypt*.

Ascona

Only four kilometers (two and a half miles) from Locarno is the small resort town of Ascona. It's on a corner of a bay frequently dotted with trim little yachts, and features an extensive waterside promenade with all sorts of boats for hire. What gives Ascona a character of its own is its quiet and relaxed atmosphere, and more particularly its contrast. For almost hidden behind the lively, colorful cafés and the trees on the shore road is the town's other face; an intriguing muddle of old streets and twisting alleys filled with boutiques, antique shops, bookbinders, galleries and craft shops, all surrounding the eye-catching church tower. True, some are there to catch the tourist, but the scene is pleasant and unexpected, and the emphasis on art, culture and craftsmanship is an indication of the way Ascona has attracted artists, writers, musicians and composers. By the lakeside you will probably see artists displaying their work, although some of what you see is decidedly tawdry.

In the surrounding districts craftsmanship is also highly developed. Baskets, bags, mats and woven cloths come from nearby valleys; ceramics with highly colored fanciful designs of birds and animals, from the Ascona region. Rustic pottery, decorated trays and platters,

THE TICINO

and wooden *zoccoli* (or clogs) and other quality goods are produced here.

Excursions from Locarno and Ascona

From Locarno and nearby Ascona there are countless contrasting day and half-day trips up valleys, among mountains, and on the lake. One of the best starts is the center of Locarno. By cable railway you can go to Orselina, where an aerial cable car whisks you up to Cardada at 1,234 meters (4,050 feet) before the final trip by lift to Cimetta (1,508 meters, 4,950 feet). From both there are magnificent views of Lake Maggiore and the Alps, as well as wonderful mountain hikes, and if you need sustenance you can get a meal or a snack at either place. In winter there's skiing on the snowy slopes.

A quick and pleasant introduction to the many valley excursions is to the Centovalli, which runs from near Locarno due west toward Italy. To the frontier it's a 38 kilometer (24 mile) round trip by road, or you can join one of the little tram-like trains which weave their way up the valley from Locarno to Domodossola. Named the Centovalli ('valley of one hundred valleys') because of its many, often gorge-like lateral valleys, it is noted alike for its unspoiled character and beauty, its chestnut trees, and the rustic simplicity of its villages, although Intragna, at the entrance to the valley, is on a rather grand scale and boasts, at the church of San Gottardo, Ticino's highest belltower.

One of the ancient customs still practised in the Centovalli is the game of *boccia,* which has a slight resemblance to bowling. One day, so the story goes, a bowler's ball struck the painting of the Madonna on the side of a church wall in Rè, a few miles over the border in Italy. A stream of blood appeared on the face of the Madonna and the player was so overcome by his experience that he ended his days as a hermit in the mountains. To this day, on April 30th each year, residents of the Centovalli make a pilgrimage to Rè to commemorate the legend.

To Valle Maggia and Val Onsernone

The Valle Maggia has a good highway and is also served by postal bus. At Bignasco the valley splits into Val Lavizzera, noted for dairy farming and cheese-making, and Val Bavona, a dramatic gorge with compact stone-built mountain villages and many waterfalls. From San Carlo, where the road ends at the head of Val Bavona, you can now go by cable car up to Robiei (2,010 meters, 6,500 feet) where, in the silent beauty of peaks and glaciers, there is a new 40-bed economy-grade hotel.

Through the centuries the Valle Maggia has suffered violent floods, notably in 1747 when Avegno was inundated, and again in 1834 when Peccia was destroyed. This century the mountain waters have been harnessed by the creation of artificial lakes which feed an elaborate system of hydroelectric generators, built inside the mountains.

Typical of the Valley Maggia are the rough-hewn dry-stone *grotti,* often with a solid wall of rock behind them. These are wine vaults for Ticino wines—the red Merlot, which can be excellent, and the white Nostrano, primarily a cooking wine. In Ticino, a restaurant with tree-shaded, granite tables where you can eat, and drink wine from a *boccalino* (small pottery jug), is often known as a grotto. You'll see many of them.

In the town of Maggia one attraction is the church of Santa Maria delle Grazie di Campagna, a curious blend of the elegant, with its frescoes, and the rustic, with its wood-beamed ceiling. Hanging in the church are many ex-votos, paintings done by country folk in thanksgiving for favors granted through prayer. Painstakingly realistic and yet naive in their execution, they are a typical expression of the folk art of this area.

The Val Onsernone, sheer and deep, has a winding road passing through several old villages. Connected to Locarno by bus, the region is the center of the straw industry. Since the 16th century this straw work has found ready markets, but many emigrated to Tuscany, Piedmont, and Belgium to carry on their craft.

The most beautiful of all the valleys near Locarno, according to many, is the Valley Verzasca. Wild and scenic with many waterfalls, the region is largely unspoiled and undeveloped. A well-surfaced though sometimes narrow road goes from Gordola, a few kilometers east of Locarno, to Sonogno, about 24 kilometers (15 miles) up the valley; postal coaches cover the route. Just beyond the village of Sonogno there's a small café where you can enjoy a simple but good meal in the open air. In Brione you can visit a castle, as well as a church with remains of 14th-century frescoes in the style of Giotto, depicting the life of Christ. Primarily, however, this valley is one of natural beauties —campers, hikers, and photographers should find their paradise here.

Around Lake Maggiore

A fascinating excursion by car or postal coach from Locarno is to the tiny dry-stone hamlet of Indemini, clinging to the grassy slopes of Mount Gamborogno. After crossing the River Ticino you skirt the shore, leaving the highway at Vira-Gamborogno to climb steeply on an excellent road, with the entire northern (Swiss) end of Lake Maggiore spread out below you. Later on the Passo di Neggia, about five kilome-

THE TICINO

ters (three miles) before Indemini, both Swiss and Italian sections are visible. Indemini has no streets—only steep paths—but it has a café with a balcony looking across stone roofs to the chestnut trees and a valley beyond. Mountain flowers and herbs scent the air, and clusters of stone cottages seem camouflaged against their background. It is worth going on beyond Indemini to enter Italy, rejoining the lakeside at Maccagno for the lovely drive back along the shore (in Switzerland again). The round trip is 80 kilometers (50 miles).

On the other side of the lake, the drive from Locarno to Porto Ronco by the upper road takes you through villa-studded wooded hills with occasional views of the lake far below. It then descends dramatically to the picturesque lakeside village of Porto Ronco, from which the two beautiful little Brissago Islands can be seen. Both are nationally preserved botanical gardens for exotic trees and plants, the larger island being accessible by steamer.

Bellinzona, Crossroads of Ticino

Located in the surprisingly flat and wide valley of the River Ticino, Bellinzona is not only the capital but also the crossroads of the canton. Northwards, highways go to three important and historic passes (the San Bernardino to Chur and the Grisons; the Lukmanier, or Lucomagno, to Disentis; and the St. Gotthard to Andermatt and central Switzerland) as well as to a recently developed one, the Nufenen pass to the Rhône valley. To the west the road goes to Locarno. Southwards there's a fine new motorway to Lugano and Milan.

With a key position astride important trade routes, small wonder that over the centuries Bellinzona has been fought for and bandied about from one overlord to another with almost monotonous regularity. Nearly 1500 years ago there was a settlement where the town is now. Later it came under the sway of the Bishop of Como. In the Middle Ages Bellinzona was the subject of many bitter disputes, and was kicked around like a football by the Bishops and feudal overlords of Como and Milan. The Swiss of Uri bought the town for 2,400 florins in the early 15th century only to lose it in the battle of Arbedo three years later. Finally, in 1503 the town was ceded to the Swiss of Uri, Schwyz and Unterwalden, who brought it three centuries of peace, but only at the expense of a harsh rule which lasted until 1803—the year that Bellinzona became part of the newly created canton of Ticino.

With this long and turbulent history in mind, and the town's strategic situation, the visitor will hardly be surprised to find Bellinzona dominated by three fine 13th- to 15th-century castles and some formidable walls. One—the Castello Grande or San Michele (often called the castle of Uri)—is on a hillock near the town center. Close by, on a hillside overlooking the station, is the second, the well-restored Castello di Montebello (or Castle of Schwyz), now a museum. Some 150 meters (500 feet) higher up the hill is the last of the trio, the Castello di Sasso Corbaro (or Castle of Unterwalden), from the terrace of which you'll get a fine view of the town and the Ticino valley.

Valle Levantina and Val Bedretto

Busiest of the valleys north of Bellinzona (it carries all the road and rail traffic using the Gotthard route) is the Valle Levantina, down which flows the River Ticino. Despite its heavy traffic the Levantina between Biasca and Airolo is a splendid wild alpine valley, well-wooded and with waterfalls streaking its sides. As you go along it you will realize that it forms the transition between the subtropical southern Ticino and the truly alpine north. Stop a while at Giornico to visit the well restored 12th-century church of San Nicalao with its unusual carvings of animals and mythical beasts, most particularly in the crypt. Incidentally, it was here that a few hundred Swiss defeated thousands of Milanese in 1478 at the battle of Sassi Grossi.

At Airolo the road ahead quickly steepens to climb the St. Gotthard. But if you turn left you'll enter Val Bedretto where a good but narrow road goes through magnificent alpine scenery to the recently much improved Nufenen Pass close to the source of the River Ticino.

From Biasca one can also head up Val Blenio and the pretty Valle Santa Maria, which together form the approach to the wild desolation of the Lukmanier pass.

These valleys—even busy Levantino—take the traveler through forests of chestnut at lower levels and conifers higher up; into rustic villages with Romanesque buildings, past milky mountain torrents and waterfalls, and among some of the finest alpine scenery. But for the adventurous, prepared to accept roads which may be steep and sometimes rough, there are many more side valleys where the scenic beauty and silence is all but overwhelming.

PRACTICAL INFORMATION FOR THE TICINO

GETTING AROUND. By train, steamer and post-bus you can see almost every corner of this colorful part of Switzerland. The region is bisected by the main railway line from the St Gotthard running right down to Italy with a branch to Locarno.

THE TICINO

In addition there are a number of smaller private railways and a variety of both mountain and cable railways. The line up Monte Generoso from Capolago Lago is particularly attractive. The post-bus network is one of the best in Switzerland, reaching into the lovely and completely unspoiled valleys. On both Lake Lugano and Lake Locarno (especially the former) there are steamer and large motor-launch services.

There are two Regional Holiday Season Tickets for the area, one based on Locarno and the other on Lugano. These are valid each for seven days giving unlimited travel (first class) around the town and lake and half-fare rates elsewhere (see page 25).

A motorway runs from the southern end of the Ticino valley (and indeed is extending right up that valley) to the Italian border.

HOTELS AND RESTAURANTS. Nearly all the hotels that we include in our listings below have a wide range of rooms, a good many of which may well fall into a lower grading than that which we have given here. The best advice is always to check beforehand with the hotel (we have provided phone numbers to facilitate this).

AIROLO. *Delle Alpi* (I), tel. 881722. Central and comfortable. *Motta & Poste* (I), tel. 881917. Central and quiet.

ASCONA. *Casa Berno* (L), tel. 353232. Quiet hotel in own grounds with pool and sauna. *Castello del Sole* (L), tel. 351165. Lakeside hotel with indoor and outdoor pools, tennis, gymnasium and sauna; comfortable and quiet. *Delta* (L), tel. 351105. All facilities in this excellent hotel. *Eden Roc* (L), tel. 355255. Luxurious lakeside hotel in own grounds; tennis, 2 pools and sauna. *Europe au Lac* (L), tel. 352881. Quiet lakeside hotel with 2 pools. *Acapulco au Lac* (E), tel. 354521. Quiet hotel by lake with waterskiing and indoor pool. *Castello-Seeschloss* (M), tel. 351803. Central, quiet and comfortable; pool. *Sasso Boretto* (M), tel. 357115. Good family hotel; sailing and indoor pool. *Tamaro au Lac* (M), tel. 353939. Atmospheric and quiet. *Villa Veratum* (M), tel. 353577. Breakfast only; small, central and atmospheric; pool. *Luna* (I), tel. 353607. Quiet and central; facilities for the handicapped. Breakfast only. *Mulino* (I), tel. 353692. Ideal family hotel; quiet and in own grounds.

Restaurants. *Da Ivo* (M), Via Collegio (tel. 351031). Recommended. *Monte Verità* (M), tel. 351281.

BELLINZONA. *Croce Federale* (I), tel. 251667. Near the station and very quiet; sauna. *Unione* (I), tel. 255577. Central but quiet and in own grounds.

BRISSAGO. *Camelia* (I), tel. 651241. Central, but very quiet hotel in own grounds. *Mirto au Lac* (I), tel. 651328. Lakeside hotel with sailing and waterskiing; very quiet.

CAMPIONE. In Italy, but this enclave uses Swiss money etc. *Grand Hotel* (M), tel. 687031. Outdoor pool.

COLDRERIO. *Motel Mobil* (I), tel. 464881. Central and with restaurant but otherwise undistinguished.

FAIDO. *Milano* (I), tel. 381307. Medium-sized hotel in own grounds; very quiet. *Faido* (I), tel. 381555. Central and small.

GANDRIA. *Moosman* (I), tel. 517261. Small and very quiet lakeside hotel.

LOCARNO. *La Palma au Lac* (L), tel. 336771. Beautiful situation on lake; waterskiing, indoor pool and sauna. *Reber au Lac* (L), tel. 336723. Lakeside hotel with tennis and pool. *Esplanade* (E), Minusio (tel. 332121). Traditional hotel with huge gardens; tennis and pool. *Muralto* (E), tel. 338881. Fine view of the lake; central; facilities for the handicapped. *Park-Hotel* (E), tel. 334554. Lovely gardens in this lakeside hotel; outdoor pool and facilities for the handicapped. *Quisisana* (E), tel. 336141. High above town with splendid view, indoor pool and gymnasium. *Beau-Rivage* (M), tel. 331355. Central and quiet. *Remorino* (M), tel. 331033. Breakfast only; quiet in own grounds with pool; ideal for children. *Dell'Angelo* (I), tel. 318175. Atmospheric and central. *Du Lac* (I), tel. 312921. Central; facilities for the handicapped. *Villa India* (I), tel. 311210. Small, quiet family hotel in own grounds.
Restaurants. *La Palma au Lac* (M–E), vl. Verbano 29, Muralto (tel. 336771). Another of Switzerland's outstanding restaurants. *Oldrati* (I–M), vl. Verbano 1, Lungo-Lago, Muralto (tel. 338544). First class spot.

LOCARNO-ROBIEI. *Val Bavona* (I), tel. 991226. New hotel situated among peaks and glaciers.

LOSONE. *Losone* (L), tel. 350131. Very superior lakeside hotel with facilities for children and the handicapped; very quiet.

LUGANO. *Eden Grand Hotel* (L), tel. 542612. Cure facilities, airconditioning, 2 indoor pools, one with seawater, waterskiing and sauna in this quiet lakeside hotel. *Splendide Royal* (L), tel. 542001. Old fashioned elegance in furnishings, but modern in all other respects; indoor pool and facilities for children. *Admiral* (E), tel. 542324. 2 pools, sauna and gymnasium; facilities for the handicapped. *Alba* (E), tel. 543731. *Bellevue au Lac* (E), tel. 543333. Central and with pool. *Du Lac-Seehof* (E), tel. 541921. Waterskiing, sauna and pool; by the lake. *Europa au Lac* (E), tel. 543621. Smart lakeside hotel with indoor pool. *Béha* (M), tel. 541331. Central and with facilities for the handicapped. *Cristina* (M), tel. 543312. Tropical garden with heated pool. Tennis, water sports, and San Salvatore nearby. Recommended. *De la Paix* (M), tel. 542331. Pool. *Meister* (M), tel. 541412. Fine family hotel with pool. *Nizza* (M), tel. 541771. Park with heated pool. Excellent cuisine. Panorama bar. Splendid views. Recommended. *Walter au Lac* (M), tel. 227425. Central. *Rio* (I), tel. 228144. Small, simple and very reasonably priced.

Restaurants. *Bianchi* (E), Via Pessina 3 (tel. 228479). *Al Portone* (M–E), Viale Cassarate 3 (tel. 235995). Excellent. *Grotto Grillo* (M–E), Via Ronchetto 6 (tel. 511801). *Cina* (I–M), Piazza Riforma 9 (tel. 235173). First class. *Locanda del Boschetto* (I–M), Via Casserinetta 40 (tel. 542493). Very good. *Del Tiglio* (I–M), Via Merlina 6 (tel. 515470). *La Tinèra* (I–M), Via dei Gorini 2 (tel. 235219).

LUGANO-VEZIA. *Motel Vezia* (M), tel. 563631. Large hotel with pool; in own grounds.

LUMINO. *Motel Lumino* (M), tel. 291252.

MELANO. *Motel Lido* (I), tel. 687971. Lakeside hotel in own grounds with pool and facilities for the handicapped. *Park-Palace* (I), tel. 687795. At lakeside.

MELIDE. Restaurant. *La Romantica* (E), tel. 687521. Built in the 18th century as a stopover for the King of Savoy en route to Italy and now a small and extremely comfortable restaurant and nightclub in fine gardens; private beach.

MENDRISIO. *Stazione* (I), tel. 462244. Central and with facilities for the handicapped.

MORCOTE. *Olivella au Lac* (L), tel. 691731. Superior lakeside hotel with indoor and outdoor pool, waterskiing, sailing and sauna; facilities for children. *Carina* (M), tel. 691131. Lakeside hotel in historic building; fine views plus waterskiing and pool. *Rivabella* (I), tel. 691314. Small lakeside hotel; in own grounds and very quiet.

PONTE TRESA. *Del Pesce* (I), tel. 711146. Lakeside hotel with waterskiing and pool; plus facilities for the handicapped. *Zita* (I), tel. 711825. Pool. Golf course nearby.

RIAZZINO. *Motel Riazzino* (M), tel. 641422.

VIRA GAMBAROGNO. *Touring Hotel Bellavista* (M), tel. 611116. In own grounds with pool and wonderful views; very quiet rooms. *Viralago* (M), tel. 611591. Lakeside hotel with gym, indoor pool, tennis, sauna and facilities for children.

MUSEUMS. Bellinzona. *Museo Civico*, Castello di Montebello. Collection reflecting local history.

Bissone. *Casa Tencalla*. Italian Renaissance building furnished in the local style of the 17th century.

Castagnola. *Villa Favorita*. The finest private art collection in Europe. In over 20 beautifully appointed rooms is displayed the collection of Baron von Thyssen —including works by many major artists. Open from Good Fri. to 2nd Sun. in Oct., Fri./Sat. 10–12 A.M. and 2–5 P.M., Sun. 2–5 only.

Ligornetto. *Vincenzo Vela Museum*. Displays many sculptures by this 19th-century artist who became popular in Italy. Closed in winter.

Locarno. *Museo Civico/Museo d'Arte Contemporanea*, Piazza Castello 2. Interesting collection of local historical exhibits and modern art.

Lugano. *Villa Ciani*, City Park. A permanent printing exhibition and art gallery specializing in loan exhibitions.

Melide. *Swissminiatur*. Fine models (1/25th size) of typical or famous Swiss buildings, castles, steamers, trains etc. Closed in winter.

Meride. *Museo Deifossili* (Fossils Museum). Interesting small collection of the Monte San Giorgio fossils of evolutionary importance.

SPORTS. Golf, 18-hole course, open all year, Lugano Golf Club, Magliaso. There are many tennis courts about the town, two lighted at night, and a covered court, Lido Tennis Club (consult the official guide). Fishing, lake and river, Mar.–Oct.; licenses at the Municipio, Piazza Riforma. Boats for hire. Riding, Mario Roggiani, Crespera 7; S. Pedretti and Hubertus, both at Origlio; Scuderia "Roby," Bedano. Bathing at Lugano's huge lido with heated pools, lawns, buffet/restaurant.

USEFUL ADDRESSES. *Ente Turistico*, Tourist Office, Lugano, next to the Kursaal, Riva Albertolli 5, tel. 091–214664. *American Express*, c/o Danzas, Piazza Manzoni 8; *Cook's*, Riva Caccia 1; *English Church*, Via Clemente Maraini; *Christian Science Church*, Via Ciseri 7; *Synagogue*, Via Maderno 11. *British Vice-Consulate*, Via Maraini 14a, Loreto.

Car Hire. *Avis*, Via Adamini 4; *Hertz*, Via C. Maraini 14; *Europcar*, Via Ciani 5; *Budget*, Via San Gottardo 6.

WINTER SPORTS. Though not renowned for its winter sports, facilities are nevertheless available in the Ticino.

Ascona, 205 meters (670 feet); skating and curling.

Locarno, 205 meters (670 feet); 1 funicular railway, 1 cable car, 4 lifts, 12 km. of downhill runs, 3 km. of cross-country trails, 2 km. of ski-hiking trails; curling, ski schools.

Lugano, 275 meters (900 feet); 2 funiculars, 1 cable car, 1 lift, 1 cogwheel railway, 15 km. of downhill runs, 50 km. of cross-country trails, skating.

ENGLISH-FRENCH-GERMAN-ITALIAN VOCABULARY

LANGUAGE/30

For the Business or Vacationing International Traveler

In 27 languages! A basic language course on 2 cassettes and a phrase book ... Only $14.95 ea. + shipping

Nothing flatters people more than to hear visitors try to speak their language and LANGUAGE/30, used by thousands of satisfied travelers, gets you speaking the basics quickly and easily. Each LANGUAGE/30 course offers:
- approximately 1½ hours of guided practice in greetings, asking questions and general conversation
- special section on social customs and etiquette

Order yours today. Languages available: (New) POLISH

ARABIC	GREEK	KOREAN	SERBO-CROATIAN
CHINESE	HEBREW	NORWEGIAN	SPANISH
DANISH	HINDI	PERSIAN	SWAHILI
DUTCH	INDONESIAN	POLISH	SWEDISH
FINNISH	ITALIAN	PORTUGUESE	TAGALOG
FRENCH	TURKISH	VIETNAMESE	THAI
GERMAN	JAPANESE	RUSSIAN	

To order send $14.95 per course + shipping $2.00 1st course, $1 ea. add. course. In Canada $3 1st course, $2.00 ea. add. course. NY and CA residents add state sales tax. Outside USA and Canada $14.95 (U.S.) + air mail shipping: $8 for 1st course, $5 ea. add. course. MasterCard, VISA and Am. Express card users give brand, account number (all digits), expiration date and signature.
SEND TO: FODOR'S, Dept. LC 760, 2 Park Ave., NY 10016-5677, USA.

ENGLISH-FRENCH-GERMAN-ITALIAN VOCABULARY

ENGLISH	FRENCH	GERMAN	ITALIAN
Come in!	Entrez! (ahn'tray)	Herein!	Avanti!
Can anyone here speak English?	Y a-t-il ici quelqu'un qui parle anglais?	Spricht jemand hier englisch?	C'è qualcuno che parla inglese?
Do you speak English?	Parlez-vous anglais?	Sprechen Sie englisch?	Parla inglese?
Do you understand?	Comprenez-vous?	Verstehen Sie?	Capisce?
I don't understand	Je ne comprends pas	Ich verstehe nicht	Non capisco
Don't mention it	Pas de quoi	Bitte sehr	Di niente
I beg your pardon	Pardon	Verzeihung	Mi scusi
Good morning	Bonjour	Guten Morgen	Buon giorno
Good day	Bonjour	Guten Tag	Buon giorno
Good evening	Bonsoir	Guten Abend	Buona sera
Good night	Bonne nuit	Gute Nacht	Buona notte
Good-bye	Au revoir	Auf Wiedersehen	Arriveder La, Arrivederci
How are you?	Comment allez-vous?	Wie geht es Ihnen?	Come sta?
How much...many?	Combien?	Wieviel?	Quanto...quanti?
I don't know	Je ne sais pas	Ich weiss nicht	Non so
No	Non	Nein	No
Yes	Oui	Ja	Sì
Please speak more slowly	Parlez plus lentement, s'il-vous-plaît	Bitte, sprechen Sie langsamer	Parli più lentamente, per favore
Sit down	Asseyez-vous	Setzen Sie sich	S'accomodi
Thank you very much	Merci bien	Danke sehr	Grazie mille
There is, there are	Il y a	Es gibt	C'è, ci sono
Very good...well	Très bien	Sehr gut	Molto bene
What is this?	Qu'est-ce-que c'est?	Was ist das?	Che cosa è questo?
What do you want?	Que voulez-vous?	Was wünschen Sie?	Cosa desidera?
Please	S'il vous plaît (silvooplay)	Bitte (bi'teh)	Per piacere, per favore

ENGLISH	FRENCH	GERMAN	ITALIAN
What is your name?	Comment vous appelez-vous?	Wie heissen Sie?	Come si chiama?
With pleasure	Avec plaisir	Mit Vergnügen	Con piacere
You are very kind	Vous êtes bien aimable	Sehr freundlich	Lei è molto gentile
Sunday	dimanche	Sonntag	domenica
Monday	lundi	Montag	lunedì
Tuesday	mardi	Dienstag	martedì
Wednesday	mercredi	Mittwoch	mercoledì
Thursday	jeudi	Donnerstag	giovedì
Friday	vendredi	Freitag	venerdì
Saturday	samedi	Samstag	sabato
Is there . . .	Y-a-t'il . . .	Gibt es . . .	C'è . . .
—a bus for . . . ?	—un autobus pour . . . ?	—einen Autobus nach . . . ?	—un autobus per . . . ?
—a dining car?	—un wagon-restaurant?	—einen Speisewagen?	—una carrozza ristorante?
—an English interpreter?	—un interprète anglais?	—einen englischen Dolmetscher?	—un interprete inglese?
—a guide?	—un guide?	—einen Führer?	—una guida?
—a good hotel at . . . ?	—un bon hôtel à . . . ?	—ein gutes Hotel in . . . ?	—un buon albergo a . . . ?
—a good restaurant here?	—un bon restaurant ici?	—ein gutes Restaurant hier?	—un buon ristorante qui?
—a sleeper?	—une place dans le wagon-lits?	—einen Schlafwagen?	—una cuccetta nel vagone letto?

VOCABULARY

ENGLISH	FRENCH	GERMAN	ITALIAN
Is there . . .	Y-a-t'il . . .	Hat man . . .	C'è . . .
—time to get out?	—le temps de descendre?	—Zeit auszusteigen?	—tempo di scendere?
—a train for . . . ?	—un train pour . . . ?	Gibt es —einen Zug nach . . . ?	—un treno per . . . ?
Thank you	Merci	Danke	Grazie
Where is . . .	Où est . . .	Wo ist . . .	Dov'è . . .
—the airport?	—l'aéroport?	—der Flugplatz?	—l'aeroporto?
—a bank? (money exchange?)	—une banque? (change?)	—eine Bank? (Wechselstube?)	—una banca (un ufficio di cambio)?
—the bar?	—le bar?	—die Bar?	—un bar?
—the barbershop?	—le coiffeur?	—ein Coiffeur/Friseur?	—un barbiere?
—the bathroom?	—la salle de bains?	—das Badezimmer?	—la sala da bagno?
—the ticket (booking) office?	—le guichet?	—der Billettschalter?	—lo sportello?
—a chemist's shop (drug store)?	—une pharmacie?	—eine Apotheke?	—la farmacia?
—the movies (cinema)?	—le cinéma?	—das Kino?	—il cinema?
—the checkroom?	—la consigne?	—die Gepäckaufbewahrung?	—il deposito bagagli?
—the British (American) Consulate?	—le consulat (américain) d'Angleterre?	—das englische (amerikanische) Konsulat?	—il consolato (d'America) d'Inghilterra?
—the Customs office?	—la douane?	—das Zollamt?	—la dogana?
—a garage?	—un garage?	—eine Garage?	—un autorimessa?
—a hairdresser	—un coiffeur?	—ein Coiffeur?	—un parrucchiere?
—the lavatory?	—les toilettes?	—die Toilette?	—i gabinetti?
—the luggage?	—les bagages?	—das Gepäck?	—i bagagli?

VOCABULARY

ENGLISH	FRENCH	GERMAN	ITALIAN
—the museum?	—le musée?	—das Museum?	—il museo?
—the police station?	—le poste de police?	—die Polizei?	—la polizia?
—the post office?	—le bureau de poste?	—das Postamt?	—l'ufficio postale?
—the theater?	—le théâtre?	—das Theater?	—il teatro?
—the railway station?	—la gare?	—der Bahnhof?	—la stazione?
—a tobacconist?	—un tabac?	—ein Tabakladen?	—una tabaccheria?
When... (At what time...)	Quand... (A quelle heure est)	Wann....	Quando... (a che ora)
—is lunch?	—le déjeuner est-il servi?	—ist das Mittagessen?	—è il pranzo?
—is dinner?	—le dîner est-il servi?	—ist das Abendessen?	—si cena?
—is the first (last) bus?	—part le premier (dernier) autobus?	—geht der erste (letzte) Autobus?	—parte il primo (l'ultimo) autobus?
—is the first (last) train?	—part le premier (dernier) train?	—geht der erste (letzte) Zug?	—è il primo (l'ultimo) treno?
—does the train leave (arrive)?	—le train part-il (arrive-t-il)?	—geht der Zug ab (kommt der Zug an)?	—parte (arriva) il treno?
—does the theater open?	—ouvre-t-on le théâtre?	—wird das Theater geöffnet?	—si apre il teatro?
—will it be ready?	—sera-t-il-(elle) prêt?	—wird es fertig sein?	—sarà pronto?
—does the performance begin (end)?	—la séance commence-t-elle(finit-elle?)	—beginnt (endet) die Aufführung?	—comincia (finisce) la rappresentazione?
—can I have a bath?	—pourrai-je prendre un bain?	—kann ich ein Bad nehmen?	—posso fare il bagno?

VOCABULARY

ENGLISH	FRENCH	GERMAN	ITALIAN
Which . . .	Quel est . . .	Welches ist . . .	Qual'è . . .
—the way to . . . street?	Par où va-t-on à la rue . . . ?	Wie komme ich zur Strasse?	—la strada per . . . ?
—the best hotel at . . . ?	—le meilleur hôtel de . . . ?	—das beste Hotel in . . . ?	—il migliore albergo di . . . ?
—the train (bus) for . . . ?	—le train (autobus) pour . . . ?	—der Zug (Autobus) nach . . . ?	—il treno (l'autobus) per . . . ?
What is . . .	Quel est . . .	Was ist . . .	Qual'è . . .
—the fare to . . . ?	—le prix du voyage à . . . ?	—der Fahrpreis nach . . . ?	—il prezzo per . . . ?
—the single fare?	—le prix d'aller?	—der einfache Fahrpreis?	—il prezzo per l'andata?
—the round trip (return) fare?	—le prix d'aller et retour?	—der Preis der Rückfahrkarte?	—il prezzo per andata e ritorno?
—the price?	—le prix?	—der Preis?	—il prezzo?
—the price per day?	—le prix par jour?	—der Preis pro Tag?	—il prezzo per giorno?
—per week?	—par semaine?	—pro Woche?	—per settimana?
—the price per kilo?	Combien le kilo?	—der Preis pro Kilo?	—il prezzo al kilo?
—the price per meter?	Combien le mètre?	—der Preis pro Meter?	—il prezzo al metro?
—the matter?	Qu'est-ce qui se passe?	—los?	—Che c'è?
—this?	Qu'est-ce que c'est?	—das?	—Che e questo?
—the French (etc.) for?	Comment dit-on . . . en français?	Wie sagt man . . . auf deutsch?	—Come si dice . . . in Italiano?

313

VOCABULARY

ENGLISH	FRENCH	GERMAN	ITALIAN
Have you . . .	Avez-vous . . .	Haben Sie . . .	Ha . . .
—any American (English) cigarettes?	—des cigarettes américaines (anglaises)?	—amerikanische (englische) Zigaretten?	—delle sigarette americane (inglesi)?
—a timetable?	—un indicateur des chemins de fer?	—einen Fahrplan?	—un orario?
—a room to let?	—une chambre à louer?	—ein Zimmer zu vermieten?	—una camera libera?
—anything ready? (food)	—quelque chose de prêt?	—etwas fertig?	—qualcosa di pronto?
—any fruit?	—des fruits?	—etwas Obst?	—della frutta?
How long?	Combien de temps?	Wie lange?	Quanto tempo?
How often?	Combien de fois?	Wie oft?	Quante volte?
I want . . . would like . . . need	Je désire . . . je voudrais	Ich brauche . . . Ich möchte . . . Ich bitte um	Vorrei . . .
—my bill	—mon compte	—meine Rechnung	—il conto
—the chambermaid	—parler avec la femme de chambre	—Ich möchte mit dem Zimmermädchen sprechen	—parlare con la cameriera
—a dentist	—consulter un dentiste	Ich brauche einen Zahnarzt	—consultare un dentista
—a dictionary	—un dictionnaire	Ich brauche ein Wörterbuch	—un dizionario
—a doctor	—consulter un médecin	Ich brauche einen Arzt	—consultare un medico
—to buy . . .	—acheter . . .	Ich möchte . . . kaufen	—comprare . . .
—something to drink	—prendre quelque chose à boire	Ich möchte etwas trinken	—qualcosa da bere

SWITZERLAND and LIECHTENSTEIN

Key to Map ②& ③
- ┼┼┼┼┼ Railway
- ▲ Mountain peak
- ─── Motorway with junctions
- ─ ─ ─ International throughroute
- ─ ·· ─ Regional throughroute
- ─── Main connecting road
- ✈ Airport
-)(Mountain pass

LANGUAGES
- Swiss German
- French
- Italian
- Romansh

Boundary of canton — Map ①

1. ZURICH
2. BERNE
3. LUCERNE
4. URI
5. SCHWYZ
6. NIDWALDEN
7. OBWALDEN
8. GLARUS
9. ZUG
10. FRIBOURG
11. SOLOTHURN
12. BASLE-STADT
13. BASLE-LAND
14. SCHAFFHAUSEN
15. APPENZELL AUSSER-RHODEN
16. APPENZELL INNER-RHODEN
17. ST. GALLEN
18. GRISONS
19. AARGAU
20. THURGAU
21. TICINO
22. VAUD
23. VALAIS
24. NEUCHÂTEL
25. GENEVA
26. JURA

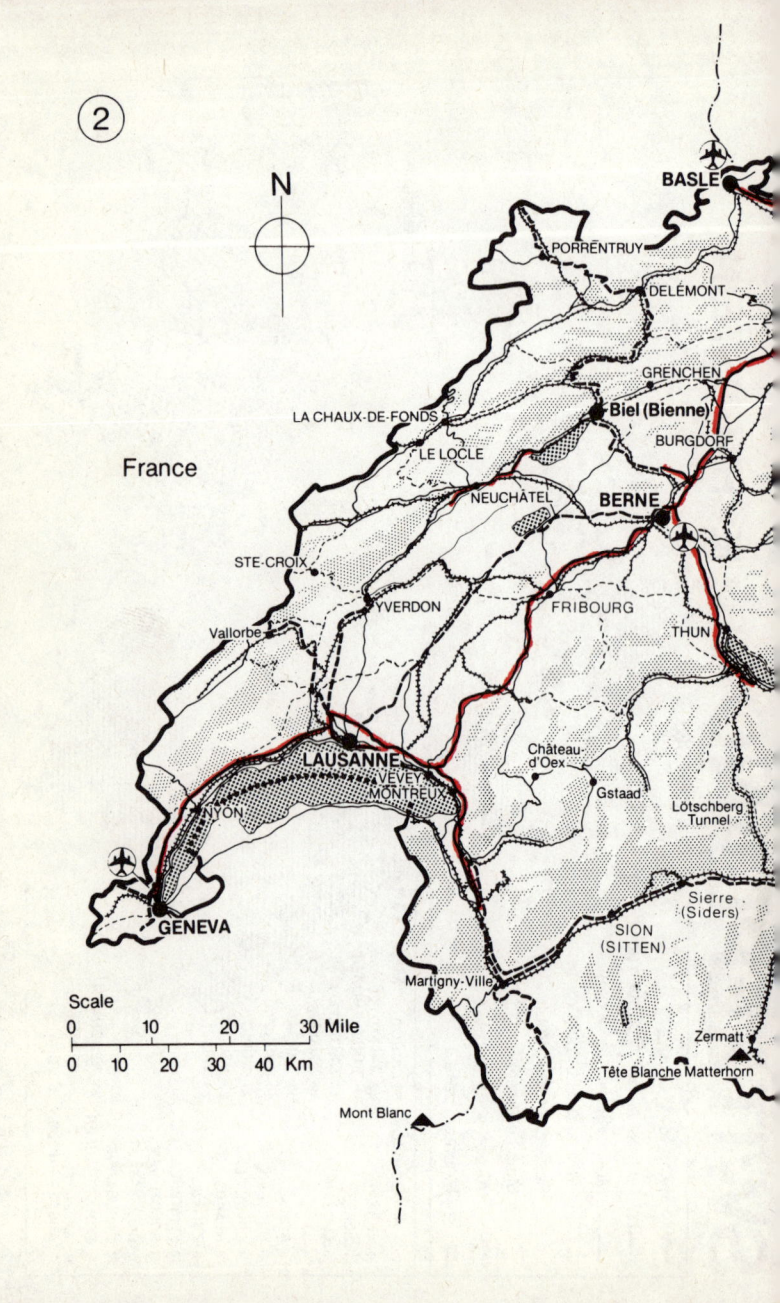

②

N

France

BASLE
PORRENTRUY
DELÉMONT
GRENCHEN
LA CHAUX-DE-FONDS
Biel (Bienne)
LE LOCLE
BURGDORF
NEUCHÂTEL
BERNE
STE-CROIX
YVERDON
Vallorbe
FRIBOURG
THUN
LAUSANNE
VEVEY
MONTREUX
Château-d'Oex
Gstaad
Lötschberg Tunnel
NYON
Sierre (Siders)
SION (SITTEN)
GENEVA
Martigny-Ville
Zermatt
Tête Blanche Matterhorn
Mont Blanc

Scale
0   10   20   30 Mile
0 10 20 30 40 Km

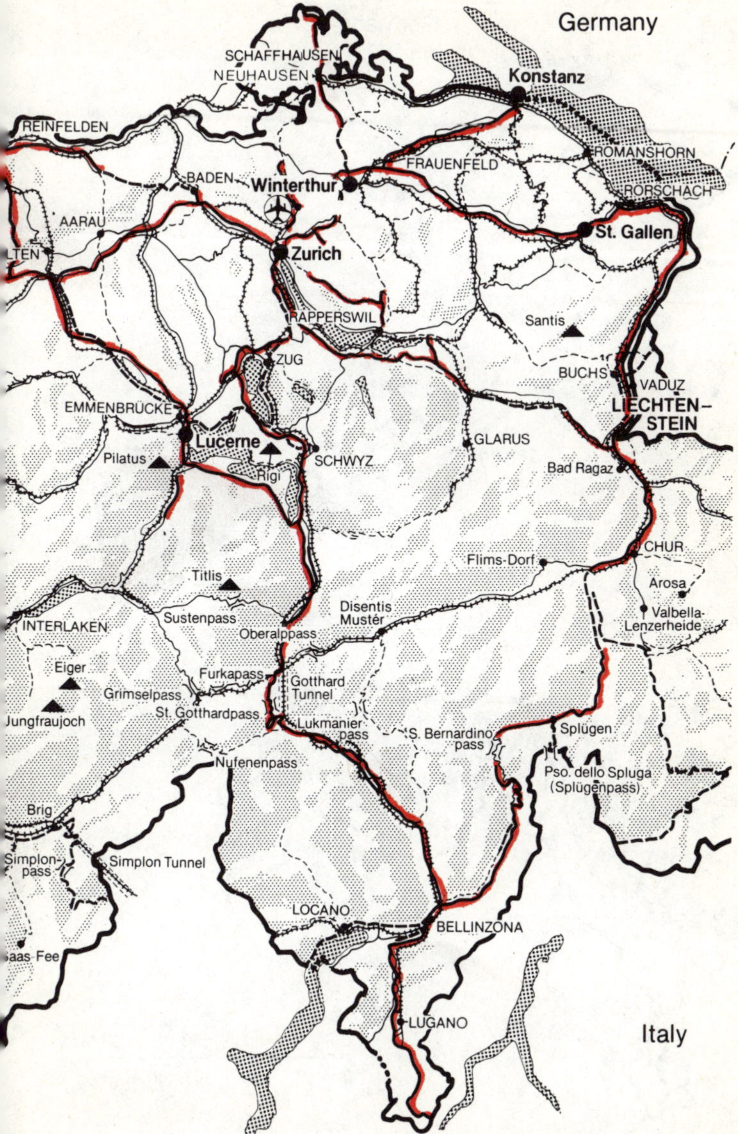
Germany
SCHAFFHAUSEN
NEUHAUSEN
Konstanz
REINFELDEN
ROMANSHORN
FRAUENFELD
BADEN
Winterthur
RORSCHACH
AARAU
St. Gallen
LTEN
Zurich
Santis
RAPPERSWIL
ZUG
BUCHS
VADUZ
LIECHTEN-STEIN
EMMENBRÜCKE
GLARUS
Lucerne
Pilatus
SCHWYZ
Rigi
Bad Ragaz
CHUR
Flims-Dorf
Arosa
Titlis
Disentis Mustér
Valbella-Lenzerheide
Sustenpass
INTERLAKEN
Oberalppass
Eiger
Furkapass
Gotthard Tunnel
Grimselpass
St. Gotthardpass
Jungfraujoch
Lukmanier pass
S. Bernardino pass
Splügen
Nufenenpass
Pso. dello Spluga (Splügenpass)
Brig
Simplon-pass
Simplon Tunnel
LOCANO
BELLINZONA
Saas-Fee
LUGANO
Italy

Germany
3
Konstanz
ROMANSHORN
FRAUENFELD
RORSCHACH
St. Gallen
Santis
BUCHS
VADUZ
LIECHTENSTEIN
Austria
GLARUS
Bad Ragaz
Klosters-Dorf
Klosters
CHUR
Flims-Dorf
DAVOS PLATZ
Arosa
Valbella-Lenzerheide
Valpera
Disentis
Mustér
Albulapass
Splügen
S. Bernardino
pass
St. Moritz
Bad
Pontresina
Pso. di S. Maria
(Umbrailpass)
Pso. dello Spluga
(Splügenpass)
Silvaplana
Maloja-P
N
BELLINZONA
LUGANO
Italy
Scale
0
10
20
30 Mile
0
10
20
30
40
Km

INDEX

Speak a foreign language in seconds.

Now an amazing space age device makes it possible to speak a foreign language *without* having to learn a foreign language.

Speak French, German, or Spanish.
With the incredible Translator 8000—world's first pocket-size electronic translation machines—you're never at a loss for words in France, Germany, or Spain.

8,000-word brain.
Just punch in the foreign word or phrase, and English appears on the LED display. Or punch in English, and read the foreign equivalent instantly.

Only 4¾" x 2¾", it possesses a fluent 8,000-word vocabulary (4,000 English, 4,000 foreign). A memory key stores up to 16 words; a practice key randomly calls up words for study, self-testing, or game use. And it's also a full-function calculator.

150,000 sold in 18 months.
Manufactured for Langenscheidt by Sharp/Japan, the Translator 8000 comes with a 6-month warranty. It's a valuable aid for business and pleasure travelers, and students. It comes in a handsome leatherette case, and makes a super gift.

Order now with the information below.

To order, send $69.95 plus $3 p&h ($12 for overseas del.) for each unit. Indicate language choice: English/French, English/German, English/Spanish. N.Y. res. add sales tax. MasterCard, Visa, or American Express card users give brand, account number (all digits), expiration date, and signature. SEND TO: Fodor's, Dept. T-8000, 2 Park Ave., New York, NY 10016-5677, U.S.A.

INDEX

(The letters H and R indicate hotel and restaurant listings.)

Liechtenstein listings are at the end of the index.

See "Facts at your Fingertips" pages 3–34 for general information on getting to and staying in Switzerland.
See also "Practical Information" at the end of each chapter for information on local transportation, shopping, sports, entertainment and museums.

Aarau, 128, H133
Aarburg, 129
Aareschlucht, 110
Adelboden, H118
Aesch, 129
Aeschi, 104, H119
Agra, 293
Aigle, 243–4
Airolo, 302, H303
Aletsch (glacier), 109
Alt-St. Johann, 190
Altdorf, 153–4, 159, 163, HR169
Alter Spital, 254
Altnau, 199
Amden, 191
Amsteg, H169
Andermatt, 154, H169, R170
Angenstein (castle), 129–30
Anniviers, 250
Anzère, 248, H256
Appenzell, 191–2, HR200
Arbon, 199, H201
Ardez, 223–4
Arenenberg (castle), 196
Arlesheim, 130
Arolla, 249
Arosa, 234–5, HR236
Arth-Goldau, 156
Ascona, 298–9, HR303

Aubonne, 261
Avants, Les, 267
Avenches, 140
Axenstrasse, 160

Bad Ragaz, 191, HR201
Bad Schinznach, 128
Baden, 128, H133
Balsthal, 129
Basle (Basel), 123–7, H130–1, R131–2
Beatenberg, 103, H119
Beatenbucht, 103
Beiva. *See* Bivio
Bellinzona, 301–2, H303
Berne, 93–100, map 97, H114–5, R115–6
Bernina, 231
Beromünster, 128
Bex, 244
Biasca, 302
Biel (Bienne), 146, HR119
Bignasco, 299
Bioux, Les, H273
Birr, 128
Bissone, 296
Bivio, 232
Blauherd, 252
Blausee, 112
Blausee-Mitholz, 112

321

INDEX

Blue Lake. *See* Blausee
Boltigen, 111
Bönigen, H119
Boniswil, 128
Bossaye, 270
Bottighofen, 199
Bourg-St. Pierre, 246, HR256
Brassus, Le, 269, H273
Braunwald, HR201
Bremgarten, 128
Bretaye, 243
Brienz (lake and town), 101–2, 110, H119
Brig, 253–4, HR256
Brione, 300
Brissago, 301, H303
Brugg, 128, H133
Brunnen, 163, HR170
Bulle, 139, HR147
Burgdorf, H119
Bürgenstock, 157, H170

Campione (Italy), 294–5, H304
Capolago, 293
Carona, 293
Cassongrat, 234
Castagnola, 292, 295
Casti. *See* Tiefencastle
Caumasee, 234
Caux, 267
Celerina, 227, HR236
Centovalli, 299
Champéry, 244, HR256
Champex, 246, H256
Charrat, HR256
Château d'Oex, 139, HR273
Châtel-St.-Denis, HR147
Chaux-de-Fonds, La, 143, HR147
Chenalette, La, 247
Chesières, 243
Chexbres, 266, HR273

Chillon, 267–8
Chur, 219–20, HR236
Col des Mosses, 139
Coldrerio, HR304
Collina d'Oro, 293
Colombier, 145
Comacina (island), 295–6
Constance (Germany), 196–7
Constance (lake), 127, 195–6, 198–9
Coppet, 261, HR273
Cossonay, 269
Côte, La (district), 262
Crans, 249, HR256
Crésuz, H147
Crissier, R273
Cully, 266

Davos, 220–2, HR237
Delémont, 144, HR147
Diablerets, Les, H274
Diavolezza, 231
Diessenhofen, 195
Dino, 294
Domleschg (valley), 233
Dornach, 130

Ebenalp, 192
Egerkingen, H133
Eigergletscher, 108
Eigerwand, 108
Einsiedeln, 161–2, H170
Eismeer, 108
Ems, 234
Engadine Valley, 221–31
Engelberg, 158–9, HR170
Eschenz, 195
Estavayer-le-Lac, 146, HR147
Eugensberg (castle), 196
Evian-les-Bains (France), 268
Evolène, 249, H256

INDEX

Faido, H304
Faulensee, 104, H119
Felskinn, 252
Findeln Rothorn, 252
Flims, 234, HR237
Flüela Pass, 222
Flüelen, 163, H170
Flums, 191
Flumserberg, 191, H201
Fribourg, 136–7, H147–8, R148
Frick, 128
Friedrichshafen (Germany), 198
Ftan, 224

Gais, 191
Gandria, 295, H304
Gemmi, 250
Gempenach, H148
Geneva, 276–83, map 280–1, H284–5, R285–6
Geneva (lake/region), 260–70
Gentilino, 293
Gersau, 163, H170
Giessbach (falls), 110
Giornico, 302
Glacier Express (train), 254
Glarisegg, 195
Glarus, 192–3, H201
Gletsch, 254–5
Glion, 267, HR274
Gontenbach, 179
Goppenstein, 113
Gornergrat, 252
Gottlieben, 196
Grächen, 252–3, H256
Grandson, 145
Grialetsch (glacier), 222
Grimentz, 250, H257
Grimsel (pass), HR257
Grindelwald, 109, 113, H119
Gruyères, 138–9, H148
Gstaad, 112, H119

Guarda, 223
Gunten, 103

Hallwil (lake), 128
Hasli (valley), 110–1
Haudères, Les, 249
Haute-Nendaz, 249, H257
Heiden, 200, H201
Heimwehfluh, 105
Hergiswil, H170
Hilterfingen, 103
Hölloch (caves), 161
Horn, H201

Indemini, 300–1
Interlaken, 104–5, HR120
Iseltwald, 110
Isérables, 247–8

Jaun (pass), 111
Jorat, 265
Julier (pass), 231–2
Jungfraujoch, 106–10
Jura Mts., 142–6

Kandersteg, 112–3, H120
Kehrsiten, 157
Kleine Scheidegg, 107, H120
Kleintitlis, 159
Klewenalp, 163, H170
Klosters, 220, HR237
Kruezlingen, 196–8, HR201
Küssnacht am Rigi, H170

Laax, 234, HR237
Landquart, 220
Langenbruck, 129, H133
Längfluh, 252
Laufboden, 191
Laufen, 129
Laufenburg, H133

INDEX

Lausanne, 262–5, H270–1, R271–2
Lauterbrunnen, 106–7
Lavaux (region), 266
Lenk, 111, H120
Lenzerheide, 232–3, HR238
Leukerbad, 250, H257
Levantina (valley), 302
Leysin, 243, H274
Liestal, 129, H133
Ligornetto, 296
Lindau (Germany), 198
Locarno, 297–8, HR304
Locarno-Robiei, H304
Locle, Le, 143, HR148
Loeche-les-Bains. *See* Leukerbad
Losone, H304
Lucerne (Luzern), 150–3, H165–6, R167–8
Lucerne (lake), 153–4, 159–64
Lugano, 290–2, H304–5, R305
Lugano-Vezia, H305
Lumino, H305

Maggia (town & valley), 299–300
Mainau (island, Germany), 198
Maloja (pass), H238
Mannenbach, 196
Marécottes, Les, 245, H257
Mariaberg, 199
Mariastein, 130
Martigny, 244–5, H257
Matterhorn, 251–2
Meilen, 180
Meiringen, 110, H120
Melano, H305
Melchsee-Frutt, H171
Melide, R305
Menaggio (Italy), 295
Mendrisio, 296, H305
Menziken, 128

Merligen, 103, H120
Mittelzell (Germany), 196
Moléson-Village, 139
Mont Cervin. *See* Matterhorn
Montagnola, 293
Montana, 249, H257
Montbovon, 139
Monte Generoso, 292–3
Montreux, 267–8, HR274
Morat, H148
Morat-Meyriez, H148
Morcote, 293–4, H305
Morges, 261–2, HR274
Morgins, 244, H257
Mount Pilatus, 155–6, H171
Mount Rigi, 156–7, H171
Mount Santis, 190
Mount Titlis, 157–8, 159
Moutier, 144
Münsterlingen, 199
Muntelier, H148
Muotta (valley), 161
Muottas Muragl, 226–7
Mürren, 106, M120
Murten, 139–40

Neuchâtel (Neuenburg), 140–2, HR148
Neuhausen, 194, H201
Niederzell (Germany), 196
Niouc, 250
Noirmont, Le, 145
Nyon, 261, HR274

Oberhofen, 103
Oberiberg, H171
Oberzell (Germany), 196
Oensingen, 129
Oeschinen (lake), 113
Olten, 129, H133, R134
Orbe, 269
Orselina, 299

INDEX

Orsières, 246
Ospedaletto, 295
Ouchy, 265

Paccots, Les, HR147
Paradiso, 292–3
Payerne, 140
Piz Nair, 227
Planachaux, 244
Plattjen, 252
Ponte Capriasca, 294
Ponte Tresa (Italy), 294, H305
Pontresina, 230–1, HR238
Porrentruy, 144–5, H148
Porto Ronco, 301

Rangiers, Les, 144
Rapperswil, 180–1, HR201
Rè (Italy), 299
Reichenau Castle, 234
Reichenau Island (Germany), 196
Reichenau-Tamins, 234
Reichenbach (falls), 111
Reinach, 128
Rheinfelden, H134
Rhine (falls), 127
Riazzino, H305
Riddes, 247–8
Rietberg, 226
Rigi, 156–7, H171
Riva San Vitale, 296–7
Roc d'Orsay, 243
Rochers-de-Naye, 267, H274
Rolle, 261, HR275
Romainmotier, 269
Romanshorn, 199, H202
Romont, 138
Rorschach, 199–200, HR202
Rosenlaui, 111
Rothenbrunnen, 234
Rütli, 163

Saanen, 112
Saanenmöser, H121
Saas Fee, 252, H257–8
Saignelégier, 145, HR148
St. Bernard (pass), 245–7
St. Cergue, 269
St. Gall. See Gallen
St. Gallen, 189–90, HR202
St. George (monastery), 195
St. Gingolph, 268
St. Gotthard (pass), 289
St. Imier, 144
St. Luc, 250
St. Margrethen, 200
St. Maurice, 244
St. Moritz, 227–30, HR238
St. Mortiz-Bad, 229
St. Moritz-Dorf, 229–30
St. Peter's Isle, 146
St. Sulpice, 262
St. Ursanne, 144
Ste. Croix, 143
Salvan, 245
Samedan, 226, HR238
Sarraz, La, 269
Sauvabelin, 265
Savognin, 232, HR239
Schaffhausen, 193–4, H202
S-chanf, 226, H239
Schillerstein, 163
Schilthorn, 106
Schlattli, 161
Schöenenwerd, 129
Schuls. See Scuol
Schwägalp, 190
Schwarzsee, 252
Schwarzhorn, 222
Schwyz, 160–1, H171
Schynige Platte, 105
Scuol, 223–4, HR239
Seelisberg, 163, H171
Seengen, H134

INDEX

Sembrancher, 245–6
Sierre, 249
Sihl Valley, 179
Sihlwald, 179
Sils-Baselgia, 230, H239
Sils-Maria, 230, H239
Silvaplana, 230, H239
Simmental, 111–2
Simplon, 254, HR258
Simplon (pass), 253–4
Sion, 248, HR258
Soleure. *See* Solothurn
Solothurn, 129, HR134
Sonogno, 300
Sonvico, 294
Spiez, 103, HR121
Splügen, H239
Stäfa, 180
Stalla. *See* Bivio
Stans, 157–8, H171
Stanserhorn, 158
Steckborn, 195–6
Stein-am-Rhein, 195
Stoos, 161, H171
Sundlauenen, HR121
Sunnega, 252
Süs. *See* Susch
Susch, 222–3
Swiss National Park, 224–5

Tamina Gorge, 191
Tannenbodenalp, 191
Tarasp, 224, HR239
Tellsplatte, 163
Teufen, 191
Thielle, H149
Thonon (France), 268
Thun, 102, HR121
Thun (lake), 100–1, 103
Thusis, 233
Tiefencastel, 232
Toggenburg Valley, 190–1

Torrent, 250
Tourbillon, 248
Treib, 163
Tribschen, 152
Trogen, 192, H202
Trümmelbach (falls), 106

Uetliberg, 179
Ufenau, 180
Unterwasser, 190, H202
Unterzell (Germany), 196

Val Bavona, 299
Val Colla, 294
Valbella, 232–3
Valère, 248
Vazerol, 232
Verbier, 245, HR258
Verzasca (valley), 300
Vevey, 266–7, HR275
Villars, 243–4, H275
Villeneuve, 268, H275
Vira Gambarogno, H305
Visp, 251
Vitznau, 156, H171
Vulpera, 224, HR239

Waldenburg, 129
Walensee, 191
Wartegg, 199–200
Wasserauen, 192
Weesen, 191, HR202
Weggis, 162, H171
Weissenburgbad, 111
Weissfluhjoch, 220–1
Weisshorn, 222
Wengen, 107, H121
Wengernalp, 107
Werd, Isle of, 195
Wil, 190, H202
Wilderswil, 105, H121
Wildhaus, 190, H202

INDEX

Winterthur, 181
Wohlen, 128
Wolfgang, 220

Yverdon, 146

Zermatt, 251–2, HR258
Zernez, 224
Zinal, 250, 259

Zofingen, H134
Zug (lake & town), 164, HR171
Zugersee, 164
Zuoz, 226, H239
Zurich, 173–9, map 177, H182–4, R184–5
Zurich (lake), 180–1
Zürichberg, 179
Zurzach, HR134
Zweisimmen, 111, H121

LIECHTENSTEIN

Balzers, 210, H214, R215
Bendern, H214
Bettlerjoch (pass), 211
Eschen, H214, R215
Gaflei, 211
Gamprin, H214
Malbun, 212, H214, R215
Mäls, 210
Masescha, 211, H214

Nendeln, H214
Sareiserjoch, 212
Schaan, 211, H214
Silum, 211, H214
Steg, 211, H214
Triesen, 211, H214, R215
Triesenberg, 211, H214, R215
Vaduz, 207–8, 210, H214, R215
Wildschloss, 211

National Travel Club

Over 75 Years of Service To Our members

You Are Cordially Invited To Join!

Membership brings you 14 money-saving benefits and services INCLUDING a subscription to TRAVEL-HOLIDAY magazine AND $50,000 travel accident insurance coverage ($75,000 IMMEDIATELY with an initial 2-year membership) for ALL your travels ANYWHERE in the world and for the ENTIRE TERM of your membership. You enroll JUST ONCE (at incredibly low annual dues)—No monthly payments to make or bother about.

NO OTHER TRAVEL CLUB GIVES YOU SO MUCH FOR SO LITTLE

Over a HALF MILLION
members consider these benefits indispensable:

- $50,000 Travel Accident Insurance ($75,000 on renewal; Immediately with initial 2-year membership
- Subscription to TRAVEL-HOLIDAY magazine
- Travel Information Service
- Book Discounts (25% savings)
- Routing Service
- Travel Digest Evaluation Program
- Avis, National & Hertz Car Rental Discounts
- Mediguide Service
- Travel/Holiday Fine Dining Guide
- Mail Forwarding Service
- Discount Pharmaceutical Service
- Discount Film Processing
- Car/Puter-Discount Auto Pricing & Buying Service
- Membership Card & Club Emblems

*Accident insurance provided by
Nationwide Insurance Company, Columbus, Ohio.*

National Travel Club

Travel Building, Floral Park, N.Y. 11001

Please enroll me as a member for the term indicated:
- ☐ 1 Year **($50,000** travel accident insurance) $14.00
- ☐ 2 Years **($75,000** travel accident insurance) $27.00
- ☐ **I enclose remittance**

Charge to my ☐ MasterCard ☐ Visa ☐ American Express

Acct. # _____ Exp. Date _____

Name _____
(Signature if charging)

Address _____

City _____ State _____ Zip _____

$3.00 additional per year for Foreign & Canadian postage

FG-1A